THE HISTORY OF ROCK CLIMBING IN COLORADO

Jeff Achey
Dudley Chelton
Bob Godfrey

Foreword by
Michael Kennedy

THE MOUNTAINEERS BOOKS

Published by
The Mountaineers Books
1001 SW Klickitat Way, Suite 201
Seattle, WA 98134

© 2002 by Jeff Achey, Dudley Chelton, Bob Godfrey

All rights reserved

First edition, 1977. Second edition, 2002

No part of this book may be reproduced in any form, or by any electronic, mechanical, or other means, without permission in writing from the publisher.

Published simultaneously in Great Britain by Cordee, 3a DeMontfort Street, Leicester, England, LE1 7HD

Manufactured in Canada

Project Editors: Kathleen Cubley and Julie Van Pelt
Editor: Don Graydon
Cover, book design, and layout: Mayumi Thompson
Black and white digital imaging: Dudley Chelton
Cartographer: Tracy Martin

Cover photograph: *Tracy Martin and Jonathan Thesenga on* Astrodog, *South Chasm View Wall, Black Canyon of the Gunnison* (Photo: Jeff Achey)

A catalog record for this book is available at the Library of Congress.

 Printed on recycled paper

Foreword 4
Preface 5
Acknowledgments 7
Introduction 8

Part One
THE EARLY DAYS: DARING AND DISCOVERY 10

  1. From the Foothills to the High Peaks 12
  2. New Techniques, Steeper Rock 19
  3. State of the Art in the Fifties 24

Part Two
THE SIXTIES: ANYTHING IS POSSIBLE 28

  4. A Much Bolder Boulder 30
  5. The Great Faces 38
  6. Black Canyon of the Gunnison 49
  7. The Free Climbers 56
  8. Colorado Springs 71

Part Three
THE SEVENTIES: FREE AND CLEAN 77

  9. Eldorado Freestyle 80
10. Drilled Angles and Golden Jamcracks 96
11. High and Wild 103
12. The West Slope 112
13. Colorado National Monument 123
14. Granite Dreams 126
15. A Woman's Place 137
16. Freeing the Walls 143
17. Boulder: End of an Era 147
18. Second Bloom in the Garden 154
19. A Gentler, Freer Diamond 157
20. Rockaneering 163

Part Four
THE EIGHTIES: GYMNASTICS IN THE SKY 170

21. Winds of Change 173
22. Mountain Madness 182
23. Back in the Black 190
24. Trashy Little French Crags 198
25. Bolt-er, Colorado 205
26. The Busy Years 211

Part Five
THE NINETIES AND BEYOND: THE MADDING CROWD 219

27. Industrial Rock 222
28. Big Walls in the Nineties 230
29. Into the Future 242

Colorado Rock-Climbing Ascents and Events 249
A Note About Sources 251
Index 252

Foreword

When I moved to Colorado in the early 1970s I was caught between two worlds. A photography student and soon-to-be college dropout, I'd taken a summer job running the darkroom at a photography school in Aspen, but within a few weeks of my arrival a budding fascination with rock climbing had eclipsed any artistic ambitions. All too soon climbing, any kind of climbing, ruled my days. I couldn't wait to tie into the end of the rope, and fighting fear and inertia and uncertainty became more important than paying the rent, or working, or going to the movies with my girlfriend. Climbing wasn't just a good thing, it was the only thing.

Colorado was the perfect place for one so obsessed. Having grown up in the dull gray cities of the Midwest, I was entranced by the mountains and the space and the infinite blue skies of the West. More than anything, though, Colorado's crags, canyons, and high mountain faces had captured my soul. Within a few hours of home lay a cornucopia of rock, hundreds of routes waiting to be discovered and savored. Who could resist the alpine delights of Rocky Mountain National Park, the convoluted granite of Independence Pass, the clean slabs and cracks of the South Platte? Even the soft sandstone of the Garden of the Gods had its own unique charm. And who wouldn't fall in love after their first Eldorado route, an intricate puzzle of square-cut edges and subtle sidepulls, precision footwork and delicate balance?

That essential appeal hasn't faded in the years since I first came to Colorado. Tying into the end of the rope and stepping off the ground is still an act of faith, a yearning for the perfection of a single move unsullied by the minutiae of daily life. But the hedonistic pleasures of Colorado's seemingly endless variety of rock only partially explains the drive, perseverance, and imagination of the visionaries and dreamers among us—people like Albert Ellingwood, Layton Kor, Jim Erickson, Roger Briggs, Jimmy Dunn, and the dozens of others who have brought the state's crags alive.

The first edition of *Climb!* was the first and most successful attempt to capture in print the spirit and energy of Colorado rock climbing and climbers. Bob Godfrey and Dudley Chelton's landmark effort was more than just history; beautifully illustrated with black-and-white photos, many of the best by the authors themselves, *Climb!* was a celebration, tick list, who's who, repository of myth and personality, and call to arms. Long out of print, a copy of *Climb!* on your bookshelf was a sign that you took climbing seriously. Indeed, it was one of the formative influences for a whole generation of climbers growing up in the 1970s and 1980s.

Jeff Achey is a prominent member of that generation, an author of hard first ascents in Eldorado, the Black Canyon, and other Colorado areas both well-known and obscure. His skill and audacity on rock is complemented by a firm understanding of history, a keen ear for dialogue, and a staunch belief in the ideals of boldness, tenacity, and commitment. When we worked together at *Climbing* magazine in the 1990s, Jeff's talents as a writer, researcher, photographer, and raconteur were a welcome addition to an already strong editorial staff, although his good-natured sandbagging on the boulders and propensity for powerful dynos in the gym left some of us shaking our heads. In teaming with Chelton on this revised and expanded edition of *Climb!*, he has done justice to the efforts of his forebears and created a book every bit as essential as the first edition. The tales and photos herein will be an inspiration for your own adventures, whether you're sending a 5.14 at Rifle or doing your first 5.7 on Lumpy Ridge.

—*Michael Kennedy*

Preface

First published in 1977, the original *Climb!* became something of a cult classic. Bob Godfrey and Dudley Chelton created an image of Colorado rock climbing that influenced a generation, both with gripping tales and startling black-and-white photography. The book sold out the original hardcover printing and a softcover second printing and has been out of print for many years.

I was among that generation influenced by *Climb!*, having moved from the East Coast to Colorado the year before its publication. Twenty years later, as photo editor at *Climbing* magazine and looking for an historical Colorado climbing photograph, I telephoned Dudley Chelton. I expressed my admiration for his book, and at the end of our conversation he mentioned that he wished an updated edition could be written.

Several major events had transpired that made it difficult for Dudley to take on the task of updating the book—a considerable task, since twenty-five years of fast-paced rock climbing had taken place since the first edition of *Climb!* Dudley moved to California in 1975 and drifted away from climbing altogether eight years later to pursue other interests. Bob died in 1988, taking his own life after beginning to experience the debilitating effects of Parkinson's disease.

Several years later, Dudley and I began this project together. I am honored to be a part of the continuing effort to document the colorful history of rock climbing in Colorado.

During the course of writing this edition I learned a lot about the old book: funny stories from its research, the names of the anonymous climbers in its photographs, that the photographic style had been inspired by techniques described in an appendix of John Cleare and Tony Smythe's book *Rock Climbers in Action in Snowdonia*. I learned that most of Bob's archives had been lost. Fortunately, Dudley's original films were still intact, as were the original printing plates from the first edition of *Climb!* What I did not realize then was just how much work lay ahead. If I had, this edition would never have come to pass.

This updated edition of *Climb!* condenses the history in the original edition and adds twenty-five years of new adventures. I take full responsibility for the extensive editing of the original text, and for any flaws in its current form. The material from the late 1970s on, as well as several earlier sections, is all new. As in the original book, noted climbers have contributed essays, greatly adding to the breadth and richness of the story. The information herein is as sound as I have been able to make it, but is surely not without inaccuracies. For these I apologize. Suggestions and corrections for future editions can be posted at *www.paintedwall.com*.

The text was only half the battle. Most people remember *Climb!* as a picture book, and an even harder act to follow was its photography. Rather than gathering

The original cover of Climb!

from existing "photographs of opportunity," as most mountaineering books had, Dudley and Bob took most of the photographs specifically for *Climb!* Finding the older historical photos involved an impressive archeological effort on Bob's part, while the striking 1970s photos were mostly the work of Dudley.

The imagery of *Climb!* made a big impact in its day, which we knew would be impossible for us to replicate in this new edition. Instead, we turned to those who could. The twenty-five years since *Climb!*'s first edition had provided inspiration to a new breed of climbing photographer, many of whom revered the original edition of *Climb!* and graciously consented to sharing the images they had produced of the great modern climbs as they unfolded. Amateurs and professionals alike contributed their work in the spirit of a shared love of Colorado climbing.

Here, Dudley made a major contribution to the new edition of *Climb!* Though the film images used for the original edition looked just as stunning in 2000 as they did in 1977, the reproduction quality in the book itself was decidedly dated. Dudley scanned and digitized the black-and-white imagery for this new edition, which allowed for major improvements in the reproduction of the original photographs. The result is that the standard-setting images that appeared in the original *Climb!* appear again here, but better. Most of the post-1975 photos were originally taken in color. When electronically scanned, the full-color images allowed for fine control of tones and contrast using techniques akin to a traditional black-and-white photographer's use of dodge-and-burn and colored filters. By improving the old and adding the best of the new, we think we've rivaled the photographic impact of the original.

The original edition of *Climb!* was accused of being Boulder centered. This bias was justifiable—Boulder was then and continues to be the center of Colorado climbing. Nevertheless, Boulder is only part of the story, and in more recent years, even Boulder climbers have done much of their notable climbing farther afield in areas such as Rifle. For earlier times as well, the new edition gives more coverage to historic areas such as Aspen and Colorado Springs.

Deciding what to include and what to leave out of this book was painful. After those decisions were made and a massive work assembled, the decision making began all over again as the manuscript was edited to a manageable size. Needless to say, this book contains only a fraction of the worthy rock-climbing activity that has taken place in Colorado.

Several criteria were used in choosing what to include. First, we drew an arbitrary line between rock climbing and mountaineering and generally omitted climbs better covered in a Colorado mountaineering history, such as William Bueler's excellent *Roof of the Rockies* (Colorado Mountain Club Press, Golden, CO, 2000, third edition). The climbs described, generally first ascents at the highest standard of the day, are those that involved a particularly interesting new challenge, technique, or style, or were otherwise influential. Many of the routes have become often-repeated classics, increasing their historical interest if not their significance. Others have definitely not become classics, for good reasons, but have established themselves in the mythology of Colorado climbing because of the desperate adventures of those who first climbed them. In some cases, climbs and events have been included simply for their richness in the spirit of the times.

For many people, rock climbing is simple recreation, not an exercise in challenging the impossible or a forum for existential definition. This book is a poor record of such climbers and their climbs. Instead, we pursue events perpetrated by devotees and fanatics who forged the cutting edge of the times. The tales, however, should be of interest to all who climb rock.

—*Jeff Achey*

Acknowledgments

Neither edition of *Climb!* could have been written without the help of countless people. During the creation of the first edition, Jim Erickson and Steve Wunsch were the most long-suffering in the attempts to portray events of the seventies. Bob Culp was a constant source of information, inspiration, and good-humored tolerance of our attempts to make sense of the most complex period in Colorado's climbing history—the 1960s. We visited his store many times, overused the telephone, and eventually the mess took shape. Roger Briggs, a thinker and writer spanning several important eras, helped debug the draft chapters.

Thanks also to: David Rearick, Walter Fricke, George Hurley, Larry Dalke, Pat Ament, Huntley Ingalls, Steve Komito, Jack Turner, Tex Bossier, Stanley Sheperd, Bill Forrest, Royal Robbins, Wayne Goss, Jim Logan, Layton Kor, Cleve McCarty, Ray Northcutt, Harvey T. Carter, Tom Hornbein, Dale Johnson, Carleton Long, Melvin Griffiths, Joe Stettner, Baker Armstrong, and Ralph Squires for helping keep the pre-1970s climbing history straight.

Ken Wilson of *Mountain* magazine, Nan Babb of *Mountain Gazette,* Alistair McArthur of the Colorado Outward Bound School, Linda Morehead, and Grant Barnes assisted in editing and publishing of the first edition.

Special thanks to the following "photographic assistants" for their willingness to climb the routes of Dudley's choice, at the time of his choice, sometimes multiple times in a day: Roger Briggs, Mark Norden, Bruce Adams, David Breashears, Bill Briggs, Bob Wade, John Ruger, Hunter Smith, Chris Reveley, Steve Wunsch, Dick Nystrom and the numerous other climbers whose stems, laybacks, hand jams, and mantels of 1974 and 1975 are immortalized on the pages of *Climb!*

This second edition was especially enriched by the photographic archives of Pat Ament, Topher Donahue, Charlie Fowler, Chris Goplerud, Stewart Green, Dan Hare, Michael Kennedy, Glenn Randall, Beth Wald, and Ed Webster, who had the interest and talent to capture events and people of the 1970s through the 1990s.

Thanks to Henry Barber, Pat Bingham, Michael Benge, Michael Kennedy, and John Long, and especially Lou Dawson for their help with the Aspen chapters. Thanks to Bryan Becker, Leonard Coyne, Jim Dunn, Steve Cheyney, Bob D'Antonio, Ian and Stewart Green, Martha Morris, and Earl Wiggins for helping unravel the mysteries of Colorado Springs climbing. Thanks to Chris Archer, Crusher Bartlett, Roger Briggs, Steve Diekhoff, Charlie Fowler, Christian Griffith, Colin Lantz, Alan Lester, Steve Levin, Mark Rolofson, Richard Rossiter, and Alec Sharp for their diverse perspectives on the Center of the Known Universe, Boulder.

Special thanks to Steve Levin for allowing endless bivouacs in his living room, to Beth Bennett, Phillip Benningfield, Wayne Goss, Jeff Hollenbaugh, Steve Levin, Matt Samet, and Annie Whitehouse for generously contributing essays, and to Tracy Martin for creating the map.

Thanks also to: The *American Alpine Journal*, Bob Barron, Bobbi Bensman, Eric Bjørnstadt, Jim Collins, Mike and Tommy Caldwell, Chip Chace, Les Choy, *Climbing* magazine, Andy Donson, Bill Forrest, Kennan Harvey, Bill Hatcher, Lynn Hill, Steve Hong, Huntley Ingalls, Fred Knapp, Layton Kor, Ace Kvale, Randy Leavitt, Jim Logan, Jeff Lowe, Craig Luebben, Alison Osius, *Rock & Ice* magazine, Ken Sauls, Jim Surette, Amanda Tarr, Ken Trout, Kris Walker, Robert Warren, Kent Wheeler, Mark Wilford, and Robbie Williams.

To these people and everyone else who assisted and endured our quest to record the first century of Colorado rock-climbing history, our eternal gratitude.

Introduction

Mention Colorado to the average citizen and you conjure images of the Rocky Mountains. Mention it to the rock climber and you conjure mythical cliffs—Eldorado Canyon, Black Canyon of the Gunnison, the Diamond, Rifle.

Colorado has some of the most advanced rock climbs in the world, but difficult routes alone do not make for an interesting climbing history. People do. In the towns below the crags, vibrant enclaves of mountain culture thrive, with ever-changing casts of characters inspired by, and sometimes obsessed with, the rocks. Boulder has one of the largest and most intense climbing communities in the world. Other towns—Estes Park, Fort Collins, Colorado Springs, Aspen, Durango, Telluride—have their own climbing tribes, each proud and distinct. For decades, the state has been a melting pot of climbers from across the country. Writers go to New York. Actors go to Hollywood. Climbers go to Colorado.

The result is a wild synergy, played out on one of the most diverse collections of cliffs anywhere. Every day of every year for over a century, climbers have been exploring Colorado rock, and thousands have left their mark. The highlights are recorded here, climbs that have redefined the concept of what is possible.

Climb! begins with stories of primitive times, when climbers first ventured onto vertical rock, surmounting overhangs with now-comical equipment and technique, risking falls on ropes made from hemp. There are turn-of-the-century tales of the steak fries once held at Chautauqua Park, when the more adventurous members of a local hiking group contemplated scaling the untrodden face of the Third Flatiron. The more recent climbs are no less daring: the first ascent of Redgarden Wall, the Diamond, and the Painted Wall. Quite a few worthy stories begin with an old Ford, piloted by Layton Kor, speeding down the road toward another first ascent. Later, Steve Wunsch works up the precarious face of *Jules Verne* in Eldorado Canyon, risking a fifty-foot fall and climbing into legend. Across the state at about the same time, another first ascent: Jim Dunn on an overhanging off-width he has no gear to fit, two days up a wall in the Black Canyon, out of water, out of options, and desperate for the top.

As modern times approach, tales of raw adventure give way to a more complicated game. Lynn Hill emerges from behind the shadow of her hulking boyfriend John Long to nab the first free ascent of Telluride's hardest crack and launches into a career as a rock superstar. Boulder divides into camps during the offensives of the great Bolt War. Sport climbing appears, with its own breed of drama. Colin Lanz races down to Shelf Road before the French A-Team arrives to steal his prized project. Matt Samet pries off huge blocks from the overhanging cliffs of what was once called Box Canyon, as rock music blares from the boom box below. Throughout the diverse history, one element remains constant. Whether set among ten-foot boulders or on a 2,000-foot wall, these are tales of climbers following their passion.

At the center of it all, there is rock—psychedelic sandstone, shining granite, bulging limestone. Sometimes it is impossibly smooth, other times it is seemingly made to be grasped and climbed. It allows moments of surpassing joy, and of abject terror. Regardless, Colorado climbers have made this rock their home and managed to squeeze from it something of value: a thrill, a lesson, a signpost of achievement, a way of life. Their story is here.

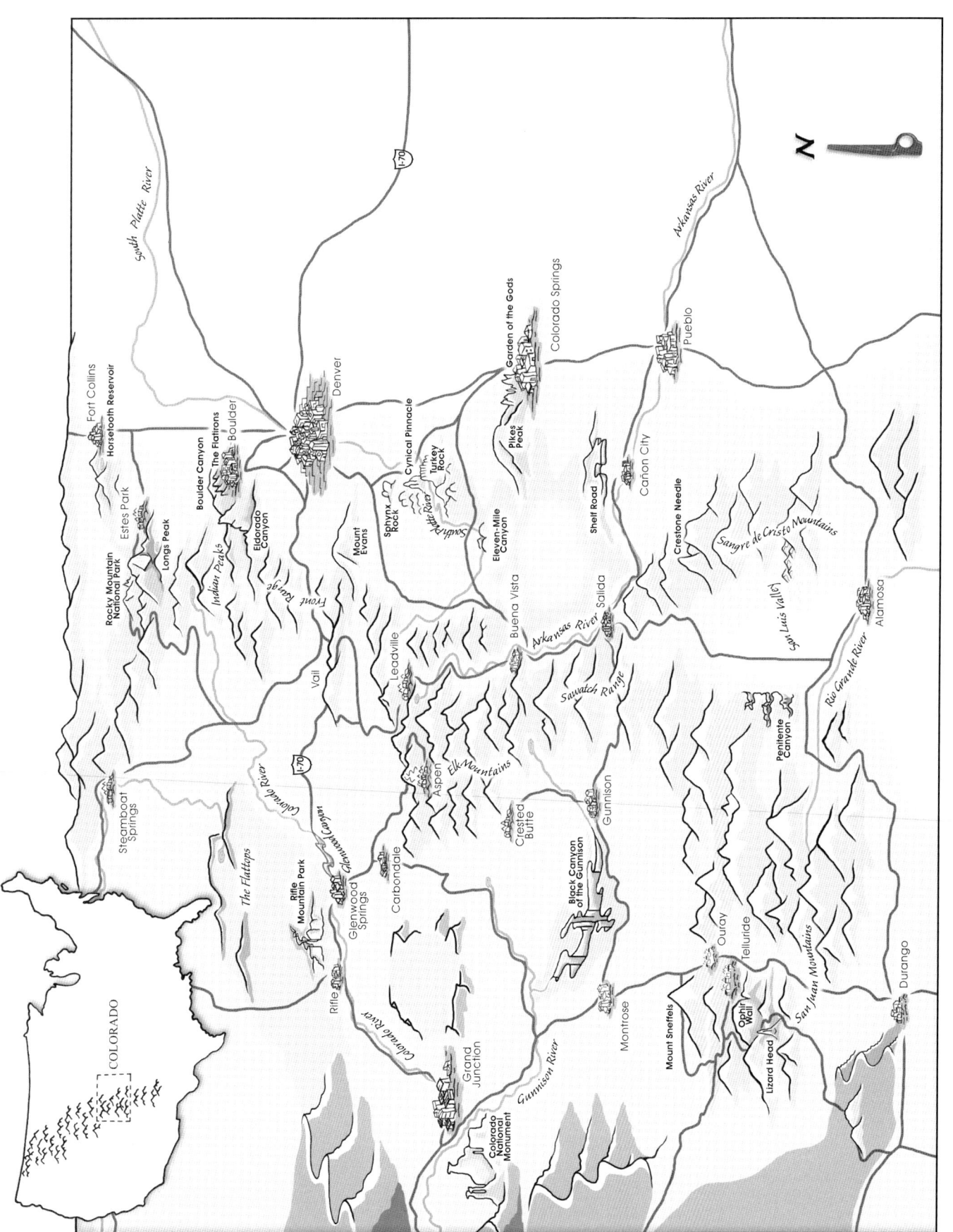

Part One

THE EARLY DAYS: DARING AND DISCOVERY

Colorado is a mountainous state, and rock scrambling has been part of its history since the Utes roamed and hunted the high country and white surveyors mapped the land. Rock climbing as a discipline in itself took shape somewhat later, in the early 1900s.

At the turn of the century, with frontier days still a recent memory, Boulder was a small university town, a social and cultural melting pot on the edge of the Great Plains. Just west of town lay the Flatirons, a series of large sandstone slabs that turned the hillsides of Green and South Boulder Mountains into labyrinths of hidden canyons. Boulder had become a favorite summer retreat for well-to-do Texans, some of whom enjoyed mountain hiking, and the rocky nature of the Boulder foothills led the more intrepid hikers onto the state's earliest true rock climbs.

Another cradle of early Colorado rock climbing was the Garden of the Gods, near Colorado Springs. This cluster of brilliantly colored sandstone fins was a well-known landmark of the Pikes Peak region and played a distinctive, formative role in Colorado climbing on into modern times.

In addition to its eye-catching outcrops, Colorado has hundreds of peaks exceeding 13,000 feet in elevation. Many of these are little more than lofty humps, but others feature steep, rocky escarpments. Colorado mountaineering has a history all its own, but the high peaks played an important role in the state's rock climbing. Most notable is Longs Peak, a craggy 14,255-foot summit northwest of Boulder. Other key peaks include the steeper summits of the Sangre de Cristo range in south-central Colorado, and others in the San Juans in the southwest corner of the state.

Early Colorado rock climbing developed largely independently, but with occasional infusions of climbers and techniques from abroad. Advancements were erratic and haphazard well into the 1940s.

Opposite: *A Rocky Mountain Climbers Club party near the top of the Third Flatiron in 1919. This is the earliest known photograph of rock climbers in Colorado.* (Photo: Earnest Greenman)

1. From the Foothills to the High Peaks

In 1896 a group of Boulder hikers formed the Rocky Mountain Climbers Club, whose main activity was hiking and scrambling, in the Flatirons as well as the Indian Peaks on the Continental Divide directly west of Boulder. One hundred miles to the south, exploratory rock climbing at Garden of the Gods started in 1914. Farther into the mountains, adventuresome individuals began to make high-peaks ascents that crossed the fuzzy line into true rock climbing.

The Flatirons

Chautauqua Park was a favorite meeting place for the Rocky Mountain Climbers Club, and the Flatirons provided a backdrop to steak fries and hikes on Green Mountain. The east face of the Third Flatiron presented a single, unbroken sweep of rock almost 1,300 feet high, formidable from Boulder but gentler and more inviting from its base. It wasn't long before the more adventurous members of the RMCC considered scaling it. In 1906, Floyd and Earl Millard dared the feat. The east face of the Third Flatiron was the earliest recorded rock climb in the state, followed by east-face ascents of the First Flatiron and routes on the south flanks of the Third.

Rudolph Johnson, a Swede who practiced law in Boulder during those years, was a particularly active member of the RMCC and one of the group's top rock climbers. He described climbing on the First and Third Flatirons in a 1923 *Trail and Timberline* article:

> *In climbing either Flatiron with a party I have always used a rope, and it has been a life saver several times, but the first man up or the last man down gets no advantage of the rope. As to footwear, I prefer wearing hob nailed boots, but have found rubber soled shoes, or even stockinged feet to be satisfactory, except in wet weather, when rubber is exceedingly dangerous, while hob nails will stick anywhere on any sort of rock in any sort of weather.*
>
> *I am not recommending the Flatiron climb for any except the most foolhardy rock climbers, but to mountaineers who want real thrills no better climb can be found.*

The Flatirons above Boulder, Colorado. Eldorado and Boulder Canyons lie just out of sight on the left (south) and right, respectively. (Photo: Dudley Chelton)

Aerial view of the northern Flatirons from the southeast, with Longs Peak in the background (Photo: Dudley Chelton)

What a delicious adventure climbing must have been in those days, with so little known of technique, and equipment virtually nonexistent.

Johnson's remarks about the use of a rope indicate changing times. Until 1920, it was generally felt that using a rope on the Third Flatiron was somehow cheating. Ralph Squires, who was president of the Rocky Mountain Climbers Club in those days, was alive and active in Boulder in 1977 when the first edition of this book was written. He said that most rock climbers of the day "scorned the use of a rope in rock scaling," though occasionally a rope was carried to protect novice members of the party. Squires recollected that the first man up would tie the rope around his waist, sit down on a handy ledge, and let the other members of the party use the rope for a handhold as they climbed up.

Prominent in the Rocky Mountain Climbers Club at that time were Ernest and "Ma" Greenman. Ernest arrived in Boulder in 1896 and worked as a surveyor on the local narrow-gauge railway. He loved the Third Flatiron and climbed it over one hundred times. His photographs, meticulously inscribed with names, places, and dates, are the earliest records of technical rock climbing in Colorado.

Another prominent early Boulder climber was Baker Armstrong, who began his long climbing career in 1911 at the age of five. Armstrong hiked and climbed in the Boulder region until the late 1960s and was noted for his slow Texan drawl, indefatigable patience, and interest in the welfare of beginning climbers.

At some time after an unroped ascent of the Third Flatiron with Ernest Greenman, Armstrong came across a book containing a picture of a climber descending a rock face by wrapping a climbing rope around his body and using the friction gained to slide down. The new method was called rappelling. Borrowing a hemp rope from a friend, Baker took the book, climbed solo to the top of the Third Flatiron, and prepared to use the new method to lower himself over the steep west side. A spike of rock provided a secure attachment for the rope. Spreading the pages of the book out beside him, he tried to figure out the correct way of wrapping the rope. His first effort almost ended in disaster, as he turned upside down as soon as he put his weight on the rope. He managed to right himself, and his next attempt proved successful.

Clubs played a significant role in introducing newcomers to climbing, and Colorado's best-known mountain club originated in 1912. In that year, James Grafton Rogers of Denver started the Colorado Mountain Club. It was more broadly based than the Rocky Mountain Climbers Club, both geographically and in its activities. Very little rock climbing took place in the club's early days, and this group, too, was involved mainly in hiking and ascents of easy peaks. Many early CMC members were businessmen, and one of the goals of the club in those days was to spread propaganda about Colorado and to attract new residents from the Midwest and East Coast. The CMC journal, *Trail and Timberline*, would also become an important vehicle for spreading information before the advent of guidebooks or rock-climbing magazines.

Garden of the Gods

Colorado Springs, like Boulder, lies at the meeting point of the Great Plains and the Rocky Mountains. Close to town is a crenellated series of brightly colored rock spires up to 300 feet high—the Garden of the Gods. The rock is a soft sandstone—so soft that the holds come and go under the hands and feet of climbers. Both the nature of the rock and the background of the early climbers led to a local school of climbing with a style, technique, and philosophy significantly different from those in the Boulder area. The differences are evident to this day.

The influence of European mountaineering was felt more strongly in Colorado Springs than in Boulder, due to the early activities of Albert Ellingwood, a student at Colorado College in Colorado Springs. In 1910, Ellingwood attended Oxford University in England on a Rhodes Scholarship. He went on outings with the very active Oxford Mountaineering Club, climbing in Wales, the Lake District, and the Alps, and brought his newfound skills back to Colorado.

Ellingwood returned to Colorado Springs in 1914 and

Garden of the Gods from the northwest. Tower of Babel and North Gateway Rock are in the foreground with South Gateway and Kindergarten Rock (a.k.a. Gray Rock) to the right. (Photo: Chris Wood)

embarked on a series of climbs the likes of which Colorado had not seen before. He knew how to use a rope to belay a climber, and brought back soft-iron pitons from Europe. Crude as his techniques were, they allowed him to go where other Colorado climbers had not yet dared. Though the Boulder Flatirons had been scaled, there were as yet no technical climbs near Colorado Springs. Just outside town, the colorful, fantastically shaped summits of the Garden of the Gods beckoned.

Ellingwood, equipped with hemp rope, a soft-iron piton or two, nailed boots, and a taste for adventure, embarked on several notable climbs, including the west face of Gray Rock and *Ellingwood's Chimney* on Keyhole Rock. Ellingwood's climbs generally connected ramps and chimneys with the occasional short headwall, with the odd passage as difficult as 5.6 (although no such ratings system existed at the time). In 1914 and 1915, they were the most advanced climbs of the day, and along with ascents of the Third Flatiron, marked the start of technical rock climbing in Colorado.

Climbing the Peaks

Most of Colorado's prominent high peaks were climbed in the nineteenth century—Pikes Peak in 1820, Longs Peak in 1868. In 1871, the eccentric Reverend Elkanah Lamb became the first person to explore the great east escarpment of Longs Peak with an epic descent of the face. Lamb descended to Broadway ledge via a line (now known as Kieners) just north of the Notch Couloir, traversed Broadway, and then dropped down the steep snow chute that would appropriately become known as Lamb's Slide.

The 1920s saw a few high-peaks climbs that definitely qualified as more than rock scrambles, and in these we can begin to discern the rock-climbing spirit. Outstanding among the earliest climbs were two ascents led by Albert Ellingwood.

In 1920 Ellingwood and Barton Hoag made a climb in the San Juan Mountains southwest of Telluride that to this day is considered hazardous and bold. Lizard Head (13,113 feet) is probably the most difficult-to-attain 13,000-foot summit in Colorado, a spectacular 400-foot tower of rotten volcanic rock. The crux section is now rated 5.7, with very loose rock. Ellingwood and Hoag's ascent, done with hemp rope, nailed boots, and three soft-iron pitons, took about four hours from the base of the summit tower.

Ellingwood's other outstanding high-peaks rock climb was in the Sangre de Cristo range about seventy miles southwest of Colorado Springs. The east escarpment of the Crestone group is a convoluted rock wall a mile wide and averaging over 1,000 feet high. At Crestone Needle, one of the escarpment's two 14,000-foot summits, the wall reaches its maximum height of almost 2,000 feet and forms a graceful, gradually steepening buttress. In 1924, Ellingwood led Eleanor Davies, Marion Warner, and Stephen Hart up this superb route—known as the *Ellingwood Arête*—encountering several steep 5.7 pitches near the summit.

Robert Ormes and Jim Munroe below Lizard Head in 1932
(Photo: Mel Griffiths)

Another historic rock climb of the early 1920s took place on Longs Peak. The great east face of Longs—by far the most famous escarpment in Colorado—towers nearly 2,500 feet above the icy, wind-dappled waters of Chasm Lake. Forming the south side of the cirque are the lower cliffs of the Ships Prow and the long couloir of Lamb's Slide slanting up toward Mount Meeker. On the north is the Chasm View Wall, a 500-foot precipice. Between Lamb's Slide and Chasm View lies one of the most impressive mountain faces in the Rockies, capped by the dead-vertical Diamond, 950 feet high and situated entirely above 13,100 feet.

A climber approaching the east face of Longs Peak passes tree line well before reaching Chasm Lake, and beyond there the landscape is starkly alpine. Jumbled boulder fields alternate with perennial snowfields and, where soil has managed to cling, dense carpets of low-lying alpine plants. Colors are vivid—the blue-black sky, golden granite, and showy clusters of blue and white columbine, demure green gentian, deep pink Parry primrose. The high-altitude sun is intense, but even on a sunny day in July or August the breeze has a bite to it.

By the early 1920s the east face had seen two descents, but had yet to be climbed from the bottom. Several Colorado parties had been plotting an ascent, but in the summer of 1922, Professor J. W. Alexander of Princeton University scooped the local climbers and made an unroped solo of a line that began on the ledges and slabs just north of Lamb's Slide. The route, about 5.5 in difficulty, is known today as *Alexander's Chimney,* and it was the first of many ascents in what would become one of the most distinctive rock-climbing arenas in Colorado.

Not long after Alexander's ascent, two Bavarian brothers brought Colorado rock climbing to a new level. Paul and Joe Stettner were experienced climbers from one of the leading rock-climbing centers of the world, the limestone ranges of Germany and Austria. Joe immigrated to Chicago in 1925, and Paul joined him the following year. Obtaining two Indian Chief motorcycles, the pair toured Illinois and Wisconsin searching out low-lying rocks. They found some climbing, but yearned for real mountains. In early September 1927 they assembled their equipment, loaded the motorcycles, and headed west for Colorado.

The Stettners carried a few European pitons, and the carabiners they had were probably the first in Colorado. They had not been able to find a rope in Chicago, however, and hoped to purchase one when they arrived

The eastern escarpment of the Crestone group in the Sangre de Cristo range. The Ellingwood Arête *takes the left skyline ridge.*
(Photo: Steve Bartlett)

The great eastern cirque of Longs Peak in Rocky Mountain National Park. The first ascent of the face began in chimneys near the left margin of the photo, ascending to Broadway, the obvious, snow-covered ledge system that curves across most of the east face. After a short traverse along Broadway, the ascent followed a line near the prominent snow-filled Notch Couloir, traversing right to finish just left of the dramatic Diamond face. (Photo: Bob Godfrey)

in Colorado. After spending a day in the Garden of the Gods, during which they climbed the Kissing Camels, they headed for Longs Peak.

At the Longs Peak Inn they found a rope, but its owner refused to sell or lend it, warning that it was too late in the year for a major climb. Eventually they found 120 feet of thick hemp rope at the general store in Estes Park. The pair knew of Alexander's route, but were looking for a harder line. Their experiences on the high-standard routes of Hans Dülfer and others in the Alps had taught them that even apparently sheer rock faces could be climbed. They spent the night in the timberline cabin below the east face of Longs and the next morning examined the face through binoculars. They settled on a line about 200 feet right of *Alexander's Chimney*.

Joe was pessimistic as they headed up toward the face, suspecting that some of the cracks might be icy. "We can worry about that when we get there," Paul replied. Upon reaching the face, they swapped their nailed boots for felt-soled climbing shoes. Paul led, with Joe climbing second, carrying their pack.

Partway up the climb they arrived in a flat-floored alcove. The rear wall of the alcove was vertical, with small holds, but Paul was able to free climb it with a few pitons for protection. In subsequent years this section sprouted so many pitons that it became known as the Piton Ladder, and was often climbed as such. Joe, struggling up with the pack, fell while following, but Paul was well belayed and lowered Joe to a good foothold. Snow began to fall as they reached Broadway, but they continued rap-

Cary Huston on Alexander's Chimney *in 1952* (Photo: Tom Hornbein)

idly up *Kieners* and gained the summit of Longs six and a half hours after beginning the climb.

In 1927 the *Stettners Ledges* of Longs Peak and Lizard Head in the San Juans were the most difficult high-mountain rock climbs in the United States, unmatched until 1931 when Robert Underhill and Fritiof Fryxell climbed the famous north ridge of the Grand Teton in Wyoming. No other climbs surpassing them in daring and technical difficulty were to occur in Colorado until the mid-1940s.

A small group of energetic climbers emerged in southwestern Colorado during the late 1920s, calling themselves the San Juan Mountaineers. The driving force behind the group was Dwight Lavender, who was Colorado's authority on rock-climbing equipment during the early 1930s. He manufactured his own pitons, pioneered countless high-mountain rock ascents, and authored numerous articles on climbing before dying of polio at age twenty-three.

The San Juan Mountaineers were extremely active in the Needles and Grenadiers in the southern San Juans and on the spectacular rock pinnacles of the Sneffels Range near Ouray. They also made the first technical climbs in the Black Canyon of the Gunnison, with adventurous ascents of some of the rock "islands" along the rim.

Throughout the 1930s and 1940s, Lavender, Mel Griffiths, Gordon Williams, and others did many excellent rock climbs in the San Juans, including the impressive north face of Mount Sneffels. These climbs are little known, and it has been said that none of them advanced the state's rock-climbing standards beyond what had been achieved years earlier on *Stettners Ledges*. It might be said, however, that in the more important psychological sense, *Stettners Ledges* had little to do with Colorado rock-climbing standards. The Stettner brothers simply dropped in, blitzed up a climb that seemed to them rather ordinary by the standards of their home area, the eastern Alps, and then left, without influencing the general standard of Colorado rock climbing at all. For years, the route went unrepeated.

For ongoing climbing in the Colorado high country in the 1930s and '40s, the San Juan Mountaineers represented the cutting edge. An excellent account of the group's activities, as well as other historical information and route descriptions from the San Juan range, is found in *The San Juan Mountains,* by Robert F. Rosebrough (Johnson Books, Boulder, 1986).

In 1947 Joe Stettner, then forty-six, again visited the San Juans and made an ascent that stood out as a major rock climb of significant difficulty—the 1,200-foot east face of Monitor Peak in the Needles Range. The intended route was rather unremarkable, but the ascent eventually took a much bolder line up the face. Stettner, John Speck, and Jack Fralick had climbed several hundred feet up the main

Joe and Paul Stettner get their first view of the Rockies, 1927 (Photo: Joe Stettner collection)

Joe Stettner on the Kissing Camels, Garden of the Gods, 1927 (Photo: Paul Stettner)

Joe Stettner on the first ascent of Stettners Ledges, Longs Peak *(Photo: Paul Stettner)*

weakness on the face, encountering very poor rock. At one point, Speck fell, causing a near disaster. Fralick's account in *Trail and Timberline*, December 1947, describes the incident:

> *I was unable to hold him and keep my feet in doing so. Checking his rope instinctively, and perhaps too rapidly, I stopped the running of the rope, but was pulled off and down to the next ledge about five feet below. Our combined fall came heavily on Joe, but he held us on the piton and karabiner through which he was anchoring me. John and I were able to quickly take our weight off the rope, and the incident was soon forgotten. However, only Joe's caution in anchoring me, while I belayed John, had saved the day.*

Higher, an overhang barred progress up the team's intended line. They drifted right toward the center of the face until a steep crack promised a way up. Stettner made two unsuccessful attempts to start the crack. "These spoke eloquently of its great difficulty," wrote Fralick, "but Joe's only comment was his request for a shoulder stand." Using a rope sling and Speck's shoulders, Stettner managed to get started in the crack, which then required a thirty-foot, all-out layback to reach the first resting place. This and one other shoulder stand were the only points of direct aid used on the ascent.

The crack led the party onto steep rock to the right of the large groove system they had been following, and they now found themselves committed to finishing the climb via the great central face. The climbing proved difficult and sustained, but the rock was firmer. Nine hundred feet up the wall, with darkness coming quickly, the three decided to bivouac for the night. The remaining 300 feet the next day presented sustained difficulties, including another crux passage, called the "140-foot Lead." Later parties reported this lead to involve intricate and poorly protected face climbing of about 5.8 in difficulty.

The east face of Monitor was the first recorded multiday technical climb in Colorado. Stettner considered it the most difficult route of his career, more severe than the north face of the Grand Teton or the *Stettners Ledges* route on Longs Peak. Monitor's east face would not see a second ascent until 1968.

The east faces of Monitor Peak (13,635 feet) and Peak Thirteen (13,705 feet) in the San Juan Mountains. The Stettner route takes the smoothest face on the left-hand peak. (Photo: Jeff Achey)

2. New Techniques, Steeper Rock

Little climbing exploration took place in Colorado—or anywhere—during the war-stricken 1940s, although mountaineering techniques were refined by the U.S. Army's 10th Mountain Division, which had a Colorado base at Camp Hale near Leadville. After the war, technical advancements came quickly.

Although the hemp and manila ropes of the 1930s were quite strong, with a tensile strength of up to 2,000 pounds, they possessed virtually no elasticity, so the shock load of a leader fall was quite likely to snap the rope. Thus, part of all early rock climbers' training was the famous admonition, "The leader must not fall."

In 1947 the Sierra Club published an important paper by California climbers Dick Leonard and Arnold Wexler called "Belaying the Leader," which described the *dynamic belay,* in which the belayer allowed the rope to slide before gradually bringing the falling leader to a halt. Properly executed, a dynamic belay could safely arrest a severe lead fall without snapping the rope.

During the war the U.S. Army had carried out studies of climbing ropes, concluding that nylon ropes were far superior to ones made of natural fibers. By the late 1940s army-surplus nylon ropes were available to civilian climbers. The greater durability and flexibility of nylon ropes and the new dynamic belaying methods opened the door on a radical concept: that a leader fall might be seen as a calculated risk rather than certain suicide.

More technical advances were afoot. The 1948 *American Alpine Journal* carried an article by Fred Beckey, a climber from the Pacific Northwest, that presented a short description of "contraction bolts" and their use in rock climbing. These devices, and similar ones, could be placed in drilled holes and used for protection or direct aid on blank, crackless sections of rock on which pitons were useless. Bolts would play a significant role in Colorado rock climbing from the 1950s to the present, in the creation both of new climbs and of controversy.

Garden of the Gods

Climbing at Garden of the Gods advanced little between Ellingwood's day and World War II. Ellingwood had died young from illness in 1934, but passed on his rock-climbing techniques and philosophy to a fellow professor at Colorado College, Robert Ormes, whose thirty-foot plummet (caught by Bill House) on New Mexico's Shiprock in 1937 may be the most famous fall in American rock-climbing history. Ormes would later author Colorado's original peak-climbing tome, *Guide to the Colorado Mountains*, now in its tenth edition (Colorado Mountain Club Press, Golden, CO, 2000).

Robert Ormes, Colorado College professor and author of the first comprehensive guide to the mountains of Colorado, in the 1930s (Photo: Mel Griffiths)

The British style of climbing that Ellingwood had learned emphasized a minimum use of pitons and mechanized methods. Like Ellingwood, Ormes was an intellectual, and a self-imposed, Spartan discipline in rock climbing appealed to his sense of aesthetics. Even if there had been no stylistic bias against pitons, they were of limited use in the Garden of the Gods, which featured soft, friable rock with few piton cracks.

Following World War II, army climbers from Fort Carson made a number of ascents in the Garden, employing numerous pitons and a pragmatic if rather inefficient aid-climbing style. These included some classic climbs, such as *West Point Crack* and the North Ridge of Montezuma's Tower.

A colleague of Ormes at Colorado College was Harvey Carter, whose son, Harvey T. Carter, began rock climbing in 1950, serving as a climbing instructor with the mountain troops at Fort Carson. The younger Carter would become a well-known figure in North American climbing and was a controversial character noted for his stubborn nature and verbal pugnacity. He visited almost every major climbing area in the United States, from Yosemite in the West to the Shawangunks in the East, but he was most famous for his exploits in Colorado and the desert Southwest.

In the mid-1950s, Carter tried to develop a more uniform system of rating the relative difficulty of rock climbs in different parts of the country. Carter felt that the decimal grading system that had been introduced in California failed to grasp the overall challenge of a rock climb, since it assessed difficulty simply by identifying the single most difficult move. He proposed a system he called the Universal Standard, where the amount and quality of protection, the nature of the rock, and the degree of exposure and danger would be combined with the technical difficulty of the hardest moves to provide an overall rating of each pitch. The total difficulty of a particular climb was then calculated by averaging the individual pitch grades. Carter's system was complex—and poorly received.

Carter was indeed an organizer and an innovator. During the 1950s he put on a curious event, the first National Championship Meet for competitive rock climbing, a bouldering contest held on his home turf of the Garden of the Gods. It was poorly attended, and Carter won handily. Another Carter oddity was the can of spray paint he carried on his gear sling to mark his routes. Though most of the marks have since been scrubbed off or washed away, a modern climber at Ute Pass or one of the many granite crags near Pikes Peak might still come across a faded red spot at the base of some crack, miles from nowhere.

More significantly, Carter devised his own protection system for the unique climbing at the Garden of the Gods. Carter's method combined early expansion-bolt techniques with durable army hardware. First, a hole was drilled, as if for an expansion bolt, but deeper. Into the hole Carter would then drive an army angle piton with its tip sawed off, and the soft steel of the pin would bend and conform to the hole. These drilled angles eliminated the problem of damage to cracks caused by repeated insertion and removal of pitons, as was the style in Boulder and California at this time. Carter felt that a drilled angle, well placed, was bombproof. With this newfound security, he and his contemporaries embarked on a series of bold face climbs.

Carter wanted to preserve the free-climbing traditions in the Garden of the Gods. To this end, climbs were designed and graded according to a prescribed amount of protection. Carter was careful to position drilled protection so that it could not be used for direct aid on crux moves, but was sufficiently close to provide adequate safety in case of a leader fall. Among Carter's best climbs of the day were *New Era*, a steep crack and dihedral climb on the east face of Kindergarten Rock, and a free ascent of the North Ridge of Montezuma's Tower, a 130-foot freestanding rock fin and probably the Garden's most popular climb of all time.

Boulder and the Flatirons

By the mid-1940s, the large faces of the Flatirons were laced with routes. The wildest rock climb yet made in Boulder was the Maiden, an airy pinnacle high in the Flatirons, climbed in October 1944 by Roy Peak and Mark Taggart. The route began on the west edge of the rock, surmounted a short wall, and traversed a narrow ridge to a spot called the Crow's Nest. Though the climbers had barely started to ascend, the hillside dropped away below and they had now gained 100 feet of exposure. From the Crow's Nest, they embarked boldly out onto the sheer north face, gaining the east ridge and easier climbing to one of the most satisfying summits in the Boulder region.

In Colorado Springs in the 1950s, climbers emphasized free climbing, with ropes used for protection in the event of a fall but direct aid being used only as a last resort to overcome short sections. Around Boulder, however, the wealth of firm and often overhanging rock was luring climbers into a more technical style of climbing. One standard-setting climb was the *Northwest Passage* route on the north side of the Third Flatiron, done in 1949.

The members of the first-ascent party were students at the University of Colorado—Tom Hornbein, Bob Riley, and Dick Sherman. Two short pitches—one of which included a tension traverse—led the team to a stance below a smooth wall. Here they made the first recorded attempt in Colorado to drill bolts to pass a blank section, but their hardware-store equipment foiled the attempt and they resorted to a lasso move instead.

The next obstacle was a jutting, body-length overhang, where Riley experimented with a number of options. Hanging on tension, he hammered in a piton, well out in the overhang, tied a foot loop in the lead rope, and clipped the rope through the piton. The intention was that Riley would step into the loop, the belayer would pull on the rope, and Riley would slowly rise above the overhang. Instead of rising, Riley sank, and ended up

Climber on the Skid Row *section of the 1949* Northwest Passage *route on the Third Flatiron. The troublesome overhang is visible at the top of the photo.* (Photo: Dudley Chelton)

Bob Riley, Tom Hornbein, and Dick Sherman atop the Third Flatiron after the first ascent of Northwest Passage *in 1949* (Photo: Tom Hornbein collection)

dangling in space and had to be hauled back to the belay ledge. Finally, with a different foot-sling arrangement, Riley engineered his way over the overhang. This climb, standard setting as it was, demonstrated the backwater nature of Colorado climbing. Even though Riley, Hornbein, and Sherman were among Boulder's top rock climbers, they were completely unaware of the aid-stirrup techniques that had been in use in Europe and California since the 1930s.

Hornbein pioneered a much more popular Third Flatiron route the next year, a striking vertical crack up the rock's steep west flank. At 5.7, *Friday's Folly* became the most-repeated hard climb in the area for years to come.

Also in 1950 a young Boulder climber named Dale Johnson would help bring Colorado climbing into the modern age. Johnson had seen a photograph of the great French climber Gaston Rébuffat climbing the underside of a huge overhang in the Alps. With Phil Robertson and Bob Sutton, Johnson set out to make such a climb himself. On a granite crag in Boulder Canyon called Castle Rock, Johnson found just the place—a piton crack out a massive roof directly above the dirt road that circled the crag.

Johnson devised a complicated two-rope system that was strenuous for leader and belayers alike, and in an exhausting effort managed to work his way out the fifteen-foot roof, a first for this kind of climbing in the Boulder region. The so-called *Practice Roof* sits only twenty

A 1970s ascent of the popular Friday's Folly *on the Third Flatiron, established by Tom Hornbein and Harry Waldrop in 1950* (Photo: Dudley Chelton)

feet off the ground and has been climbed countless times since Johnson's first ascent. Fishermen have often watched in amazement as a spidery figure, encased in a cocoon of tangled ropes, inched across the underside of the roof. Sometime during the early 1950s, James Peterson used a rather unconventional technique for belaying the roof. He anchored the climbing ropes to the bumper of his car and carried out his belaying responsibilities from the driver's seat, moving the car back and forward to give the leader the appropriate amounts of slack and tension.

Hardware was improving. Raffi Bedayn of California produced the first aluminum carabiners, which lightened the load considerably for the equipment-intensive direct-aid climbing that had captured the imaginations of Boulder climbers such as Johnson. Roy Holubar, a Boulder outdoor shop owner, employed a local blacksmith to manufacture steel pitons that were stronger than either European imports or the ubiquitous army-surplus pins.

Expansion bolts were also coming into use. Johnson was an early connoisseur of bolts, and he and his companions would occasionally head up to the cliffs, select a blank wall, and drill a row of expansion bolts just for practice. Climbers wandering the Boulder Flatirons today may still happen upon these old bolt ladders, which often end in the middle of nowhere.

Johnson also used bolts to make short work of coveted routes, and great controversy surrounded the introduction of such powerful technology into Boulder climbing. One seminal route was the *East Ridge* of the Maiden. This elegant line on Boulder's showpiece pinnacle had turned back the efforts of several parties at a crackless headwall at midheight. By drilling three bolts for direct aid, Johnson and party were able to surmount the obstacle without difficulty and make the first ascent.

In October 1953, the *East Ridge* party of Johnson, Dave Robertson, and Cary Huston assembled for an attempt on another spectacular Maiden climb, this one up the overhanging northwest side. A year or two previously, Brad Van Diver had pioneered a dizzying free rappel from the summit of the Maiden to the Crow's Nest. Johnson and crew planned to start at the Crow's Nest and work up the overhanging face just left of the rappel line. They had three 120-foot climbing ropes, one length of eighth-inch parachute cord for ferrying equipment up and down, carabiners, a large number of pitons of different sizes and shapes, three drills, and eight expansion bolts. The bolts, from the local hardware store, were of three different types: a lead-shield bolt with a diameter of three-eighths of an inch, a self-driving Phillips Redhead, and an inch-and-a-half-long split-rivet type.

Staggering under the weight of his equipment, Johnson immediately faced ten feet of steep free climbing—no mean feat carrying forty pounds of iron—and he was relieved when the rock steepened and he could step into his aid slings. It took Johnson twenty-five minutes to drill his first bolt hole, and two and a half hours to drill the next three. Suspended from the "diaper seat" sit-harness he had devised for the Castle Rock roof, Johnson was forced to lean back at a twenty-five-degree angle and

Dale Johnson at the Crow's Nest before the first ascent of the Northwest Overhang of the Maiden in 1953 (Photo: Johnson collection)

A busy day on the Maiden, near Boulder, in 1956. Climbers are visible on summit, the notorious rappel, and in the Crow's Nest, while Dale Johnson makes the first ascent of his second route on the spire's western overhangs. Johnson's historic 1953 route climbs the overhanging headwall forming the upper left skyline. (Photo: Cleve McCarty)

pound on his drill at arm's length above his head.

By now, Johnson was tired of drilling. Two or three increasingly poor piton placements brought him underneath an overhang. There was a crack above, which would accept only the tip of a piton driven in about a quarter of an inch. Whispering a silent prayer and shouting "Red alert!" to his anxious belayers, Johnson clipped in a foot sling and gingerly transferred his weight to the piton. The next instant, the piton went flying past his head and he followed it downward. As he fell he waited for the jerk of his last half-driven piton being pulled out by the impact of the fall. By some miracle it held. Robertson grasped the belay ropes tightly and brought Johnson to a stop after a free fall of some twelve feet. Johnson climbed back up and finished the route, the *Northwest Overhang*, without further incident.

Johnson's fall on the Maiden is the first recorded event of its kind in Colorado climbing. He knew his piton placement was suspect, and he took a calculated risk when he weighted it. This was unprecedented—but new belaying techniques and better ropes would make such calculated risks increasingly common.

3. State of the Art in the Fifties

In the 1950s, Colorado rock climbing began to pick up momentum. Free-climbing standards were steadily rising, and success on unlikely artificial climbs such as the Maiden overhang led to much speculation about ascents of the bigger, sheerer faces.

To many climbers (then and now), the east face of Longs embodied the essence of Colorado rock climbing. In the 1950s, that essence was of wild imaginings and potential climbs yet undared. Colorado's best climbers scanned the unclimbed Diamond and the equally sheer lower east face, right of the Stettner route—and hesitated. Elsewhere in Rocky Mountain National Park were other imposing walls, unclimbed but surely not unclimbable. Near Boulder, climbing had focused on the Flatirons and the friendly crags of Boulder Canyon. Soon, Boulder climbers would begin to explore the towering canyon walls behind the nearby resort of Eldorado Springs.

Closing In on the Diamond

In the twenty-five years since the climb of *Stettners Ledges* in 1927, no significant advancements had been made on the east face of Longs Peak, though much climbing had been done. One notable route was the pinnacle of *Zumie's Thumb*, high above the top of Lamb's Slide, done in 1951 by the *Friday's Folly* team of Tom Hornbein and Harry Waldrop, along with Dexter Brinker.

More significant was *The Window*, done by Bill Eubanks and Brad Van Diver in August 1950. *The Window* was the first climb to encroach—albeit marginally—upon the massive rock wall above the right half of Broadway ledge, the Diamond. Named for a remarkable hole in the rock at the apex of its main feature, *The Window* route climbed into the large, right-facing ramp just left of the Diamond proper before exiting left through the "window" onto *Kieners*. No single pitch on *The Window* was quite as hard as the Piton Ladder pitch on *Stettners Ledges*, but the average standard of the route was higher. Also, *The Window* route and *Stettners*, both 5.7, could be done consecutively for a classic grand tour of the east face, with 1,300 feet of rock climbing.

Another significant achievement on Longs was the successful ascent, after much effort, of the *Hornbein Crack* below Chasm View. Tom Hornbein had tried to lead this dead-vertical dihedral several times, finding very poor protection in the wide crack. He was thrown a rope from above during two of his attempts and climbed the crack with an overhead belay, before finally managing the lead in the summer of 1953. At solid 5.8, it was one of the hardest crack pitches in the state at the time, and poorly protected to boot.

The *Hornbein Crack,* and the easier *Chasm Cutoff* done around the same time, were the first routes to climb out from the right side of Broadway ledge. The great Diamond had now been closely flanked on both sides. Hornbein and crew had also traversed out across Table Ledge from above *The Window* to survey the great precipice. Colorado

A climber traverses Table Ledge in 1952, exploring for a possible Diamond route. (Photo: Tom Hornbein)

climbers were making ready for the first attempts on the Diamond, but an unforeseen obstacle would foil them.

In 1954, after three months of intensive preparation, Dale Johnson and Bob Sutton felt ready to make an attempt on the Diamond. In anticipation of prolonged sessions in aid stirrups, Sutton's wife had made him a special pair of pants with a zipper in the seat. The climbers had also manufactured many Continental-style wooden wedges for direct aid in wide cracks. The equipment would never be put to the test. "Rather than marching up there to the Diamond and just trying it," Johnson recollected, "we went over and told the rangers at park headquarters what we had in mind. The Park Service immediately forbade it."

The climbers had a long and heated discussion with the rangers, to no avail. There was no stated policy against climbing the Diamond, but knowing that the climbers planned to use expansion bolts, the rangers made it clear they would take action against the climbers for defacing the rock. Indeed, the new bolt technology was an important component of Johnson's optimism that he could climb the Diamond. Nevertheless, Johnson felt that this was merely an excuse to keep them off the face. Johnson made several attempts to obtain permission for a Diamond ascent over the next few years, and each time was refused.

In 1954, the hardest routes in the high peaks were still Lizard Head and the east face of Monitor in the San Juans, the *Stettners* and *Window* routes on Longs, and the *Ellingwood Arête* in the Sangre de Cristos. Standards had not advanced since the 1920s.

On the crags it was the twilight of an older and more traditionally based period of rock climbing in Colorado, which reached its apex with such Boulder Canyon routes as *Cozyhang* on the Dome, done by Mike O'Brien and Jim Crandle in 1953, and *Empor* on Cobb Rock, by George Lamb and Dallas Jackson in 1954, as well as *Friday's Folly* on the Third Flatiron. The activities of Hornbein—later, with Willi Unsoeld, to make the first ascent of the West Ridge of Mount Everest—and of Johnson heralded the approach of a new era.

Redgarden Wall—First Ascent

Eight miles to the south of Boulder lies Eldorado Springs Canyon, whose steep walls have been preeminently important in the development of Colorado rock climbing. Today, one drives into the canyon through the modest remains of the old spa, so fashionable in the 1930s that Dwight D. Eisenhower spent his honeymoon there. Once in the canyon first-time visitors are immediately impressed by the size and steepness of its colorful walls—and are sure to develop a crick in the neck from attempting to see

Ivy Baldwin on the Eldorado Canyon high wire, 1907 (Photo: Ed Tangen, Carnegie Branch Library for Local History, Boulder Historical Society Collection)

the top of precipitous cliffs. A steep, somber, 300-foot wall rises abruptly on the south side of the road, so close that one can step directly onto it from the open door of a car; this is the Bastille. For many years a steel cable stretched from its top to the opposite side of the canyon, some 300 feet above the rushing creek. Between 1906 and 1949, Ivy Baldwin—stuntman, balloonist, tumbler, parachutist, and circus clown—walked the wire eighty-nine times, the last crossing on his eighty-second birthday.

Across South Boulder Creek lies the Wind Tower, cheerfully dappled with bright yellow lichens, and just up-canyon lies the immense, sprawling mass of Redgarden Wall. Painted in colors of flame red and brilliant orange, and subtly garbed in traceries of yellow lichens, it leans skyward in a formidable series of vertical walls, intricate crack systems, and intimidating overhangs. Pigeons wheel around its upper reaches in dizzying swoops, leading the eye across vertigo-inducing walls. In places, the cliff is more than 600 feet high.

In 1956, Chuck Murley, Cary Huston, Dick Bird,

and Dallas Jackson made the first attempts to climb Redgarden Wall. The *Northwest Passage* and the *Northwest Overhang* on the Maiden, steep and technical climbs though they were, were both relatively short. The terrain of Redgarden looked just as fierce, and the wall was four times as high. The team could discern only one significant line of weakness on the face of Redgarden, a sort of groove system flanked by a jutting, overhanging buttress on one side and a steep, smooth face on the other. Unfortunately the groove did not reach the ground.

Sandwiched between steep walls on the right and a line of overhangs to the left was the only possible start to the climb, featuring a steep layback crack. Bird led this pitch—later known as the *Birdwalk*. On this and the following attempt, the four reached a point some 600 feet up the wall, but were stopped by the last pitch, where it was necessary to move out right from a small cave.

The terrific exposure, rather than pure difficulty, stalled the party here. On the final attempt, the trio recruited Dale Johnson, the local ace, who was given the honor of leading the initial *Birdwalk* pitch, which he found quite difficult. At the final impasse, Murley decided to have one more go before handing the lead over to Johnson. This time the psychology was right, and Murley pushed through to the top.

The *Redguard Route* followed a direct line up a huge, impossible-looking cliff, and the team had expected sections of direct aid. The route was sustained in difficulty, but the team was pleasantly surprised to find a continuous line of cracks and holds, enabling the route to be climbed free at 5.7 or 5.8. Later the same year, Ray

Climber on the Birdwalk *pitch of* Redguard *in 1974* (Photo: Dudley Chelton)

Northcutt, Dallas Jackson, and Cary Huston climbed the first two pitches of *Redguard*, and then traversed left onto the large feature now known as the Upper Ramp, ascending this remarkable ledge system nearly to its end and topping out via a steep fissure called the *Chockstone Chimney*.

These ascents opened up what was to become the most intensively climbed rock face in Colorado. In a similar manner, another landmark climb of 1956, on Hallett Peak, opened up the faces of Colorado's high peaks.

On the North Face of Hallett

Ray Northcutt was from Boulder and had begun climbing while doing military service with the mountain troops at Fort Carson near Colorado Springs. Noted for his dedication to physical fitness, he ran a minimum of a mile each day up a steep mountainside, bouldered frequently on Flagstaff Mountain, and included one hundred chin-ups in three sets as part of his training routine.

At Fort Carson, Northcutt met Harvey T. Carter. In

Aerial view of Redgarden Wall and Wind Tower, showing the 1956 routes. Left to right: Upper Ramp with Chockstone Chimney *exit,* Redguard, *and* Recon. *(Photo: Dudley Chelton)*

1956 the pair decided to attempt a major high-mountain objective—the north face of Hallett Peak in Rocky Mountain National Park. The striking 800-foot high escarpment had been climbed by an obvious gully line, *Hallett Chimney*, but its main buttresses were untouched.

The massive face had a gloomy north-facing aspect, and the height of the mountain, 12,713 feet, added the potential perils of lightning and high-mountain storms. The line they hoped to climb had no precedent in Colorado: the buttresses of Hallett were steeper and less broken than anything yet done on the east face of Longs Peak.

Northcutt and Carter's first attempt took them some 500 feet up the westernmost buttress, where they found themselves on a steep slab beneath a large overhang. Northcutt led a frightening passage here, with difficult climbing and very poor protection. Routefinding problems and the difficulty of the lower face had consumed most of the day. Preferring not to risk a night on the face, the pair retreated.

They returned on July 28, confident that their previous experience would allow them to complete the climb in a day. Again reaching the overhang, Northcutt took tension from the rope, skirted the lip, and lodged himself in a tight chimney. The chimney led to a roomy ledge, and the major difficulties of the climb were behind them. They moved rapidly up the final 300 feet of easier rock, spurred on by the rumble of thunder to the west.

Even though the *Northcutt-Carter* route was significantly easier than Tetons rock climbs such as the *South Buttress Direct* on Mount Moran and the direct north face of the Grand Teton, both done three years earlier, this was not evident at the time. The climb was a major psy-

Ray Northcutt on the first ascent of the Northcutt-Carter *route on Hallett Peak.* (Photo: Harvey T. Carter)

chological accomplishment for Colorado, and the climbers told thrilling stories to their friends. Northcutt published a full account in the *American Alpine Journal*, and the route gained a formidable reputation. The second ascent, however, would deflate this notoriety considerably, and help establish a long-lasting rivalry with the climbers of California.

Yvon Chouinard read the *American Alpine Journal* report and was intrigued. Northcutt's account had left little doubt as to the route's difficulties, and Chouinard, who had been involved in some of the most difficult climbing in Yosemite Valley, felt it was worth a trip to Colorado. In July 1959, Chouinard and Ken Weeks hiked in to Hallett Peak.

Arriving in midafternoon, they decided to climb a couple of pitches that evening and leave fixed ropes to give them a head start the next day—common practice for the big walls of Yosemite Valley. They started up at four in the afternoon. The first two pitches went quickly, so they decided to go a little farther. Finding the difficulties moderate, they kept going, following a more direct line than Northcutt and Carter's, and reached the summit with enough daylight to enjoy the view.

The entire climb had taken the Californians a total of four hours. Clearly, Colorado standards were still far off the pace.

The north face of Hallett Peak, Rocky Mountain National Park. The 1956 route takes the right-most buttress leading to the apparent summit. (Photo: USGS)

Part Two

THE SIXTIES: ANYTHING IS POSSIBLE

It has often been said that the 1960s were the golden age of Colorado rock climbing. That description is based on a complex mixture of myth spiced by fact; on a flavor of wildly improbable new climbs; and by the appearance of a small group of individuals possessing tremendous technical ability and daring, coupled with the rich personal idiosyncrasy that is the stuff of legend. The 1960s were a time when the electric energies of a handful of climbers sparked reactions between personality and the flow of historical events that, firework-like, left blurred retinal after-images for later generations.

The 1960s were more a state of mind than a sequence of years: the era really had its origins in the late 1950s, perhaps around 1958. In that year, the sheer northeast face of Spearhead in Rocky Mountain National Park was first climbed by a party including Richard Sykes and a young climber named Dave Rearick. In Yosemite, Warren Harding and team completed the monumental climb of *The Nose* of El Capitan. Throughout the country, the pioneer climbers of the late 1950s were showing that, with a dash of optimism and a reasonable sprinkling of good luck, anything was possible. Action replaced inhibition, and the doors were thrown open for a flood of energy to be loosed on the mountains.

Before the 1960s, rock climbing had been widely considered the poorer cousin of mountaineering, an activity practiced aggressively only because most of the country lacked the venues for proper alpinism. In the 1960s we find the roots of a rich rock-climbing culture that was almost completely independent of mountaineering. Up through the 1950s, climbing had been a sport and a weekend activity. In the 1960s, for many key characters, climbing became a complete way of life.

Opposite: *Climbers on the last pitch of* The Naked Edge *in Eldorado Canyon* (Photo: Bob Godfrey)

4. A Much Bolder Boulder

In 1956 a tall, gangly youngster began to hang around the periphery of Boulder's core group of climbers, which included Cary Huston, Dallas Jackson, Stanley Shepard, Dick Bird, and Dale Johnson. This newcomer would be seen at The Sink, a tavern on the Hill near the University of Colorado, around tables in the university cafeteria, and during chance meetings at Gerry's, the local climbing shop. His ears would prick up when the latest climbing was mentioned, but he was apparently too shy to directly approach the local hard men. The youngster's name was Layton Kor.

Soon, rumors began to trickle back to the group about a crazy individual who had been seen climbing solo on the rocks of Boulder and Eldorado Canyons. Members of the group began placing bets on how long he would live. The most optimistic wager was three months.

Before long, however, it became apparent that Layton Kor would survive, and that he possessed unusual rock-climbing ability. He was tall—six feet, five inches—strong, and agile. After his initial hair-raising solo climbs, Kor was hooked, and rock climbing became the driving force in his life. During the following ten years he was to become the most influential figure in Colorado's rock-climbing history.

The summer of 1957 was Kor's second year of climbing, and he was ready to attempt a major new line. The climb he had in mind would broach a sheer section of Redgarden Wall to the right of the *Redguard* route. He made one unsuccessful attempt on it, then persuaded Ben Chidlaw, a law student at the university, to accompany him on a second attempt.

Kor's line picked its way up a remarkably blank section of wall, singularly lacking in cracks and other prominent features. Undaunted, Kor flowed up the wall, chatting encouragingly to Chidlaw, who felt somewhat overwhelmed by the whole business. At the crux, an unprotected 5.7 bulge on the third pitch, Chidlaw had to shout up to Kor to "stop talking and concentrate on the climbing." The crux passed uneventfully after this admonition and the pair soon stood atop Layton Kor's first major new route, *The Bulge*. They were back in Boulder by 10:00 A.M. Shortly after this ascent, Kor rappelled down the route

Paula Crenshaw and Sue Giller on the crux pitch of The Bulge *in the mid-1970s* (Photo: Bob Godfrey)

A Much Bolder Boulder   31

Bob Culp on the second pitch of Grand Giraffe *(Photo: Bob Godfrey)*

Buttress near Estes Park with Kor in 1958, commented: "There's a fine line that should be reached where you keep your belayer relaxed, and yet let him know that the climbing is hard. Kor could never find this line. He always struck terror into the hearts of his belayers."

Kor's old Ford was a familiar sight near Boulder in the early 1960s. He usually drove at sixty miles an hour—on the straights, over hills, through turns, and probably through the narrow gate of Eldorado Canyon as well.

T2

In 1959, Kor picked out an intricate line left of upper *Redguard* that led directly to the summit of Tower 2, the easternmost of Redgarden Wall's summits. Kor invited Gerry Roach, a young, relatively inexperienced climber (later to summit Mount Everest), to accompany him. Roach's account captures the flavor of climbing with Kor in 1959:

> *"Want to go climbing tomorrow, Gerry?"*
> *"Sure, Layton, what's up?"*
> *"Uh, just a route in Eldorado. I'll pick you up at four A.M."*
> *"Four A.M.! Must be some route."*
> *The other climbers in the room all gave me looks of impending doom. They obviously knew something I didn't but, in my eighteen-year-old enthusiasm, I paid no heed. At 4:30 A.M. Layton's car roared into Eldorado. "Damn, it's still dark."*
> *"Watcha expect, Layton, it's the middle of the night."*
> *We sat in the car for a while and at the first hint of dawn we were off.*
> *"Hey, this is Redguard." I protested.*

Redgarden Wall, showing (left to right) Yellow Spur, Grand Giraffe, T2, *and* The Naked Edge *(Photo: Bob Godfrey)*

and placed a bolt at the crux for the benefit of future parties. Even with the bolt, the exposed, poorly protected climbing still inspires respect in modern climbers.

Improbable and bold, *The Bulge* was a fitting start for a climber who was to become noted for his ability to examine any cliff and pick out a line of ascent. Kor refused to be daunted by impossible-looking rock, and he possessed a rare intuition for finding hidden lines of holds on apparently blank walls. Many of Kor's climbs are masterpieces of routefinding. Those who climbed with him have said that he just seemed to *know* where a climbable line existed.

At first, Kor had difficulty finding partners because he was unknown to the local climbers. Later, as word of his exploits spread, he continued to have difficulty finding partners—because of his interest in only the most difficult climbs and his hair-raising ways of tackling them. Chuck Alexander, who made the first ascent of Sundance

"Just wait," was all Layton said as he disappeared upwards.

The first three pitches sailed by in dim confusion and finally in the light of day we started the fourth pitch, off the Upper Meadow. As Layton moved up, lichens tinkled down through the air well away from the rock. We were into it now. Higher up Layton got into trouble. I had followed him many times but had never seen him so gripped. He did some incredible stems that I knew my mere six-foot-two could not duplicate. As soon as I reached the same spot Layton announced, "If you can't make it up in thirty seconds I'll start hauling! This route's gotta go!"

"Thirty seconds? Jesus!" I looked around frantically for a hold, found one, pulled up and had just about worked out the crucial combination when Layton hollered, "Time's up!"

"Wait, Layton, I'm making it!" Too late. With a great "This route's gotta go," Layton began hauling on the rope. I came up sputtering and protesting but Layton could only think about the fifth pitch.

He tiptoed across a difficult traverse and nailed a steep crack. As I followed, Layton employed another tactic—he launched into an incredible nonstop patter: "Atta-boy-just-keep-inching-along-grab-that-knob-great-move-hang-on-just-keep-inching-along."

At the top of the fifth pitch a rack of biners and hardware jammed behind a large flake. Layton became furious and yanked so hard that the entire flake system we were on shook and shook. As I pondered our anchors the rope slipped away and jammed fifty feet below. I lowered Layton and he free climbed back up the steep crack on finger jams, an impressive display.

Higher, after Layton had run out eighty feet of rope, I suggested that he place a piton. He did, but I was able to pluck it out with my fingers. "Yeah, well I didn't want you to get too worried...."

As we shook hands on top it began to dawn on me what we had done. T2 was open.

Kor and Roach had started *T2* by climbing the first two pitches of *Redguard Route*. A few months later, Kor and Charles Roskosz added an independent start, beginning on the overhang now known as *Old, Bad Aid Crack*, and then traversing left to what is now the standard *T2* line.

Northcutt's Crack

One day in 1959 Ray Northcutt, fitness buff and bouldering specialist, was at the foot of the Bastille in Eldorado Canyon. "See that crack?" said his companion, pointing to a thin crack that rose fifty feet in a dead-vertical groove before ending in blankness. "Layton free climbed it the other day." In fact, Kor and Stan Shepard had made the first free ascent of the *Bastille Crack* earlier that year, but not via this much more difficult start.

The story, however, was enough for Northcutt. Tying in to the rope with his informant as belayer, he set off up the crack. Through his mind kept going the words, "If Kor can do it, so can I." The crack was steep but offered good holds—for most of the way. About forty feet up, a thin horizontal crack led right, toward the *Bastille Crack*. With a good piton for protection, Northcutt made an extremely difficult series of free moves and joined the *Bastille Crack* proper. At this point, Northcutt's belayer informed him that he had made up the story about Kor's free lead.

The *Northcutt Variation* was the first lead in the Boulder area to receive a 5.10 rating. In fact, modern guidebooks rate the pitch 5.10d—very close to 5.11—

The Bastille Crack, *Eldorado Canyon's earliest major rock climb, first ascended by unknown U.S. Army climbers in 1954 or 1955. The* Northcutt Variation *reaches the belayer's position from a thin crack down and left.* (Photo: Dudley Chelton)

John Ruger begins the crux moves of the Northcutt Variation *to the* Bastille Crack, *one of the hardest leads in the country when first free climbed by Ray Northcutt in 1959. Interestingly, Northcutt's ascent was accomplished the same year that the standard route was first climbed free.* (Photo: Dudley Chelton)

The first Yosemite 5.10 was the upper pitch of *Crack of Doom* by Chuck Pratt and Mort Hempel in May 1961. One of John Gill's variations on Baxter's Pinnacle in the Tetons, done in 1958, is supposedly 5.10, while in Big Cottonwood Canyon near Salt Lake City, *Goodro's Wall,* a definite 5.10, is reported to have been free climbed by Harold Goodro in 1949.

The Grand Giraffe

By 1960, Eldorado Canyon had a number of impressive climbs, including the *Yellow Spur* on Redgarden Wall, and the *West Buttress* and *Northwest Corner* of the Bastille, all three masterminded by Layton Kor. In 1960 Kor roped in George Hurley to attempt another new route on Redgarden Wall. Hurley was a quiet, unassuming figure, easy to overlook against the more extroverted characteristics of his contemporaries—one of many who grew up in the shadow of Kor—but his climbing would

The Bastille in Eldorado Canyon. Several early routes are visible, including the Bastille Crack *on the lower left face, and the* West Buttress, *with climber. The* Northwest Corner *begins on the prominent pillar between the two routes, while* Outer Space *takes the steep headwall on the left side of the summit block.* (Photo: Dudley Chelton)

ascent in 1959 was far ahead of its time. Some climbers have questioned if Northcutt actually climbed the pitch completely free, since he might have climbed the crack, at 5.9, but not the crux moves where the climb moves up and right across the face. When interviewed in 1976, Northcutt remembered the climb clearly and stated that he had indeed climbed the crux moves completely free.

The *Northcutt Variation* was one of the earliest 5.10 leads in America. In the Shawangunks of New York, the earliest 5.10 was *Retribution,* done by Jim McCarthy in 1961. California's first official 5.10 was *Dave's Deviation* at Tahquitz, by Tom Frost and Joe Fitschen in 1960.

span over four decades and include countless first ascents from the sandstone towers of Utah to the granite of New Hampshire.

"When Layton Kor and I first climbed the *Grand Giraffe*, we thought we were on an extremely hard, maybe even a desperate climb." Hurley said of the 1960 first ascent with Kor. "To some extent the desperate quality was part of Layton's style. He liked to wonder aloud about the human possibility of whatever we were doing. 'It's awful,' he'd say, or, 'Don't fall or we'll both go,' as he leered down a hard lead. Usually he was just having fun, but on the chimney pitch of the *Grand Giraffe* I was not laughing."

This pitch was a very strenuous off-width squeeze, rated 5.10 in modern guidebooks. The name for the climb, Hurley continued, "was a takeoff on the Grandes Jorasses and a way of debunking ourselves and our efforts in a canyon in the foothills of the gentle Rockies. We looked to European climbs with awe and reminded ourselves that Eldorado was a practice area, a *klettergarten*. It was only later, after we had climbed in Europe, that we realized that Colorado climbs deserved serious respect."

In 1960, Kor developed a strange lung disease and departed for a starvation diet at a Texas sanatorium. On his return to Colorado he had lost forty pounds and was a confirmed vegetarian. Bob Culp noted that seeing him lustily devour two huge heads of lettuce in rapid succession on a bivouac ledge was a unique experience. "Lotsa energy in lettuce!" he would mutter between gulps. Kor's lung disease allowed him to regularly prevail upon his climbing partners to carry all the gear up to the base of the climb. Once there he would suddenly perk up, grab the equipment, and lead off at breakneck speed.

Kor's flurry of activity between 1961 and 1963 resulted in some of Eldorado Canyon's most popular and memorable climbs, including *Blackwalk* on the eastern flank of Redgarden; the great Roof Routes including *Le Toit, Kloeberdanz, Guenese, Psycho,* and *The Wisdom; Super Slab* and the *Diving Board* on Redgarden's upper walls; and *Outer Space* and *X-M* on the Bastille. These were done in the best style of the day: rapidly, employing both aid and free-climbing techniques. Other outstanding climbers on the scene included Bob Boucher, Bob Culp, Dave Dornan, Dave Rearick, Rick Horn, Huntley Ingalls, Paul Mayrose, and Jack Turner—a group that formed the heart and soul of Boulder climbing and shaped the scene of the early 1960s.

"Climbers Rescue Youths Off Wall"

On a snowy Christmas day in 1961, Kor and Jack Turner climbed a spectacular line they named *Rosy Crucifixion* that traversed out above the great Redgarden roofs. The following day they made the first ascent of an obvious rock formation high above the canyon floor. As they huddled in their jackets and froze their hands in a leaning, 200-foot dihedral system, they daydreamed of warmer climates, naming their route *Rincon* after the balmy California surfing area near Santa Barbara. Shortly after these first ascents, Turner was sitting at home on a cold, snowy evening when the phone rang. It was Kor.

"Turner, we gotta go climbing."

"For God's sake, why?"

"There are a couple of kids stuck up on the *Yellow Spur*. The Rocky Mountain Rescue just called. We gotta go and get 'em."

Kor picked up Turner and sped down to Eldorado at a speed that turned the gently falling snowflakes into horizontal bullets. Rocky Mountain Rescue was there. Everyone and his friend seemed to be there. Chaos reigned. Hours had been spent discussing the situation, and an eight-foot-diameter searchlight bathed the scene in eerie yellow light, revealing only snowflakes.

"Come on, Turner!" yelled Kor, charging up the hillside. At the foot of Redgarden, Kor tied into the rope and disappeared into the gloom, swimming his way 150 feet up the snow-filled chimney system of *The Dirty Deed*. Turner quickly followed. A traverse ledge led across to the *Yellow Spur*, where two shivering sixteen-year-olds from Boulder High School huddled in the dark on a snow-covered ledge. The *Rocky Mountain News* the next day trumpeted a banner headline: "Climbers Rescue Youths Off Wall."

Layton Kor and George Hurley sort gear near Kor's famous Ford, in 1962 (Photo: Huntley Ingalls)

Layton Kor on Ruper *in 1961* (Photo: Charles Roskoz/Pat Ament collection)

This unusual meeting was the beginning of great partnerships—the youngsters were Larry Dalke and Pat Ament. After their snowy meeting on the *Yellow Spur*, Kor, Dalke, and Ament became regular climbing companions.

X-M

In the spring of 1962, Pat Ament got a phone call from Kor. "Ament, you gotta get down here right away. Bring all the money you can get hold of. There's somebody here selling Chouinard equipment. It's incredible."

Chouinard's legendary chrome-moly-steel pitons were light years ahead of the soft-iron hardware the Boulder climbers were using. Ament immediately phoned Larry Dalke. The two pooled all their money—about one hundred dollars—and shot off down to Kor's trailer. They were soon the proud possessors of a selection of Chouinard pitons. "Bugaboos were our favorites," recalls Ament of the sturdy blade pitons that seemed particularly suited to the cracks of the Boulder region.

Kor, Dalke, and Ament also purchased some of the fabled RURPs—Chouinard's Realized Ultimate Reality Pitons. RURPs were about the size of a razor blade, intended for hairline cracks, and would just about hold a climber's weight, provided he didn't do anything radical, like cough. Shortly after this equipment bonanza, Kor led the apprehensive Ament into Eldorado, hoping to climb a direct start to one of the recent new Bastille routes, *Outer Space*. Ament's account tells of their adventure:

Pat Ament and Larry Dalke in Boulder in 1962 (Photo: Layton Kor/Pat Ament collection)

It was a fiasco for both of us. The head of my hammer flew off and landed on top of somebody's car. Layton was screaming at me. I was standing there trying to figure out how to get the pitons out without a hammer, and here comes the haul line down the cliff with Layton's hammer tied to it, swinging across the wall around the corner, missing my head by about two inches.

I didn't know anything about direct aid and I had a desperate time seconding the first pitch because I couldn't reach Kor's pitons. At the belay ledge, he clipped some RURPs on me and said, "This is all you'll need for this pitch." I reached over and tapped a RURP in and said, "I can't believe this is gonna hold me." He said, "Sure it'll hold you." I said, "You sure?" He said, "I'll show you." So we changed belay for a minute and he went out and stepped right up on it without testing it. Didn't know if I'd placed it well or not. "See, they hold!" He was about two hundred pounds. I said, "Oh my god!" I was terrified that I'd have to catch him if it gave way and he took a fall. Catching him was a major feat. He came back, and up I went placing RURPs.

The day before we did the climb we'd been to see a science fiction movie. It was about rocket ships going up into outer space. The name of the ship in the movie was Rocketship X-M. *We were heading up directly to* Outer Space, *so it seemed very appropriate. We decided to call the route* X-M.

For Kor, *X-M* was just one more new climb, but for Ament it was a powerful lesson in psychology. Ament would soon emerge as a brilliant and distinctive climber in his own right. And the RURPs? "RURPs assumed almost magical significance for us," recalls Ament. "We'd go screaming down to Eldorado in Layton's old car. He'd look across at me and say, 'Got the RURPs?' 'Gosh, Layton, no. I thought you had 'em.' Around we'd spin, bald tires squealing, and tear back to Boulder to get them."

The Naked Edge

Stanley Shepard was a small, wiry, intellectual Boulder climber, known for a high level of energy, spirited sense of humor, and great humility. Shepard aspired to do major new climbs, but seldom pulled them off. "We were under the influence of the slow drama of Ray Northcutt's great project, the *Diagonal*," he noted, "and were very slow ourselves. We would do the first couple of leads of a climb, come back to Boulder and tell everybody who would listen how hairy it was, and wake up a day later to find out that Kor had gone out and done it in a couple of hours." Summarizing his activities, Shepard wrote: "My ability to visualize a climb and to name and publicize it far exceeded my ability to get up." In fact, Shepard pioneered many adventurous climbs, including a striking line on Castle Rock in Boulder Canyon later to be known as *Athlete's Feat*.

Surveying Redgarden Wall one day, Shepard saw a possible climb up the magnificent southeastern edge of Tower 2, beginning from the edge of the Upper Ramp some 250 feet off the ground. Shepard was surely not the first to imagine this line, but his name for it would endure. He climbed the route in his mind, naming it for a current movie starring Gary Cooper and Deborah Kerr, *The Naked Edge*. This climb, one of the all-time classics of the western United States, became the scene of many dramas during following years.

In 1961, Bob Culp and Jack Turner made the first attempt on *The Naked Edge*. From a ledge near the bottom of the Upper Ramp, Culp led up a spectacular but easy aid crack and placed two bolts for a belay at the bottom of a steep slab. Turner climbed past and attempted to free climb the slab, but lack of protection turned him back. Culp tried, and also retreated. Subsequently, Shepard and Bob Boucher made an attempt, envisioning a complete line from the ground. They began with the

Redgarden Wall from the southwest. The Naked Edge *takes the central buttress, roughly following the line of sun and shadow.* (Photo: Dudley Chelton)

Layton Kor on the fourth pitch of The Naked Edge *during the second ascent* (Photo: Pat Ament)

original *T2* start, continuing direct up the line now known as *Old, Bad Aid Crack*. They, too, were turned back by the unprotected slab. A bolt now protects this slab, but the original climbers trying *The Edge* refused to place bolts on any of the route's blank sections.

Next, Kor persuaded the young Steve Komito to accompany him. Instead of trying to free climb the slab, Kor moved right to an incipient crack beneath the overlap on the slab's outer margin. A few tenuous piton placements found Kor in extremis. Komito recalls: "Kor was shrieking that he was going to come off at any moment and just clean me right off the slab. I was petrified!" Kor managed to lower to the belay and the two made a disheveled retreat.

In 1962, after success on many hard new Eldorado routes, Kor and Culp returned to *The Naked Edge*. This time Kor finished the frightening second pitch—then a solid A4 lead. Later, as with so many of Eldorado's aid routes, it became much easier as subsequent ascents deepened hairline cracks. Kor and Culp continued upward, finding excellent climbing. They climbed through a leaning chimney high on the upper wall, then moved left into a steep inset to finish. The basic line of *The Naked Edge* was finally climbed. Kor and Rick Horn returned in 1964 to complete the line as it is known today, moving right from the fourth-pitch chimney into a hanging dihedral on the most overhanging section of the final edge.

During the early years of the 1960s, Boulder's aid routes—including the roof routes in Eldorado Canyon; the *Nordwand* on the Matron on the slopes of Bear Peak; and the *Red Dihedral* on the Mickey Mouse Wall south of Eldorado—involved some of the most difficult artificial pitches in the country. Lacking the soaring cracks and predictably sound granite of Yosemite, Eldorado aid climbs ascended relatively short but supremely improbable faces, connecting flakes and seams with hook moves and free climbing. After making an early ascent of the notorious *North America Wall* in Yosemite in 1973, Colorado Springs climber Jim Dunn whimsically commented, "It was good practice for the harder aid routes in Eldorado."

5. The Great Faces

Before the great advances in Eldorado Canyon in the early 1960s, other breakthroughs took place in the higher peaks. In 1958, Dale Johnson and Ray Northcutt made a formal application for permission to climb the Diamond on Longs Peak, submitting photographs, ability certificates, and detailed plans. As in 1954, the climbers were refused permission. The Park Service ban applied only to the Diamond's main face, however. On the lower east face, between *Stettners Ledges* and *North Chimney*, was a massive expanse of blank rock as big as the Diamond. A thin crack system slanted diagonally up this face, and Northcutt felt there was the prospect of a route. Learning from past mistakes, he kept his mouth shut and didn't ask permission for an attempt.

The Diagonal

Northcutt's first attempt on the Longs *Diagonal* was in August 1958, with George Lamb (who four years earlier had established *Empor* on Cobb Rock in Boulder Canyon, one of the toughest climbs in Boulder at the time). They climbed far enough up the slanting crack system—clearing the prominent overhang 250 feet above Mills Glacier—to persuade Northcutt that the route was possible. In September of that year Northcutt met Layton Kor, and the pair agreed to attempt the route together the following summer.

Northcutt and Kor climbed together regularly during the spring of 1959, and on the first weekend of July they made their first attempt on the *Diagonal*. Conditions on the face were very wet, making the climbing difficult and necessitating a good deal of direct aid. In the early afternoon a storm came in, bringing heavy rain. The line was exposed to stonefall washed off from Broadway, and as the rocks went bouncing by, Northcutt and Kor retreated, leaving fixed ropes to their high point.

The following weekend they returned to the face and prusiked back up their fixed ropes. Three more pitches up wet cracks took them to a point two-thirds of the way up the face. Ahead of them the nature of the rock changed; the diagonal crack system became shallow and the piton placements poor. To the right, a system of holds and small ledges offered promise of a traverse line, the goal being a

Ray Northcutt begins the long traverse on the Diagonal, Longs Peak, 1959 (Photo: Layton Kor)

large dihedral system leading straight to Broadway, about 200 feet to the right.

Northcutt led across the traverse, which involved some difficult face climbing. Another storm caught the team high on the face. They made an epic retreat, leaving fixed ropes once again. Soon after, they returned, prusiked their lines, and completed the traverse into the summit dihedral. Two hundred feet higher, at long last, the pair finished the climb to Broadway. It was the first Grade V route in Colorado.

The *Diagonal* traverse generated quite a controversy in following years. Northcutt claimed to have free climbed the whole way across, but subsequent parties were unable to repeat this feat. Northcutt's difficult route on the Bastille, however, suggested that he might have pulled off a similarly unlikely stretch of free climbing on the *Diagonal*.

In 1960, while making the second ascent of the *Diagonal*, Dave Rearick and Bob Kamps were unable to free climb a blank slab at the right side of the traverse, resorting to a forty-foot diagonal rappel. On the third ascent, Larry Dalke and Pat Ament reported a similar experience. During the late 1960s and 1970s, Northcutt's free traverse became something of a legend, with climbers holding varying opinions on what had occurred.

When interviewed in 1975, Northcutt cleared up the mystery. An afternoon storm had caught him and Kor near the right side of the traverse, and they rappelled off, leaving fixed ropes in place. When they returned, Northcutt said, they got off their fixed rope at an advantageous spot slightly below the point from which they had initially rappelled, then continued the climb. The questionable forty feet that had stopped the later parties had been bypassed by the rappel off the face.

The *Diagonal* was a tremendous climb that has held its reputation well to the present time. It was Northcutt's masterpiece, culminating a decade during which he had become an acknowledged master in Colorado climbing. Soon after, he dropped out of climbing completely.

The Diamond

In 1954 and 1958, the Park Service had refused permission for Colorado climbers to attempt the Diamond. In 1959, after their Hallett Peak climb, Yvon Chouinard and Ken Weeks sneaked up to Broadway for a clandestine attempt on the Diamond, but a major storm moved in and they were compelled to retreat.

In 1960 the Park Service finally relented and issued application blanks for a Diamond attempt to all parties that had previously expressed interest. Johnson contacted Northcutt, but he had not climbed seriously since the *Diagonal* the year before and felt that he was unprepared for an attempt. As Johnson searched for a companion, application blanks also went out to two California climbers, Dave Rearick and Bob Kamps.

Rearick and Kamps had climbed extensively in Yosemite Valley. They made the fifth ascent of the *Steck-Salathé* route on Sentinel Rock together, and with Royal Robbins, Rearick had made the third ascent of the Northwest Face of Half Dome, the country's first Grade VI. Visiting Colorado for the summer, the pair had made the second ascent of the *Diagonal* and clearly had the experience and confidence for a multiday climb on the Diamond.

At this time Colorado climbers had only soft steel pitons, which, especially in the smaller sizes, bent easily as they were hammered and removed from cracks. Rearick and Kamps had brought with them prototypes of the revolutionary Chouinard chrome-moly steel pitons that would cause Kor, Ament, and Dalke such excitement two years later. These were much more durable than the

The Diamond of Longs Peak (Photo: Jeff Achey)

The east face of Longs Peak, showing (left to right) the Diagonal, Yellow Wall, *and* D1 *routes (Photo: Bob Godfrey)*

soft steel pitons and came in a wider variety of sizes, with "knifeblades" for hairline cracks, and "bong bongs" for cracks up to five inches wide. In 1960, after checking out their climbing record and their equipment, the Park Service gave Rearick and Kamps permission to go ahead with an attempt on the Diamond.

It was drizzling steadily as the climbers and a support party fixed ropes in *North Chimney* to make it easier and safer to carry equipment up to Broadway and the base of the Diamond. Rain continued that evening, and the climbers spent the night in the shelter cabin at Chasm Lake. The next day dawned cold and windy, but it had stopped raining and Rearick and Kamps headed up the fixed ropes to the foot of the wall. In the rather matter-of-fact report they prepared for the Park Service, they described the start of the climb:

> *The actual climbing began at 9:30 A.M. on August 1. The first pitch, 140 feet, is easy free climbing. The second pitch is moderate to difficult face climbing on sound rock, leading to an overhang slanting to the right. The third pitch involves direct aid to ascend the right edge of this overhang, and ends on a grass-covered platform with a large (loose) boulder, easily visible from Chasm View. The fourth pitch starts up the inside of the corner above, gaining thirty feet by difficult free climbing until direct aid is necessary. Easy "nailing" brings one up to the conspicuous six-foot overhang above, and it was passed with a single piton. Increasingly difficult nailing is encountered in the wide grass-filled crack leading from here up to the Ramp. On the first ascent this section was being drenched by water falling from the chimney near the top of the Diamond.*

Rearick and Kamps placed the first bolt of the climb to reinforce the belay stance at their high point, and then rappelled to Broadway for the night, leaving their ropes in place. After spending a comfortable night on Broadway, they ascended their lines to the Ramp. The next 400 feet of the wall leaned outward. The rock, sheltered from the weathering action of rain and running water, lacked the hard veneer of the lower slabs, but thanks to the overhanging nature of the rock, the climbers were behind the water that was falling from the upper cracks.

Two pitches higher they found a ledge measuring two feet wide by seven feet long. After climbing one more pitch above the ledge and fixing a rope, they settled in for the night on this tiny aerie. Rearick's comment in his report was simply that the temperature was about forty degrees, and that their down jackets kept them comfortable—a rather laconic notation considering their exposed perch and the historic nature of their ascent. With the exception of the top pitch, which contained several large blocks of ice, the next day's climbing proved relatively straightforward, and they reached the top of the Diamond at 1:15 P.M. Their route would be known simply as *D1*.

Rearick and Kamps' ascent had been followed by daily gripping stories in the local newspapers and on radio, and a half-page account of the adventure appeared in *Time* magazine. They received a hero's welcome in Estes Park, finding themselves the star attraction in the summer rodeo parade.

Dave Rearick leaving the D1 *bivy ledge on the first ascent of the Diamond* (Photo courtesy the *Denver Post*)

Bob Kamps, Dave Rearick, and the Diamond, in 1960 (Photo: Glen Prossen/Pat Ament collection)

The first ascent of the Diamond, though historic, proved relatively straightforward, and would doubtless have been accomplished earlier had the Park Service not intervened. Rather than being an ultimate, the ascent was to prove only the beginning of a series of events in the 1960s in which the concept of the impossible was seized roughly by the scruff of the neck and shaken up so as to be unrecognizable.

Northwest Face of Chiefshead

The next great high-country climb was the work of Colorado's own, Layton Kor and Bob Culp. Culp, an active pioneer in Eldorado Canyon, would become one of the wise men of Colorado rock climbing. He climbed almost everywhere in the state and recounted his adventures in a tersely humorous style, both verbally and in writing. For many years he owned the famous Boulder Mountaineer climbing shop, a hub of the Boulder rock-climbing scene for over three decades.

Culp had a number of near-death experiences during his early climbing days. On one occasion he was standing unroped on a ledge near the top of a pinnacle in Gregory Canyon, trying out a new hand jam espoused by British climber Joe Brown. Just as he inserted his hand in the crack, the ledge on which he had been standing collapsed. The jam failed, Culp fell over backward, landed on another ledge below, and was pummeled with debris. Bruised and bleeding, he crawled back to his car and drove to the University of Colorado hospital, where he spent a week in bed.

A short time later, Culp was attempting a new route near Boulder Falls. Protection was very poor, and he free climbed into a position where he faced a 100-foot ground fall. Culp reached an impasse and was shocked to find that he had exerted so much energy that he could no longer climb down. Terrified, he clutched the rock until his arms were in such intense pain that he could no longer stand it. His fingers loosened on the holds, but as he began to slide he felt something holding him by his waist. His jacket had snagged on a tiny nubbin of rock. He rested his full weight on his jacket, slowly regaining his strength until he was able to pull up with his arms and place a sling on the nubbin that held him. Standing in this sling, he was able to step up to good holds and finish the lead.

Culp and Kor made many outstanding climbs together, including *Ruper*, which became one of the most popular routes in Eldorado Canyon, done in a three-hour blast in 1961. In the summer of that same year, the pair set off to attempt the unclimbed northwest face of Chiefshead, a wall not quite as steep as the Diamond but notably lacking in crack systems. Culp's account in *Trail and Timberline*, November 1970, is excerpted here:

Bob Culp on Rosy Crucifixion *in 1966* (Photo: Jane Culp/Pat Ament collection)

The northwest face of Chiefshead was one of the biggest unclimbed walls in Rocky Mountain Park when Layton Kor pointed it out to me in the winter of 1960. Its remote location and forbidding appearance had discouraged attempts to climb it. Kor was excited. "The best thing left in Colorado," he boasted. "It'll take everything we've got to get up it! It's got to be climbed!"

We prepared for the climb with uncharacteristic care. During the cold, snowy months I sent away to the Dolt Hut for a collection of CCB pitons which we thought might work better than the Simonds and Army Angles we normally used. We made sporadic attempts to get into shape by climbing ropes in the CU fieldhouse and traversed the university buildings to strengthen our fingers. These sessions usually ended up with our searching the library for climbing books or photographs we might have missed.

One day at the gym we watched the wrestling team working out and Layton suggested we give it a try. After a few minutes of threshing about I was ready to call it quits but Kor was still raring to go. We were approached by the wrestlers, who seemed to be fascinated by the commotion we had caused. I waved them on to Layton. What followed was an incredible melee that left everyone rolling on the mats—those not actually wrestling were convulsed with laughter. They could do nothing with him! He had no wrestling experience but possessed an abundance of energy. I remember him frantically leaping about trying to dislodge a young man with a death grip on one of his long legs who gasped, "Just like trying to pin a giraffe!"

My first close-up view of the climb was not very encouraging. It was early June and the face was running with water. The wall loomed dark and ominous with smooth rock that seemed crackless. Kor had stayed behind at Black Lake to shake the last lingering effects of an illness and had sent me ahead with all the gear and instructions to take advantage of the light and pick out a good line. It was impossible to pick out a real line so I invented an imaginary one right up the center.

Next morning as we surveyed the climb Kor's only comment was, "Looks good as any." With some uncertainty I began climbing. Although there were seldom any cracks, the rock was fantastic and little holds seemed to sprout under my fingertips. The rope reached to a convenient ledge. The route above was uncertain but that was Kor's problem for the moment.

Pausing just long enough to grab the hardware, he was off. He had completely shaken the previous day's lethargy and was impatient to get on with it. "Move your belay down to the end of the ledge," he shouted. "I'm gonna need all the rope I can get."

Somewhat reluctantly I untied from my anchor. By the time I had re-established the belay most of the rope had been taken up. "Good flake up here," I could hear him shouting as he banged in a pin. Clipping in a stirrup he leaned back for a view of the route above. "It's gonna go, it's gonna go!" I could hear him humming happily as he moved out of sight.

Seconding the pitch gave me a preview of what was in store above: consistently difficult climbing on good but small holds with little protection. One piton driven upside down under a flake had protected the lead.

As I approached him, Kor began getting me ready for the next pitch. He always preferred to lead and had been known to try to psych out his partners so he could get all the pitches. "You're gonna love this next part," I could hear him gloating. "Perfectly smooth. No holds at all. You might get in some protection about fifty feet up." On and on.

As I started off it dawned upon me that his predictions were absolutely accurate. Reaching up at arm's length I was barely able to get fingertips on a small edge. Working my feet up on friction I pulled up. Above, about six inches further than I could reach was another tiny nubbin. Maybe with a lunge? I decided against it and stepped back to consider other alternatives. There seemed to be none. Kor was getting restless. After all we were wasting time with most of the wall above us. "OK Layton, you give it a try," I relented.

Moments later I was trying to get tied onto the belay anchor with Kor already half way to my high point and climbing rapidly. Without hesitation he pulled up on the small edge, shot up an incredibly long arm to the high nubbin, and stepped neatly up. "Good holds up here," he remarked, as he began an upwards traverse to the left which ran out the rope without a single piton.

Groaning inwardly I cursed myself for not leading the pitch. At worst I would have faced a relatively short fall. Now if I came off I was in for a pendulum halfway across the wall. With clenched teeth and pounding heart I pulled up. The nubbin looked impossibly high, but from the extreme of a thumb-tip mantel I was just able to reach it. It was good. I gradually calmed down before rejoining Kor.

"You're gonna love this next one," I could hear him beginning.

The climb progressed. Kor was a genius at routefinding. Or maybe he was uncommonly lucky. Perhaps it was just that he had the commitment to climb through whatever he encountered. Probably it was all three. At any rate, although the difficulties and uncertainties persisted, we were soon halfway up the wall. It was here that we encountered the crux.

It was Kor's lead. The rock above looked blank. Nothing new. He moved up a few feet and placed a shaky pin behind a small flake. "Probably ought to put in a bolt," he fretted, but decided against it when he thought he could see a small crack above. A few minutes later he had half the rope out and the crack was nonexistent. "This is serious up here," he shouted. "Get ready. Get ready!" Standing on a ledge barely big enough for both feet and tied to a questionable anchor, I was in no mood to think of catching a 150-foot fall.

From my ledge I could see him spread-eagled above, finger and toe tips touching the rock. He rarely paused—just long enough to scan the rock above and then he was moving on. Such was his commitment that he was able to bring to bear the full focus of his immense drive without even entertaining the idea of retreating. Eventually came the dreaded words. "Sorry about this but the rope won't reach. You're gonna have to come up a ways."

It wasn't so bad on my end. The climbing was reasonable, but I knew Kor was in a difficult spot. If he came off while I was climbing? . . . "Oh, well," I tried to convince myself, "it's Layton. You're probably safer here than on the drive up." Kor made it safely to a ledge.

There was a lot more to come but nothing desperate. One false start high on the wall required Layton to climb down, with me directing his feet to tiny holds. An apparently blank area that had us worried suddenly developed a perfect piton crack that ran to the end of the difficulties. By that time we hardly needed it. We used three pitons for aid and placed three bolts for belay anchors in crackless rock. The famous CCB pitons had been of no use whatsoever.

Layton Kor on the first ascent of the northwest face of Chiefshead, 1961 (Photo: Bob Culp)

We were met by our friend Huntley Ingalls, who had soloed the north ridge to take pictures. At the summit, in the fading light, we had one final surprise. Kor was hopping up and down in excitement. "Roberto, get up here! You've got to see this." There to the south was a great wall that neither of us had known about: the east face of Mount Alice. Kor lingered for the better part of a minute to enjoy the view. "Now that has got to be climbed," was his parting comment.

The Chiefshead route, now known as *The Path of Elders*, was an impressive achievement in 1961. Though comparable in length and difficulty to the great *Diagonal* on Longs, first done just two years earlier, it was a completely different undertaking, employing a bold, lightning-fast style. Unlike the *Diagonal*, which was quickly repeated, the Chiefshead route would sit fourteen years before its second ascent, until Billy Westbay and Dan McClure climbed it in 1975, eliminating the original three points of aid and reporting long, mandatory runouts on 5.9 and 5.10 climbing.

After the *Diagonal*, the Diamond, and the northwest face of Chiefshead had been climbed, climbers looked for other challenges in the high country: new routes, speed ascents, winter ascents. Once again, Layton Kor would figure large and the east face of Longs Peak would provide the central venue.

The Yellow Wall
In the summer of 1962, Kor set out to establish his own route on the Diamond, which had not been climbed since Rearick and Kamps' ascent two years earlier. Regulations were still strict. Prior to the attempt, each climber and support-party member was required to sign the park's five-page application form. After a lengthy check-out process, park rangers certified a team led by Layton Kor as fit for a Diamond attempt. Kor's teammates were Bob Culp and the noted Shawangunks climber Jim McCarthy, who had pioneered the earliest 5.10 climbs in the East and would play a brief but energetic role in Colorado big-wall climbing in the early 1960s.

While approaching the face, both Culp and McCarthy fell ill. Rather than abandon the attempt, Kor enlisted Charlie Roskosz from the support team. The climb—which they called the *Yellow Wall*—followed a direct line up the golden vertical flatiron forming the left side of the Diamond, with a few tricky traverses and thin-crack sections, finishing just right of a distinctive roof band near the top. Kor and Roskosz reached the summit of Longs after one bivouac on the face. Roskosz had not been authorized for the climb—his wife didn't even know he was on the face until she read about it in the newspaper a

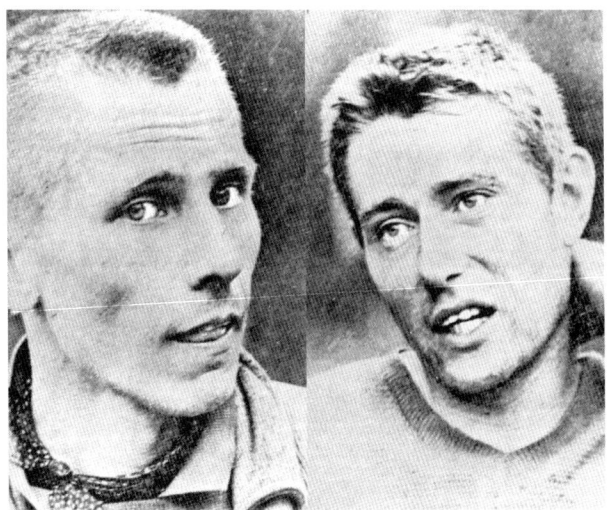

Charlie Roskosz and Layton Kor after the Diamond (Photo courtesy the *Denver Post*)

day later—and following the ascent he was called before the local magistrate and fined.

The Diamond in a Day

In the summer of 1963, Kor and Royal Robbins made the first one-day ascent of the Diamond, via the Rearick-Kamps route. Two days later, in a remarkable effort, this pair put up a route of their own—*Jack of Diamonds*—also in a single day from Broadway.

Robbins had great respect for Kor, and in a 1977 letter recalled Kor's impact on the Yosemite climbing crowd:

> Kor was a phenomenon. He was the first climber to break the hegemony which Californians had long enjoyed in Yosemite. Until Kor arrived, it was folk wisdom among Yosemite climbers that everyone who came there—no matter how they might star on their home ground—every climber on his first visit to Yosemite suffered a decline in his personal estimation of his climbing worth. Yosemite would inevitably take the piss out of the arrogant visitor. This was mostly due to the peculiar nature of Yosemite climbing, which tended toward holdlessness and strenuousness. But Layton wasn't daunted. He astonished us all by his ability to immediately do the harder routes in the Valley, and in record time as well!

In the same letter, Robbins described the phenomenal pair of one-day Diamond ascents, beginning with the repeat of the Rearick-Kamps route:

> It's a long but lovely walk up to Chasm Lake. I remember more the loveliness, at this distance, than the length. Embedded in my memory are pictures of the pines and twisted aspen, the fresh stream bubbling downward, the wildflowers, and, up high, the meadows and lakes. It has always been a wonder to me that the Colorado Rockies, which appear so desolate, barren, and dry from a distance, can present to the visitor such an abundance of alps, wildflowers, lakes, and streams.
>
> There were a number of parties camping in and about the stone shelter at Chasm Lake when Liz, Layton and I arrived. We were ambitious to make the second ascent of D1, because of its reputation as a Yosemite wall in an alpine setting, and also simply because the Rearick/Kamps route was an elegant line up a stunning face. We were doubly ambitious, for we hoped to get up in a day.
>
> I knew there was no one in the country, perhaps in the world, at that moment, with whom I stood a better chance of climbing the Diamond in one day than with Layton Kor. He was fast. Kor, in fact, had never developed the knack of climbing at any speed other than flat out. He was always in a hurry, and climbed every route, even the most trivial, as if he were racing a storm to the summit....
>
> I had great respect for Kor, and this would grow during our ascents of the Diamond. But, more than re-

Layton Kor on the first ascent of Yellow Wall, *the Diamond's second route, in 1962* (Photo: Huntley Ingalls)

spect, I liked Layton. He was a climber's climber, which is to say, he didn't play to the crowd, and he climbed for the right reasons, that is, to satisfy himself. He wasn't the sort of fellow to step on a piton and later claim a free ascent, because to him that would be utterly pointless. It wasn't what others thought of his climbing, but what he thought, that counted. Kor was one of the very few highly competitive climbers who never criticized the efforts and achievements of others. He was interested in action, life, joking conversation, and plans for the next climb. In fact, although he never talked about religion, Kor was a sort of natural Christian, generous when others were wrong, and not in the habit of finding fault with his neighbor. There was one exception to this. I once heard Layton express scorn for a Coloradan who had made a tasteless bolt route up one of Kor's favorite sandstone spires in the Utah desert.

During the afternoon of July 12, Layton and I left the shelter cabin and trod the fine brown granite along the south shore of Chasm Lake. We were soon on Mills Glacier and then followed Lambs Slide to Kiener's Traverse, which brought us to North Broadway, and a several hundred foot descent to our bivouac at the base of the Diamond. It was comfortable, and our sleeping bags assured a good night's sleep.

Our ascent went smoothly, except for a ten-foot fall when Kor pulled an aid pin. The icy chute at the top of the wall provided interesting variety to what was otherwise a straightforward, if difficult, technical rock climb. That Rearick and Kamps had climbed this route with only four bolts was evidence not just of their technical competence, but even more of a stern, anti-bolt discipline which had its roots in Yosemite climbing at that time; a discipline which, though occasionally violated, would later prevail in American mountaineering.

According to Bob Culp's prodigious memory, we did D1 in sixteen hours. Sounds about right. At any rate, we reached the refuge before dark.

After two days rest, we were back on Broadway, this time by way of the 500-foot North Chimney. This approach was shorter, but not without its dangers. We climbed it unroped with packs, and at times I felt we were engaged in a daring enterprise. There were several unpleasant passages, and at the top a steep section of loose rock. Layton swarmed up it, but I was thwarted by a hold out of reach. Kor, seeing my distress, lowered a vast paw, which I gratefully clutched and used to reach safe ground.

Hoping to avoid a bivouac, we started even earlier than we had on D1. I remember Kor swarming up the first pitch, pulling off a great block of loose rock which crashed down the North Chimney. By noon, the winds were being rude and clouds swirled overhead. Now, to lead was a pleasure and to belay a cold hell. Not that either of us fiddled about on the leads. We were competing against each other, yes. After all, each of our lives was given to climbing, and we both wished to excel.

I quote from a note about the ascent which appeared in the 1964 American Alpine Journal: "Racing against the setting sun to avoid a bad night in slings, Kor led the last pitch, a long, strenuous jamcrack. On my last reserves I struggled up this final pitch, topped the Diamond, and shook the hand of a great climber."

It was a long walk down. Mile after mile through the night I paced steadily behind Kor, through the Boulderfield—which seemed an enormous area. Kor showed no signs of weakening, and I forced myself to thrust my legs forward, long strides trying to match his. I wouldn't weaken. I would keep up behind this natural force that wouldn't slow down. Aching feet, legs, back. Mind numbed, but there was the light of the shelter; crowded, sordid, smelly, but warm and welcoming. I well remember Liz, but, oddly, I can't recall booze. Ah, I have grown so sophisticated that I can't imagine a climb like that with a walk like that, not being followed by wine, as well as love.

The Diagonal Direct

When Layton Kor and Ray Northcutt climbed the *Diagonal* in 1959, Northcutt had been the driving force. Four years later, Northcutt had dropped out of Colorado climbing and Kor was its unrivaled star. Viewing the line anew, Kor felt it might be possible to follow the *Diagonal* crack more directly to Broadway rather than making the long traverse. In 1963, he spent a week climbing on Longs' lower east face with Tex Bossier, doing several new routes including the *Gray Pillar*. They decided to attempt the so-called *Diagonal Direct*. In a 1975 interview, Bossier told of the desperate adventure this was to become.

I had dropped out of school and had a job as a hod carrier working for Kor. He just loved to shout, "Hey, mud!" . . . We decided we were going to try the direct finish on the Diagonal. I had expected the thing to be tremendously difficult from its reputation. I was very apprehensive. We were using direct aid where we didn't need to in the lower sections, but there wasn't any really extreme climbing. We were climbing very fast.

A thing that slowed us down was bolt chopping. When Northcutt first climbed the Diagonal, the only pitons around were ex-army, and he placed a lot of bolts to make things secure. A lot of them were belay bolts. I was kind of irritated at Kor doing this. I just wanted to say, "To hell with the damn bolt, let's go!" He had style in his mind in those days. If a bolt was there and it wasn't supposed to be there, then you were supposed to get rid of it.

We got to where the traverse started. Didn't take us too long to get there. About four hours. Right there, a storm came in. It started to rain. We talked about it, and under the circumstances it looked harder to do the traverse than to go straight up. We also thought it wasn't going to be that bad, and we didn't want to go down, but the nature of the climbing changed dramatically. The face became scooped out with boilerplate slabs, and the cracks were very shallow.

The storm was really getting bad. Rain was severe. We still thought we were better going up. We had a feeling about the difficulties of retreat and thought it was safer to continue. Water from the upper part of the wall was channeled down the crack system. It was coming down the rope and ending up in my swami belt, just like a waterspout. I was freaked out. Then it started getting cold, but we were committed. It was getting later and later and we were making extremely slow progress. It started to turn into snow and ice, and the wall started to freeze up. Fog also was coming down. Kor was off somewhere above, and we couldn't even see each other. It was extremely cold by this time. I would go into uncontrollable shivering and cramps on the belays. I had the feeling that if we didn't get off the climb that day, I'd never be able to live through it.

It turned into a full-fledged, full-blown storm. There was a ranger with a telescope on Mount Lady Washington, and he said it was a hell of a storm. We just weren't prepared for the conditions. We didn't have any bivouac gear. We had down jackets, but they were completely soaked before the temperature dropped. We had no idea where we were in the fog. I have no idea how difficult the climbing really was. We were really scared. In the guidebook they mention Kor getting knocked out of his stirrups by an avalanche. That's true. I heard this hollering, and screaming, and cursing. "What's going on?" I shouted. We were enshrouded in fog and I couldn't see him.

We started leaving pitons in place. We didn't even clean the last pitch of the climb. I kept thinking, "What's gonna happen if we get stuck? Who is there to come and rescue us? There's only one person in the whole of the United States who can get me off this climb, and I'm with him! If I get stuck, that's it."

Kor belayed me to Broadway. We got the pack up and were going to coil the haul rope. Part of it was over the edge, down the face, and it got stuck! Kor said, "To hell with it!" That was unprecedented. Never in my whole climbing career had I even considered abandoning a rope.

We started to traverse Broadway. There are some hairy-assed spots on Broadway. I knew Kor was pressed. He led off on a traverse. There was freshly fallen snow over previous icy snow. He sank in up to his knee in the new snow. There was one steep place, fifty to sixty degrees. The ledge was very narrow, with the Diamond above you and that whole lower wall below. Kor nailed in a piton for a belay and said, "On belay." Crossing in his footsteps, I got about half way across when some of the snow gave way and I half fell over backwards. One leg stayed in the step. I was on my back with my head looking down the lower wall. The whole panorama of the face went by as I fell backwards. I expected to go shooting off into space and take a horrible pendulum across to Kor. It was in slow motion. Everything was on film through my eyeballs. But one of my legs stayed.

I got straight up and went over to Kor. He's got one knifeblade in, that you could take out with your fingers! That you could take out with your fingers, for God's sake! I was about eighty feet horizontal to him when I slipped. I said, "God, Layton. This thing would just never have held." "I know, I know," he said. He said that when he saw me fall over backwards, his heart just went into his throat and he knew we were both dead. I said, "Look, if the belays are going to be like this, should we stay roped?" "Yes," he said, "we stay roped."

We got down to the shelter and the storm lasted for days. Next day we looked up and could see the wall. It was encased in ice. If we'd been up there, we'd just have been a goddamned icicle along with everything else. I said to Kor afterwards, "I don't think I would have made it if we'd had to stay the night up there." Kor replied, "Yes you would. You'd have made it if I had to stay up all night and beat on you with my hammer." But the way he said that, I also had the feeling that he didn't know for sure whether he would have made it or not.

Kor and Bossier had experienced the full brunt of the conditions that Northcutt had so feared during his attempts on the *Diagonal*. Events proved that his concerns were justified. The relatively low angle of the *Diagonal* had exposed Kor and Bossier to water, snow, and rocks coming down the face from Broadway and the Notch Couloir. The Diamond, in comparison, was relatively safe. Its overhanging walls deflected falling debris out beyond the range of climbers. After stories of Kor and Bossier's epic filtered down, the *Diagonal Direct* did not receive a second ascent until 1975, by Michael Covington and Billy Westbay. They found the climbing hard, and they discovered the pitons in the last pitch up to Broadway, silent witnesses to an epic of years gone by.

The Diamond: First Winter Ascent
Wayne Goss was a young Boulder climber who had learned much from Layton Kor during his beginning years. By 1966 he was an expert climber in his own right. Goss had a grand project in mind—a winter ascent of the Diamond. Climbers had long talked about it, but no serious attempt had been made.

It was no fluke that Goss, and not Kor, was the prime motivator behind this ascent. Kor had recently returned from a fateful trip to Europe, where in February 1965 he joined the legendary American alpinist John Harlin in an attempt to climb a direct route on the North Face of the Eiger in winter. Harlin was killed when a fixed rope broke. Kor was greatly distressed by Harlin's death, and on his return to Colorado his attitude toward climbing vacillated between disinterest and his old enthusiasm. Later that year, Goss asked Kor if he would be interested in the Diamond project. Kor said he was not.

Goss teamed up with Bob Culp for an attempt on Christmas Eve 1966. They reached Broadway and established a bivouac. The next morning they heard over their two-way radio that a big storm was moving in—and also that three youths who had attempted to climb Longs the day before had not returned. Abandoning their attempt but leaving their equipment on Broadway, Goss and Culp headed down, found the lost youths, frostbitten after a night out, and helped them down the mountain.

Later that winter, Goss and Culp managed to persuade Kor to join them in another attempt. The trio and their support party from Rocky Mountain Rescue arrived at the Chasm Lake shelter cabin on the afternoon of March 4. That night, six inches of snow fell. The team headed up Lamb's Slide, but Culp, who had been feeling ill, soon returned to the cabin. After a struggle up to Broadway, a bivouac, and two pitches of climbing up a new line, Goss and Kor retreated in bad weather. Snow continued and their supplies dwindled.

After a brief retreat to Boulder, Kor and Goss returned. Their proposed route up the Diamond was an entirely new line they would call the *Enos Mills Wall*, named for a former guide and naturalist on Longs Peak. Kor's account of the climb, published in *Trail and Timberline* in 1967 under the title "On the Granite Wall," is excerpted here:

> It was always nice to be moving, for while in motion the warmth seeped through our systems and chased out the

Aerial view of Longs Peak in winter (Photo: Dudley Chelton)

> cold and misery we endured on the silent stances. About noon I began the fifth lead of the climb. This airy experience followed a wide crack on the edge of a 100-foot pillar. I had nearly reached its top when a protruding piton tore a large hole in my down jacket. Unable to stop, I continued struggling up the bad-width crack until some small footholds provided rest. The now-useless down spiraled like falling leaves toward Goss, who hung in slings seventy-five feet below. It was very late in the day when I left the comfort of a two-foot ledge on top of the pillar and began hammering long pins deep into the ninety-degree wall. If we were lucky, a bivouac ledge awaited us at the end of the lead.
>
> One hundred feet up, the rock became rotten and the smooth diagonal overhangs stopped all progress. I was trying desperately to place a piton on my left when the tiny angle holding my weight popped out and a terrifying twenty-foot plunge into the dusk followed. When it ended I was swinging upside down squinting toward Goss, whose bright smile showed it had been an easy catch.
>
> I quickly climbed hand over hand up the rope, drove a larger piton into the same crack and once again studied the traverse to the left. A thin sling hooked over a tiny knob held my weight, while I nervously placed a poor piton upside down beneath the roof. Using this for

Wayne Goss on the first winter ascent of the Diamond (Photo: Layton Kor)

balance, I left the little security I had and tiptoed on the very edge of my double boots across a slab, which ended in an overhanging snow-filled corner. It had turned completely dark as I hung from my tortured fingers, placing several pitons to secure the belay.

"Lightning" Goss, who was in remarkable shape, removed all the pitons in just a few minutes, and soon headlamps cast out two beams halfway up the Diamond.

"Just above is the bivouac," I told Wayne, not really sure of anything except how lousy I felt. As Wayne belayed I sighted along the flickering light, which cut into the darkness, yielding a one and a half inch crack. Three aid pitons put me on a small snow shelf fifteen feet above Wayne and with the last of my energy I stamped out a small ledge in the snow. Again I placed the necessary belay anchors and began hauling up the packs, which felt like three mail bags full of lead. Soon a bright shower of sparks lit up the large piton on which Wayne was hammering, and before long he pulled out the last piton of the day. I slowly worked my way into the sleeping bag while Wayne, without a word, dug through the packs removing food, cooking gear, and other items we would need for the night. After joining me in idle comfort, he fired up the stove to provide us with the only food we could consume, hot raspberry Jell-O.

Even though we had to remain sitting all night, it was warm, reasonably comfortable, and we only woke up occasionally to change positions. Morning arrived with the sun gods and their yellow warmth which we thankfully absorbed along with more hot Jell-O.

Stiff swollen fingers kept us from smiling as we sorted out the mess from the night before. After things were a bit straightened out, more pounding, which inserted our metal spikes, carried us up a huge overhanging open book above the bivouac. One hundred and twenty feet up I crawled into another sling belay, a position which was overhanging Goss and the bivouac site by ten feet. We carefully nailed the last seventy feet of the open book up to and over a three-foot roof; then belayed thirty feet above in slings from a horizontal crack system. This thin and brittle crack cut all the way across the Diamond to the well-known Table Ledge. The view at this point was quite spectacular as everything below to Broadway was overhanging.

Artificial climbing on the Diamond in winter, as we were finding out, is a slow and delicate process, and our snail-like pace was almost sure to provide us with another "bivvy" on the wall. The next rope-length was even more rotten and every well-placed piton sent granular, red rock dashing all over the mountain. After I had climbed another 130 feet, the last ten of which consisted of a horizontal traverse on "spooky" knife blades, I set up the fifth hanging belay of the climb. While Wayne removed the pitons I viewed the crack system forty feet to the left where I had joined the master of technical climbing, Royal Robbins, on a one-day ascent of the wall.

Once again darkness set in and as our headlamps were giving us trouble, we almost expected a night in slings on the blank wall. Both Wayne and I agreed to make the top if at all possible, as we were still worried about the unsettled weather. Fifty feet above, another large roof provided a strenuous ten minutes and a spectacular view into the depths. Above the overhang the crack widened and an occasional free move was needed to eliminate the use of expansion bolts as our biggest pitons (four inches) were not large enough. After many minutes of struggling with rope slings and my headlamp cord I somehow managed to force several pitons deep into the icy crack, setting up the last belay of the climb. Wayne soon shared my position at the hanging "spaghetti gardens."

After a few minutes rest we changed places and I led into the night with a blinking headlamp until the wild blast of the wind told me it was all over. We arrived at the top of the wall at about 10 P.M. and bivouacked on the spot. The wind kept us awake most of the night and our short walk to the summit of Longs the next morning was a tiring, breathless undertaking. Even that was soon over and I shook hands with my tremendous partner for the first winter ascent of the Diamond—an experience we would long remember.

6. Black Canyon of the Gunnison

In 1960, Bob LaGrange returned from a sightseeing trip to the Black Canyon of the Gunnison River, in southwestern Colorado. Bubbling with enthusiasm, he showed

Aerial view looking upstream through The Narrows of the Black Canyon of the Gunnison. The North Chasm View Wall is hidden below the lowest protruding buttress in the bottom of the photo. Mirror Wall *climbs the face and ridge on the opposite side of the canyon just upstream, ending on the brush-covered "island" at the right of the photo. (Photo: Jim Neu)*

The main, southwest face of North Chasm View. The original 1963 route ascends the obvious diagonal weakness before exiting straight up through roofs at the top. (Photo: Jeff Achey)

Layton Kor color slides of massive granite cliffs bigger than either of them had climbed before. A few days later the pair assembled their equipment and drove to the canyon. They engineered a complicated descent and then climbed a 1,700-foot route that began just downstream of the sheerest portion of what is now known as the South Chasm View Wall, finishing near the Chasm View overlook on the South Rim.

Layton Kor beginning the crux lead of the Diagonal, *with Jim McCarthy and Tex Bossier at the belay* (Photo: Layton Kor collection)

just turned eighteen—along with Easterners Jim McCarthy and Will Bassett. Kor had just returned from a trip to Yosemite during which he and Steve Roper established the *West Buttress* route on El Capitan, and he was lamenting the fact that while Yosemite now had a half dozen Grade VI climbs, Colorado had none. Talk turned to the possibilities that surely existed in the Black Canyon. Within days the foursome was camped on the canyon's North Rim.

The sight of the vast gorge had a sobering effect on the Easterners. McCarthy was initiated that evening with a Swisher Sweet cigar—fitted with an exploding device. In the morning, the team pioneered a brush-choked and technical descent to the canyon floor and headed up the North Chasm View Wall via the obvious weakness—a 2,000-foot diagonal ramp and crack system. The climbing was mostly reasonable, but the rock was poor, hauling the bags was strenuous and unpleasant, and progress was slow. Bad weather forced a re-

A series of new routes ensued: the longest rock climbs in Colorado. Approximately twenty-five major ascents would be done in the Black Canyon of the Gunnison by the mid-1960s, including most of the prominent walls and arêtes of the canyon's most dramatic section, The Narrows. Though the Black Canyon lacked the altitude and harsh storms of Longs Peak, the climbs were huge—nearly twice as long as the Diamond routes. Sections of horribly loose rock were common, and conditions on the sunny walls could be unbearably hot. Crack systems were seldom continuous, as they were on the Diamond. Retreat from high on the walls meant countless rappels back into the canyon's depths, followed by a grueling gully climb to the rim. Consequently, once under way, ascents tended to take on a do-or-die quality.

One night in 1963, a group of climbers was gathered at Steve Komito's old house on University Avenue in Boulder, participating in the favorite household activity: talking rock. Kor was there, as was Tex Bossier—

Layton Kor and Larry Dalke, around the time of their ascent of North Chasm View (Photo: Larry Dalke collection)

The 1,600-foot southeast face of North Chasm View. The 1964 Kor-Dalke route ascends the center of the sheer face just to the right of the wall's profile. The obvious deep gash, known as Ament's Chimney or Chasm Gap, was first climbed by Pat Ament and Fred Pfahler in 1965. (Photo: Jeff Achey)

treat and a two-day hiatus. Bassett, feeling ill, bowed out of the attempt, which progressed laboriously. Kor, McCarthy, and Bossier had already made two bivouacs when they reached a point high on the face where the diagonal line died out into a series of large overhangs with decomposed rock.

Kor, after studying the overhangs for a while, turned to his partners and in an ominous voice said, "I think I'd better lead this pitch. I'm not married." His joking remark would soon prove to be all too apt. Kor would later say that it was one of the most difficult artificial pitches he had ever climbed, and it took him eight hours to lead.

Despite the difficulties of Kor's headwall pitch, the climb seemed to fall short of the mythical Grade VI standard. Nevertheless, the North Chasm View route, now known as the *Diagonal,* was an impressive climb, later to be the site of further adventure as free climbers ventured onto the canyon walls.

The next year, over two days in June, Kor and Larry Dalke climbed North Chasm View's southeast face, which Kor had passed under while approaching the *Diagonal.* Here they found some of the canyon's best rock, and compared their route to the *Steck-Salathé* on Sentinel Rock in Yosemite, one of the classics of the era. Despite such superlatives their "South Face" route went unrepeated for a decade.

Unlike the Diamond, whose routes saw regular repeats, the Black Canyon was not popular among climbers of the 1960s. In addition to being ominous and intimidating, the canyon was remote: construction of Interstate 70 west of Denver did not begin until 1967, and even with Kor driving, the canyon was an eight-hour backroads drive from Boulder compared with the hour needed to reach Longs Peak. Nevertheless a small group of climbers loved the Black Canyon, and it provided them with many fine climbs.

Mirror Wall

Most of the early Black Canyon climbs were masterminded by Kor. Some were not. Pat Ament was introduced to the canyon by Kor at age sixteen. In 1965, when he was nineteen, Ament returned with Fred Pfahler to make the first ascent of a route on North Chasm View Wall. Known as *Ament's Chimney,* this was a claustrophobic line whose crux pitch featured a horrific, unprotected chimney negotiated with feet on one wall, hands on the other.

Ament's account of another route, the *Mirror Wall* on the first buttress upstream from South Chasm View, illustrates the adventurous nature of many 1960s' ascents, in the Black Canyon and elsewhere, that took place in Kor's shadow. The account of the climb with Roger Briggs is excerpted from Ament's book *Swaramandal* (Vitaar, Boulder, 1973).

The sounds of white water reach the rim of the canyon where Roger Briggs and I stand . . . staring down. We contemplate dropping a rock and watching it fall. We turn away and walk through a land of trees, sagebrush, and desert silence and descend a gully between the walls.

Ute Indians have a superstitious dread of the Black Canyon and fear evil spirits that dwell in its depths. Winds run through the bends in the canyon like living things. At the bottom, 2,000-foot walls loom above us. The waters of the Gunnison flow westward.

It is autumn and evening. Before sacking out, my fifteen-year-old comrade and I are challenged by slick, water-polished boulders that submerge in spring. A kaleidoscope of astral light flashes on the rocks, reflecting a fifty-foot flame fueled by driftwood. A night in the deeps.

Huge, jagged, white-pink pegmatite bands that cross the walls are visible, lit by rays that bleed in through the narrowness overhead. A night of sounds and imaginings. Memories of other times, other climbs

The Mirror Wall *team in 1966: Pat Ament in Yosemite, and Roger Briggs (during the first free ascent of the* Northwest Corner *of the Bastille)* (Photos: Pat Ament collection)

in the canyon . . . first with Kor . . . then Fred Pfahler and I in a 1,500-foot chimney; the chimney ending with a "death lead," my lunging, risking a 200-foot fall; friends waiting for us on top telling us we look as if we've been fished out of the river.

"Be weird if the water rose tonight," I say to Roger.

Roger and I begin nailing a thin, unflawed, 600-foot crack at dawn, hacking our way upward into the expanses of the walls.

A traverse 80 feet left where the crack ends takes us across the top edge of a recess, which plunges toward our campsite. An elegant, 200-foot corner rises from a ledge we are on. I climb up 50 feet in the twilight but return. We bivouac on the ledge.

A light supper . . . cheese, meat, and water. The sounds of the river and the world below.

Morning. The exposure returns. Scattered clouds and colder temperatures. The top of the corner. Intuition and 500 feet. A collage of cracks, blocks, and pillars. My friend is subdued, has a far-away look, wonders if I know what I am doing. I wonder too. The ranger is on the rim and shouts down to us, "Will you make it today?"

"Yes!" I holler back. Roger seems to cheer up. We reach the summit at dark, stumbling, crawling up a brushy trough like a grave.

Our ride from Boulder to the Black Canyon a one-way affair, we have to figure a way back. The ranger drives us to Montrose, his headquarters seventeen miles southwest. We sleep in the city park, the next morning (trying to hitchhike) suffer police interrogation and have to walk to the ranger's office to borrow bus fare to Grand Junction—the nearest town north. Out of food, hungry, we steal an apple as we pass a fruit stand and snitch candy bars at the bus station. The stationmaster is a chubby Ben Franklin fascinated with us, and takes inventory over the top of his bifocals as we leave. The bus is full of Navajo Indians who sing the duration of the ride in the dusk.

Grand Junction's freight yards. The track. The night and wind. A switchman opens a caboose for us. "Warm up. Go to sleep if you want. They'll wake you later," he says.

The caboose has an other-worldly air about it. Briggs resembles a corpse as he dozes. He is really not the silent, stoic type, but he is worried about his parents, how they will react. He will miss a day of school. He has never ridden the freights. His face is expressionless except for a particular boyish smile now and then as I boggle his mind with stories of breaking my wrist, a voyage down the Yellow Spur, *swinging off* Supremacy, *and* Layton *. . .*

Finally I shut up. Roger is tall and thin, with a long, gazelle neck and funny glasses. He is studious, a dean's son, places pitons the way I do . . .

A switch-engine slams us. We run out, a train humming, and jump on as it goes. Steel and motion.

We wake up in blackness, suffocating in diesel smoke in the Moffat Tunnel, passing under the Continental Divide, close to home. We wonder if it is day or night. The train's horns blast. We hit East Portal and meet morning, blue skies, and mountain valleys where a foot of snow has fallen.

The Southern Arête

Downstream from North Chasm View are a series of buttresses called the Arêtes, which feature some of the most unusual—and frightening—rock in the state. Unlike the granitic rock of Chasm View, the rock of the Arêtes is highly metamorphosed, banded in shades of pink, gray, and brown, some of it flint hard, some the consistency of sawdust. The Arêtes culminate in the Painted Wall, the tallest cliff in Colorado.

The southwestern edge of the Painted Wall is the tallest of the Arêtes, a sweeping 2,200-foot line rising directly out of the river. Kor spent considerable time on the South Rim admiring the Painted Wall and looking for a direct route, during which time he picked out several flanking lines. He climbed the *Northern Arête* (on the northeastern edge of the Painted Wall) in 1962. In fall 1966, Kor set out with Larry Dalke, Wayne Goss, and Mike Covington to make an attempt on the so-called *Southern Arête*. The downstream side of the buttress yielded weaknesses that could be managed without ropes—or so Kor hoped. They would begin there, aided in their approach by the low water of late autumn. Kor wanted to complete the route in a day, using lightweight tactics and two semi-independent teams of two. Goss tells the story of the climb:

> Michael Covington and I drove down from Steamboat in his Porsche and met Larry and Layton about 9:30 at night in Gunnison. We drove in tandem down the twisty dirt road to the top of SOB Gully. The plan was for a light, fast ascent and I guess that program applied to the bivouac the night before the climb. It was November, but we slept in the cars in our lightweight down jackets.
>
> At 3:30 A.M., prodded by a mix of cold, claustrophobia, and general discomfort, we got up. Frost coated the windshield. Layton promised, "Once we get going it'll be fine." He was fresh from the Alps, where early starts were de rigueur. I hate them. We had no breakfast and packed little or no food. Layton was wearing odd-looking French La Foque boots with a rubber flap over the laces, and the rest of us wore tight-as-you-can-bear Kronhoffer klettershues. We had no bivy gear, and one flashlight for the group descent down SOB. I was anxious, and Layton said something like "We are so strong. If we can't do this nobody can." I was reassured.
>
> I have no memory of the descent, which means it must have been bad. In the faint predawn glow we hiked the canyon floor and pussyfooted around the rock tongue where the wall met the water, to the place Layton thought we should start. At that time the route was simply the left edge of the Painted Wall. There was nothing romantic about it. Only years later, when I looked at the wall from the South Rim, did I sense its mass and wild, tangled geology.
>
> We matter-of-factly worked up a complicated series of ramps, soloing. Larry led the way, showing us the moves. We hardly spoke. I was sleep-climbing. We roped up for one hard crack pitch, then, worried about the delay, resumed soloing. I woke up a little when the sun lit up the dihedral we were stemming up . . . farther apart than before, because we could see better, still rarely speaking. We were having fun. A snapshot is imprinted in my mind—looking down between my feet on tiny footholds, seeing Covington maybe thirty feet below, and below him the pink dihedral swooping downwards for hundreds of feet to the canyon floor.
>
> At last, coming upon a section of off-widths and overhangs, we geared up in earnest. Michael recalls Larry taking that first pitch, and Larry remembers Layton leading it. Michael and I jumared. Partway up one of the first pitches, Larry popped a RURP—a minor aid fall—and then worked through the difficulty. We mixed up the teams and the leading, always in the name of efficiency. First it was Larry and Kor, then Michael and Kor. We hauled the packs on the toughest pitches. Often we simul-climbed. Larry recalled losing his piton hammer at some point, and free climbing into an inside corner, "weeding out major bushes so we could pass."
>
> Our mood while roped climbing was dramatically different than when we were soloing. Where before we were quiet, now we screamed and yelled. Before we had moved with careful deliberation, now we threw ourselves at the climbing. Earlier we had been meditative, now we were driven by Layton's ever-present sense that something awful might happen—"Gotta hurry, man."
>
> The climbing was hard and the routefinding complex. Layton had photographed the wall and committed the photos to memory. We had no choice but to trust his sense of where we were and what line to follow. He never got it wrong. We knocked off ten pitches before it got so dark we couldn't move.
>
> Calm returned a little, and Michael suggested we sit tight for an hour and wait for the moon. We did, and all our previous tension and energy went into shivering. Still no food, no more water. The moon appeared. We thought we could almost see the top, so we tied two ropes together and launched Layton up a slab that was part real and part shadow. He put in no pro at first, so that the knot wouldn't keep him from running the pitch out as far as necessary.
>
> After about 200 feet, Kor topped out. Larry followed and left ropes in place for Michael and me. We simul-climbed, but it must have taken a while, because Larry and Kor had a small fire going by the time we heaved ourselves up onto the glorious flat. The canyon walls released their big squeeze on us and offered open sky and stars. It was cold. We debated whether to build a huge bonfire or make the hike back.
>
> We hiked. For me it was an exhausting trek. We had to be careful to avoid the small side canyons that would plunge us back down into the canyon. Larry remembers the hike wasn't bad, but I don't trust him—once, during a storm on Longs, he took my pack and strapped it on over his own so that we could move faster. He didn't complain then either.
>
> We reached the cars, drove to Crawford—nothing open; drove to Delta—nothing open. Layton and Larry turned south to Montrose, where they found food and spent another night in the car. Michael and I, driven by something—maybe some residual, intense Kor-like need to keep moving—headed back to Steamboat.

The Painted Wall: First Attempts

Perhaps the most spectacular formation in the Black Canyon is the 2,200-foot Painted Wall, the largest cliff in the state. White veins of pegmatite zigzag through gray and purple gneiss. The rock is brittle and fractured, and much of the wall overhangs.

By the end of 1966, Kor had climbed both edges of the wall, and from these climbs and the opposite rim he studied the daunting face for a route. In 1967, Kor, Culp, and Dalke made an attempt on the face.

They started in the center of the wall, first gaining a large grassy terrace. Immediately above, they encoun-

The Painted Wall, tallest cliff in Colorado. The 1967 route takes the far-left arête. (Photo: Jeff Achey)

tered shattered rock, worse than anything they had previously climbed in the Black Canyon. For most of two days they persevered. After 500 feet of difficult, loose climbing, they arrived beneath a massive overhang. Culp recounted the action in a tape-recorded interview in 1975:

> *The ceiling went way off to the left and then up. It was Kor's lead. He went nailing around the overhang and was busy on the pitch for two or three hours. Dalke and I were hanging in slings dozing and freezing. A storm was moving in, and it was getting late on in the afternoon. It was a long pitch, continuously overhanging, and ended up nowhere, just at a couple of pins on more overhanging wall. Kor had done two or three RURP placements in a row. In some places he had done sky hooks in a row. It was a fiercely difficult artificial pitch.*
>
> *When my turn came to jumar, there was no rope left to lower me out. I put my jumars on, tied the pack on, turned off my mind, and jumped. I took a fantastic pendulum and ended up way out from the rock. There I was hanging on the rope with Kor cackling down, "You should see the expression on your face."*

The next section of the wall looked worse—rotten and continually overhanging. Dalke led up a little way and said he didn't think it would go. Kor made an attempt and after an hour had made little progress. Reluctantly, they prepared to rappel. Culp's account continues:

> *The sickening thing was that, to get off, we had to rappel from the two bad anchor pins clear to the end of the hauling line, which ended up twenty feet from the wall. From there, the plan was to pendulum in underneath a big ceiling, and we had no idea if it could be done. Kor took off first. We just hung there watching. He rappelled down, then disappeared under the ceiling. He pendulumed back out, and then he swung back under and grabbed onto something, apparently a pin, and eventually secured himself. It was one of the most horrifying descents I've ever made.*

Later, Kor and Dalke tried the Painted Wall again, but abandoned the attempt. Later still, Goss and Rusty Baillie made attempts on the wall, but were also unsuccessful. Baillie, a South African native who taught at Prescott College in Arizona and worked in the summer for Outward Bound in Lake City, Colorado, would become particularly obsessed with the wall and return time after time—with results to be recounted later.

Layton Kor: End of an Era

By 1967, after a decade of phenomenal climbing, Layton Kor had firmly established himself as Colorado's leading rock climber. His name evoked respect throughout the climbing world. Kor's legend was based on more than technical ability on rock. He had, in Bob Culp's words, a "sheer animal energy" that would see him through the worst situations—and would also inspire caution in his climbing partners.

Kor traveled widely and gained a reputation as one of climbing's most colorful characters, with a boisterous manner, lusty good humor, and steady supply of ribald jokes. His strength was prodigious and gave him the potential to deliberately, or inadvertently, abuse those with whom he climbed. Yet, invariably, Kor's contemporaries looked on him with admiration, with love, and, above all, with respect. He frequently took them to the brink of disaster, but like a father telling a young son a horror story, he could always transform the horror to pantomime and assure a happy ending.

The key to Kor's paradox lies in the fact that his sterner characteristics were balanced by a constant, underlying quality of childlike glee. Despite his oaths and crudeness, Kor was a perpetual innocent. His toothy grin, raucous laughter, and sheer delight in the exuberant expression of his physical energies softened him and made his potentially overwhelming qualities lovable.

After ten years of high-standard routes, Kor's interest in climbing was waning. In the wake of the Eiger tragedy that took the life of John Harlin, Kor began to reconsider his involvement. Harlin had possessed tremendous strength, both of will and body, and the realization of Harlin's mortality hit Kor hard. By 1968 it was becoming clear to Kor that climbing offered only a short-term solution to his driving inner needs.

Those who knew Kor closely in 1968 say that he regretted some of his escapades. A small-town boy originally, and a bricklayer by trade, Kor had come from a religious family. His climbing had taken him to many parts of America and to Europe. It was a giddy whirl of new experiences, and like many others during the '60s, Kor experimented with life. Charismatic, he was attractive to women and his affairs became legend. In Yosemite, and at the Vagabond Club in Leysin, Switzerland, drugs were commonplace.

In the summer of 1968, Kor climbed a last route in the Black Canyon of the Gunnison with Bob Culp. The two spent the night on a bivouac ledge discussing spiritual matters. Shortly after this, Kor chose to forsake climbing and become a devoted Jehovah's Witness.

7. The Free Climbers

Up through the mid-1960s, top Colorado climbers generally treated short climbs as practice—for long routes in the high mountains or for big-wall ascents. Aid-climbing prowess was most revered, along with speed, and hard free climbing was typically done to save time or avoid

Bob Wade approaching the 5.9 finger crack of T2, *first led free by Dave Rearick in 1962* (Photo: Dudley Chelton)

even harder aid climbing. Working on free moves when a hard section could be quickly aided was almost unheard of. Style was as important then as it would be later, but good style meant minimizing bolt placements and moving fast. With so many sheer faces and big walls still untouched, repeating an existing route just to eliminate a few aid moves seemed mundane and pointless.

Despite the emphasis on speed and big climbs, there were hints of a free-climbing revolution to come. Free-climbing standards in Colorado were already quite high. Eldorado Canyon was rich in open face climbing that proved difficult to aid. Northcutt, Kor, and Culp were all capable of impressive free climbing. The *Grand Giraffe* off-width, done in 1960, still commands respect, and the unprotected 5.9 traverse along the lip of the *Psycho* roof (1962) was—even with the bolt added on the second ascent on Kor's request—notoriously "psycho." On the boulders of Flagstaff Mountain, Culp climbed the very difficult face of Red Wall before 1960. In the high mountains, Kor and Culp's 1961 ascent of the northwest face of Chiefshead was almost all free climbing, up to 5.9 with poor protection.

Prior to the 1960s, competition was a vague factor in Colorado climbing. Free climbing brought stricter definitions, which enabled climbers to more precisely evaluate their efforts and compare themselves to others. Once such comparisons became possible, they were inevitable.

Free climbing required new rules, yet, no one agreed on exactly what these rules were. Ambiguous techniques such as resting on protection or placing protection on aid were no longer just tactics—they became points of contention. Some of Colorado's most impressive early free-climbing efforts were tainted by controversy as climbers ironed out the rules of their new game.

Dave Rearick

Dave Rearick, noted for the first ascent of the Diamond with Bob Kamps in 1960, was one of the first climbers in Colorado to pursue free climbing as a worthwhile end in

Opposite: *John Ruger on the crux first pitch of* T2 (Photo: Dudley Chelton)

Dudley Chelton leading on the second 5.10 pitch of Athlete's Feat. *The sloping mantel on pitch one is visible just down and right of the belayer, while the two upper 5.10 pitches are out of sight above the leader.* (Photo: Bob Hritz/Dudley Chelton collection)

itself. A Yosemite veteran before moving to Colorado, he had climbed extensively in California with Royal Robbins and Chuck Pratt, both early proponents of the movement to climb routes completely without the use of direct aid.

Rearick's style was slow and meticulous. A graduate student, and later to become a professor of mathematics at the University of Colorado, Rearick enjoyed the problem-solving aspect of working out free moves on unlikely sections of rock. He also was a self-taught gymnast.

In 1962, Rearick and Bob Culp made a routine ascent of *T2* in Eldorado Canyon, and Rearick managed to free climb the striking fourth-pitch finger crack. He then wondered if he could climb the complete route free. One obvious obstacle was the large overhang at the start of the route.

Returning another day, Rearick placed a bolt at the lip of the overhang, above a large talus spike sticking up from the ground a few feet left of Kor's start. Standing on the spike, Rearick could reach good holds at the lip. With the bolt for protection, a few hard pulls took Rearick over the overhang. (The talus spike is gone now and the

start is much harder.) A few days later Rearick and Culp came back and made the first all-free ascent of *T2*, now one of Eldorado's most famous long free climbs.

Rearick made other landmark free-climbing efforts in Eldorado, including the second pitch of *Vertigo* on Redgarden Wall in 1963 and *Werk Supp* on the Bastille in 1964. Also in 1964, in Boulder Canyon, Rearick led the strenuous third-pitch layback crack on a route soon to be known as *Athlete's Feat,* which for a few months vied with the unrepeated *Northcutt Variation* on the Bastille as the hardest free lead in the Boulder area.

Royal Robbins
Sardonic, witty, a specialist in groan-inducing puns and sweat-inducing climbs, Royal Robbins, Yosemite's most prolific author and first ascensionist, possessed a superb gamesmanship approach to rock climbing. Competitive by nature, he delighted in measuring his abilities against the best standards of the day, pushing new routes at home and abroad—and free climbing classic aid routes.

In the summer of 1964, the year after climbing the Diamond with Kor, Robbins returned to Colorado with his mind set on free climbing. He teamed up with Pat Ament, who had become a protégé of Rearick in the new discipline, and Ament showed Robbins many promising local routes that might yield to a strong free climber. Robbins' visit would take Colorado free climbing a quantum leap forward, and his plucky attempts made as big an impression as his actual successes.

In Boulder Canyon, Robbins and Ament tried *Country Club Crack*, an impressive vertical-to-overhanging crack system on Castle Rock that had been first climbed

Liz and Royal Robbins, 1968. Note the early nut in Robbins' hand. (Photo: Pat Ament)

on direct aid by Ted Rouillard and Cleve McCarty in the busy year of 1956 and recently attempted free by Rearick. The crack did not reach the ground, and the first twenty feet was the site of one of Colorado's earliest bolt wars. The scars can still be seen today, where climbers of differing opinions placed, chopped, and replaced their metal studs. Robbins made his statement on the issue, aiding the smooth slab without bolts. He then clipped the rope into a carabiner, descended, and added a modern exclamation point by free climbing the very thin face. This in itself was a remarkable feat. Today, these moves, well polished from so many climbers popping off, are considered solid 5.11, the hardest on the entire climb. Robbins was climbing without chalk, in footwear more akin to hiking boots than modern rock shoes.

The crack climbing soon began. Above the face, Robbins climbed easily to a ledge and belayed Ament up. The imposing second-pitch cracks rose above. Robbins passed Rearick's high point and, still free climbing, turned a roof a mere fifteen feet from the top. Above, however, lay a flared, overhanging crack, too wide for finger jams, too thin for hands, where Robbins struggled and finally

The very thin opening face moves of Country Club Crack, *first climbed free by Royal Robbins in Kronhoffer boots in 1964* (Photo: Dudley Chelton)

Country Club Crack, *one of Boulder Canyon's most spectacular lines, first ascended by Ted Rouillard and Cleve McCarty in 1956. The climber is just below the free-climbing high point reached by Royal Robbins in 1964.* (Photo: Dudley Chelton)

gave it up. He used two pitons of aid to finish the climb. Three years later, Ament would return to *Country Club* and climb it all free.

Robbins had better luck on another Castle Rock aid route, which many consider even harder. Dave Rearick had recently free climbed the third pitch, an extremely strenuous overhanging layback, but the remaining sections of aid featured much thinner cracks that were nearly as steep. The first-pitch bulge featured no crack at all. Robbins managed to free all three remaining pitches of aid. With five short pitches, including four of 5.10, this route was the most continuously difficult free climb in the country in 1964. The first-pitch crux has lost some holds since 1964 (it's now considered 5.11), but has also gained an overhead protection bolt. It wasn't much easier when Robbins pressed out the committing, Yosemite-style mantel move protected by thin, upward-driven pitons below his feet. Robbins named the route *Athlete's Feat*.

Shortly after, on Lumpy Ridge near Estes Park, Robbins roped up below a dramatic route on Sundance Buttress first climbed, with some aid, by Layton Kor and Jack Turner two years earlier. After several hundred feet—and three 5.9 pitches—Robbins found the crux. In what for 1964 was considered a rather alarming display, he battled with a fist-size roof crack, taking four or five leader falls before finally clearing the roof and then squirming up the wide crack above. Another 5.10 roof crack and a long flare waited still higher, but Robbins also succeeded in free climbing these. On a roll with his puns, he renamed the Kor-Turner route *Turnkorner*. One modern guidebook writer called it "the quintessential crack climbing testpiece of this grade at Lumpy."

In the 1960s the old admonition that "the leader must not fall" still rung in climbers' ears. *Turnkorner* and other Robbins routes showed a disregard for this rule that shocked many Colorado climbers. Yet ropes and equipment had improved, and such willingness to take leader falls was proving a safe tactic that would figure extensively in the future.

With Dave Rearick and Dan Davis, Robbins attempted another Lumpy Ridge climb, this one among Colorado's most impressive cracks, the 400-foot *Crack of Fear* on the Twin Owls. Kor and Paul Mayrose had made the first ascent the previous year, which involved lots of hard free climbing in off-width cracks—too wide to hand jam, too narrow to chimney—as well as some precarious direct aid from six-inch bongs. The second-ascent team was hoping to climb the route free.

Rearick led the first pitch, a long 5.9 flare, and the team assembled below a steeper section of crack. Robbins tackled the daunting second pitch, free climbing a fierce, sustained, round-edged off-width. Above, the crack narrowed and bulged left. Robbins struggled, and finally resorted to two aid pitons to finish the lead. Interestingly, this bulge had been free climbed by Kor. Robbins attempted to jam the overhanging jog in the crack, while Kor, stepping off a bolt and facing the other direction, had grasped the crack's edge and exited in an undercling—the standard tactic on modern ascents.

The route did go all free in 1966. Chris Fredericks, a visiting Yosemite climber, was fresh from first ascents of some of the country's fiercest free climbs: in the Valley he followed Chuck Pratt up *Twilight Zone,* and led the equally difficult *English Breakfast Crack*. He had met Kor in Yosemite and shared crack-climbing stories, and he arrived in Colorado primed to free the notorious *Crack of Fear.*

Fredericks' companion was Jim Logan, a skinny, in-

Opposite: *Roger Briggs on the crux of* Country Club Crack *in 1974* (Photo: Dudley Chelton)

Looking up Turnkorner *on Sundance Buttress, Lumpy Ridge, with the crux overhangs visible* (Photo: Dudley Chelton)

experienced Boulder kid whom Pat Ament had graciously introduced to Fredericks as "a 5.10 climber"—solely on the basis of Logan's lead of the twenty-foot long *Final Exam* on Castle Rock. Unknown to Fredericks, Logan's previous crack-climbing experience was zero. The evening before the climb, Dick Erb showed Logan the finer points of crack-climbing technique—in his living room.

Fredericks got his money's worth as he led up the strenuous second-pitch crack. Logan watched in awe as Fredericks, in the most strenuous off-width position imaginable, locked one arm in the crack and with the other, plucked a piton off his rack, inserted it overhead, grabbed his hammer, and with the dexterity of a master carpenter backhanded the pin home. He then holstered his hammer, clipped his rope through the pin, spun out of the crack, and laybacked through the jog in the crack that had defeated Robbins.

Despite his limited off-width skills, Logan managed

Jim Erickson on the first pitch of Crack of Fear, Twin Owls, *1971. All but a few moves of this ferocious climb were led free by Layton Kor on the route's first ascent in 1963.* (Photo: Dudley Chelton)

to climb the second 5.10 of his career. Sitting on the belay ledge at the top of the pitch, Fredericks could not see Logan seconding, but could hear very unusual hammering noises. Logan was so thin that he could squeeze all the way inside the crux crack, and the odd noise was Logan removing Fredericks' protection bongs—by hammering them straight out from the inside.

Castle Rock and Lumpy Ridge are granite crags, and the climbing style is familiar to Yosemite-trained climbers. Another legendary Yosemite climber to visit Boulder in the 1960s was Chuck Pratt, who in 1965 made a free ascent of the short but wildly overhanging *Umph Slot* on the Dome in Boulder Canyon. Though climbers of slim build can climb this route as a moderate squeeze chimney, Pratt was not slim. As an off-width crack, the *Umph Slot* is very close to 5.11.

Granite cracks were Robbins' forte, but his skill extended onto Eldorado sandstone. With Pat Ament, Robbins free climbed the last few remaining moves of aid on one of Eldorado Canyon's very best routes, the *Yellow Spur*, cruising the exposed seventh-pitch "piton ladder" that had recently thwarted Ament and Rearick, and following Rearick's now-standard *Arête Variation* to the top.

Pat Ament

In 1964, at age seventeen, Pat Ament joined Bob Boucher for a new route on the Diamond—the *Grand Traverse*, the wall's longest line. Within a few years Ament would make the third and fourth ascents of Northcutt's *Diagonal* on Longs Peak, put up difficult new routes in the Black Canyon of the Gunnison, and establish severe aid routes in Eldorado Canyon, including *Jules Verne*, *Evangeline*, *Temporary Like Achilles*, *Apple Strudel*, *Fire and Ice*, and *Centaur*.

One of Ament's most famous climbs, however, was only thirty feet long. At the west end of Eldorado Canyon lies a small fin of quartzite, its back wall absurdly overhung and split by a hand- and finger-size fissure that Dave Rearick had named *Supremacy Crack*. Rearick showed the crack to Ament, who in an account written for the first edition of this book, described the first attempts.

> *We arrived underneath the overhanging crack and dislocated our necks studying it. Dave scrambled the easy way to the top, doubled the rope down from a piton anchor, returned, and had me tie in. . . . A fall meant a sixty-foot swing above the river, and the bottoms dropped out of our stomachs when we thought about it. Instructed to practice the swing in order to get rid of the fear of it, I made a move upward, reluctantly glanced with wide eyes at Rearick's happy face, was overcome with a weak, hysterical sensation, and let go. I was like a ball of gum spinning slowly away from him on a long strand of hair.*

Ament did not succeed that day, nor did he expect to. He later played on the crack with various partners—Rearick, Culp, Bossier—who belayed with amusement and incredulity. Eventually, Ament's attitude toward the crack began to change. He thought he might, in fact, be able to do it.

> *Instead of viewing it as fun, it became a fevered, exotic dream. . . . With Roger Rauback belaying I found myself mesmerized to the rock, struggling, applying a certain integration of mind and touch, and succeeding. Roger's face seemed to get red and puffy as he exclaimed, somewhat belatedly, "You did it!"*

One afternoon in 1966, after a quick ascent of *Ruper* with Royal Robbins and the famed British free climber

Don Whillans, Ament returned to *Supremacy*. The route had already developed quite a reputation, and Ament half-expected one or the other of these two climbers to put his accomplishment in perspective, perhaps with an effortless lead.

> *I expected a day of refreshing humility and was sure that the myth of* Supremacy *would be dissolved. Whillans hinted that routes like* Supremacy *were a six pence a dozen in England. On* Ruper, *he had led both the crux pitches entirely unprotected and exhibited amazing form. On the* Ruper *crack, the rope from Whillans ran down freely to me and was between Royal and the rock. Royal stood unanchored, and I whispered nervously to him, "If Whillans falls, he'll yank you off." "I'll take that chance," Royal replied.*

Ament never got to see what Whillans could do on *Supremacy,* since by that time Whillans had elected to do nothing more that day than belay and take it easy.

Robbins tried *Supremacy* first; he went a few moves up the crack and placed a *nut,* a strange protection device that Ament had never seen.

> *It was hard to know what to make of Royal's machine nuts with slings through them, apparently the newest of his creative whims. The easiest and most efficient method of protecting such a lead was at hand, but I didn't know it. I grabbed some pitons, a few carabiners, and a hammer!*
>
> *First to belay, Whillans provided added incentive by keeping a lot of slack in the rope and staring soberly into space. I jammed up the first crux, hung there with one hand half-wedged, placed a piton, clipped the rope through, and lowered to the belay. Whillans gave Royal the rope and went off to lie in the sun. I led past the second crux, hung again by a poor hand jam, placed a second piton, clipped in, and again returned for a breather. By this time, Whillans was flat on his back on his blanket beside the river.*

Pat Ament on Supremacy Crack *in 1976, eleven years after the first ascent. This short overhanging crack became one of the more famous in Colorado, and one of the first to be given the 5.11 grade.* (Photo: Tom Frost/Pat Ament collection)

Ament rested next to Robbins until he was prepared to launch up the strenuous crack a third time. By now the rope was strung over halfway up. Ament climbed to the piton, proceeded higher, placed a third piton quite near the top, clipped his rope through it, and once again weighted the rope. This time, instead of lowering, he rested briefly on the piton, then finished the lead to the top.

Down by the river, Whillans appeared to have drifted off into a deep sleep. Robbins followed the crack, using aid only through one short section. After discussion with Robbins, Ament called *Supremacy Crack* 5.11. It was one of the first pitches in America to receive that grade.

Note that the lead was done with a tension rest—occasioned by the substantial effort required to hammer in the piton protection. Modern climbers who have grown up with well-established free-climbing rules might insist that the rest point disqualifies the lead. Ament himself suggested recently that a more accurate grade might be 5.11 A1.

This, however, is hindsight. Many free ascents of the 1960s through the 1980s did not conform to today's "redpoint" standard, yet they held to other stylistic nuances that have been discarded in modern times. In 1966, the modern rules of free climbing were far from established, and adding an aid suffix to Ament's ascent obscures the mentality of the times. Ament was but a young upstart, and Royal Robbins, godfather of the free-climbing game, supervised and sanctioned the *Supremacy* ascent. Whether or not Ament's feat is judged today as a free lead does not change its importance. Such relentlessly overhanging climbing was unprecedented, and the lead of *Supremacy Crack* opened the door on a new realm.

Supremacy was the beginning of a spree of free climbs by Ament, the next of which were the *Northwest Corner* of the Bastille and the overhanging dihedral of *Vertigo* on Redgarden Wall, both in Eldorado Canyon. Both of these 1966 ascents became famously controversial, a state of affairs that had more to do with Ament's personality and the transitional state of the sport than with intentional cheating.

On the *Northwest Corner,* Ament first aided up past the crux, noticed a hold that might allow for a free ascent, and then lowered and finished the lead free using the overhead protection. On *Vertigo,* Eldorado Canyon's second 5.11, Ament claimed the free ascent after freeing only the crux moves, not the upper section of the dihedral that his friend Larry Dalke had previously free climbed.

Ament was vague about describing his tactics, and

Opposite: *Roger Briggs on a 1974 ascent of the* Northwest Corner *of the Bastille. In 1966, at age fifteen, he accompanied Pat Ament on the first free ascent.* (Photo: Dudley Chelton)

Roger Briggs on a 1974 ascent of the crux dihedral of Vertigo, *Eldorado Canyon* (Photo: Dudley Chelton)

when the facts came out, critics claimed he had cheated and lied. Ament was nineteen, egotistical, and eager for recognition. The degree to which he honestly felt that these were valid free ascents, and the degree to which he was engaged in building his own myth, became questions of considerable speculation. "Climbers disdain me, take shots at me," he once wrote "but not as cheap as mine at them."

Such squabbles tormented the career of one of Colorado's truly visionary climbers. Ament's free ascents in 1967 included *Country Club Crack* and *Tongo* on Castle

Pat Ament on Flagstaff Mountain. The climb is Richard Smith's Smith Overhang, *one of the standard-setting bouldering routes of 1967.* (Photo: Pat Ament collection)

Rock, and *Super Slab* on Redgarden. Also that year, in Yosemite, Ament led the *Center Route* on the Slack, which, with Tom Higgins' free ascent of *Serenity Crack*, was considered the Valley's first 5.11. (Both cracks were later downgraded; a small block fell out of the Slack crack, leaving a hand jam, and *Serenity* was widened by pitons.) Ament's boulder problems on Flagstaff Mountain—such as the *Right Side of the Red Wall* (1967) and *First Overhang* (1968)—were among the first in the area hard enough to qualify for John Gill's elite "B" scale. Ament's hard mixed lines in Eldorado were equally impressive.

Ament imagined free climbing Eldorado aid routes such as *The Naked Edge, Outer Space*, and the *Diving Board* years before such feats were to become realities. He served as an important mentor to several outstanding climbers, notably Roger Briggs (his belayer on *Vertigo* and *Northwest Corner*) and later Christian Griffith (who would become a leading force in Colorado climbing in the mid-1980s).

A poet and musician, Ament's ups and downs on the rock face were accompanied by erratic emotional swings, from heights of poetic wonderment to bouts of despair. His writings are among the most sensitive and unusual in all of climbing literature, ranging from an early autobiography and numerous instructional and guide books, to biographies of John Gill and Royal Robbins, to a whimsical treatment of Mount Everest, to dozens of magazine articles from the 1960s through the present day.

Larry Dalke

Another visionary force in the mid-1960s was Larry Dalke—the other youth rescued, with Pat Ament, off the *Yellow Spur* on that snowy Christmas in 1961. On a summer day in 1964, Dalke headed up the Redgarden Wall's *Green Spur* carrying the usual stirrups and direct aid equipment, but when he reached the aid portion of the climb, he decided to try and free climb it—and surprised himself by succeeding. This nonchalant approach was characteristic of Dalke, who became one of the most impressive free climbers of the '60s. Other notable Eldorado pitches Dalke led free include the poorly protected third pitch of *Kloeberdanz* (5.10, 1965), the outrageously exposed overhanging hand crack on the last pitch of *The Naked Edge* (5.10+, 1966), and the original finish to the *Yellow Spur* (thin 5.10, 1967).

Dalke also was interested in solo climbing difficult aid routes. The standard self-protection system of the time was similar to that used today, except that the climber

David Breashears on a 1975 ascent of the exposed final jamcrack on The Naked Edge, *first climbed free by Larry Dalke in 1966. During a routine aid ascent, a fixed pin pulled while Dalke was clipped to it, causing a short fall, whereupon Dalke swarmed up the crack sans aiders.* (Photo: Dudley Chelton)

Dick Nystrom on a 1975 ascent of the final, exposed bolt ladder on the Yellow Spur, *free climbed by Larry Dalke in 1967* (Photo: Dudley Chelton)

Dalke also soloed *Psycho* in Eldorado Canyon, with its notorious stretch of unprotected free climbing along the lip of its roof. The pitch was solid 5.9 and Dalke knew he would not find stances that would allow him to slide his Jumars. Once above the roof he simply pulled up about a third of the rope, tied off to it, and began free climbing along the lip of the roof with a huge loop of rope hanging from his waist, making the 5.9 section look like 5.4.

Dalke possessed peculiar blind spots, for example an inability to judge the difficulty of moves. "Am I at the hard part yet? Where does the hard part start?" he once called to his partner, while right in the middle of a crux. Another side of Dalke's character was his reverence for the mountains. In a very simple way, he perceived beauty all around him, commented on it frequently, and would make difficult moves to climb around a flower without damaging it. Dalke's motorcycle was his other passion in life. He disliked authority and loved to drive the highways at a hundred miles an hour, keeping one eye open for the police. He didn't always see them in time, and they caught him one night after a high-speed chase through the streets of Boulder with his girlfriend riding double.

Larry Dalke on the first pitch of X-M *during the first free ascent in 1967* (Photo: Larry Dalke collection)

attached himself to the rope with prusik knots or Jumar ascenders instead of a modern device designed specifically for the task. With the rope anchored at the belay, the climber moved upward, sliding the prusiks or ascenders along the rope as needed for protection. At the end of each pitch he would rappel down and prusik back up the rope to recover his pitons, in effect, covering each pitch three times.

The Matron, a large, free-standing rock near the Maiden on the slopes of Bear Peak, featured a sheer north wall ascended by one of the most serious aid routes in the Boulder area in 1967, known as the *Nordwand*. Layton Kor, at the peak of his expertise, had required a number of attempts to lead it. With his self-protection system, Dalke soloed the route in four and a half hours, a feat of wall-climbing prowess that spun heads in the 1960s like a modern-day free solo of *The Naked Edge*.

One of the 1960s' most impressive displays of free climbing was Dalke's 1967 ascent of *X-M*, a Kor-Ament route on the Bastille that he had done twice before. The first pitch ended atop a massive flake with an off-width crack on its left side. The original line of the pitch had been a thin aid crack just to the flake's left, and Dalke's original idea on that day in 1967 was just to do the off-width crack. He was pleased and surprised when he was able to free climb to the top of the flake.

Above the flake, Dalke faced a steep slab leading off to the left. The aid moves required the thinnest pitons—RURPs had been used on the first ascent—and Dalke decided to attempt the pitch free. A bolt partway across the slab gave him something to go for. He placed a very poor piton, then went for it. The first moves were 5.10. He made it to the bolt, easier climbing, and a belay.

The next pitch was no easier. "I knew there was a ledge up there," Dalke recalled in 1975, "but you have to commit yourself. It wasn't really a lunge. It's just that once you're up there, you just can't get down, because the sequence of moves up to that point is complicated."

Four years passed. Better climbing shoes made their appearance before *X-M* got a second free ascent, by two young up-and-coming climbers, Duncan Ferguson and Jim Erickson. Their report affirmed Dalke's skill and boldness. The technical, poorly protected sections were both mid-5.10.

Though not as strenuous as some of Robbins' and Ament's earlier climbs, *X-M* was hard in a new way. Ahead of its time, it possessed intricate technical and psychological difficulty, undertaken in pure free-climbing style—characteristics that were to become hallmarks of Boulder's most difficult rock climbs of the 1970s.

John Gill

The enigmatic John Gill already had become a legend among rock climbers when he moved to Colorado in the summer of 1967. Gill grew up in the South, where a high-school girlfriend got him interested in rock climbing. On an early vacation to Colorado, in 1954 at age sixteen, Gill climbed the Maiden in the Boulder Flatirons and soloed the east face of Longs Peak. That fall he enrolled at Georgia Tech, where he dabbled in gymnastics, especially rope climbing and the rings. At about the same time he began to work out short but increasingly difficult climbs on the small rocks of Alabama and Georgia—a decidedly odd pursuit now well known as bouldering.

Opposite: *Bruce Adams belays Mark Norden on the frightening crux moves on the second pitch of* X-M *in 1974. A fall would land Norden—and possibly Adams—in the chimney visible below.* (Photo: Dudley Chelton)

Later, Gill worked out specific tricks and training exercises for bouldering, including a one-arm front lever and a one-finger pull-up, and he was the first person to use gymnastic chalk for rock climbing.

As an air force meteorology officer, Gill studied at the University of Chicago and was then stationed in northeastern Montana. By 1959 he was gaining notoriety for fierce ascents at various areas within striking distance of his base, including the *Red Cross Overhang* in the Tetons' Jenny Lake boulders and *Sometime Crack* at Devil's Lake, Wisconsin. His unroped 1961 route on the north face of the Thimble in the Needles of South Dakota, an uncharacteristically risky ascent, quickly became legendary. Gill pioneered miniature routes in areas across the country—City of Rocks, Idaho; Veedauwoo, Wyoming; the Beartooths of Montana; Dixon Springs in southern Illinois; Elephant Rocks, Missouri; the Shawangunks of New York. In 1967, Gill began studies for a Ph.D. in mathematics at Colorado State University in Fort Collins.

Some of Gill's early Colorado routes—for example those at the now-closed Split Rocks area north of Boulder—featured less-than-vertical face climbing on tiny holds. The more he bouldered, the more Gill preferred acrobatic and aerobatic moves. By happy coincidence, the rocks near Fort Collins offered fantastic opportunities for this kind of climbing. The best place to see Gill's work is at the Mental Block and Eliminator boulders at

John Gill demonstrates a one-finger pullup in Fort Collins in the late 1960s. (Photo: John Gill collection)

Gill on his route Ripper Traverse *near Pueblo, Colorado, in 1979* (Photo: Jeff Achey)

Horsetooth Reservoir. These two rocks sport seven Gill routes, each marked with a still-visible white painted arrow. All done in the fall of 1967, these are by no means Gill's hardest climbs, but are among his most elegant.

Gill invented a grading system for boulders, modeled after one used in gymnastics, with grades of B1 (a difficult boulder problem), B2 (an exceptionally difficult boulder problem), and B3 (an unrepeated boulder problem). Only dedicated boulderers could make use of this scale, which began at approximately 5.11.

Gill rejected the notion of bouldering as merely practice climbing. He shared his vision of the activity in an essay, "American Bouldering—An Alternative to the Risk Ethic," written for the first edition of this book and excerpted here.

> *In spirit, bouldering is the quintessential kinesthetic experience in climbing. It is the soul of rock climbing: the fascinating acrobatic synthesis of man and rock. It is an intensely personal art form, the measure of its gratification directly proportional to the style and grace of the artist, and the intensity of its impact varying with difficulty.*

Gill was more than a powerhouse on the rock. His climbing often had spiritual aims, and his essay provides food for thought for the modern climber.

> *It is possible that severe competition in rock climbing and the direction such competition is taking, coupled with personality conflicts and perennial ethical disputes, will result in some climbers rejecting mainstream philosophy and accepting a more personal, transcendental concept of climbing. Unpublicized solitary bouldering can offer access to a spiritual rapport superseding the desire for a reputation or for human companionship.*

John Gill's best climbing spanned two decades, from 1955 to the mid-1970s, and he left mini-masterpieces at major rock climbing areas throughout America. For a detailed look at Gill and his work, see Pat Ament's book *John Gill, Master of Rock* (Stackpole Books, Mechanicsburg, PA, 1998).

Dan Stone samples John Gill's Right Eliminator *at Horsetooth Reservoir near Fort Collins. Note the painted arrows, which Gill used to indicate his finer routes up until the late 1960s.* (Photo: Jeff Achey)

8. Colorado Springs

Colorado Springs is different from Boulder in every way. It is rougher and more industrial, less hip, less affluent, and has a strong military influence. Where Boulder has NCAR, the National Center for Atmospheric Research, Colorado Springs has NORAD, the North American Aerospace Defense Command, a strategic radar-information processing center, buried inside Cheyenne Mountain so as to be impervious to nuclear attack. Colorado Springs is home to the Air Force Academy, as well as Fort Carson, whose soldiers often trained in climbing and made notable Colorado first ascents including the *Bastille Crack* in Eldorado Canyon and the North Ridge of Montezuma's Tower in the Garden of the Gods. On the other hand, Colorado College attracts its share of liberals and studious Easterners to the Springs and had a climbing tradition of its own. It might be that the schizophrenic nature of the town has led to the unusual qualities in many of the climbers.

Colorado College had a mountain club, but in the late 1950s Harvey T. Carter established his own club that focused on technical climbing. Known simply as TCC—The Climbers Club—this group held monthly meetings that welcomed college students, veteran climbers (few of whom attended), and youngsters from the local neighborhoods. It was a Boy Scouts sort of organization. Carter had made up small triangular TCC patches to sew onto one's shirt, and moms would serve Kool-Aid during the featured slide presentations.

Layton Kor visited from Boulder a few times (he spent part of his boyhood in Colorado Springs), giving shows about the desert and the Black Canyon and climbing with the local kids. Other slide shows featured Carter's own desert exploits. These shows helped inspire the Colorado Springs climbers' dominance in the Utah desert and the Black Canyon in the 1970s and 1980s.

Despite such an apparently organized climbing scene, there was a backwater feel to Colorado Springs climbing. Even in the early 1960s one still had to drive to the Holubar Mountain Shop on Pearl Street in Boulder to purchase a carabiner.

In the Spotlight

Among the youngsters drawn to Carter's club in 1958 were the eleven- and twelve-year-olds Steve Cheyney, Richard Borgeman, and Herby Hendricks, who lived in Pleasant Valley, close to the Garden of the Gods. A few years ahead of them were Pete Croff, Bob Stauch, and Art Howells. This gang of boys became excellent free climbers, and Croff was particularly gifted. By 1960 they were riding their bikes to the Garden and scrambling all over the major formations. Among their many antics was a ritual nighttime ascent of the *Plus 4 Crack*.

The name of this climb derived from its difficulty. At that time, various systems were in use for rating climbs. The Decimal System, universal in the United States today (in a significantly altered form), was still a California phenomenon. In other areas such as the Tetons, the open-ended National Climbing Classification System (NCCS), with its F1 through F11 grades for free climbing, was preferred. Harvey T. Carter had his own rating system, which according to Cheyney, "was so complicated that even Harvey couldn't explain it without getting confused." Suffice it to say that a moderately severe climb of the day would warrant a grade of Plus 3 or 4, thus the *Plus 4 Crack*.

Historically speaking, the *Plus 4 Crack* was only important as social commentary, and some background is necessary to appreciate its significance. Lyda Hill was a wealthy Texan with many holdings in the Springs area. She owned the top of Pikes Peak and its tourist concession, the visitors center concession in the Garden of the Gods, and a posh club that overlooked the Garden from a mesa to the east. At night, for the benefit of her Garden of the Gods Club patrons, Hill would shine a powerful spotlight onto North Gateway Rock, illuminating the hole at the Kissing Camels.

The spiritual landlords of the Garden of the Gods, however, were the youngsters, and their antics were designed to prove it. Their unroped scrambling extended from fierce boulder problems to fifty-foot climbs on Red and White Twin spires and Easter Rock to frolicking traverses of the major formations. They knew every gully, ramp, ridge, and crack on North Gateway. As it turned out, Lyda's light illuminated quite a bit of prime climbing terrain. Near the east side of the hole in the Camels, beginning on a ledge about 300 feet off the ground, was the *Plus 4 Crack*.

The boys' intimate knowledge of the terrain allowed easy passage up the pitch-black Tourist Gully and out onto the upper east face. From a ledge rose the crack, which began as a difficult overhanging slot—Plus 4 climbing, or about 5.8—then eased off a bit for another twenty-five feet, finishing atop North Gateway. It made for an impressive solo, which, as the boys well knew, would be visible to any tipsy lady or gentleman who might happen to be studying the illuminated rocks from the observation bay at the Garden of the Gods Club. Soloing the *Plus 4 Crack* was a statement of skill and defiance, truly in the spirit of Springs climbing at the onset of the 1960s.

Opening the Gateway

The west face of North Gateway Rock is the most spectacular wall in the Garden of the Gods. The north end terminates in the Tower of Babel, a partly detached spire. Farther south, the wall is split by a deep recess, the so-called Tourist Gully, notorious then and now for luring the uninitiated into positions from which they cannot descend. Rising above this gully is the gently angled Finger Face, which is topped by the landmark of the Kissing Camels.

In 1960, an adventurous Phoenix climber named Rick Tidrick was active in the Garden of the Gods. The previous year he had made the first ascent of Zoroaster Temple, the most spectacular summit in the remote interior of the Grand Canyon and, at 5.8, a difficult and adventurous ascent for the day. Obviously comfortable on soft rock, Tidrick edged his way up the Garden's most impressive climb yet, which followed the main diagonal weakness on the Finger Face before making a dramatic exit right to the south ridge. Tidrick used Carter's new drilled-piton method, establishing protection every twenty to sixty feet. Later known simply as *Tidrick's*, in 1960 this delicate face climb was the testpiece of the Pikes Peak region. Tidrick also climbed with Kor during this time, and in 1961 the pair established the very popular *Anthill Direct* on Redgarden Wall in Eldorado Canyon.

A few years later, Pete Croff and crew extended the *Tidrick's* line into a grand, left-arching traverse beneath the Kissing Camels, ending at the top of the Tourist Gully. The six-pitch, all-free route was technically a touch harder than *Tidrick's* and much longer, involving free climbing up to 5.9 with long runouts. On a small ledge at the top of the fourth pitch, Croff made a remarkable discovery—an old high-top, hook-lace ladies boot. It was an unusual place indeed to find such a relic, and speculations about

Vintage "drilled angles" on Pete and Bob's, North Gateway Rock, in the 1970s *(Photo: Steve Levin collection)*

the owner of the mysterious boot gave rise to the name of the climb, *Psychic Grandma*.

By 1960, the Finger Face was laced with climbs but the steep, potholed central section of North Gateway still had no routes. Two climbs would soon fill the gap. Mike Borghoff, outside the circle of the young Garden elite, established *Borghoff's Blunder*, which ascended directly to a prominent groove marking the south end of Hollywood and Vine ledges. Though Borghoff was sometimes called "the mad bolter" (one of his early bolt lines can still be seen below the Crow's Nest on the Maiden near Boulder), his North Gateway ascent was almost all free. Soon after this ascent, Pete Croff, mostly with Bob Stauch, began working on a significantly more ambitious line to the right. Sometimes accompanied by Cheyney, the pair worked for almost a month, after school and on weekends, on their great project, *Pete and Bob's*.

Garden climbers were still experimenting with their protection systems at this point. Carter's army-angle method required deep holes that were three-eighths of an inch to half an inch in diameter, and somewhat time-consuming to drill. Croff found that he could pound an army wafer piton—a short, narrow knifeblade-size, ring-eyed pin—into a shallow hole only a quarter-inch wide, cutting the drilling time considerably.

The first feature of *Pete and Bob's* was a crack that began in a pothole about thirty feet off the ground. Fifteen feet up the blank face leading to the pothole, Croff quickly drilled a small hole and pounded in a wafer pin. He clipped in, pleased with the speed of his placement, climbed an-

Opposite: *John Sherwood and Jim Solder on a 1970s ascent of* Tidrick's, *the hardest route in the Garden of the Gods in 1960* (Photo: Ed Webster)

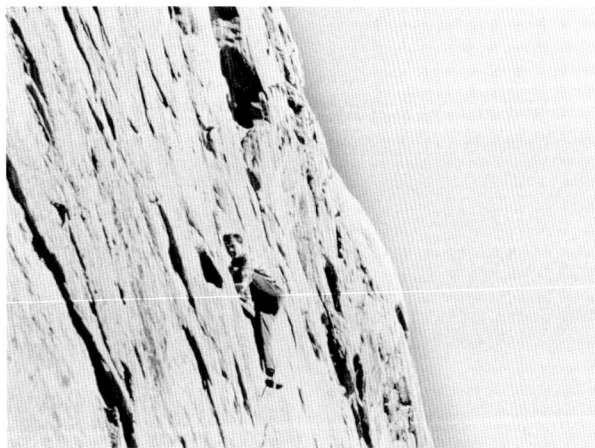

Pete Croff on the first ascent of Pete and Bob's, *North Gateway Rock, in 1961* (Photo: Pete Croff collection)

other two feet, and slipped. As he slid down the face, the rope came tight on the wafer pin, which held for an instant, then ripped out. Croff landed on the ground next to Cheyney. After this episode, the wafer pin fell out of favor.

The next day Croff reached the pothole and the crack above, which was quite difficult, and he used a point of aid near its end. From the end of the crack it would have been easy to join *Borghoff's* and reach Hollywood ledge, but the object was to reach the striking, unclimbed slab that hung like a blank canvas below the summit of North Gateway. To do so, Croff drilled a long, horizontal bolt ladder to reach a small ledge perched below the slab. At a bulge above, another shorter bolt ladder led over a bulge and directly into the route's second crux—5.9 face climbing. The two-pitch slab above offered fantastically exposed climbing. When finally complete, *Pete and Bob's* was by far the longest and most involved climb in the Garden.

Gary Ziegler and John Auld also made a number of major ascents in this era, including the *Pipe Route*, which in 1961 was the most direct route yet on the Garden's second-most impressive wall, the west face of South Gateway. Along with Harvey T. Carter and Layton Kor, these two climbers would also help pioneer the first routes on the sandstone towers of Colorado National Monument.

Murder of the Impossible
In the early 1960s, the proudest achievements of climbers in Boulder were highly unlikely aid lines such as the *Northwest Overhang* on the Maiden and the Eldorado Canyon Roof Routes. Later, Boulder would make a major transition into free climbing.

This transition was much more dilute in Colorado Springs, not because Springs climbers got stuck in the piton age, but because they had never really had one.

Pete and Bob's was one of their most artificial climbs, and its aid climbing consisted of simple bolt ladders that served to connect up the "real" climbing, which was free. Very little actual nailing took place in the Springs. If a line couldn't be done predominantly free, it generally wasn't climbed.

The locals' lack of aid-climbing prowess was demonstrated by two particularly prominent climbs. On the north side of the Tower of Babel was one of the Garden of the Gods' rare natural lines, a steep and impressive thin crack and flake system. Another thin crack line split the west face of South Gateway Rock—a shorter crack but almost as obvious. The technique and hardware needed for these ascents, however, were foreign to the Springs climbers. Both lines—*Anaconda* and *Kor's Corner*—went unclimbed until 1965, when they were led by Layton Kor of Boulder.

Local climbers did try their hand at the artificial climbing that was all the rage elsewhere. Carter's drilled-angle technique allowed routes to go anywhere, and climbers did a few purely artificial *direttissimas,* such as *Angle Tangle* on North Gateway by Cheyney, Croff, and

Layton Kor and John Auld on the first ascent of Anaconda (Photo: Harvey T. Carter)

Stauch. Once these routes were done, however, repeat ascents were devoid of challenge. When the local climbers read Reinhold Messner's famous article in *Mountain* magazine lamenting the technological "murder of the impossible," they had the voice of authority verifying what intuition had already told them. Garden aid climbing quickly died.

Free climbing had always been the foundation of Colorado Springs climbing, but ironically the lack of a real "aid era" inhibited its development. Using direct aid, Boulder climbers of the 1960s made routine ascents of impressively steep and smooth faces. Once the free-climbing concept took hold, a Boulder climber could stand in his slings, inspect the terrain, and wonder. If he chose to try a pitch free, his efforts would benefit from previous knowledge of the rock features, fixed protection, and the assurance that he could always go back to aid if the going got tough. Pat Ament had aided the *Northwest Corner* of the Bastille and *Vertigo* on Redgarden Wall before making his landmark free ascents in 1966, and Larry Dalke had first aided *X-M* and the last pitch of *The Naked Edge*. Boulder free climbing through the end of the 1970s would consist almost entirely of freeing old aid routes.

In Colorado Springs, however, while absolute standards lagged behind, most of the early, standard-setting free climbs were first ascents on untouched rock, not repeat ascents of familiar old aid routes. Though the resulting routes were thus easier in the Springs, the actual feats of climbing were of a higher standard than the grades reveal.

The young Colorado Springs climbers lived in the shadow of their Boulder brethren, but they were more talented than they realized. In the summer of 1963, Croff, Cheyney, Stauch, and Richard Borgeman set out for Longs Peak to repeat Layton Kor's new route on the Diamond, the *Yellow Wall*. It was an improbable mission, probably doomed to failure.

On their way through Boulder, however, the teenagers stopped for information at the house of Pat Ament. Ament wisely recommended that the boys warm up on some of Boulder's harder climbs, and directed them to *T2* in Eldorado, which had seen only two all-free ascents. The boys first climbed *Jackson's Wall Direct,* one of the harder free routes in Boulder Canyon at the time, then went to Eldorado where they managed the third free ascent of *T2*. They never did continue on to the Diamond, but they had made a fine showing on the rocks of Boulder.

The Martyr
West of the soft sandstone crucible of the Garden of the Gods lies the other half of Colorado Springs climbing—the Pikes Peak granite. Pikes Peak is one of the gentlest

Old Ironsides, one of the many granite cliffs on the flanks of Pikes Peak first explored by Harvey T. Carter (Photo: Steve Cheyney)

looking of Colorado's 14,000-foot peaks, but its flanks hide steep cirques and rock outcrops. The Barr Trail—route of the Pikes Peak Marathon that makes a round trip to the summit from Manitou Springs—takes hikers near a few of the crags, and the Pikes Peak toll road passes just above others. Countless crags dot the lower elevations of the massif.

To this day, Pikes Peak climbs are poorly documented. The crags are hard to find and the climbs scattered. Pikes Peak climbing is something shared by locals with chosen friends, but it played a significant role in local history. Carter had investigated almost every granite crag around Pikes Peak before moving to Aspen in 1963, and he passed on word of newfound crags to the young, eager members of The Climbers Club.

In the foothills ten miles southeast of Pikes Peak is a prominent rock formation called Saint Peter's Dome. In the summer of 1962, following a tip from Carter, Pete Croff and Bob Stauch went to have a look at a nearby pinnacle Carter had named the Aguille de Saint Peter. They approached the new crag, spotted a fantastic crack line on the north arête, and climbed the first long 5.9 pitch before an afternoon hailstorm drove them off.

On the next trip, Cheyney, who had been grounded by his parents during the first foray, joined Croff and Stauch. Above the first belay rose a steep, diagonal crack.

It was too wide for the boys' biggest pitons—half-inch army angles—so Croff had to climb the initial crux section unprotected. Above, a beautiful green dihedral gave easier climbing. The third pitch fell to Cheyney and began with a sixty-foot off-width—totally unprotected. A spectacular roof led to the top.

At 5.9, with continuous difficulties and scanty protection, *The Martyr* was the most demanding climb in the Colorado Springs area in 1962. From the early 1960s on, such difficult granite climbs would keep pace with the more visible activities in the Garden of the Gods, though they would remain almost completely unknown to outsiders.

Bigger Bagger

One Pikes Peak formation, which Carter had named but not climbed, was the Bigger Bagger, a granite buttress topped by a pinnacle high above timberline on Pikes' east flank. In the summer of 1968, Steve Cheyney, Bob Stauch, and Don Doucette set out to bag it.

They were dropped off along the toll road with climbing and camping gear and set off in search of the spire, invisible in one of the cirques below. After a long and circuitous hike they found the rock; the "standard" approach was only discovered years later, when a herd of mountain sheep showed Cheyney a route that connected hidden ledges into an efficient high traverse.

The team set up camp, then started up the taller, downhill side of the formation. At a notch they rappelled off, leaving fixed lines—unusual tactics that, along with the pristine alpine terrain, lent an exotic air to the expedition.

The next day's climbing was more difficult. Doucette aided a thin crack, which took them to the blank face of the final pinnacle. Stauch went up first, drilled a bolt in the hard granite, and then came down.

A superb face climber, Cheyney was also an expert on the latest footwear. Like Kor and Ament, Cheyney favored the Austrian Kronhoffers, whose Marwa soles were the "sticky rubber" of the day. Once the lugs wore off the toes, these were excellent free-climbing shoes, much better than the Italian Pivettas and Black Spiders, which were soled with slick Vibram. Today, however, Cheyney was sporting a pair of the new, state-of-the-art, blue suede Royal Robbins boots. He free climbed past Stauch's bolt and soon found himself stranded at a bulge on the smooth slab. He needed another bolt, but couldn't drill it. He edged carefully back down to devise a different plan.

The team's skimpy bolt kit was mostly composed of homemade gadgets. Doucette had modified quarter-inch nail-drive bolts so they could be pounded into very shallow holes. Cheyney went back up, top-stepped on Stauch's bolt, and drilled a half-inch-deep hole. He inserted a lead sheath, stuck the point of an eighth-inch nail directly through a loop of webbing, and pounded the nail home. He clipped a foot loop into the sling and gingerly weighted it. Three more such placements took Cheyney back to the bulge, where he could now place a real bolt. Then he stepped out of his aiders and ran out twenty feet of 5.9 face climbing to the top.

The victorious summit climbers straddled their lonely, windswept pinnacle, which was too narrow to stand on for more than a moment's balancing act. It was an all-too-flawless point of granite—devoid of cracks for a rappel anchor. Only one dull three-eighths-inch bit and a sawed-off army angle remained in their meager bolt kit. An hour of work produced one inch-deep hole. They pounded in the angle, tied it off, said a prayer, and rappelled.

A few years later, Cheyney returned with John Sherwood and climbed the pinnacle all free. Remote and spectacular, it stands today as one of Pikes Peak's most popular climbs.

Ed Webster on the final pinnacle of Bigger Bagger on Pikes Peak (Photo: Steve Cheyney)

Part Three

THE SEVENTIES: FREE AND CLEAN

By the early 1970s, society at large was beginning to call the earth a "global village," and climbers witnessed the parallel phenomenon of the shrinking cliff. Information and technology had cut the cliffs down to size. During the 1960s, rising standards pushed new lines all over the low cliffs and the high mountains of Colorado. Climbs such as the Eldorado Canyon Roof Routes showed that the steepest and smoothest pitches could be mastered. The Diamond, Chiefshead, and Black Canyon ascents showed that even the most imposing big walls were climbable.

Colorado climbing would now see a major shift: away from the techniques that had allowed the "impossible" faces to be climbed, toward a free-climbing ethic that would make those faces nearly impossible once again.

Other factors were at play. Environmental thinking was on the rise everywhere in the 1970s, and many elegant climbs had been pounded into scarred remnants of their former beauty. Free climbing required fewer damaging piton placements, which appealed to the spirit of the 1970s climber. In a similar vein, free climbing reemphasized a simpler, aesthetic side of rock climbing, which had been overshadowed by equipment-intensive conquests of huge walls. Ironically, however, despite its simplicity, free climbing sharpened the competitive side of rock climbing. The more defined rules made it easier to directly compare climbs and climbers.

The number of high-standard rock climbers in Colorado in the early 1960s could be counted on the fingers of two hands. By the early 1970s, this number swelled to more than a hundred. At the same time, information about climbing increased exponentially. In 1967, Pat Ament and Cleve McCarty published Boulder's first guidebook, *High Over Boulder*, and a revised edition came out in 1970. A steady stream of guidebooks would follow thereafter.

Specialized climbing magazines appeared. Colorado's *Trail and Timberline* had long carried climbing accounts, as had *Summit*, published in California, but these magazines were regional and devoted primarily to hiking and general mountaineering. In 1969, *Mountain* magazine appeared. This British publication had technical climbing as its primary emphasis, and during the 1970s it achieved international circulation, becoming extremely influential in the United States. In 1970, the American magazine *Climbing* appeared. Based in Aspen, Colorado, it vied with *Mountain* in importance. Other climbing magazines included *Off Belay* from the Pacific Northwest, begun in 1972, and *Ascent,* an artsy, erratically published California climbing journal, which first appeared in 1967. Magazine editors became influential opinion shapers. The reporting of the newest and hardest routes helped generate an atmosphere in which comparison and competition became increasingly important components of climbing.

Equipment was changing rapidly. Among the most important development was hammerless protection—nuts or chocks. These had their origin in Britain. Climbers of the 1940s would carry small pebbles in their pockets, and slot these into cracks in the rock. A nylon sling could then be looped over the pebble, and the climbing rope clipped in with a carabiner. During the 1950s, one of Britain's most important climbing areas was Clogwyn du'r Arddu in North Wales, the approach to which followed a cog railway. The story goes that one day a climber picked up a hexagonal machine nut that had fallen off the train, threaded it with a sling, and jammed it into a crack in lieu of a pebble. Subsequently, climbers spent many loving hours filing out the threads of various-size nuts and rubbing them smooth with emery cloth.

Metal wedges were soon being manufactured specifically for climbing, and by the late 1960s, a few climbers—notably Royal Robbins—had brought nuts to America. By the mid-1970s, most American climbers would go completely hammerless, and at the crags the old familiar clang of pitons was replaced by the thud of aluminum nuts striking against each other. The actual placement of a nut made no sound at all.

Footwear, too, saw important changes. Kronhoffer-brand kletterschuhes (German for climbing shoes) were the favorite of the 1960s. In the 1970s, smooth-soled shoes became standard: PAs (named after the original French designer, Pierre Allain), RDs (after René Demaison), and later EBs (after Edouard Bordeneaux).

Another tactic that became popular in the early '70s was use of gymnastic chalk to give sweaty fingers better friction. Chalk was first introduced to rock climbing by the boulderer John Gill and was passed on to Pat Ament and others in the 1960s. As the 1970s progressed and more climbers acquired the habit, hard routes became dotted with white, allowing—indeed forcing—a climb-by-numbers style. In a few short years, the dark sandstone walls of Eldorado Canyon sprouted white dotted lines tracing the routes. Chalk bags became part of a climber's normal wardrobe. Permanently chalked-up climbs, unknown in 1970, have been with us ever since.

Opposite: *Roger Briggs on an early repeat of the direct finish to* Vertigo *in Eldorado Canyon, a spectacular overhang first free climbed by Henry Barber in 1973* (Photo: Dudley Chelton)

9. Eldorado Freestyle

Through the 1950s, so little had been accomplished in Colorado climbing that radical development was possible. Thus the new paths that Layton Kor and partners had blazed were revolutionary. In later years, new developments were more subtle, and it became increasingly difficult for an individual climber to make a mark. With that said, certain individuals did stand out, and one of the most influential during the early 1970s was Jim Erickson.

Erickson began climbing at age fourteen at Devil's Lake near Madison, Wisconsin, in 1963. In 1966, at seventeen, he led his first 5.10 climb, and the next year he moved to Boulder to study classical music at the University of Colorado. The Devil's Lake routes were short, small-hold face climbs, and Erickson adjusted slowly to the larger and more varied cliffs of Colorado. His first experiences were not promising and began with a demoralizing string of failures.

After failing on *Redguard*, Erickson embarked on the *Bastille Crack*. Beginning the fourth pitch, Erickson saw a piton sticking out of a steep wall above, and only with much difficulty was he able to climb up to it. Though he knew the *Bastille Crack* was rated 5.7, Erickson concluded that the wall above the piton was beyond his ability. Dismayed, he descended and found an easier variation to the top. Unknown to Erickson, his escape route was the normal finish to the *Bastille Crack*. The line he had attempted was one of the aid pitches of *Wide Country*, a route that would later be done free at 5.11.

A few days later, Erickson picked out an obvious crack system on the Wind Tower. Looking in the guidebook, he found the climb: *Black Jack*, rated 5.8. Still smarting from his "failure" on the *Bastille Crack*, he decided to give it a try. Two hours later he was back down at the stream again, having failed to make any headway. This failure, too, was a fluke. *Black Jack* had had only one ascent, in 1963, and it was Layton Kor who had called it 5.8. Only in 1973 did *Black Jack* receive its second ascent, by Duncan Ferguson and Dudley Chelton, who confirmed its long-suspected 5.10 rating and its lack of protection.

Erickson's confidence improved when he managed a free ascent of the *Yellow Spur*. In the fall of 1968, he made a trip to the Shawangunks in New York and saw the impossible-looking overhangs the local experts were free climbing. Upon his return to Colorado, he picked out Eldorado's most Gunks-like aid route, *Tagger* on the Wind Tower, which featured a large overhang on the second pitch. With Jim Walsh, Erickson free climbed the route, his first major free ascent in Colorado. Finally, one of the 1970s' great free climbers had hit his stride.

That same year, Erickson watched a pair of climbers nailing the overhanging section of an old Kor route on the west face of Redgarden. The aid crack skirted a parallel

A 1974 ascent of the Tagger *overhang on the Wind Tower, Jim Erickson's first major free ascent in Colorado. Erickson was inspired by a resemblance to climbs at the Shawangunks of New York, which he had visited just before his free ascent of* Tagger *in 1968.* (Photo: Dudley Chelton)

Jim Erickson on Grandmother's Challenge *in 1974* (Photo: Bob Godfrey)

crack that was too wide for pitons, but looked good for free climbing. Soon after, Erickson tried and succeeded on his second Eldorado free route, *Grandmother's Challenge*.

Erickson explored the guidebook for more aid routes. In 1969, he free climbed *Rincon*, rating it 5.9+ (it is now considered 5.11). Another notable climb was *Blackwalk*, on Redgarden Wall near *The Bulge*. Attempting this climb represented a leap in confidence. Whereas most previous free-climbing objectives had originally been A1 or A2, *Blackwalk* carried an A4 rating, indicating that the aid section was long and sustained and that good protection would not be assured. On his first attempt, Erickson took a long fall onto an old quarter-inch aid bolt, dragging his surprised belayer across the ground. At the time, this fall was considered quite reckless, a quantum leap be-yond the short, safe falls Robbins and others had taken on their free-climbing projects. Returning later, Erickson completed the moves, and the very long runout beyond, without further incident. If A4 could go free, who knew what might be possible?

In 1970, Duncan Ferguson and Steve Wunsch joined Erickson at the forefront of Boulder free climbing. These two were the first of a new wave of Colorado climbers: those who had never learned direct aid, and to whom free climbing was the only way to climb.

Ferguson was tall and athletic and practiced yoga. He led Eldorado's *T2* only a few months after taking up

John Ruger approaching the crux of Blackwalk, *the first of Eldorado's A4 routes to be climbed free. The old aid bolt near his right hand is the last protection on the pitch.* (Photo: Dudley Chelton)

climbing, demonstrating amazing natural talent. In 1970 he contributed his first major free climb, *Cosmosis*, an overhanging dihedral on Bell Buttress in Boulder Canyon.

Ferguson climbed brilliantly but assiduously avoided the public spotlight. He loved to challenge the elements, a trait that would later make him one of the country's most daring and pioneering ice climbers. He once free soloed *Werk Supp* (5.9) on the Bastille in a rainstorm, wearing socks over bare feet, and he soloed the *Wind Ridge* at night, in a blizzard. A master thin-face climber, in 1974 and 1975 Ferguson quietly established some of Eldorado Canyon's hardest "mind control" climbs, among them *The Uplift* on the Whale's Tail and a little-known 5.11 journey on the Bastille that climbed directly up through the top of the *Northcutt Variation* dihedral.

Steve Wunsch, circa 1975 (Photo: Bob Godfrey)

Wunsch was tall, lanky, and had a smooth, flowing style. His climbing travels would take him as far afield as England and East Germany, and he made important free ascents in Yosemite and the Shawangunks. An articulate critic of the climbing scene, Wunsch developed into a key figure influencing free-climbing philosophy and developments nationwide.

The Naked Edge—Free

Around 1967, Pat Ament began to prepare himself for an outrageous free ascent. He had already done the route on aid several times, and knew it well. He had made free ascents of numerous other aid routes around Boulder that, in style and difficulty, matched what would be found on his dream climb. These included *Country Club Crack*, a 5.11 jam crack; *Super Slab*, with its exposed 5.10 face climbing; and *Super Squeeze*, a 5.10+ chimney slot on the Dome in Boulder Canyon. These successes, coupled with Ament's visionary imagination, were leading toward an all-free ascent of Eldorado's ultimate line, *The Naked Edge*.

Events would intervene before he could realize his dream. Ament was a musician and artist, enmeshed in the experimental Boulder counterculture of the 1960s. One night on Flagstaff Mountain, a young friend had a bad LSD trip, ran away as Ament tried to calm him, and finally had to be tackled by police at the top of a cliff in

Duncan Ferguson at the Macky "Pits," a state-of-the-art 1970s training facility located outside a basement entrance to Macky Auditorium on the University of Colorado campus in Boulder (Photo: Dudley Chelton)

Redgarden Wall viewed from below, showing (left to right) Psycho, Guenese, Kloeberdanz, Jules Verne, *and* Diving Board. *These routes were all established in the years 1962 to 1967 and were first climbed free between 1971 and 1975.* (Photo: Jeff Achey)

Gregory Canyon and taken to the hospital in a straitjacket. The aftermath of the incident, with the guilt and accusations, was devastating. "I was so upset by that experience that I stopped climbing," Ament said. "My nerves were absolutely shattered." Ament had met Jim Erickson at about this time, and passed on his dream of free climbing *The Naked Edge* to the young Devil's Lake climber.

In 1969, Erickson made his first attempt on *The Naked Edge*. After free climbing two thirds of the steep finger crack on the first pitch, he fell and retreated. The following year he tried again. By 1971, free climbing *The Naked Edge* was Erickson's foremost ambition. He wrote the following for inclusion in the first edition of this book:

> *It is 6:00 A.M. on September 26, 1971. Steve Wunsch and I sit wide-eyed in Boulder's IHOP trying to consume enough pancakes and coffee to achieve consciousness. Yesterday we completed the third completely free ascent of* Country Club Crack. *Today we are poised for an equally presumptuous attempt:* The Naked Edge, *a spectacular classic regardless of how it is climbed, but to date all the parties to do it have employed direct aid techniques virtually the entire distance. We are to try it completely free.*
>
> *Memories of previous attempts drift by: three times on aid, two times free, five times failure. No reason today will be different. Steve is excited to try, and needs someone to humor him, and belay.*
>
> *Mounds of sausage, Swedish pancakes, and coffee coagulate, inhibiting enjoyment of the clear morning air and blue sky. Like stuffed pigs, we waddle up and wander up 200 feet of moderate rock to the start. The first pitch brings memories of pumped arms, lowering on the rope and a ten-foot fall. Thankfully, Steve wants to lead it.*
>
> *Steve climbs upwards, meticulously and irresistibly, to near my previous high point, sets a piton, and lowers down to rest. He smiles beneath his twisted, stringy blond hair, and my hopes begin to bubble. My turn. Five feet higher, into a critical fixed pin, before I*

David Breashears on the first pitch of The Naked Edge, *generally considered the climb's technical crux* (Photo: Dudley Chelton)

Sex after death?" Wunsch departs for Yosemite, leaving Achilles brooding.

Sunday, October 3, 1971. 6:30 A.M. I turn off the ignition. A predawn blast of wind shakes the car. I open the door just as another freezing gust hits, and slam it instantly shut. Duncan Ferguson and I exchange nervous glances, afraid that our mutual cowardice might shatter the myth of the hard man. I tentatively turn on the heater. Duncan rationally replies that we could sort our gear in the car. Thank God. We both breathe unconscious sighs of relief. Twenty guilt-ridden minutes later we manage to summon enough courage to leave the security of the car and brave the fifty-degree weather. No mere rock climbers here.

Mark Norden leading the second pitch of The Naked Edge *in 1975* (Photo: Dudley Chelton)

stumble and ride the elevator back down. Only five more difficult feet remain. Excitement boils as Steve climbs up and finesses past my fall with a bridge. When he gets to the belay I burst with happiness. Five minutes later I've followed the strenuous pitch and I'm standing at Steve's side with a grin as wide as Niagara, jumping up and down like a six-year-old going to the circus for the first time. Another ten minutes and I've calmed down enough to start climbing again.

Up a beautiful slab, around the edge to a smooth, twenty-foot headwall. I carefully reverse moves here for almost an hour, until I unlock the combination to a single 5.10 move. Steve follows and leads the 5.8 pitch above rather easily.

Here the climbing becomes exposed and spectacular as it moves up the outward leaning edge."

Steve dubs it impossible. I give it a disheartened try, but it is late so down we come, pondering the ultimate metaphysical questions: "Is there life after birth?

Steve Mammen on the flared and exposed chimney on pitch four of The Naked Edge. *After making the second free ascent with Roger Briggs, Henry Barber called this pitch the most psychologically demanding of the climb.* (Photo: Dudley Chelton)

The bottom of the first pitch: I watch silently as sun slowly evaporates the shadows, revealing the crisp colors of the sandstone canyon. We are absolutely alone, a uniquely aesthetic experience. I look at Duncan, then at the spotless sky. Today will be a perfect day.

Climbing the lower pitches, we reach my high point well before noon and leapfrog protection up the prow into a flared, overhanging slot. My knicker knee rips trying to get in and, after a fall, I lower to Duncan. Next try I make it, and then Duncan makes it look easy. The belay must be one of the most spectacular imaginable, a sloping doormat, suspended in space. For almost an hour we rest, enjoying the insecurity of this singular place.

The final pitch towers still farther above, like the bow of some great battleship, a fitting finale. Strenuous, overhanging finger-laybacking leads around a corner. A severely overhanging hand crack pierces the prow leading upward thirty feet and out of sight. My forearms feel like melted silly putty as I struggle to rest, shaking first one arm, then the other, light years of emptiness beneath. I have but strength for one attempt.

Ten feet of hand jams leads to a fixed pin. My hands are sliding like molasses from the crack. I hastily clip in. Ten more feet. Nothing is left in my forearms except dull throbbing. Both hands slip from the crack. The next heartbeat extends for eternity. I instinctively grab the edge of the crack with both hands in a quasi-layback, pull with everything there is left, and lunge forever for a perfect hand slot with my left hand. It crunches into the crack and grinds to a stop, ripping skin as my weight puts its strength to trial, preventing a breathtakingly long fall. A few more feet and I'm allowed to rest both arms for the first time since I left Duncan. Ten easier feet lead to the top, where I put in an anchor, tie in, and collapse. Five full minutes pass before I recover the energy to pull up the rope and belay Duncan.

The free ascent of *The Naked Edge* was one of the high points of American rock climbing. *The Edge* was the dream climb of an entire generation, at a time when the game of free climbing still felt fresh and new. Ament could not have been more prophetic when he said, in his 1975 guidebook, *Eldorado*, "This is destined to become a classic, as standards advance."

By the mid-1970s, Colorado climbing would become famous less for the sheer difficulty of its routes than for their style of ascent. Much of this can be traced to Erickson, and the aftermath of his *Naked Edge* climb. On his early free climbs, especially *The Naked Edge,* Erickson took repeated falls and recognized that his eventual success had hinged on the knowledge gained during these attempts. After *The Edge*, he decided that falling gave him so much of an advantage that it spoiled his sense of adventure. Subsequently, Erickson adopted a much more restrictive style, limiting himself to only those tactics that would also be possible for an unroped solo climber. Thus, if he took a leader fall, or used protection for lowering off, Erickson would consider himself "dead," concede the game, and not attempt to lead the pitch again.

Erickson soon gave up using pitons and was also one of the very few climbers during the early 1970s who did not use chalk. He humorously referred to transgressions of his climbing principles as "tainting." In the decade or so that he was most active, Erickson accomplished more

By the end of the 1990s, history would prove both to be true. Erickson's influence contributed to a quiet revolution, one that would influence climbers all over the country and carry Colorado climbing well into the 1980s before finally giving way to a new vision.

Death and Transfiguration

One day in the early 1960s, two schoolboys attempted their first real rock climb, *The Bulge* in Eldorado Canyon. The pair's collective skill and know-how produced predictable results: near-disaster. One of the thirteen-year-olds quit climbing immediately, while the other remained determined. This youth's name was Roger Briggs.

A year or so later, in 1964, Briggs was picnicking with his family at Castle Rock. There he watched wide-eyed as Royal Robbins and Pat Ament struggled to free climb *Athlete's Feat*. Soon after, Briggs phoned Mr. Ament—as Briggs addressed him, though Pat was barely nineteen—and bashfully asked to go climbing.

Their partnership was intense and took Briggs deep into the climbing counterculture of the '60s. He found himself in tow on Ament's landmark free ascents of *Vertigo*

Roger Briggs on the initial overhanging pitch of Diving Board, *the site of a desperate struggle on his first free ascent in 1971 but later tamed by the appearance of additional fixed protection* (Photo: Dudley Chelton)

Mark Norden on pitch five of The Naked Edge. *Many climbers, including Jim Erickson on the first free ascent, have found this overhanging hand crack to be the crux of the climb. The crack was first climbed free by Larry Dalke in 1966.* (Photo: Dudley Chelton)

than one hundred first free ascents, and with each passing year he adhered more and more stringently to his free-climbing principles.

In 1977 Erickson ruefully commented, "I sometimes wonder if I've set an example that other climbers respect, or I'm just some kind of weird climbing anachronism."

Briggs on the crux slot of Diving Board (Photo: Dudley Chelton)

Roger Briggs on an early repeat of his route Death and Transfiguration, *Fourth Flatiron* (Photo: Bob Godfrey)

developed into one of the leading free climbers of the 1970s. In 1971, two months before Erickson and Ferguson free climbed *The Naked Edge,* Briggs made a memorable ascent of the nearby *Diving Board,* a crack line directly up the steepest and most exposed section of Redgarden Wall. He had originally intended to aid the line, as he had done before, but on a whim, began free climbing. Finding himself halfway through and committed, Briggs free climbed the crux aid pitch with almost no protection. He soon returned to free the last pitch, and then a year later returned with Erickson and made the first continuous free ascent. Briggs gave the *Diving Board* the common catchall grade for desperate climbs of the early 1970s: 5.9+.

The year 1972 was a transitional one for Briggs. Unlike Erickson, Wunsch, and Ferguson, who were only in-

Steve Wunsch, belayed by John Bragg, on Guenese (Photo: Dudley Chelton)

and *Northwest Corner*, following horrific Eldorado aid routes like *Canary Pass,* and hopping the freights back from a new big-wall route in the Black Canyon. His parents were distraught. As Ament's protégé, Briggs advanced rapidly and was soon climbing new routes of his own.

In 1967 Briggs made one of his earliest first ascents, *Wide Country,* a difficult aid line up the smooth wall to the right of the *Bastille Crack,* logging a frightening moment as he tentatively stepped off a sky hook and the hook and aider fell away, leaving him committed to a desperate stretch of free climbing. Times changed, and Briggs

terested in free climbing, Briggs had strong roots in direct aid climbing. He was already a veteran of the Diamond on Longs Peak, having made the second ascents of *D7* (at age sixteen) and the *Yellow Wall*. In the hidden labyrinths of the Flatirons he had discovered some of the most elegant climbs in Boulder: *The Inferno, Space-Time Inversion,* the Maiden's *South Crack*. Fresh back from Yosemite, where he had done the highly respected *Direct* route on Half Dome, Briggs was in top shape. He spotted an overhanging crack system on the north side of the Fourth Flatiron that would change his direction in climbing.

> *I had my hammer and rack of pitons, but I thought that I would do as much of it as I possibly could free before using aid. I pushed and pushed on the lower part, and kept thinking to myself that I'd go just a little farther until I could find a resting place and then start aiding. There was a large roof about two-thirds of the way up the crack, and I felt that if I could get over it free, that would be enough, and then I'd start aiding. I managed the overhang free and then realized how close I was to the top. It was only twenty-five feet away but looked outrageous. I thought to myself, "Well, I've done it all free up to here, might as well keep going." The closer I got to the top, the more determined I became that I was going to make it, and I did . . . by the skin of my teeth.*

Briggs' on-sight lead of this mid 5.11-route, *Death and Transfiguration*, was remarkable, and it transfigured him into a free climber. He stopped using pitons for protection and would soon repeat virtually all of Boulder's hardest free routes, including the second free ascent of *The Naked Edge*.

Guenese

One miserably cold day in 1972, Steve Wunsch, Jim Erickson, and Scott Stewart were sitting, hungover, at the base of Redgarden Wall. "How about *Super Slab?*" suggested Stewart. Wunsch had failed twice on that climb, and diverted attention by airily waving his arm toward the large overhang capping the wall against which they were huddled and inquiring, "Jim, what goes up there?"

It was *Guenese*. Erickson had privately entertained fantasies of free climbing the route sometime in the dimly distant future, but he felt sure that the day hadn't yet arrived. *Guenese* and the other Roof Routes were among the most intimidating aid climbs in Eldorado. The apparently featureless *Guenese* roof jutted directly out from the smooth lower wall, creating an impossible-looking combination.

Wunsch, eminently rational, pointed out that they

Wunsch on the Guenese roof (Photo: Dudley Chelton)

were in one of the few relatively warm spots in the canyon that day, and that they need not aggravate their hangovers by further hiking. In an atmosphere of lighthearted fun, they all applied themselves to the problem at hand.

They took turns leading up the wall, exchanging wisecracks, fixing protection, groaning in mock anguish, and lowering off. Suddenly, to everyone's surprise, Stewart reached the top of the lower wall. At the roof, he discovered a flake in the roof that had been invisible from the ground. The team effort took on an air of feasibility. With the rope now through the protection at the roof, Wunsch climbed to Stewart's high point. The roof extended four feet horizontally. Wunsch found it nearly impossible to rest under the roof, and with little hope of success, he grabbed the flake, stretched out horizontally, reached a good hold on the lip, and pulled over. "I don't believe it," exclaimed Erickson down below, "that's just ridiculous."

This ascent exemplified a popular free-climbing style of the 1970s—the so-called yo-yo. Climbers took turns placing progressively higher protection before falling or giving up. After weighting the rope, it was not permitted to continue climbing, nor to hang on tension and inspect the moves ahead. The overhead rope, established while free climbing, was permitted, but each would-be leader was required to free climb from the ground (or a no-hands stance) before inspecting or climbing any section above.

Henry Barber attempting the second ascent of Kloeberdanz *in 1974* (Photo: Dudley Chelton)

Obviously, by Erickson's rules, the team was shamelessly "tainting." This was normal. On the hardest routes of the 1970s and early 1980s, the yo-yo style was common.

Kloeberdanz

In 1973, Steve Wunsch made a long trip to the Shawangunks, where he climbed with John Stannard. Wunsch's Gunks trip was as eye-opening and influential as Erickson's had been. Stannard was exclusively a free climber, approached the short Gunks routes as roped boulder problems, and enjoyed working on his project climbs for months at a time. His most famous climb, the body-length horizontal roof of *Foops,* one of the country's first 5.11s, was a huge psychological breakthrough when done in 1967 and had required more than a year of attempts.

Stannard had an uncanny willingness to take leader falls onto protection—a psychological skill that was still radical in the early 1970s. Prior to his Gunks trip, Wunsch had been very conservative about falling, but he quickly adopted Stannard's tactics.

In 1973 Wunsch began working on *Kloeberdanz*, the route adjacent to *Guenese*. Protection on the crux roof was excellent and the fall safe. Wunsch took the fall fifteen times before reaching the lip. His final solution involved a spectacular lunge.

"How hard is it?" he mused in a whimsical account in *Climbing* magazine in May 1974. "5.10a for the left hand, 5.10c for the right hand, 5.10b for the right foot and 5.10d for the left foot. Like any other problem in the Flagstaff gymnasium, but we must be exact or newcomers to the area might get in over their heads and have to be rescued."

Kloeberdanz was the Colorado debut of the powerful new free-climbing psychology that Wunsch had learned from Stannard. The *Guenese* ascent had involved much falling and lowering on gear, but was attempted almost as a joke. *Kloeberdanz* was deliberate, and when completed, it seemed the ultimate in difficulty.

Jules Verne

Jules Verne, done by Pat Ament and Larry Dalke in their whirlwind year 1967, was the longest and hardest mixed free and aid route on Redgarden Wall. Early Boulder guidebooks called it a Grade V, and 5.9, A5. The aid crux was the first twenty feet, involving scary piton work above a nasty slab. In 1971, Bill Putnam, a talented Boulder climber, free climbed this section by starting on the first holds of *T2*, an arm-span right of the *Jules Verne* aid seam, and bouldering up and left out the overhang. This effort involved 5.10+ climbing with the possibility of a bad ground fall—an extremely serious lead.

A few days later, Putnam returned with Jim

Erickson. The pair repeated Putnam's necky boulder problem, and then continued much more easily for three pitches to the Upper Ramp, a large shelf halfway up Redgarden Wall. Four more pitches remained on the upper wall, the first of which turned the team back—as it would many others to come.

The fourth pitch of *Jules Verne* received a number of attempts between 1972 and 1975. It appeared to demand twenty-five feet of continuous, intricate face climbing, with a fifty-foot fall possible from the final moves. "The climbers who have attempted this pitch," Roger Briggs was inspired to write, "do not doubt that it will be free climbed some day. Such an undertaking lies in a realm which, seemingly, no man has yet entered, and epitomizes well the future of rock climbing."

Erickson and Duncan Ferguson were the first to explore the pitch, and they made a decision that would greatly delay success on *Jules Verne,* but elevate it from just another "roped boulder problem" to the landmark climb it was to become. The pair quickly realized that the hard climbing was unprotectable with nuts, but that pitons could be placed. "We had made a vow never to use pins again," Erickson said.

They tried to free climb the pitch anyway, taking turns climbing up and down. Eventually, Erickson took a short fall, and Ferguson took a much longer one. The pair retreated.

There is no doubt that, had a protection piton been placed on *Jules Verne* in 1973, one of the early attempts would have succeeded. Instead, the pitch was to remain unclimbed until 1975. The agreement not to place a piton on the fourth pitch of *Jules Verne*—a section that had originally been aided with pitons—demonstrated the Boulder climbers' extraordinary commitment to style.

Steve Wunsch tried the *Jules Verne* pitch in 1973 and again in 1974. In that year he made one of his regular visits to the Shawangunks, where he completed the first free ascent of an unusual Gunks climb called *Supercrack*. The grade of this very difficult sixty-foot overhanging finger crack would fluctuate over the next few years, ranging from its original "5.10+" to 5.13. It has now settled at 5.12c, making it by far the hardest pitch of free climbing in the country in 1974. Wunsch was obviously climbing strongly, and thin footwork was his specialty. He climbed *Supercrack* in stiff edging shoes, stemming and edging on tiny holds on the smooth face next to the crack.

In 1975, Wunsch returned again to *Jules Verne,* and with John Bragg belaying, spent most of an afternoon working on the pitch. He found placements for two #1 Stoppers—the smallest nuts then available, aluminum wedges about the size of a fingernail—and climbed almost to the end of the runout.

Bill Putnam—with a little help from his friends—making the first free ascent of the initial overhang on Jules Verne *in 1971* (Photo: Dudley Chelton)

Erickson and others watched through binoculars from the road. Wunsch climbed through the 5.10 section that had turned back all previous attempts and reached a point very close to the end of the difficulties, high enough above the #1 Stoppers that they would not have withstood the fall. It appeared that he was going to make it. He did not. Nor did he fall. In an impressive display, Wunsch painstakingly reversed each move of the pitch and regained the belay.

The following day, with Erickson belaying, Wunsch climbed back up, clipped into the Stoppers he had left in place the day before, climbed past his old high point, and completed the pitch.

Perilous Journey

In 1974, many top climbers had attempted to repeat the *Kloeberdanz* roof. None had succeeded. Roger Briggs tells of the remarkable second ascent:

My brother and I were attempting the Kloeberdanz *roof. I'd been trying it without much success when a young kid came wandering by. We were struggling, and I was finding it damned hard. He was kind of cocky and said, "That doesn't look too hard. It looks like a jug out there on the lip." I replied, "It's not a jug. Why don't you try it if you think it's that easy?"*

He climbed up and gave it one try, the way that Wunsch had done it, but couldn't do it. After a short rest, he climbed out and found a small handhold in the middle of the roof. He just hung on by one hand, found another hold, reached out to the lip of the roof, and pulled over. I couldn't believe it. He climbed it statically. I'd been trying the climb for years. John Stannard, Erickson, Henry Barber, all sorts of people had tried it. Wunsch had finally worked out his exotic dynamic combination, and everyone thought it was the only way to do it. Not only did this kid do it, but he did it statically without even thinking. Just classic.

The Kloeberdanz Kid, as he came to be known, was a seventeen-year-old named David Breashears. He had little experience on high-standard rock climbs, and not long before leading *Kloeberdanz* had been scolded for pounding pitons into the *Bastille Crack*. After *Kloeberdanz*, the local experts took the cocky teenager under their wing.

In the 1990s, Breashears would become internationally renowned as an Everest climber and filmmaker. To rock climbers, however, his greatest achievement was a seventy-five-foot climb he called *Perilous Journey*.

In 1975, Breashears' primary ambition was to lead the fourth pitch of *Jules Verne*, but Wunsch had beaten him to it. "I was really wanting to do the first free ascent," he said in a 1976 interview. "One day I got real obnoxious with Wunsch and told him that I was gonna go up there before him—this was on the morning of his last attempt. And he got kind of pissed off, so I never went up. When he did it, I should have been really happy that he had done it, but I was real disappointed. . . . I had to divert my efforts elsewhere."

Elsewhere proved to be the Mickey Mouse Wall. Reached by walking the train tracks south of Eldorado Canyon, Mickey Mouse was one of the tallest cliffs in Boulder and home to numerous impressive climbs including the big aid route *Red Dihedral*.

The lower flanks of the wall had one section that was steep and impressively blank. In 1970, George Hurley had climbed the first route on this section, *The Offset* a poorly protected 5.9 that followed a pair of offset seams. In 1974, Duncan Ferguson led the steep wall to the left of the seams, an unprotected pitch called *Duncan Donuts*. The wall was proving to be something of a testing ground for ever harder, unprotected face climbs. To the left of *Duncan Donuts* the wall jutted slightly into a steep and equally blank buttress. Wunsch commented, "It was the kind of buttress

Dan Stone approaching the crux slab during the third ascent of Perilous Journey *in 1979. After Breashears' ascent, the few climbers to repeat the route haven't bothered to carry a rope.* (Photo: Charlie Fowler)

Opposite: *Steve Wunsch and Roger Briggs attempting the fourth pitch of* Jules Verne *in 1974* (Photo: Dudley Chelton)

David Breashears on the first ascent of Krystal Klyr *in July 1975* (Photo: Dudley Chelton)

that I'd walk by and just thank God that no one would ever try to climb it." It was the site of Breashears' proposed new route.

Art Higbee and Breashears had first seen the line in 1974, and Breashears returned a number of times just to look it over. When Wunsch led *Jules Verne,* Breashears got the push he needed. He went back to Mickey Mouse with Steve Mammen and started up the route. He tried wiggling in a few tiny Stoppers behind flexing flakes, but they were worthless and he removed them. Twenty-five feet off the ground, Breashears reached a ledge an inch and a half wide, manteled, and stood in balance on the lower-angled upper wall that continued another fifty feet to the finishing ledges. It was a remarkable spot.

"I thought it was all over," Breashears said. "I'd seen a number of shadow pockets from down below, and thought they were gonna be buckets. I searched every one of 'em. There wasn't a hold in any of 'em. So, finally, I ran my hand down the last set of pockets, and found a quarter-inch bump. I thought, 'Well, I'm never gonna make this.' So, I started thinking of ways to get down. And I couldn't think of any ways to get down."

Breashears began working out the moves, climbing up and down and brushing lichen off the next holds with his fingertips. Finally he decided on his sequence. He had tiny, insecure side-pulls for his hands and faced a high step onto a slick, nickel-thin edge. He placed the toe of his EB precisely on the thin edge and committed himself. Better holds appeared. Breashears ran it out another fifty feet to a ledge and safety.

Perilous Journey has remained one of the most respected rock climbs in Colorado. Few subsequent climbs have equaled it in seriousness—and certainly not in mystique. A perfectly blank, untouched face of extreme difficulty, climbed ground-up, with no preinspection, no pitons, no protection of any sort, *Perilous Journey* grew to epitomize the Boulder ideal of the mid-1970s. The grave consequences of a fall did not indicate a lust for danger or a recklessness. Rather, they served to demonstrate that the ascent was conducted with perfect control. The climb was dangerous only if a fall was risked. Breashears' message was clear, and a statement of the times: if you found the route dangerous, you were climbing in bad style.

Soon after, Breashears returned to Mickey Mouse and climbed the left side of the same buttress in hopes of finding an even more demanding route. To his disappointment, his second route, *Krystal Klyr,* proved slightly easier and more secure, and with better protection (just enough to avert a ground fall). Discussing *Perilous Journey* and *Krystal Klyr,* Wunsch commented in 1976, "They seem like real jumps into the future to me." Erickson, never slow to respond, replied, "They sure do. You'd jump right into eternity if you fell off either of 'em."

Psycho

In 1974, Boulder free climbing had two currents. The delicate, less-than-vertical faces were ideal for pushing the limits of "mind control" climbing, such as *Jules Verne* and *Perilous Journey*. Steeper rock, with good protection, allowed climbers to push the gymnastic side of climbing with routes such as *Kloeberdanz* and *Guenese*.

The roof on *Psycho* was twice the size of the one on *Guenese* and had three bolts across it. There was a big pointy flake about ten feet down the lip. "I was thinking that if there was a foothold on the wall," Wunsch said, "it might be possible to get an undercling under the roof and just leap straight out and get the flake—just jump straight out backwards."

The poorly protected wall leading up to the roof thwarted the early free attempts on *Pyscho*. Finally, Erickson led the pitch, calling it one of the scariest in Eldorado. Art Higbee followed and prepared to try the huge roof.

As the pair huddled below the roof, Wunsch and Chris Reveley appeared below. Wunsch shouted up, "Waddya think, Art? Think it's gonna go?" Higbee bent down and whispered something to Erickson, and then tucked into a crouch. Wunsch watched, incredulous. Suddenly, with a piercing war scream, Higbee leaped out backward toward the pointy flake at the lip of the roof, just as Wunsch had envisioned.

Higbee came up about five feet short, wrenching Erickson up off his stance and leaving the pair suspended from the bolts in the roof, but the stunt had its desired effect on Wunsch.

Wunsch and John Bragg tried *Psycho* numerous times, and by 1975 it had become an Eldorado phenomenon to watch this pair attempting their itinerary of projects. To warm up, they would try to free climb *Genesis*. They would then try *Cinch Crack*, and fail on that. Then they would move over to try *Psycho*. The next day they would repeat the same thing, or a variant of it, all over again.

On one particular day they had decided to attempt the roof of *The Wisdom*. Wunsch recalled the day:

"It was a turmoil period in my brain, having to do with why I climb, or something. I realized I was pushing myself to do climbs because there was a gamut to be run. We got up underneath *The Wisdom*, and I was just sitting kicking my feet in the dirt, thinking, 'I don't wanna go climbing. I don't feel like doing this,' and generally mumbling to myself. We started talking about philosophies of climbing, and about why people do all this stuff. I suddenly thought to myself, 'I don't care about *The Wisdom*. What I really want to do is *Psycho*.' John said, 'Why don't we go and do *Psycho*?'"

Again, fall followed fall. Since the moves were close to the old aid bolts, they were short, easy falls. Then, unexpectedly, Wunsch found himself with one hand almost at the lip of the roof. Again he came off, this time with a stomach-wrenching fifteen-foot fall. (Wunsch and most of his contemporaries still used webbing swami belts in lieu of harnesses.) The bolts held, and Wunsch repositioned himself on the small belay stance. He felt a surge of excitement. Next try, he linked about ten very short, dynamic moves on small flakes, latched a good hold on the lip, and pulled onto the wall above.

Psycho would become one of the enigmatic climbs of the 1970s. There were many attempted repeats, none successful, and then in 1976, David Breashears broke off a key heel-hook flake. Wunsch's sequence was never repeated. No one can say for sure, but it is almost certain that *Psycho* was Colorado's first 5.12, and it may have been high in the grade.

Jim Michael and David Breashears attempt the Psycho *roof in 1975. Breashears later broke off a key heel-hook flake, rendering Wunsch's original climb unrepeatable.* (Photo: Dudley Chelton)

10. Drilled Angles and Golden Jamcracks

While the free climbs around Boulder in the early 1970s were becoming legendary, Colorado Springs remained out of the limelight, forging ahead in its own style.

Any area's climbing style is part tradition, part environment, and the rock itself exerts an influence. Whereas Boulder had Eldorado Canyon as its dominant venue, Colorado Springs had the Garden of the Gods. Despite their strong clean-climbing ethic on nearby granite crags, top 1970s Springs climbers all knew how to use the hammer. On the sandstone of Garden of the Gods, new routes were invariably protected by army ring pitons driven into drilled holes.

Climbing on the Garden's soft sandstone is unusual, to say the least. If the super-solid arkose sandstone of Eldorado favored thoughtfulness and precision, the sandy, unreliable stone of the Garden called for a scrappy, heads-up approach. A similar approach worked well on the granite cracks, which played an increasingly important role in Springs climbing after the discovery of Turkey Rock in 1968, about which more will be said shortly.

The social life of the close-knit Colorado Springs climbing scene centered around The Cobbler, the small mountain shop opened by Steve Cheyney in 1972. Cheyney and Dennis Jackson provided excellent boot-repair services, but were pitiful retailers. Excessive buying of gear was frowned upon by shop owners and patrons alike. Loitering was the encouraged activity. New crags and climbs, ethical debate, upcoming trips, the latest drug bust in the Garden, the new crop of Colorado College coeds—these were the subjects of commerce.

Of the many memorable gatherings at The Cobbler, one evening in the spring of 1977 stands out. Pat Ament was in town to present an artsy film featuring the bouldering of John Gill set to Ament's original piano compositions. It was a good crowd, with Gill and his wife in attendance. During the introduction, a shadowy figure appeared outside the front of the shop, leaning against the window with his forehead. It soon became clear that he was urinating against the building.

Jackson, known for neither diplomacy nor an even temper, rose in outrage from the crowd and swarmed out the door. Yelled expletives were heard, and it appeared that Jackson cuffed the man, who disappeared into the night. Quiet reigned, and Ament proceeded with his introduction.

Minutes later, a sound like firecrackers erupted in the back alley. After a moment of incomprehension, everyone hit the floor. Seven shots struck The Cobbler's alley door, and two bullets came through, one slamming the wall next to Cheyney's head. John and Dorothy Gill vanished out the front door. Ament remained standing, engrossed in his presentation.

With Harvey T. Carter now living in Aspen, Cheyney took his place as keeper of Springs tradition—now a more free-form, 1970s sort of tradition—and kept what little record existed of new climbs in a log called the Golden Book of Bullshit, which resided behind the counter at The Cobbler and contained as much scrib-

Steve Cheyney in front of his shop The Cobbler, Colorado Springs, 1979 (Photo: Ed Webster)

bling and slander as useful information. Once, when Harvey Miller suspected that Cheyney might produce a guidebook, he blacked out all entries of his new routes. The book's scrawlings did capture the many new faces on the scene—Kurt Rasmussen, Mark Hesse, Doug Snively, Jim Dunn, Billy Westbay, Stewart Green, Earl Wiggins, and others. Perhaps the most motivated of the crew was the former captain of the local high school wrestling team, Dan McClure.

In the summer of 1971, McClure rediscovered one of Pikes Peak's best crags, which he named The Pericle, a Greekish permutation of "parallel cracks," which aptly describes the main face. Side-by-side stood a half dozen towering, 500-foot crack lines. It was a granite heaven. That summer McClure and Mark Hesse did the first major line on the face, the *Feather* route, and in 1972, McClure returned frequently with various partners, camping at the base and ticking off the best lines, including the all-time classic *Arching Jam Crack* with Billy Westbay. Most of the routes were 5.9 or 5.10, punctuated by the occasional rest points of aid, eliminated later on repeats by Wiggins, John Sherwood, Ed Webster, or McClure himself. By 1974, Pericle had fifteen routes.

While McClure monopolized The Pericle, Cheyney and others made dozens of first ascents in the even more alpine North Cirque, near Bigger Bagger, site of Cheyney's first major Pikes Peak outing in 1968. One North Cirque crag, the Sphinx, featured one of the most spectacular cracks on Pikes Peak, a three-pitch line climbed in August 1973 by Doug Snively and McClure at 5.10, plus five points of aid. An overhanging alcove of orange-burnished granite on the first pitch gave rise to the name—*The Flame*—though the climb might have just as aptly been named for the sensation in the climbers' forearms. In 1975, Jim Dunn and Steve Wood climbed the line all free at 5.11.

The Crack-climbing Cradle of Colorado
Eldorado Canyon was the crucible of early 1970s Boulder free climbing. The Colorado Springs climbers of that era were partial to a very different sort of crag, discovered over a few rainy days in 1968.

Three Colorado College students—Chuck Behrensmeyer, Molly Higgins, and Jim White—were exploring the back roads south of Cheesman Reservoir in Behrensmeyer's VW bus. Beautiful but featureless domes appeared as they drove down mazes of sandy roads through the ponderosa forests in the south part of a region known to today's climbers as the South Platte, for the South Platte River that winds through its heart.

Finally the students happened down an obscure road marked with a sign for Turkey Rock Ranch Estates, about fifteen miles northwest of the town of Woodland Park. Here they sighted a different kind of crag: not a bald dome but a steep, jutting rock laced with splitter crack lines. When the weather cleared they climbed *Second Coming* (5.8), Turkey Rock's first and longest route. There were, in fact, several crags in the area, including an even steeper rock soon to be known as Turkey Tail.

The most memorable early Turkey Rock ascent took place in the spring of 1969, as Art Howells, Mike Dudley, and Don Doucette were training for the *Nose* in Yosemite. (They would succeed, becoming the first Colorado Springs climbers to climb El Capitan.) They headed to the newfound Turkey Rock for some nailing and hauling practice on what now has become a popular 5.9 free route, appropriately known as *Turkey Shoot*.

The trio simulated big-wall style as best they could. The first pitch ended with a hook traverse to a two-bolt

Jim Dunn belays Rick Westbay on Arching Jam Crack, *the Pericle, Pikes Peak, in the mid-1980s* (Photo: Jim Dunn collection)

ments rained down on the belay stance. Howells and Doucette looked at each other in disbelief. Dudley, working his way slowly up the crack, heard the shot and shouted. The rifleman hadn't noticed Dudley, but now he did. He took a new bead and fired. More granite fragments tinkled down. The helpless climbers fought off panic.

Just as suddenly as it began, the shooting ended and the gunmen disappeared into the woods. The climbers finished their ascent, moving very quickly now. When they returned to their car they were met by six Douglass County sheriff's vehicles, called out to arrest them for trespassing. Tempers flared, but in the end no charges were filed. The crag itself was on national forest land, and subsequent climbing expeditions used a northerly approach, far from Turkey Rock Ranch Estates.

With a dense concentration of hard cracks, a mild

Turkey Tail, site of Colorado's hardest crack climbs of the mid-1970s. The climber visible in the center is Earl Wiggins, on Sidewinder, *one of his many unroped solo ascents of the era.* (Photo courtesy L. Hazlett/Earl Wiggins collection)

hanging belay. Hauling practice ensued. Dudley led out on the second pitch, nailing a long crack above a roof. As Howells and Doucette huddled at the El Cap-style belay, they noticed two figures step out of the woods below. One of the men shouldered a rifle.

Suddenly there was a sharp retort, and granite frag-

Opposite: *Leonard Coyne and Jeff Achey on* The Flame, *Pikes Peak, 1979* (Photo: Stewart M. Green)

Climber on Quivering Quill, *one of the outstanding Turkey Rock climbs of 1972* (Photo: Dan Hare)

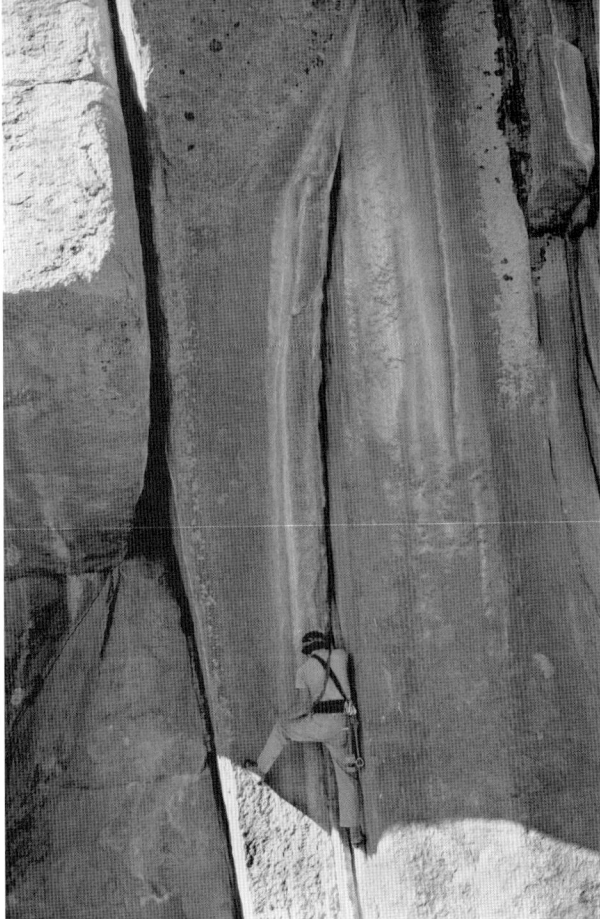

Steve Hong on a 1975 ascent of Drumstick Direct, *the hardest crack in the South Platte when freed by Dan McClure and Mark Hesse in 1972. The off-width roof crack to his left is* For Turkeys Only. *(Photo: Ed Webster)*

climate, and a long season, Turkey Rock quickly became the testing ground for pushing the limits of Springs-area free climbing. In a low-key guide to the area published in the 1980s, Steve Cheyney had this to say:

> *The Discovery Years were a short-lived period; by 1970 locals were onto the style of climbing required to be successful at Turkey Rock. We found out early that placing too much pro would ensure failure. Teetering between boldness and sanity brought out the very best in the local climbers. . . . The unknown, the sense of adventure, was fantastic. To wonder about the blank face above the end of the crack, to wonder what happened when the perfect hand crack became overhanging offwidth—obviously unprotectable—were typical Turkey Rock dilemmas. We could speculate forever but the only way to know for sure was to go out there and feel it. The formula went like this: climb as far as your mind would allow, place good pro, and go for it again.*

One standout climb was *Quivering Quill,* which, though only fifty feet long, overhung for most of its length. "Stopping to place more than four pieces in this hand and fist crack is to guarantee failure by blowout," noted Cheyney. Doug Snively and Dan McClure proved this to be the case on the first ascent in 1972, using a point or two of aid on the unrelenting crack. They soon returned to do the crack all free.

The most impressive Turkey Rock climb of the early 1970s was the free ascent of *Drumstick Direct,* another practice aid line done by Doucette, Howells, and Dudley, picked for its resemblance to the Stoveleg Cracks of the El Cap *Nose* route. The hand- and fist-size crack was intimidating enough as an aid climb, splitting the steepest section of Turkey Tail. In 1972, McClure and Mark Hesse free climbed the pitch with an unrelenting marathon of steep jamming, finishing out a finger crack through an eight-foot roof. For three years this 5.10+ pitch would remain the area's most daunting free climb, and when first done it was the most strenuous and difficult pitch on South Platte granite.

Wild Turkey

The 1975 season at Turkey Rock was frenetic. A younger crowd had appeared—including Ed Webster, Bryan Becker, Steve Hong, Mark Rolofson, and Leonard Coyne—who would all contribute new routes to Turkey Rock, but one veteran climber stood out.

Jim Dunn had been climbing about nine years by 1975. A New Hampshire native, he began climbing in Colorado Springs on the time-honored testing grounds of North Cheyenne Canyon and Garden of the Gods. Beginning in 1968 he made annual trips to Yosemite to climb the big walls. He climbed El Cap twice in 1971, making the second ascent of the *Heart* with Andy Embick and Roy Kligfield, and the fourth ascent of the *North America Wall* with Billy Westbay. The next year he embarked on an El Cap odyssey that has become legend.

The story of *Cosmos* belongs to the annals of Yosemite, and we can note it only briefly here. El Capitan was hopping in 1972—both *Zodiac* and *The Shield* went up that year, and several top climbers were vying for the "last great El Cap first"—a solo first ascent. These included Royal Robbins, who was trying the line that would later become *Tangerine Trip,* and Jim Bridwell, who was considering a line just right of the *Dihedral Wall* that had been pushed a few pitches up by a local crew.

The latter line would become *Cosmos.* There was talk that Bridwell had threatened to break the arms and legs of anyone who went up on the climb, but Dunn and Doug Snively ignored the rumors and went up anyway. A few pitches up, when Dunn popped a sky hook, the Californian team who had started the route cheered his fall from below. Higher, Snively managed to break his hand, and the pair had to retreat.

A complicated series of events followed. Dunn returned to Colorado, cashed in his college books, and came back. He recruited another partner but ended up on the El Cap line solo. Soon, he was high on the wall, past the point of no return.

The ascent did not go smoothly. Dunn made a huge pendulum and got onto a hook at its end—then popped the hook. He badly burned his hand on another fall. Baking in the heat, he apologized to El Cap for underestimating it and getting in over his head. He broke all his drill bits, which meant belay anchors were often marginal. After more than a week of climbing, he crawled onto El Cap's summit.

He bushwhacked down to the west—not the normal descent route—abandoning his haul bag and making epic rappels through the manzanita. When he walked into Camp 4, the first person he saw was Jim Bridwell. "He was looking at me," says Dunn. "Then he walked over and just put his hand out and said, 'I'm impressed. Let me cook you supper.'"

Cheyney's phrase "teetering between boldness and sanity" might have been coined specifically for Dunn. The same intensity that went into Dunn's big-wall ascents appeared in condensed form on small crags. Cheyney showed him Turkey Rock, and on consecutive weekends in January 1973, Dunn and Cheyney climbed *Crack with the Bolt* (named for a bail-out bolt partway up) and *Crack to the Right of the Crack with the Bolt*. These off-width crack climbs were not destined for popularity, but they were among the boldest existing free climbs in the area.

Billy Westbay and Jim Dunn in Colorado Springs, gearing up for the fourth ascent of the North America Wall *in Yosemite, 1971. The next year they also established a new route on the Diamond.* (Photo courtesy Jim Dunn collection)

In May of 1975, Dunn and Brian Teale took Turkey Rock climbing to a new level when they climbed what is widely considered the area's best route, *Whimsical Dreams*. Dunn raised some eyebrows when he used "New Hampshire tactics" to clean grass from the cracks on rappel, but the quality of the climb quickly quieted the fuss. Long and sustained, *Whimsical* had sections of finger crack, thin hands, a big roof, and few rests. Other Turkey Rock climbs followed, including the overhanging off-finger crack of *Turkey Turd* in May, and in August the well-named *Wadamudafuka*. All these climbs are now considered 5.11.

Dunn's Turkey Rock masterpiece was an off-width crack splitting the crag's biggest roof. A hand crack led to the roof, where a fat tube chock could be placed far up inside for protection. Here the fun began, and several days of effort were required. Dunn climbed down and out the roof on arm bars, completely sideways in the crack. Turning the lip proved the crux. Once Dunn mastered this exotic maneuver, another twenty feet of conventional, unprotected 5.10+ off-width led to the top. "Only a turkey would want to do a climb that hard," said Dunn after he finally succeeded in October 1975, naming the route *For Turkeys Only*.

There was speculation that the route might be 5.12, perhaps Colorado's first (*Psycho* was free climbed at about the same time). Although the consensus grade is now 5.11+, the crack will still turn back most 5.12 climbers who attempt it.

Garden Delights

In the early 1970s, with new granite being found every weekend, the Garden of the Gods had become a place for after-work climbing or late-night stunts. A few notable ascents did take place, such as Kurt Rasmussen's all-free ascent of *Pete and Bob's* in 1973. In 1975, another historic Garden line went free, in an effort spearheaded by Earl Wiggins.

Wiggins grew up near the mouth of North Cheyenne Canyon, a Colorado Springs city park with streams, trails, and small granite crags that he could easily reach on foot. By the time he was thirteen, Wiggins' early scrambles had progressed to technical rock climbing. His early partners were John Sherwood and Kurt Bowerman, whose father was the county coroner and cautioned the boys with appropriately morbid tales.

Wiggins was fourteen when he met Jim Dunn, then just back from his solo of *Cosmos*. When Dunn announced he was quitting the sport and selling all his climbing gear, Wiggins assembled his first rack from the sale. Dunn's retirement was brief. He bought new climbing gear, and then lured Wiggins into a tempting arrangement. Dunn was a beekeeper, and he proposed that if Wiggins helped with the hives, Dunn would pay for their climbing trips.

Unfortunately, Dunn had imported a special Italian strain of bees, which were very productive but equally vicious. Even when heavily smoked they remained agitated. Clumsy handling with gloves would send the hive into a stinging frenzy, so Wiggins had to remove the combs bare-handed. Regardless of his tactics, Wiggins suffered twenty to thirty stings every workday.

Dunn was as high-strung as his bees, and climbing trips were often worse. Once, at a hanging belay after a hard pitch in Canyonlands, Utah, Wiggins called Dunn a "big baby." Dunn lost his cool, punched out the insolent teenager, rapped off, stalked back to the car, dumped Wiggins' belongings on the ground, and drove back to Colorado. A similar fight occurred on *New Dimensions* in Yosemite. Wiggins soon learned to hold his tongue unless they were on the ground, where he could let Dunn chase him through the woods until he cooled off.

Wiggins and John Sherwood first climbed the classic Garden of the Gods aid route *Anaconda* when Wiggins was fourteen, in winter. Their ascent went smoothly, if slowly. They topped out on the Tower of Babel and rapped off at dusk into the notch of Hidden Valley. The next section of the descent required climbing a thirty-foot slab that was iced and impassable. A cold bivouac seemed inevitable. Wiggins, however, became increasingly worried about what his parents might think if he didn't show up that night. When he spotted a policeman near the parking lot, he swallowed his pride and yelled for help. Amid a kaleidoscope of flashing lights and fire trucks, the boys were extracted from the wall.

In April of 1975 the boys were seventeen and their climbing skills had vastly improved. The existing Garden testpieces were slab climbs; no one had free climbed anything as steep as *Anaconda,* and the boys became possessed by the idea. They used the original hanging belay that had been used for the aid climb, a tactic that gave them no advantage whatsoever, and which located the belayer directly in the path of a fall from the second-pitch crux. Over the course of several days, Wiggins and Sherwood took turns punishing each other on this fall. Finally, Wiggins held on through the thin, strenuous moves for the free ascent. Sherwood quickly followed. As they were relaxing at the belay above the crux, Dunn walked by. They dropped him a rope and he joined them on the Garden's first 5.11.

A few months later, Wiggins and Dunn repeated the climb. Wiggins avoided the awkward belay by leading the crux in one long pitch. Dunn climbed through into an overhanging hand crack. Dunn was wearing the typical climbing harness of the day: a swami belt made of a length of webbing wrapped a few times around the waist and tied. In the hand crack, Dunn noticed that the swami seemed unusually loose. Visual examination led to a shocking discovery—he had wrapped the swami but forgotten the knot. Wiggins knew to disguise his mirth as Dunn scrambled frantically to secure himself before his swami belt dropped off like oversize trousers.

Jim Dunn, belayed by Earl Wiggins, on an early free ascent of Anaconda. *Dunn is about to discover that his swami belt is untied.* (Photo: Bob Godfrey)

11. High and Wild

In the 1960s, big-wall aid climbing was considered the ultimate form of rock climbing, and this feeling lingered into the 1970s for many climbers even as the free-climbing game gathered force. Many Colorado climbers made regular trips to Yosemite, while a dedicated few—such as Harvey T. Carter, Bill Forrest, Jim Dunn, Earl Wiggins, and Jeff Lowe—pioneered the early sandstone big walls in Utah's Fisher Towers and Zion National Park.

Big-wall techniques had progressed rapidly in the 1960s. One revolutionary new tool was the Jumar rope clamp, a European device originally designed for crevasse rescue and first used for climbing by the Colorado team of Layton Kor, Huntley Ingalls, and George Hurley on the first ascent of the Titan in the Fisher Towers in 1962. Jumars hit Yosemite two years later when Royal Robbins and others used them on the second ascent of the *Dihedral Wall* on El Capitan. Jumars replaced prusik knots, greatly speeding the process of climbing fixed lines and giving rise to the now-standard fixed-rope method of following aid pitches. The Californians devised a new method of bag-hauling that employed Jumars and foot slings, allowing much heavier loads to be hoisted with relative ease. Other brand names of ascenders were soon introduced, but *jumar* became the generic word for the tool and for the technique of using it to ascend a rope.

By 1970, Colorado climbers' normal arsenal included a full range of hard-steel pitons, jumars, and hammocks for hanging bivouacs. Colorado had nothing to rival El Capitan in sheer scale, but it had the striking and uniquely alpine Diamond face on Longs Peak and big walls in the shadowy gorge of the Black Canyon of the Gunnison. Both areas were still rich in unclimbed rock, awaiting the feats of a new generation.

The Diamond—Solo

In 1970, Bill Forrest was rapidly becoming one of Colorado's most innovative and adventurous climbers. He had quit his job as a Denver schoolteacher and begun a small business manufacturing climbing equipment. Soon another Colorado climber, Kris Walker, became partner at Forrest Mountaineering. Forrest and Walker made several influential innovations, such as exchangeable-pick ice tools and the single-point suspension hammock, and played a key role in the development of spring-loaded camming devices.

Forrest loved the deserts of the West and explored many remote walls and towers in Arizona, New Mexico, and Utah. He was unusually comfortable on bad rock, as demonstrated by a spree of climbs in 1968 and '69 that included major first ascents on Shiprock, New Mexico, Baboquivari Peak, Arizona, and the mud spires of the Mystery Towers near Moab, Utah. Rusty Baillie once said of Forrest, "He could arrange safe anchors on an overhanging talus slope."

In 1970, Rocky Mountain National Park revised its climbing regulations, legalizing solo climbing. Telling only close friends of his intentions, Forrest immediately planned a solo ascent of the Diamond. His account of the 1970 climb, from the 1971 *American Alpine Journal*, is excerpted here:

> As I hiked up the Longs Peak trail toward Chasm View on the morning of July 23, I felt prepared. For weeks I had gotten myself into and out of every solo climbing situation that I could think of. My mind, body, technique and equipment were together—I felt ready to take care of myself on the wall, and planned to have some fun. But lugging my eighty-pound pack up to Chasm View wasn't fun—at times it seemed absurd. Under the imposing wall, I thought of myself up there—alone with my big bag—and the whole scheme appeared ridiculous. That was the plan—to do it as my own thing—no outside help. Because the plan was so beautifully simple, it became less ridiculous, more worth doing. I hustled my bag and body to the bivouac cave on Broadway by late afternoon.
>
> On Friday, I climbed four pitches up the Yellow Wall route and set up a hammock bivouac. The day's climbing had been good for me. I knew that I was going to go ahead with the climb; I liked it. It kept me busy all the time—leading, descending, cleaning and hauling. I worried some about the weather, it seemed too warm that night, and I was concerned about the new route ahead, but I was tired and fell asleep quickly.

Long before dawn, I was awakened by a terrible roar as an avalanche of rock cascaded down the North Chimney. Sparks shot through the darkness and the mountain seemed to groan and lurch, but my anchors held and the bottom didn't rip out of my hammock. I couldn't get back to sleep, and I hung in the chilly breeze waiting for the beautiful sunshine.

Saturday was one of the most memorable days of my life. It started with salami and then a very exposed free traverse. It was cold and windy, but I climbed the traverse with surprising confidence and then nailed up to a very exposed belay at the base of my new route. Thirty feet of easy nailing brought me to an evil crack— too wide to jam, too narrow to chimney. I cursed, prayed, chickened out, and finally got with it and struggled. I didn't dare lose my composure, but it was awfully awkward. I fought and flailed. That crack took my best, but once up it, I was glad it was there; it added zest to the route. Above the crux, the crack narrowed and offered fun nailing and nutting to Table Ledge, which I reached just before dark.

That night I was full of confidence. Not even a bad storm could keep me from getting up the remaining pitches. I kept telling myself to be cautious, to keep making the right moves. The lights of the big cities on the Great Plains glittered and winked far below me as I sat on my little ledge. I was so close to turning an idea into a reality that I almost got choked up and sentimental as I made a meal of peanuts and oranges in the dark.

On Sunday morning, I climbed three pitches to the top of the Diamond. There were a few bad pins and I had to make a small pendulum to get to an exit crack, but everything went smoothly despite occasional snow flurries. As I was working up the last few vertical feet, I heard a voice. It was my friend, Don Briggs. I broke my solemn rhythm and lunged for holds and then the hands of that wonderful friend who hugged me mightily. Gary Garbert, my long-time desert climbing partner, soon joined us. Happily united, we scrambled up the talus to the top of Longs Peak.

Forrest established a major variation to the *Yellow Wall* during his solo, and his passion for style is evidenced by certain details, such as carrying his own supplies to Broadway and his early mastery of nutcraft when most other Colorado climbers still used only pitons.

Right Side of the Diamond

Centuries of running water has glazed the surface rock on the great vertical flatiron of the Yellow Wall, but the Diamond's Right Side misses out on this weathering process. It is too steep. Right of *D1*, Table Ledge is a mere joint, often an overhang, not the possible escape route it is on the Yellow Wall. Retreat of any sort is harder on the Right Side, since the overhanging wall complicates the rappels. In short, the Right Side is a sterner Diamond, and in 1971 it was almost untouched.

Two early Right Side routes were put up solo, by teenagers. Kris Walker had started climbing seriously just a couple of years earlier, when he joined a winter mountaineering club and met another young Colorado climber by the name of Ray Jardine. They hit it off and started knocking off routes along the Front Range.

In 1971, Walker, age nineteen and quite inexperienced, made the second solo of the Diamond, via a new route called *Waterhole #3* on a steep and untouched portion of the Right Side—quite an outing for even a veteran climber. By the age of twenty-one, Walker would give up serious climbing, but his brief wall-climbing career was impressive.

The career of the other teenage Diamond soloist of the early 1970s would span decades and involve some of the most extreme climbing ever seen, anywhere. In 1973

Bill Forrest at the top of his Diamond solo, 1970 (Photo: Don Briggs)

The early Diamond solo lines (left to right): Bill Forrest, 1970; Kris Walker, 1971; Jim Beyer, 1973

an unknown seventeen-year-old named Jim Beyer established *Sunshine* near the wall's right edge, the debut ascent of one of the great solo wall climbers of all time. From the 1970s on through the 1990s, Beyer would compile a far-flung list of extreme solos from the Fisher Towers and Arches in Utah, to the Tetons and Yosemite, to the granite spires of the Karakoram.

Other early Right Side routes were largely the work of the local Fantasy Ridge guides—the *Dunn-Westbay* (1972), *Its Welx* (Hesse and McClure, 1973), and *Queen of Spades* (Hesse and Snively, 1974). On *Its Welx*, Mark Hesse and Dan McClure endured a raging early June storm. They awoke after a violent, sleepless night in hammocks to find their ropes, gear, and the entire wall encased in a thick sheet of ice, which later fell from the face in great flying blades.

One last notable alpine wall-climb of this era was a new Longs Peak route done in 1974 by Ron Olevsky and Bob Dodds. Beginning on smooth slabs near *Field's Chimney*, the pair did several hard aid pitches to reach easier cracks, then Broadway, the route's halfway point. From there, they continued up a line near the left edge of the Diamond. The sheerest possible plumb line on the offset faces of the Diagonal Wall and the Diamond, this route was called the first Grade VI on Longs. The lower route has fallen into obscurity, but the Diamond portion has become one of the most traveled on the face: *Pervertical Sanctuary*.

First Ascent of the Painted Wall

In 1971 the tallest cliff in Colorado was still unclimbed—not for lack of attempts. The 2,200-foot Painted Wall in the Black Canyon of the Gunnison had a fearsome reputation. The rock was a dark and ancient granitic gneiss, fractured into precarious flakes and hanging blocks and laced in abstract patterns with intricate bands of pink and white pegmatite that gave the wall its name. Drilling anchor bolts in the iron-hard rock had proved extremely difficult, and broken bits had ended several attempts on the wall. Other sections of rock were so decomposed that piton placements simply crumbled away.

Adding to the difficulty, the wall lacked continuous crack systems and was guarded everywhere by huge roof bands. High-standard free climbing was obligatory, mixed with difficult aid, and falling rock was a constant danger. Further, there was an indefinable quality to the wall that spooked many parties. "The Painted Wall presents problems other than those of routefinding and climbing," wrote Karl Karlstrom in *Climbing* magazine in July 1973. "The wall has an aura of strangeness about it that created another sort of obstacle. I experienced a feeling of anxiety, an empty sensation in my stomach as if I were out of place in a forbidden world."

The Painted Wall stood as the one objective that had managed to repeatedly defeat Layton Kor, and in 1972 it was cloaked in an Eiger-like aura of danger and difficulty. Kor's last attempt had been with Rusty Baillie, the adventurous South African native who lived in Arizona in the winter and ran Outward Bound courses in Colorado in the summer. Baillie and Wayne Goss tried the wall in 1968, and Baillie returned in July 1971. None of these attempts came close to completing a route, and there were spectacular, epic retreats from high on the wall. Baillie and Goss failed when they made a decisive tactical error—descending the gully in their underwear due to the summer heat. They suffered massive cases of poison ivy.

By 1972, the Painted Wall was the most conspicuous objective in American big-wall climbing. At one point, Baillie had invited Bill Forrest to attempt the wall with him, but the plans never materialized. Now, Forrest and Kris Walker—the Diamond soloists—laid their own plans. Walker studied the Painted Wall from the South Rim overlooks and assembled a composite telephoto image that showed the wall in great detail. Forrest and Walker spent hours in Denver poring over the mazelike photograph of the Painted Wall, envisioning a route.

Neither climber was familiar with the Black Canyon. They arrived at the North Rim and assumed that once on the canyon floor they could hike freely downstream. With little thought, and fortunately with only a light load of gear, they embarked on a reconnaissance down what is now known as the Cruise Gully. Finally on more level talus, they headed downstream but soon found themselves cut off far from the Painted Wall by cliffs descending directly into the river.

On Sunday, April 23, they descended the SOB Gully,

Bill Forrest, Kris Walker, and the gear they used for the first ascent of the Painted Wall, behind them (Photo: Bob Godfrey)

downstream of the impasse, hefted their gear a mile down-canyon, and camped at the foot of the Painted Wall. That night, Forrest lay in his sleeping bag, contemplating what lay ahead:

"All I could see was this enormous piece of rock towering up into the sky. Every detail was clear in the evening light. I could see huge overhangs everywhere. At the top of the wall was a line of the biggest overhangs I had ever seen. We were pretty confident that we could climb everything else on the wall, but we just didn't know about those overhangs on top."

The pair had picked a line near the wall's left margin, passing to the right of a brushy terrace low down, connecting a series of subtle dihedral systems, and finishing through massive roofs just below the summit. The groovelike features that comprised much of the route were to be a continuing hazard, since they funneled falling rock. On the fourth pitch, Forrest dislodged a thirty-pound block, which crashed onto his thigh and then grazed Walker's ear as it fell past. Such incidents would prove all too common.

Two days of difficult and dangerous climbing took them to a point 800 feet up the wall. On Tuesday afternoon a storm moved in, and when they awoke on Wednesday, snow had fallen. The snow was no problem, but both had raging poison ivy rashes. Abandoning the attempt, they hiked out, leaving fixed ropes in place.

Their return schedule was expedited when they heard that the Zion wall climber Jeff Lowe was planning a Painted Wall attempt. Lowe would, in fact, show up on the canyon rim to check on the team's progress. Two days after hiking out, Forrest and Walker returned, hauling 200 pounds of equipment, food, water, and calamine lotion to their high point.

April 30 found Walker on the thirteenth lead. He touched a large block, which shifted and began to slide. He grabbed it and tried to jam it back into place. "I couldn't get it to stay up there," Walker said. "If it fell, it'd come right down the rope and hit Bill. I eased it onto my lap as best I could. I could barely lift it—it felt like a hundred pounds. There was a channel in the wall near me. I thought if I could get it into the channel, it would fall away to the left and clear Bill completely. I yelled down to Bill. He looked up. I let the thing go."

The rock didn't quite make the channel. Instead, it headed directly toward Forrest. "I looked up as Kris called," Forrest said. "I could see a huge rock plummeting down toward me. I thought I was a goner." The rock whistled past and exploded into fragments just a few feet from Forrest.

The next day, 1,500 feet up the wall, their crack system dead-ended. Walker led a pendulum that took them to a long groove system full of loose rock. Stones dislodged by the leader funneled down onto the belayer. By now they were alert to this hazard and at each anchor they strung their haul bag uppermost. The second man would hide beneath the bag to belay the leader. On the twenty-first pitch, a watermelon-size rock cut loose and hit the belay station, taking out a water bottle, food bag, and jumar. The crack system continued for 500 feet. They called it Death Valley.

Belay anchors required great creativity, and even so were often marginal: equalized, tied-off pins in questionable rock. The pair had an extraordinary ambition—to climb the wall without expansion bolts. No Grade VI climb anywhere had ever been established boltless. Now nearly

2,000 feet into their route, they had not used their drills.

Once above Death Valley they were directly under the summit overhangs. "They looked absolutely enormous," Forrest said. "I still had no idea if we could find a way through them. But there was no other way but up. We were too far up the wall to consider retreat."

The next day, May 4, found Walker and their bags hanging from five tied-off angle pitons in a crumbling white band, and Forrest leading through the much-feared summit overhangs, the twenty-fourth pitch of the climb. "It was the pitch I'd been wanting," he later said, "an ultimate physical and technical challenge where success was imperative but doubtful."

Well into the pitch, with his rope changing directions five times, Forrest reached an impasse. The pins below him had been so poor that he didn't dare to lead back down. He made yet another tension traverse, which ended just out of reach of a hairline crack. Poised on a hook, fearful that any fall would strip all his pins from the wall, Forrest felt he had pushed to the limit. After a short, terse conversation with Walker, he drilled a shallow hole—the only one on the climb—and pounded in a bolt. It went in only halfway. Walker would clean it with a light hammer blow as he followed.

The crack led Forrest to a stance and cracks where he could belay. The lead had taken him five and a half hours. Walker's pitch was almost as hard, with more free climbing. He could see the top and climbed for it like a man possessed, but the rope came up short. He strung a hanging belay from bongs in a rotten pegmatite crack, excruciatingly close to level ground. A short chimney pitch took them to the top of the wall.

Forrest and Walker's first attempt took three days; the final push took five more. The difficulty, objective danger, and great commitment of their journey left no doubt: their Painted Wall route was a Grade VI, the first in Colorado. This 1972 near-boltless ascent of a fierce, much-tried objective was one of the landmark accomplishments in American big-wall climbing.

The Dragon Route

Layton Kor had given up on the Painted Wall, and on climbing in general, but he had passed on the legacy of his route to another climber, Rusty Baillie. After his attempts with Kor and Goss, Baillie enlisted an Arizona team to attempt the Painted Wall. They made their first attempt in 1971.

Scott Baxter, a southern Californian attending the University of Northern Arizona in Flagstaff, was one of the most skilled and accomplished climbers of the early 1970s, and almost completely unknown outside the backwater of Arizona climbing. A founding member of the legendary Syndicato Granitica, which pushed state-of-the-art climbs up the walls of Granite Mountain and elsewhere, Baxter's exploits included first ascents such as the *Pan American Route,* the original line on the huge and remote Gran Trono Blanco on the Baja Peninsula of Mexico. His partner on that route was Karl Karlstrom, the "Blonde Giant," another talented Flagstaff climber. Baillie convinced these two that Colorado's Black Canyon had a wall worthy of their attention.

The *Dragon Route,* as it would come to be called, was shorter but steeper than Forrest and Walker's line, and tackled the central portion of the face. Three hundred feet of approach climbing led to a brushy terrace where the route began in earnest. The remaining 1,800 feet to the summit were overhanging.

Above the terrace, two leads of 5.9 free climbing led to the beginning of a hidden but more or less continuous crack system that ended in huge roofs about 600 feet up. Located here was the route's only real ledge, dubbed Kor's Cave because of the sheltering roofs just above it. Kor's high point lay just above.

The fractured rock of the Painted Wall was unnerving, and it took Baillie, Baxter, and Karlstrom four days to reach Kor's high point. The Arizonans had scouted the route through binoculars from the opposite rim, and it appeared that a long crack system reached down to a

Forrest and Walker on the crux twenty-fourth pitch of their Painted Wall route, 1972 (Photo: Bob Godfrey)

Sharp, overhanging rock on the lower section of the Dragon Route; *Mark Synnott climbing, 1996* (Photo: Jeff Achey)

point 600 feet above and 200 feet left of Kor's Cave. They would have to make a long traverse to reach this summit crack. Karlstrom was in the lead.

"I climbed up, then pendulumed, then did some skyhook moves, and then stopped," Karlstrom later wrote in *Climbing* magazine. "The rest of the traverse looked hopeless. . . . We had all been getting increasingly uneasy about committing ourselves to the wall. The strange aura had been working on us slowly as we climbed and it finally took control of me on that last lead."

The team retreated, a memorable epic for the younger climbers. They vowed never to return, but over the course of the winter back in Arizona, Baillie—the "snake charmer"—coaxed the daunted team. By spring he had succeeded in clouding their memories and restoring their confidence. By the summer of 1992 they were back, this time with a fourth member, David Lovejoy.

The team was more comfortable with the wall this time, in part due to the personal dynamics. "Baillie provided the spirit and the passion," wrote Karlstrom, "Baxter was amazingly good at finding his way past blank-looking, desperate aid sections, and I was well suited for hauling the heavy sacks. David Lovejoy provided the laughter that helped ease the strangeness of the wall."

Just before launching their attempt, the team heard a rumor that "a Frenchman, Chris Jones, Bill Forrest, and Royal Robbins" had climbed the Painted Wall. Soon, rumor gave way to the straight story of Forrest and Walker's successful first ascent of the Painted Wall.

The climbers were crestfallen. With the great prize claimed, a powwow ensued in Flagstaff. Baillie's passion to climb the wall was undimmed. Their route was more central, he argued, the climbing unusual, and the route might be a classic in its own right. "It was an interesting meeting," Karlstrom wrote. "We were basically talking about climbing motives and our own rationales." They resolved to go on with their attempt.

On a hot June day, the foursome set out down SOB Gully with six new ropes and food and water for twelve days. They reached their high point without difficulty. Baxter led out on the traverse that had turned back Karlstrom.

The goal of the traverse was the Summit Crack, which was completely invisible from the wall. From the climbers' position this section looked like a hopeless voyage across vertical rock, studded with roofs, leading nowhere. Below the traverse line, the wall was undercut by a massive sector of rotten rock, effectively cutting off a straight-down retreat. They called this passage the Stygian Traverse. In Karlstrom's words, "like the River

The Painted Wall, showing the Forrest-Walker (left) *and* Dragon *routes* (Photo: Jeff Achey)

Styx, once one has embarked upon the journey across, there is little hope of returning."

Blocking out thoughts of where his efforts might lead him, Baxter completed a complicated pitch with several tension traverses that put him far out to the left at a small stance where a bolt anchor was needed. Here began another battle that nearly turned the team around. The rock on the Painted Wall is among the hardest anywhere. Baxter broke their first drill bit trying to get in a belay bolt, and then Karlstrom, after jumaring up on Baxter's marginal anchor, broke several more.

Exasperated, the team held a hanging conference with members strung out across the wall from various anchors, shouting their opinions back and forth across the face of the wall. They managed to analyze and solve the drilling problem—saliva from the blow tube was causing the bits to bind in the very tight holes. With good belay bolts set, they kept their enthusiasm and moved forward. Baxter led another A4 pitch, the hardest yet, through a band of decomposed yellow rock, ending in a sling belay among large roofs. They knew the Summit Crack was close. One more difficult lead by Lovejoy led out left, around a roof, through a pegmatite band, and into the Summit Crack.

Two more strenuous days elapsed before the team topped out. They had been nine days on the wall, including six nights in hammocks—the longest yet spent on any Colorado wall, a distinction that would stand until 1980.

The *Dragon* would eventually become the "standard route" on the Painted Wall, repeated regularly if infrequently. Its traversing, diagonal nature keeps the belayer far safer from rockfall than on the *Forrest-Walker* route, the rock is better, and the difficulties more even. Still, the *Dragon* is arguably the hardest and most committing standard route on any major wall in the country outside of Alaska.

The Nose of Chasm View: First Attempts

Climbers love to speak of "last great problems," knowing full well that when one is surmounted, another will be invented in its place. In the early 1970s, with the Diamond laced with climbs and the Painted Wall surmounted by two routes, the "last great problem" in Colorado wall climbing was "the Nose" of North Chasm View Wall in the Black Canyon.

The Chasm View Nose was no hidden treasure. Nearly 2,000 feet tall, it sat directly across from the same popular scenic drive as the Painted Wall. Any climber to visit the Black Canyon had seen it, an elegant, uncanny half-size replica of *The Nose* of El Capitan.

A few early attempts had been made. Michael Covington was particularly enamored with the line, and on one attempt his partner had been a teenaged Jim Dunn, making his first acquaintance with the Black Canyon. Later, Earl Wiggins' first Black Canyon climb would also be a Nose attempt. In 1972, shortly after the Painted Wall ascents, Wayne Goss and Jim Logan of Boulder headed down to try the Nose.

The Nose of North Chasm View. Early attempts focused on the left-facing dihedral system to the right of the Nose proper, which proved impassable above midheight. Goss and Logan escaped onto the flakes visible to the dihedral's right, soon joining the 1964 Kor-Dalke route, visible as a vertical crack rising from the shadows. (Photo: Jeff Achey)

In 1969, Logan was in prime shape, climbing in Yosemite, where he did four Grade VIs in two weeks—a Valley record. A few months later he was in combat in Vietnam. Now he was back in Boulder, his nerves were shot, and Goss was helping him in the best way he knew how, by taking him climbing.

They drove to the South Rim, scoped the buttress with binoculars, drove around to the North Rim, and began. They descended the gully and started up the natural line closest to the toe of the buttress. The easy cracks and chimneys were cursed with dense pricker bushes, and made for desperate hauling. They bivouacked on a series of bushy ledges 400 feet up, in the rain. Above, the terrain became steeper.

The next morning, none too early, they headed up into a huge copper-colored dihedral, the most conspicuous feature of the lower buttress and the line of all early Nose attempts. The nailing grew thin. Goss led a long aid pitch, placing all his knifeblades, many of them only a few millimeters into the hairline crack. Finally he placed a bolt, disgusted at his own cowardice. This was the tone of the climb; they were climbing at a high standard, but felt incompetent and "off." They were distracted. They were twenty-five years old, and a variety of thoughts absorbed them. Rather than making history on a "last great problem," they were escaping the world, taking refuge in their obscure art in a desolate western canyon.

Goss eventually found cracks good enough for a belay. A large flake loomed overhead, held to the wall by forces unknown. Logan headed up, laybacking around the flake, willing it to adhere. The crack above was as rotten as the one below was thin. Logan continued another thirty feet until, half height on the Chasm View Wall, the line blanked out. What had appeared from the South Rim to be the continuation of the dihedral proved to be nothing more than a shadow, a mere groove in blank, overhanging rock whose surface flaked away when touched.

To stay near the Nose, Logan and Goss would have to somehow move out left. There were no visible crack systems to use or to go for. Down and right, Logan could glimpse the edge of what appeared to be a grassy ledge, invisible from the belay. Logan placed a nut, lowered, and pendulumed right. It was now late in the day. Goss had been hanging in slings for hours, and when he finally joined Logan on a flat and spacious ledge, his face lit up with delight.

The night was fine and they relaxed for the first time since leaving the rim. They sat in the moonlight, ate, and weighed their options. Logan had back-cleaned the upper part of the pitch but left the line hanging through his highest nut.

The next morning, with little ado, they pulled the line and followed the unclimbed crack system directly above their bivy ledge. This took them even farther right, away from the crest of the buttress. Soon, they joined Kor and Dalke's 1964 route on the southeast face. On their third day, they reached the rim, about 200 feet right of the Nose proper, unsure of exactly what they had accomplished. They had pioneered a fine route, destined to be repeated, but it was not "the Nose."

The Eighth Voyage of Sinbad

By 1974, El Capitan had fifteen routes but the southwest face of North Chasm View Wall, the Black Canyon's most Yosemite-like face, had only one, the *Diagonal* route put up by Kor, Bossier, and McCarthy in 1963. This followed a relatively easy ramp system for most of its 2,000-foot length. The surrounding rock was laced with obvious features and cracks, all untouched.

By 1974, Jim Dunn was becoming one of the country's

Dean Tschappat, Black Canyon big-wall pioneer, in 1979 (Photo: Ed Webster)

best-known climbers. A Yosemite wall veteran, he also was pioneering short, hard free routes in Colorado and New Hampshire and establishing a new generation of desert tower climbs in southeastern Utah that featured 5.10 and 5.11 free climbing up parallel-sided cracks—a bold enterprise before the advent of spring-loaded camming devices. Dunn was particularly renowned for his skill in off-width cracks, and this expertise would come in handy in the Black Canyon.

In spring of 1974, Dunn and Dean Tschappat set out on a major road trip, and their first objective was to add a second line to the southwest face of North Chasm View. They studied the line from the South Rim, then drove to the North Rim, sorted their gear, and descended to the base of the wall. They began near the *Diagonal* and headed up the wall to its left.

The climbing was straightforward, with mostly good rock and lots of free climbing, but the weather was brutally hot. They went light, bringing no sleeping bags, too little water, and no bolts. High on the wall on the second afternoon, they were out of water. Tschappat led a pitch that disappeared onto a ledge. Above was a distinctive, slanting crack they had noticed from the opposite rim. Tschappat, dry-mouthed, yelled down the grim news: "It won't go!"

Dunn jumared to Tschappat's stance. When he arrived, he saw the problem—a leaning, round-edged fissure about eight inches wide. They were 1,500 feet up, barely a rope length from the top of the wall, and they had absolutely no gear to fit the crack that was the only route to the top.

Dunn looked at Tschappat, then at the crack, and said, "Put me on, I'm going for it." He grabbed some RURPs, bongs, and tube chocks, and then started climbing. The crack looked hard, but Dunn figured he could always slither back down if things got out of hand.

The crack was deceptive, leaning to the right and entering the wall at the angle of the lean. The combined effect, not apparent until Dunn had climbed into it, produced a severely overhanging crack, much more difficult than it appeared.

Dunn squirmed up fifteen feet before he realized his predicament. Sliding down was out of the question—the crack would spit him straight out. Dunn spied a thin seam in the wall above and headed for it. Hanging from an arm bar, he pulled a RURP from his rack and pounded it in. "I got some pro!" he yelled. Relieved, he clipped in a sling, gave it a tug, and the RURP ripped out in his hand.

Dunn was now twenty-five feet above the ledge with no protection and no way to climb down. Any time he wasn't moving up he started to slip out. Now he was tiring.

Fifteen feet higher the crack pinched down. If he could reach there, he thought, he might be able to place a tube chock. The climbing was no harder, but it was insecure and exhausting. A fall was unthinkable. Forty feet above the belay, Dunn was within arm's reach of the constriction. He grabbed the tube off his gear sling and wedged it overhead. It wobbled on its edges. He thrutched higher, grabbed his hammer, pounded on the tube until it buckled and wedged fast, and clipped in his rope.

From the tube he could place an endwise bong, the last of his gear that fit the crack. Above, the wall kicked back off vertical and the difficulty eased a grade. The worst was over. Dunn continued up another fifty feet of 5.10, finding a few constrictions narrow enough to take his biggest hexes. Finally he reached a roof, a horizontal crack, and belay anchors. He fixed the rope, rapped to the ledge, and the pair spent a long, thirsty night.

In the morning, the day's heat seemed to arrive before the sun. They jumared the fixed rope and Tschappat led through. Though large roofs above the belay blocked his view, Tschappat knew his lead should take them to the top—and to water. He led out right, placing endwise bongs in the back of a flaring wide crack and camming his largest hexes against loose rocks sitting in the flare.

Tschappat started thinking about the three-foot section of rope that they had noticed was black and stiff. He could see it on his lead line, a few feet below him. Tschappat wondered if motor oil or battery acid had gotten on the rope, and as he got farther out from good protection, he grew more and more concerned that the chemically weakened rope would snap in a fall. Soon all he could think about was the rope breaking. Every aid placement seemed about to pop.

Tschappat turned the first roof only to find another waiting. He started up a short crack, free climbing now, which amplified his fears about the rope. Committing himself, he latched the crack below the second roof. It flared downward, offering no good holds. Tschappat's strength was failing rapidly. He tried to down-climb but slipped.

As he fell he imagined the damaged rope stretching and parting like chewing gum. Suddenly, he flipped upside down. His foot had caught in a sling, stopping his fall before his weight came onto the rope. He scrambled upright and aided back up to the roof, now grimly determined and beyond fear. He traversed the second flare, turned the roof, and moved up onto easy ground. A short easy pitch led them to the top of *The Eighth Voyage of Sinbad*.

Back at the campground, only a hundred yards away, they dropped their loads, drank their fill, and sat in a daze on the picnic table. An hour later they discovered the rope contaminant. In the trunk of their car was a sticky spill—from a honey jar. The next day they hit the road, en route to Zion and a new route on Angel's Landing.

12. The West Slope

To the west of the Continental Divide lies Colorado's West Slope, a vast, mountainous area sprinkled with ranches, small towns, and clusters of peaks rising high above timberline. Although the cities on the eastern edge of Colorado's Front Range, particularly Boulder, always have had the most climbers and the highest standards of difficulty, much activity took place far from this "urban corridor." In the early 1970s, two of Colorado's most famous mountain towns—Aspen and Telluride—forged their own distinctive climbing identities.

Aspen

Nowadays, Aspen is second home to Middle Eastern princes and Hollywood movie stars, and Lear Jet capital of the world, but it was a much more down-to-earth place in the 1960s. Jet-set affluence and ostentatious mansions were mostly absent. Aspen was a retreat for artists and intellectuals, skiers, and general mountain characters. Laws were loose, and the bars eclectic and rowdy. The town had intellectual and political clout. The Aspen Institute had opened there in 1950, and would broker such landmark meetings as the first international global climate conference, in 1962, and the 1990 Aspen Summit, where George Bush and Margaret Thatcher conferred during the Gulf War.

The Aspen climbing scene, too, had an influence that belied its out-of-the-way location. Even though the best local rock climbs were only marginally important, the culture was rich, speckled with traveling climbers, and Aspen's overall influence on Colorado climbing was significant.

In the 1960s a large percentage of Aspen's thousand-odd residents were hard-core mountain enthusiasts. The U.S. Army's 10th Mountain Division had trained at nearby Camp Hale during World War II, and many veterans had settled in Aspen, founding businesses and building the ground floor of a new multibillion-dollar industry: skiing. Aspen opened some of the country's earliest ski lifts in 1946. Many of the early ski instructors were European—some accomplished alpinists—and ever since, the Aspen scene has been colored with Old World traditions. Skiing, peak climbing, mountain hiking—such were the pastimes of the average Aspenite in the 1960s. The town's official European sister city was Chamonix.

Aspen's early rock climbing was inhibited by the very small, but very steep nature of the cliffs. The best effort of

Harvey T. Carter after the first ascent of Independence Buttress *in Glenwood Canyon, 1975* (Photo: Michael Kennedy)

the early days was the first ascent of Lower Grotto Cliff in 1959, by David Michael and others via the still-popular *Grotto Traverse.* Two years later, Harvey T. Carter visited Aspen and added a very steep mixed free and aid line directly up the same cliff, calling his route *Intelligentsia.* In 1963, Carter moved from Colorado Springs to Aspen. He worked on the ski patrol for many years and brought to town a passion for rock climbing that added a new dimension to Aspen's already strong mountain heritage.

Longtime local outdoorsman Dave Farney opened a summer camp-cum-mountaineering school called Ashcrofters a few miles out of town, which soon gained an excellent and widespread reputation. Surrounded by wilderness, it was a mountain paradise for twelve- to eighteen-year-old boys, with a rough-hewn soccer field, swimming pond complete with zip line, A-frame huts for sleeping, and a big central mess hall (now the site of the Pine Creek Cookhouse restaurant).

The Ashcrofters instructors were knicker-clad and seasoned, and some explained the basics of rope work in thick European accents. Among the Ashcrofters alumni were some famous climbers of the future, including Jonathan Wright, who was killed in 1980 in a Himalayan avalanche that also injured Yvon Chouinard and Rick Ridgeway, and in 1968 a young Easterner named Henry Barber, about whom more will be said leter.

Aspen's best rock was on the many small, subalpine crags up the Roaring Fork River toward Independence Pass. Here, Carter ferreted out new crags and added routes to the known ones, making first ascents of such well-known lines as *Twin Cracks* on the Grotto Wall, *Ultra Edge* on Weller Slab, and *Right Side of the Plaque.* On Whirlpool Rock, Carter did his hardest Aspen free route, known simply as *Carter's Corner,* a solid 5.10 done in 1964.

Carter also left another legacy in Aspen, this one undertaken in 1970 in partnership with Dick Bird—fellow Aspen ski patroller and retired United Airlines pilot, but best known in our context as leader of the crux *Birdwalk* pitch of *Redguard* during the first ascent of Redgarden Wall near Boulder in 1956. Carter and Bird started a modest, black-and-white magazine. The idea was to produce the first American magazine to focus on "the real thing," technical climbing, and Carter hoped to both spread information and build a more national climbing community. Carter ran *Climbing* magazine for only two years. He had strong opinions and a forceful presentation, and dealings with his free-spirited contributors and advertisers were not always smooth. Never much of a businessman, Carter sold the magazine to Bil Dunaway, a 10th Mountain Division veteran.

Among Dunaway's adventures was the first ski descent of Mont Blanc above Chamonix, done with the great French alpinist Lionel Terray. He was publisher and editor of the *Aspen Times,* and thus well equipped to float a marginal specialty magazine. Dunaway owned a printing company in partnership with a German immigrant named Fritz Stammberger, who took over as editor of *Climbing* in 1972.

Stammberger was handsome and dashing, locally famous for skiing the cliff-studded face of North Maroon Bell, the town's "postcard peak." Stammberger inspired an extreme-skiing tradition, in which local climbers played a leading role. One, Chris Landry, would become the first to ski Mount Rainier's Liberty Ridge. In 1978, Steve Shea starred in one of the first extreme ski films, Bob Carmichael's *Fall Line,* during which he made the second ski descent of the Grand Teton. One memorable cut, used for years on the pre-show lead for the TV program *The American Sportsman,* showed Shea cart-wheeling down the length of the rock-strewn Kochs Couloir on Middle Teton. Lou Dawson, another Aspen rock climber, would become the first person to ski all fifty-four of Colorado's 14,000-foot peaks and would later author the classic off-piste skiing book *Wild Snow.*

Stammberger ran *Climbing* magazine until he disappeared in Asia in an obscure mountaineering incident cloaked in rumors of international espionage. Several short-lived interim editors followed until 1974, when the magazine was handed off to a newly arrived climber, photographer, and college drop-out named Michael Kennedy. Kennedy would eventually buy *Climbing* and run it for twenty-five years, first from the *Times* basement and then from down-valley offices in Carbondale, during which time the sport of climbing would change almost beyond belief, and the magazine would grow into a slick, full-color expression of the times.

The Aspen Climbers
In the early 1970s, Aspen had a core group of devoted rock climbers who, in the tradition of their town, were mountain generalists. Skiing, ice climbing, and hard winter ascents on the nearby 14,000-foot peaks alternated with sunny rock climbing. They were a powerful bunch and would advance world standards in several disciplines, notably extreme skiing, ice climbing, and Alaskan and Himalayan superalpinism. Their summer playground was the steep crags of Independence Pass.

Perhaps the most dedicated rock climber of the bunch was Lou Dawson, a New Jersey native who had moved to Aspen during high school, spent a season with Ashcrofters, and took up rock climbing. Dawson became the archetypal 1970s "climbing bum." He drove a beater VW Bug that sported a bolt-on Plexiglas sheet for a roof and

Lou Dawson bouldering at Independence Pass in 1976, sporting typical garb of the day: bandolier chalk bag and EB climbing shoes with hand-sewn leather side panels (Photo: Michael Kennedy)

a plywood bed board in place of a passenger seat. Only the hand brake worked, leading to exciting moments on the long hill down into Aspen from the famed, low rent "barndominiums" where he sometimes resided. Dawson would drive to Yosemite and live out of his Bug for months at a time, and he used the same car for dinner dates with the rich Aspen girls, letting sheer outlaw cachet make up for his lack of funds.

Steve Shea, a ski mechanic, was the most European of the Aspen rock climbers. His excursions were not to Yosemite but to Chamonix, where he learned much from Chamonix alpinists such as Jean-Marc Boivin. In turn, Shea introduced the locals to waterfall ice climbing, a discipline in which Aspen was at the cutting edge in the early 1970s. In Aspen, Shea's house was the favored site for slide shows and the attendant debauchery.

At first glance Larry Bruce, another Aspen climber, might have been mistaken for a garden-variety hippie and was among the climbers who went at their sport with a certain "divine guidance." At one point in the early 1970s Bruce dabbled in a fad called "Name it and pray it," the object of which was to advance one's lot through prayer. Bruce invested all his money in gold—then prayed. A few weeks later, in one of its wildest fluctuations in history, the gold market went through the roof. With the wind-fall, Bruce headed to Yosemite, where he casually soloed 5.10 climbs, certain that he was under the protection of Jesus. At other times, Bruce's passions would turn to motorcycle racing, firearms, and aid climbing. He married the extremely accomplished climber Molly Higgins, co-discoverer of the South Platte's Turkey Rock, and together the pair authored the first Aspen climbing guidebook as well as numerous first ascents.

Other characters filled out the scene: Steve Kentz, Bruce Kumpf, Hank Barlow, and of course Harvey T. Carter. Carter made huge contributions to Colorado climbing, but his ideas and routes were often the subject of ridicule. This was due to both his pugnacious personality and a general misunderstanding of his rather obtuse ideas.

Ungenerously called Bolts Carter by some, he did indeed favor fixing protection pitons or bolts on his climbs and had a few good bolt ladders to his credit in Garden of the Gods and the Fisher Towers. Carter—against the grain of American climbing at the time—leaned toward the traditional European conception of "opening" a route, which subsequent climbers could then repeat with minimal equipment. Carter was not necessarily trying to reduce risk. He felt that boldness and calculated risk were essential components of good climbing, but he felt that a route should have a precise level of risk, as determined by the first ascent party.

One problem with "clean climbing," in Carter's view, was that indiscriminate use of nuts could allow a climb to be overprotected. If only fixed protection was used, the level of challenge for all repeat ascents would be uniform. Above all, Carter sought uniformity and unity—through his clubs, his organized competitions, his meticulous notes, and his magazine. His Universal Standard rating system was an attempt to classify the rock climbs of America under one system that acknowledged all the elements he considered important and relevant—exposure, risk, the continuity of the climb. If Carter's system had been simpler and his personality more winning, American climbing might have been steered toward different aspirations than the well-protected gymnastics increasingly encouraged by the Yosemite Decimal System.

Grotto of Horror

Carter's rating system never caught on, but his risk ethic rubbed off. Appropriately, early 1970s climbs at the Grotto walls on Independence Pass often took their names from H. P. Lovecraft horror novels, of which Dawson was particularly fond. *Necronomicon,* an impressive, overhanging crack line on the Upper Grotto, was the "book of the dead" often carried by a Lovecraft character called the *Mad Arab*—another climb at Grotto Cliffs. A horrific creature from another dimension was the *Mind Parasite,* a

Denny and Bill Forrest of Denver—who had recently met as fellow instructors at the Colorado Outward Bound base camp in Marble—climbed the wall's most obvious line, *Cryogenic,* left of the wall's first direct route, *Intelligentsia.* It was their first climb together, done as a warm-up for an attempt on the Diamond. In 1968, visiting East Coast climber John Reppy free climbed the first pitch to produce one of Aspen's earliest and best known 5.10 leads. A few years earlier, Reppy had been responsible for the first ascent of another Colorado classic—*Flying Buttress* on Mount Meeker in Rocky Mountain National Park.

In 1973, Michael Kennedy and Lou Dawson made the first free attempts on Carter's *Intelligentsia.* After aiding the first pitch, they belayed at a ledge about sixty feet off the ground, below a steep dihedral. Dawson took the lead, feeling particularly confident since Kennedy had recently bought one of the new MSR kernmantle ropes.

The moves up the dihedral were steep and complicated. Dawson, habitually a bit reckless, had run it out fifteen feet and was starting to tire. Just out of reach was an old fixed pin. Dawson went for it, and at the end of his strength, jammed his finger though the eye of the piton. His mistake was immediately obvious—he was now unable to clip the pin, or to hold onto it for long. Seconds

A modern ascent of the first pitch of Cryogenic, *one of Aspen's earliest and most popular 5.10s* (Photo: Jeff Achey)

Michael Kennedy on an early ascent of Bruce Kumpf and Steve Shea's 1974 route Necromonicon *on Third Grotto Cliff, near Aspen* (Photo: Kennedy collection)

suitable name for a desperate 5.10+ climb that appeared on the cover of an early *Climbing* magazine.

The most obvious rock on Independence Pass is the Lower Grotto, overhanging gently for nearly 200 feet and looming directly above the road at a hairpin turn. Slow-moving Winnebagos often come to a halt to watch the Grotto climbers dangling overhead. Not surprisingly, many of Aspen's standard-setting climbs have occurred here, front and center stage. In 1965, Yosemite climber Glenn

later, Dawson went flying. It was a long fall, about thirty feet, and Dawson's weight came hard onto Kennedy's new MSR rope, which passed the test—almost. It held, but where it passed through the carabiner, friction had melted the sheath. The prized new rope had to be retired.

The Aspen crew got steadily better at free climbing. Dawson and Shea were fond of one crag called Instant Karma, located at high elevation above the Independence Pass summit. Dawson's *Kundalini* provided the most breathtaking ascent—5.10 off-width climbing at 13,000 feet. In 1974, Kennedy and Dawson free climbed *Banana Peeler,* a thin face and crack on Walls Wall, and the very short, very obvious *Urinary Tract* in Lincoln Creek Campground. These were Aspen's first two 5.11s.

Cryogenic had become very popular, and then as now, was often the scene of mass top-roping sessions with a party atmosphere. Still, in 1974, only the first pitch had been climbed free. In the 1970s it felt a bit odd to rappel from a climb before reaching the top of the cliff, and Dawson and Kennedy had aided to the top of *Cryogenic* on several occasions. Moved as they were by Boulder's commitment to pure style on first free ascents, they were

Dan Stone on the crux of Bicentennial, *Grotto Cliff, in 1978* (Photo: Jeff Achey collection)

influenced also by Carter's emphasis on "opening" a climb. Carter's philosophy made even more sense once they had scared themselves silly a few times on the overhangs above Reppy's crack pitch. Finally, in 1975, Kennedy aided out above the first-pitch belay and placed a bolt. With this protection in place they soon free climbed the pitch at 5.10+, creating what was then Aspen's most impressive multipitch free climb.

The Bicentennial

It was summer of 1976 and the nation's two-hundredth birthday was approaching. Larry Bruce, Shea, and Dawson planned a celebratory ascent on Independence Pass. On the Fourth, hordes of sightseers cruised the winding mountain road below as the climbers uncoiled their ropes at the base of the Grotto Wall.

Dawson improvised a challenging free pitch that bypassed the thin aid on *Intelligentsia* and led to the base of the dihedral where he had taken his now-legendary fall. Shea took the lead and cruised the next hard pitch, forgoing the aerial display, and the climbers gathered once again at a small belay stance. Bruce led on to the top.

They were elated with their ascent. The climbing was hard and a bit scary, but they weren't pushing the limits, Colorado's or their own. Their satisfaction came from their teamwork, from each other's competence, from their joint mastery of an environment that was totally foreign to the tourists who passed on the road below. They descended for a festive Fourth of July afternoon, and called their route *Bicentennial*.

Above the first belay on *Bicentennial* was a crack that shot directly out a body-length roof. Once *Bicentennial* was climbed, Shea and Dawson started eyeing the roof crack. Several free-climbing attempts were made, including one by a visiting Jim Erickson.

Another visitor soon tried the route. Originally from Massachusetts, "Hot Henry" Barber was rapidly becoming the most famous young rock climber in the country and had been raising eyebrows everywhere he went. In Yosemite Valley in 1973 he flashed the first ascent of the much-tried *Butterballs,* and in 1975 led *Fish Crack,* the first 5.12 in Yosemite.

Barber's connection to Colorado's West Slope went deep. His parents had sent him to the Ashcrofters camp in Aspen in the late 1960s, and after Farney moved his operation to Telluride, Barber spent several seasons working for him there. His Telluride climbs will be recounted shortly. Barber considered Colorado a second home, and in the summer of 1976, he based his globetrotting climbing trips out of Boulder and Aspen.

Hard partying, hard climbing, and supremely confident, Barber was something of a rival to the permanent

Steve Shea attempting the Bicentennial Roof, *which became Aspen's first 5.12* (Photo: Michael Kennedy)

Aspen locals. Working for Chouinard as one of the early climbing equipment reps, he made sufficient money from commissions and slide shows to leave an almost unlimited amount of time for climbing.

A month or so after the *Bicentennial* ascent, Shea took Barber out to try the roof. Shea led up, and at the roof, he grabbed a large spike of rock, which came off in his hand. Sixty pounds of stone smashed into the belay ledge inches from Barber, ending the day's outing.

They were back the next day, and Shea's faux pas dictated that he give the lead to Barber, who made quick work of the strenuous overhang. *Bicentennial Roof* was one of Colorado's early 5.12s, and the first in the state to be led without falls.

Barefoot at Lincoln Creek

In the spring of 1976, Himalayan climber and Shawangunks pioneer Fritz Wiessner invited Henry Barber, Steve Wunsch, and Rick Hatch to climb with him in his home area, the famed sandstone towers along the River Elbe near Dresden, Germany. Barber was very impressed with the Elbsandstein, where 5.11 routes were done as early as 1954, in bare feet, with minimal protection. Barber returned to the States inspired and did many barefoot ascents in the next few years, the most improbable of which was in Aspen in the summer of 1977.

Allen Porter on Dean's Day Off *in 2000. This 1977 Henry Barber climb still inspires respect in the best climbers, even those with the added advantage of climbing shoes.* (Photo: Jeff Achey)

Climbing on Independence Pass almost daily, Barber discovered a striking aid line on Lincoln Creek Cliff called *Dean's Day Off*. His first attempt to free climb the route was Dresden style. He could not have picked a worse barefoot climb. The crack, more of a seam, ran up a smooth slab dotted with tiny edges, holds that were fairly good in stiff climbing shoes, but useless in bare feet. The whole climb was tricky to protect, requiring lots of standing around and fiddling. At the crux there was the potential for a long, sliding fall—unthinkable without shoes.

After parts of two days climbing up and down, Barber mastered all the hard climbing up to the crux bulge. Repeatedly, he probed the moves and down-climbed. On one attempt, he had to grab a nut. A stickler for good style, Barber lowered off and pulled the rope before trying again.

By the third day Barber had most of the climb figured out, but he was tempted to cave in and put on his shoes. Everyone else thought the barefooting thing was silly, and several different partners were already tired of belaying him. His feet hurt.

On the fourth day, Barber climbed into the precarious fingertip layback at the crux bulge and kept going. Leaning left at first, he pinched the crack's edge and switched through to the right. His left toes grasped the crack while the right toes searched for minuscule edges on the face. He balanced up, reached a finger lock, and much to everyone's relief, jammed through to the top.

At hard-to-protect 5.11+, *Dean's Day Off* is still considered one of Aspen's more demanding leads, but Barber was a master at thin cracks, and in climbing shoes he might have dispensed with the first free ascent in an afternoon. Barefoot, the route became vastly more difficult, and personal. "Once I started I felt like I had a chance to do something really great for myself," Barber said. "The thing was, I didn't cave."

Pumping Sandstone

In 1978, the renowned California climber and writer John Long brought his boisterous energy to Aspen. On his way slowly through graduate school, he worked as a janitor at the old "Yellow Brick Schoolhouse." Late at night, Long, a veteran weightlifter, would pump iron in the small, dimly lit gym.

Long was a passionate boulderer, and he conspired with Michael Kennedy to produce a memorable article called "Pumping Sandstone," the only piece on Colorado climbing to make it into the renowned British anthology *Games Climbers Play*. In this piece, Long played bad boy of California bouldering to John Gill's gentleman master of rock.

"Back then," Long said, "Michael Kennedy and I were both gung-ho about trying to elevate American climbing writing to the level already accomplished by Conrad, Hemingway, and so forth. That's how wonderfully naive we were." Time and funds were limited, so their schedule was frantic. Long and Kennedy had to try to climb and photograph all of Gill's classic problems around Pueblo—which were not only very hard, but spread out all over the county—in a single day. On another trip they sampled the Horsetooth Reservoir boulders. After climb-

John Long on Pinch Overhang *at Horsetooth Reservoir in 1978. Long was living in Aspen and teamed up with Michael Kennedy for a* Climbing *magazine article featuring the boulder problems of John Gill.* (Photo: Michael Kennedy)

ing problems such as *Left Eliminator* and *Pinch Overhang* at Horsetooth, and *Ripper Traverse* in Pueblo, Long had new respect for the legend of Gill.

In Aspen, Long distinguished himself with several new free climbs in 1978, including the thin crack of *B-Sharp* on Difficult Cliff, and *Seventh Octave* a few feet left, which became Independence Pass's new hardest pitch, at solid 5.12. Long would also spend the summer of 1980 in Colorado, in Telluride. another unlikely West Slope town.

Telluride
On the western edge of the San Juan Mountains in the southwest corner of Colorado is another rollicking ex-mining town. A quick escape down the San Miguel or Dolores Rivers will take you to the Utah canyon country, site of warm winter rock climbing and the old hideout of the Hole in the Wall gang. *To-hell-ya-ride,* as the place was often called in the days when Butch Cassidy started his bank-robbing career there, eventually became a ski town. The bars weren't quite as rowdy (six-shooters were eventually outlawed), but a certain mountain-man sense of lawlessness persisted.

Telluride is hemmed in tightly by steep mountainsides, a wonderland of avalanche chutes and ice climbs in the winter and peerless skiing in the spring. For summer fun, a few miles outside town lies a large crag that shimmers with facets of glacier polish—the famed Ophir Wall.

The San Juan Mountaineers did some rock climbing in the Telluride area in the 1930s as they explored the nearby craggy peaks in the Wilson group, near Lizard Head Pass. The Ophir Wall was first climbed, probably in the 1950s or early 1960s, via the so-called *Post Office Crack*, the conspicuous 500-foot diagonal weakness up the middle of the wall, directly behind the tiny post office. Relic soft-iron army pitons were found on later ascents, but the original climbers left their deed unrecorded.

In 1969, David Farney closed his Ashcrofters school in Aspen and moved operations to the Skyline Ranch near Telluride. One of his early guides was one of his Ashcrofters students, Henry Barber of Boston, still an unknown climber. In the summer of 1972, Barber began a tentative exploration of the Ophir Wall, partnering with Greg Davis, another Colorado climber who would pioneer many fine routes in Telluride, Aspen, and Rocky Mountain National Park on into the 1990s.

The Ophir Wall (Photo: Michael Kennedy)

Bill Kees, original Ophir Wall Bum and MountainFilm promoter, on Honey Pot *in 1981* (Photo: Glenn Randall)

Barber was deeply inspired by his summer season in Telluride, and when he returned to the East that fall he began the free-climbing spree that would earn him international fame and the nickname Hot Henry. His battery of new free routes in New England that year would include the first 5.11s in New Hampshire (*Lichen Delight* at Cathedral Ledge) and Massachusetts (*Jane* at Crow Hill).

Telluride's 1973 season was a good one for rock climbing. Barber was back and made first ascents of some superb Ophir Wall lines, including the top-to-bottom dihedral system *Hot Wee Wee*—sort of a cleaner, harder *Post Office Crack*—and a beautiful, steep aid line that would later become a 5.12+ free route, *Morning Glory*. Barber's best route of 1973 was the conspicuous Y fist crack that splits a steep, polished facet of the central face; *Honey Pot,* done with Dave Perlman, was named after a young woman at the Skyline Ranch whose complete lack of interest in Barber inspired his summer's climbing.

Also that year, Bill Kees, the original "Ophir Wall Bum" and the godfather of Telluride climbing, added classic routes such as *Orange Peel*, with Jack Koffman. This one-pitch, 5.10 crack was hidden away in what would be known as Cracked Canyon, a remarkable slit in the right edge of the Ophir Wall, now the most popular climbing venue in Telluride.

Henry Barber on Dr. Gizmo, *Ophir Wall, in the mid-1980s. Barber established many of the earliest climbs on the Ophir Wall, beginning in 1972.* (Photo: Michael Kennedy)

The Skyline Ranch school soon went out of business, and Barber found summer work elsewhere. There were plenty of hard routes to do, if necessary, but the Ophir Wall Bums enjoyed being just that for a few years until 1977, when some strange news hit town. Royal Robbins moving to Telluride?

It sounded like a tale made up after too many margaritas. Yet Lito Tejada-Flores, Robbins' host, claimed it was true. Royal and his wife, Liz, had dropped in for a quick visit, stayed a week—and then bought a house. They wanted to move their climbing school from Modesto, California, to Telluride.

As the Bums sat on barstools in the evenings and on porches of old Ophir cabins in the brilliant midday sun, images of rock climbs flashed before their eyes. They knew the Californians would soon be exploring their crags, and they resolved to really get after it and finally climb those nice-looking cracks they had been postponing. Before they knew it, Robbins was in town and the lines were still unclimbed—but not for long.

In the summer of 1978, Chris Vandiver joined Robbins in Telluride and the Rockcraft climbing school opened for business. That year, the total Telluride route count doubled. Especially popular were the short, steep cracks of Cracked Canyon, where many excellent routes were climbed, mostly by the Californians. Particularly painful for the Ophir Wall Bums was the first ascent of *Javelin*, the best-looking crack in Cracked Canyon. Strenuous, overhanging, and attempted on several occasions before the California invasion, it was led with maddening ease by Vandiver.

As far as the Californians were concerned, however, there was all too much time for new routes. As David Farney had already discovered with Skyline Ranch, the demand for climbing instruction in Telluride was limited at best, and the Rockcraft school would last but a few years. Kees and others had much better success putting Telluride on the international climbing map. In June of 1979, they put together MountainFilm, the first film festival on the continent devoted solely to mountaineering. In future years the festival would attract the most famous mountain personalities in the world, including the likes of Warren Harding, Yvon Chouinard, Gaston Rébuffat, Walter Bonatti, Maurice Herzog, Chris Bonington, and Edmund Hillary.

In the summer of 1980, quite a collection of name climbers was gathered in this funky mountain town in the San Juans. Among them were the young California couple John Long and Lynn Hill, in town to work for Royal Robbins. In Aspen, Long had distinguished himself with several new free climbs in 1978. Hill was a talented but as yet unknown climber from Southern California who had learned her trade with Long, John Yablonski, and others of the legendary Stonemasters clan.

Long and Hill were a comical pair, Long over six feet tall, with a massive, weightlifter's build, Hill a lithe five-foot-two. They were planning a major road tour, and they began with a "working" summer in Telluride.

Hidden away on the far east end of the Mirror Wall, protected from roadside viewing, was the most compelling crack line in Ophir, a climb originally done on aid by Dan Langmade and Bill Kees, cryptically and eponomously called *Lankees*. Robbins had told Long that if free climbed, it would be one of the greatest crack climbs in the country. When he saw it, Long was equally impressed: "By any measure, this was one spectacular crack," he said in 2000, "a laser splitter up a glacier-polished wall, from pinky locks to fist jams at the top. It's one of the great ones, good as Yosemite's best."

The pair went to work on it straightaway, and with considerable struggling and falling, they worked the protection up the crack. More accurately, Long worked the

Lynn Hill in Eldorado Canyon in 1981 (Photo: Jeff Lowe)

California climber Tom Davis attempting Ophir Broke *in 1988* (Photo: Jeff Achey)

protection up; Hill was stymied by a reach move just a few feet off the ground and focused her efforts trying to solve the impasse. Long reached a point where the crack went to one inch, a terrible size for jamming, before it was finally too dark to climb. The pair returned a few days later, joined, by chance, by David Breashears, who was just beginning his career in film, working on the shooting of a commercial on the Ophir Wall.

"Lynn went up to have a try," Long said, "and damn if she didn't climb right on through." Hill had solved her boulder problem and climbed beyond Long's high point before running out of strength. Long tried again, fell, and on her next try, Hill completed the pitch. Long and Breashears were astonished, but less so than Hill. It was a major breakthrough in Hill's climbing, which had until that point always been overshadowed—at least in her own mind—by the feats of her male partners. At the time of its first ascent, *Ophir Broke,* at solid 5.12, was the hardest crack climb in Colorado, and even Yosemite had only a climb or two that were harder. "That's when I knew for certain that this woman had extraordinary talent," Long said. Hill was indeed destined for great things in climbing, including five years of dominance in the yet-to-be-conceived World Cup, and the first free ascent of *The Nose* of El Capitan.

On the way out of Telluride, Long and Hill breezed back into Aspen. They made the second ascent of Barber's *Dean's Day Off*—with the aid of climbing shoes—and repeated *B-Sharp* and *Seventh Octave*. Continuing their tour of Aspen's hardest climbs they headed for the Grotto Wall to try the *Bicentennial Roof*. At the base of the wall, just downhill from Dawson's *Bicentennial* start, they were distracted by bolts on a slightly overhanging face—the original aid start to Carter's *Intelligentsia*, the rest of which had become *Bicentennial*.

"I was in the shape of my life and wanted to prove it," Long said. "This thing was ripe for the picking." There were some obstacles to a free ascent, however, besides the difficult moves. The old bolts were poor, and the ground below the climb was strewn with ankle-shattering blocks. Long trundled the blocks he could move—and the man could move some stone—and started trying to boulder out the first moves. This proved impossible, as the landing was still too hazardous. He was going to have to rope up and trust the bolts, or give it up.

The wall appeared to ease off twenty-five feet up, but even the featherweight Hill had no intention of risking a fall onto the rusty bolts. To make matters worse, the moves put a climber in a very awkward position. "If you popped, you'd fly off the thing like you were spring-loaded," Long said. "You'd have to be a pea brain to even try it," Hill told him.

With this encouragement, Long decided to go for it. He tied in, cranked the thin opening moves, and quickly found himself committed. "By fluke, or stark terror," he made it to a rest stance. The upper section, well above the last bolt, was terrifying. Long spent about an hour arranging tiny wires and hesitating before finally eking out the moves.

Hill followed, using tiny fingerholds to get past the huge reaches Long had employed. "It was hard 5.12 for me," Long said, "and it had to be 5.13 the way she did it, with about twenty intermediate moves." In 1980, *Pea Brain* (5.12c) became Aspen's hardest climb.

13. Colorado National Monument

Colorado's West Slope terminates on the Colorado Plateau, the high expanse that extends through Utah's Canyonlands. The transition to the plateau is defined not by elevation but by the rock strata. The tilted rocks of the mountains give way in the west to the flat-lying beds typical of Canyonlands and Arches National Parks.

Colorado National Monument is another such area, located on the western edge of Colorado in the cliffs and mesas near the town of Grand Junction. The arid landscape of Colorado National Monument seems to belong more to the canyon country of Utah than to Colorado—which it does, in all senses except its position relative to an arbitrary state line.

The Monument's sandstone towers are now less traveled than their famous Utah cousins near Moab, yet they figured earlier in the history of canyon-country climbing. After the ascents of Shiprock (1939), Spider Rock and Cleopatra's Needle (1956), and the Totem Pole (1957), the spires of Colorado National Monument were the next desert towers to be climbed.

Spire climbing in the Monument had actually begun much earlier. A Missouri wanderer named John Otto

Colorado National Monument near Grand Junction. In the right foreground is Independence Monument, viewed from the south. The 1911 Otto Route gains the obvious shoulder from the north side, and then ascends the smooth rib and overhang forming the left skyline. The urn-shaped tower in the upper left of the photo is the Pipe Organ, first climbed by John Auld, Gary Ziegler, et al. in January 1961. The top of Sentinel Spire can just be seen above the cluster of towers to the right of Pipe Organ. (Photo: Ed Webster)

Bell Tower (a.k.a. the Kissing Couple) with Pharoah Point in the distance. Harvey T. Carter, Layton Kor, and John Auld first climbed both towers, as well as Sentinel Spire and Remnants Tower, in four consecutive days in May 1960. (Photo: Jeff Achey)

wrote in a letter in 1907: "I came here last year and found these canyons, and they feel like the heart of the world to me. I'm going to stay and build trails and promote this place, because it should be a national park. Some folks think I'm crazy, but I want to see this scenery opened up to all people."

Otto commenced trail work and promotion and soon persuaded the Grand Junction Chamber of Commerce to petition the Department of the Interior to designate Colorado National Monument. In 1911, President Taft signed the monument into existence.

Less than a month later, Otto completed his most ambitious "trail"—up the 500-foot fin of Independence Monument, the area's largest tower. Otto's climb joined George Anderson's engineering feat up the backside of Half Dome in 1875 and Willard Ripley and William Rogers' cowboy ladder up Devils Tower in 1893 for the wildest American climbs done by "nonclimbers." Single-handedly, Otto chiseled steps up steep troughs and faces and finally drove an iron-pipe ladder into Independence Monument's summit overhang. Each Independence Day he would make the climb to the summit and fly the Stars and Stripes.

Otto gave up his stewardship of Colorado National Monument in 1927, but the pipes were not removed until the mid-1950s, after Otto's death. The drilled holes remain, however, allowing *Otto's Route* to be "free climbed" at 5.8. Otto was eccentric and driven (at one point he was tried for lunacy), and one can only marvel at his vision to climb the daunting monolith and the feats he dared to do so.

The famous Shiprock in New Mexico had been climbed fifty times by May 1960, when Harvey T. Carter persuaded Layton Kor and John Auld to accompany him for a desert climbing trip. The trio began in Colorado National Monument at a blistering pace. There they made first ascents of four Wingate sandstone spires—Bell Tower, Sentinel Spire, Remnants Tower, and Pharaoh Point—on four consecutive days.

They climbed Sentinel Spire by the now-popular *Fast Draw* route, which got its name from an incident on the steep first-pitch aid crack. Kor (then a desert-rock novice) stood in slings clipped to a piton driven into the soft sandstone, when suddenly it shifted under his weight and began to come out. In a blur of coordinated motion that could have won a high-noon gunfight, Kor plucked a new pin from his rack, jack-hammered it into the crack, and clipped in before the pin he was standing on could pull out—the "fast draw."

After their four days in Colorado National Monument, the intrepid trio continued on to Monument Valley, but Navajo patrols put an end to their ambitious itinerary of climbing objectives. A year later, with the Boulder climber

Layton Kor on an early repeat of Long Dong Wall *on Bell Tower, January 1962* (Photo: Huntley Ingalls)

Ed Webster and Mark Norden make an early free ascent of Fast Draw *on Sentinel Spire, 1979* (Photo: Stewart M. Green)

Huntley Ingalls, Kor returned to the desert to make the first ascent of Castleton Tower, the third ascent of the Totem Pole, and the year after, in 1962, the first ascent of the Titan.

Auld made several return trips the next winter to Colorado National Monument with various Garden of the Gods partners—Gary Ziegler, Jim Dyson, Bob Doane, and John Kuglin—to climb the Pipe Organ and Grandview Spire, located north and south respectively of Independence Monument, as well as Egypt Rock. A disturbing future lay ahead for this prolific Colorado Springs climber; years later, Auld would be convicted of the rape and murder of a Colorado College student and serve life in prison in Cañon City.

In the gentler world of rock climbing, the Monument fell into a long, quieter period, with most of the major spires now climbed. In the summer of 1970, Michael Dudley and Fletcher Smith, also of Colorado Springs, added a major variation to Otto's route on Independence Monument, a relatively easy chimney on the sunny side of the formation. This was the first probe onto the great south face, which would later be the site of several major climbs.

Dudley returned the next spring with Art Howells and Don Douchette—the same team that had endured the "turkey shoot" debacle the previous year. This trio already had experience with big routes on soft rock, having teamed with Carter and others on the first ascent of

West Side Story in 1967, one of the biggest routes in the Fisher Towers of Utah. Over the course of several days in May 1971, they pioneered a direct route up Independence Monument's 500-foot south face, the Monument's hardest route, a Grade IV, 5.8, A4.

Throughout the early 1970s, Carter continued to do an occasional climb in Colorado National Monument, generally on his way between Aspen and his major projects in the Fisher Towers, the most famous of which were the *Sundevil Chimney* and *Scheherezade* routes on the Titan in 1971 and 1973 respectively.

From 1976 to 1978, Ron Olevsky—an enigmatic Zion climber, anarchist, semi-legal firearms collector, and pioneer of *Pervertical Sanctuary* on Longs Peak—visited the Monument, soloing many of the old routes and adding some of his own. At about the same time, Andy Petefish moved to Grand Junction and brought a new standard of climbing to the area, beginning in 1978 with a free ascent of the *Fast Draw* route on Sentinel Spire. Petefish did numerous new climbs in the Monument and on the Black Canyon-like rock of nearby Unaweep Canyon, on through the mid-1980s. These, like the later Monument routes and other climbs throughout the state, contributed to the richness of Colorado climbing, but not to the thread of its history, and must unfortunately go undocumented here.

Pete Athans on the first ascent of Sundial Dihedral, *Independence Monument, 1986* (Photo: Ed Webster)

14. Granite Dreams

In the mid-1970s, rock climbing in the mountain towns progressed casually, in studied contrast to the intensity of the urban Front Range, where the sandstone of Eldorado Canyon captured the spotlight. In a sort of Never-Never Land between the two extremes were a pair of historic granite areas: Lumpy Ridge, just outside the town of Estes Park, and the sprawling region southwest of Denver known as the South Platte. In these places the unique crack and thin-face climbing skills that are characteristic of granite climbing were taken to new levels, producing some of Colorado's finest rock climbs.

The history of Lumpy Ridge and the South Platte is spotty. One or the other area figured prominently for a time, then fell off in significance. Thus, only the highlights are collected here, and the story reaches backward and forward in time more than in other chapters.

Lumpy Ridge

Since the 1960s, Lumpy Ridge has been the main "rest-day" area for those who come to climb in the high peaks of Rocky Mountain National Park. However, for many climbers, then and now, it is a destination in itself.

Steve Komito in his Estes Park boot shop, circa 1975 (Photo: Bob Godfrey)

The crags of Lumpy Ridge. Sundance Buttress is the tall formation farthest left and was first climbed by Layton Kor and Chuck Alexander in 1958. (Photo: Dudley Chelton)

Some of the state's earliest hard free climbs were Lumpy Ridge lines, including *Crack of Fear* and *Turnkorner*. In 1965, Layton Kor had also done *Slippage* on the Pear, initiating the Lumpy Ridge tradition of hard, scary slab climbs.

Of the early routes involving some aid climbing, Steve Hickman and John Bryant's *J-Crack* (1964) was the most striking. The next year, Paul Mayrose and Hans Leitinger climbed *The 44,* the first line up the popular Fat City sector of the Book. In 1970, the more popular variation, *Fat City Crack* (5.7, A1), was added by Bill Forrest and Ray Jardine, the latter a Colorado Springs climber who would go on to great renown as one of the early pioneers of 5.12 crack climbing in Yosemite Valley, and as the originator of Friends camming devices.

The Estes Park climbing scene gained considerable autonomy in the 1970s, and the energy of Rocky Mountain National Park and Lumpy Ridge climbing was bumped up a notch. Steve Komito moved his boot shop to Estes from Boulder, and Michael Covington opened the Fantasy Ridge climbing school. Komito and Covington were both passionate climbers, but their greater contribution was to give home, heart, and soul to the Estes Park scene.

Originally from Steamboat Springs, Covington was a gifted singer and poet, befriended by Simon and Garfunkel and offered a recording contract in New York, but he had opted for the simple life of a mountain guide. His lifelong friend Wayne Goss called him "always cheerful, the epitome of good sense in the mountains . . . generous and loving to his family and friends, and loved by all children and dogs . . . a humble climber with many first free ascents he let others claim, very brave and smart on the sharp end." Covington employed a talented group of young guides, a rowdy bunch mostly from Colorado Springs, including Billy Westbay, Dan McClure, Doug Snively, and Mark Hesse.

Komito played godfather and landlord to a parade of itinerants, and an ever-changing "family" lived in or near his shop. One might walk into the unlocked shop at three in the morning and find Billy Westbay passed out against the stereo speakers, from which Cream's *Crossroads* was still blaring. In the morning, a couple might crawl out of the old ambulance that was broken down in Komito's driveway and stumble over to get in line for the bathroom. Beneath the boot racks, the floor would be covered with the sleeping bags of dozing climbers. More "housebroken" types, such as Chris Reveley and Duncan Ferguson from Boulder, occasionally rented a room in Komito's house. Others pitched in for a cheap apartment above the grocery store in Allenspark, close to Longs Peak.

It was an all-star cast. Snively was the "steady Eddy"

Dudley Chelton on Gollum's Arch, *one of the fine Lumpy Ridge free climbs of the early 1970s* (Photo: Bill Briggs)

Michael Covington bivouacked on Broadway, Longs Peak, 1976 (Photo: Earl Wiggins)

of the group—meaning he was always game, for a climb or an all-night party. Hesse was halfway between his early crag-climbing days (he had made second free ascents of such Boulder testpieces as *Death and Transfiguration* and *Vertigo Direct*) and later exploits in the mountains, such as his 1982 solo of the 9,000-foot South Face of Denali and a huge fall down the Hornbein Couloir while trying a solo blitz of Everest.

Billy Westbay, the youngest brother of the Westbay clan, was growing up into one of Colorado's most adventurous climbers. He would soon attain great respect in Yosemite, where within the course of one week in 1975 he swung leads with Jim Bridwell on the first ascent of the standard-setting *Pacific Ocean Wall*, and with Bridwell and John Long on the first one-day ascent of

The Nose. But these great feats were in the future. For now, home for this adventurous lot was around Estes Park, near the crags of Lumpy Ridge and the great walls of Rocky Mountain National Park.

Among the notable free ascents of the era was the headwall finger crack of *J-Crack*, one of Lumpy's most obvious crack lines. In 1974, after several attempts, McClure managed to lead it free, followed by Westbay and Covington, for the first 5.11 on Lumpy Ridge.

On Twin Owls was another project, the overhanging left side of a seventy-five-foot flake not far from *Crack of Fear*. McClure and Westbay had been high on the strenuous off-width jam crack, and numerous attempts had gradually cleaned up the crumbly surface.

In May 1974, Jim Dunn was staying in Estes Park and McClure took him up to the crack. After their attempt, Dunn—easily infatuated with difficult, unclimbed lines—persuaded McClure to leave in all the gear. The next day, while McClure was guiding, Dunn returned with Dick

Two of Colorado's most unheralded climbers, Billy Westbay (top) and Doug Snively, in 1976. By this time, Snively had established new routes on Moses, Zeus, and Castleton Tower in Canyonlands, as well as the Diamond of Longs Peak. Westbay had recently returned from his best season in Yosemite, the highlights of which included the first ascent of the Pacific Ocean Wall on El Capitan and the first one-day ascent of The Nose. *(Photo: Earl Wiggins)*

Skip Guerin on the historic, horrific Peaches and Cream, *in 1983 (Photo: Glenn Randall)*

Dumais and after a lengthy struggle managed to finish the climb, yo-yoing on McClure's gear. Soon after, McClure made a ground-up lead of the route, *Peaches and Cream*, placing the gear as he went. For the next four years, this would be the hardest pitch on Lumpy Ridge.

The most memorable face climb of the day was *Heavenly Journey* on the Pear, done in 1974 by Westbay and George Hurley. A curving 5.10 finger crack formed the first pitch. The crack ended, but the climb continued. A frightening section of 5.10 slab climbing took Westbay well out from the belay. Higher was another crux. Ground-

Ray Jardine circa 1975 on the crux wide crack of the 1960 route Grand Giraffe, *one of the early routes on the main face of Redgarden Wall* (Photo: Bob Godfrey)

Climbers on the second pitch of The Naked Edge, *Eldorado Canyon, one of the most famous free climbs in the world* (Photo: Jeff Achey)

Bob D'Antonio on Virgin No More, *the most difficult route in Penitente Canyon when first done in 1987* (Photo: Bob D'Antonio collection)

Alison Osius, one of the top female climbers of the 1970s, later to be president of the American Alpine Club, on the crags above Redstone, Colorado (Photo: Jim Surette)

Catherine Destivelle on Rainbow Wall, *Eldorado Canyon* (Photo: Beth Wald)

Rumor Has It, *the first sport climb in Rifle Mountain Park* (Photo: Chris Goplerud)

The Diamond, as seen from Mills Glacier (Photo: Jeff Achey)

Steve Wunsch attempting the fourth pitch of Jules Verne, *Eldorado Canyon, in 1974* (Photo: Dudley Chelton)

Dick Nystrom on Art's Spar *during the shooting of the cover photo for the original edition of* Climb! (Photo: Dudley Chelton)

At right: *The Happy Trails camp, with Bryan Becker leading the Beak pitch, first ascent of* Hallucinogen Wall, *Black Canyon, 1980* (Photo: Les Choy)

Larry Bruce on the now-closed Gold Butte, *near Aspen, in 1984* (Photo: Michael Kennedy)

Roger Briggs on Diving Board *in 1974* (Photo: Dudley Chelton)

Tommy Caldwell on The Honeymoon is Over, *the most difficult free route on the Diamond* (Photo: Topher Donahue)

At left: *Pete Athans on the first ascent of* Sundial Dihedral, *Colorado National Monument* (Photo: Ed Webster)

The eastern half of Redgarden Wall after a late-afternoon rainstorm (Photo: Dudley Chelton)

Bob Beers on Topographical Oceans, *The Dome, South Platte* (Photo: Stewart M. Green)

At left: *North Chasm View Wall, Black Canyon of the Gunnison* (Photo: Jeff Achey)

Christian Griffith on his route Verve *in Boulder Canyon, one of the many state-of-the-art free climbs he established in 1987* (Photo: Dan Hare)

Kurt Smith on his route Slice of Life *in 1993, before the invention of knee bars* (Photo: Chris Goplerud)

Colin Lantz on TGV, *Mickey Mouse Wall, near Boulder, in 1993* (Photo: Beth Wald)

Bobbi Bensman on Power Bulge, *Flatirons, 1987* (Photo: Beth Wald)

Following page: *Ian Spencer-Green on* Lost Planet Airmen, *Shelf Road* (Photo: Stewart M. Green)

Mike Downing on French Fry, *Eldorado Canyon, with the Indian Peaks in the distance* (Photo: Dan Hare)

At left: *Dan Michael on his route* The Fiend *in the Flatirons above Boulder* (Photo: Beth Wald)

Bryan Becker in Escalante Canyon, one of western Colorado's many lesser-known climbing areas, in the mid-1970s (Photo: Ed Webster)

fall risk was not unheard of on 1970s face climbs, but *Heavenly Journey* was unique in that this risk came on the second pitch. In the late 1970s, someone fell on this pitch, ripping a fixed pin and sliding 130 feet down the slab. Now the bolts on a more recent nearby climb can be clipped, as one guidebook says, "to mitigate the disaster," reducing the upper runout to sixty feet.

The South Platte
The Lumpy Ridge climbers were constantly drawn into the high peaks, where they did even more impressive rock climbs. At Colorado's other granite testing ground, there was no such nearby distraction.

Both geographically and historically, the so-called South Platte is the most scattered climbing area in Colorado. Countless granite cliffs and domes dot the hills and slopes that form the basin of the tumbling South Platte River before it emerges from the mountains near Denver. The total area is over six hundred square miles. The most historically significant crags are the Dome, the Bishop, and the spire climbers call Cynical Pinnacle, all near the town site of Foxton; Sphinx Rock near Pine; and Turkey Rock near West Creek. With the exception of Turkey Rock, South Platte crags had no "climbing scene." They were explored in isolated forays by climbers from Denver, Boulder, and Colorado Springs, as well as by visitors from afar.

Many of the South Platte crags lie hidden, visible only from obscure dirt back roads in Pike National Forest or from the tops of other crags. Initiative and a taste for exploration were generally the decisive factors in South Platte first ascents, not climbing skill. Boulder and Denver climbers were the first to climb most of the Dome and Cynical Pinnacle lines, while Colorado Springs climbers had an early monopoly on Turkey Rock. New crags often were well-kept secrets until they had been thoroughly climbed.

The earliest recorded Platte climb was of the small tower called the Bishop, near the northern edge of the Platte area. In 1924 (the same year he climbed the arête on Crestone Needle), Albert Ellingwood, with Agnes Vaille and Stephen Hart, climbed the Bishop via a smooth, unprotected chimney on the west face. This route is perhaps Ellingwood's most impressive piece of pure free climbing. After lowering his companions from the summit, Ellingwood down-climbed the fissure. Today, it is rated 5.8.

In the 1930s, U.S. Army climbers trained on Lover's Leap, a 450-foot north-facing crag along Highway 285 just outside Denver where the Colorado Mountain Club also held outings. In the Pine area, one stunt of the 1940s had unforeseen historical significance. A few dynamite-happy fellows got to the top of Sphinx Rock, drilled blast holes, and tried to blow the rock in half. One loud but ineffectual charge alerted the inhabitants of Sphinx Park, who chased off the demolition team before they could topple the summit block. Later, water filled the blast holes and freeze-thaw action caused a thin but dramatic fissure—the famous *Sphinx Crack*.

Records from the 1950s are sketchy. "Mountaineering" routes such as the *Great Chimney* on Cynical Pinnacle were ascended by Colorado Mountain Club climbers in the late 1950s and early 1960s. In 1962, Gary Ziegler, Bob Doane, and Gary Boucher climbed a moderate route up Wigwam Tower (5.7), and then engineered an ambitious bolt ladder up the nearby Cap Rock Spire.

Tom Fender, who practiced martial arts, played electric guitar, and occasionally recorded with Pat Ament in Boulder, made many excellent first ascents in the South Platte in the mid-1960s. Best was the showpiece rock climb of the entire Platte, the *Prayer Book* on Cynical Pinnacle, done in 1964 with Bill Roos. On the same impressive spire, Larry Dalke and Cliff Jennings added the route now know as *Turf Spreader* in 1966, and Roos, Paul Sibley, and Carl and Bernum Arndt climbed *The Center Route* in 1968. Originally done mixed free and aid, these climbs are now considered among the best multipitch 5.10 and 5.11 crack climbs in the state.

In the late 1960s, Bill Roos and Paul Sibley made the first ascent of the *Sphinx Crack*. These two were among the many eccentric residents of the little hamlet of Eldorado Springs in the late 1960s and 1970s, and ran various climbing schools and shops, film-rigging busi-

Crags of the South Platte. The rock formation on the skyline to the left is the Bishop. The Dome is nearby to the right, and Cynical Pinnacle is in the rock formation on the right side of the photo. The rock in the foreground is part of the Top of the World formation. (Photo: Dudley Chelton)

nesses, and flophouses for itinerant climbers, a mere five-minute stroll from the rocks of Eldorado Canyon. They were also incurable gear tinkerers. Around 1966, shortly after Royal Robbins, Pat Ament, and Jim Logan braved the first all-nut ascent in Colorado—a frightening trip up *Grand Giraffe*—Sibley and Roos started the Colorado Nut Company, a first in the country, which for a few brief years produced a range of hexagonal aluminum nuts.

Sibley and Roos were responsible for a scattered collection of fine Platte climbs, including one of the area's shortest and prettiest finger cracks, *Toot Suite* (A2) on the Top of the World formation. Sibley did the first climb on Bucksnort Slabs near Pine, *The Crack of Anticipation* (a.k.a *Classic Dihedral*), in 1967 with Ron Cox and Carl Arndt, still one of the Platte's best 5.7 crack climbs. Sibley and Roos were also responsible for the popular desert-spire climb *Ancient Art* in the Fisher Towers of Utah, done in 1969.

In January 1971, Duncan Ferguson and Jim Walsh were the first to tour the large slab of the Dome near Cynical Pinnacle via a beautiful, wandering, three-pitch

Duncan Ferguson on Bishop Jaggers, *December 1972* (Photo: Dudley Chelton)

5.9 called *Bishop Jaggers*. "Jaggers" was Ferguson and Walsh's slang for long underwear, and the name was chosen to commemorate the frigid conditions they endured on the climb. Ferguson, one of the true purists of the 1970s, would lament the two bolts he placed on this climb, commenting on them even thirty years later.

The Prayer Book
Fender and Roos' *Prayer Book* was one of the most striking rock climbs in the state, and in 1974, Chris Reveley and Diana Hunter made the first attempt to free climb the 350-foot line. One moderate pitch led to a flat, spacious ledge with a fine view of the granite-flecked hills and the cascading North Fork of the South Platte River. The pair enjoyed the view a little too much and managed only one more pitch, up steep, strenuous hand cracks to a belay in an uncomfortable alcove below a roof. Much harder climbing appeared to lie above, and they rappelled off.

Steve Wunsch and Duncan Ferguson tried the line soon after. Ferguson led the crack to the alcove. The next pitch was hidden by the alcove's roof. Wunsch hand-jammed strenuously out to the lip and got his first close look at the rest of the pitch. Just over the roof, the crack narrowed to fingers and led up a long dihedral, one wall of which overhung. The climbing looked extremely strenuous and appeared to continue unrelentingly for over sixty feet.

Wunsch was intimidated but had no choice but to move—either up or down. He pulled over the roof into a

Cynical Pinnacle. Prayer Book *climbs the clean dihedral that lies just right of the left skyline.* (Photo: Jeff Achey)

Opposite: *The second pitch of* Prayer Book, *Cynical Pinnacle* (Photo: Dudley Chelton)

layback position in the dihedral. Fortunately, the steep crack provided solid finger locks and the occasional thin hand jam. Less fortunately, the lower cracks had taken a toll on Wunsch's hands, and every jam left a little blood on the rock. "It was hard all the way," Wunsch said. "My hands were hurting and I felt that if I fell I wouldn't be able to start over again. So I kept going and didn't fall." The effort gave a new moniker to the climb which endures to this day: *Wunsch's Dihedral*.

Wunsch's pitch took them to a large and spectacular ledge about forty feet below the summit of the pinnacle. Above rose a blank wall, near vertical at first, then rounding back to the summit. An old bolt ladder marked the route. A stiff wind was blowing. Their hands hurt. A session of precarious face climbing, with a dubious chance of success, seemed ill advised. They aided the bolt ladder and rappelled from the summit. On the last rap to the ground they snagged a rope, and a short hand crack would have to be climbed to free it. Each climber held out his bleeding hands and looked at them. They cut the rope and left.

The next summer, David Breashears hiked up with Steve Mammen and several friends to try the route. They were in top shape (they had just made the first ascent of *Perilous Journey* near Boulder), and in an inspired effort, Breashears free climbed—on-sight—Fender's original first pitch, a steep finger crack. In summer 1975, this was the hardest pitch in the Platte. Mammen, a master face climber and diehard crack hater, refused to follow. The whole ascent ground to a halt in the brutal midday heat after one more pitch.

That winter, Roger Briggs climbed the *Center Route*, finishing with a short, spectacular crack that joined the *Prayer Book* at the top of the leaning dihedral. From there, Briggs free climbed past the first three bolts on the summit headwall, moved left to better holds on the face, and climbed unprotected to the top for the first free ascent of Cynical Pinnacle. Now, *Prayer Book* had both the hardest crack and hardest face pitches in the Platte, and it awaited a continuous ascent.

Like Breashears, Pat Adams had made a name for himself with teenage antics on Eldorado's famous *Kloeberdanz* roof—in Adams' case it was a free solo ascent. Adams had a taste for adventure, making several visits to the Diamond before the age of seventeen. In 1976, Adams teamed with Michael Hoffman of Germany for an attempt on *Prayer Book*.

Adams went all out on the first-pitch finger crack, climbing unprotected for twenty feet with a stopper clenched in his teeth. He slammed in the nut below the crux, then gunned for the good jams. Hoffman led the second-pitch hand crack in similar go-for-broke style with just two pieces of protection, and Adams led the third-pitch dihedral to the big ledge. They took a brief rest, and Hoffman began edging up the bolt ladder. Moving left from the bolt line, now near success, his foot popped off a tiny edge and he peeled, taking a big swing and narrowly missing the ledge. Hoffman collected his wits, rested briefly on the ledge, and went back up and finished the pitch. The *Prayer Book*, the most demanding multipitch climb in the Platte—a sort of granite *Naked Edge*—was complete.

In 1978 at Turkey Rock, Leonard Coyne, Henry Lester, and Peter Mayfield put up the three-pitch *Journey to Ixtlan*, one of the Platte's most sustained routes and Turkey Rock's first 5.12. Like the famous *Tales of Power* and *Separate Reality* in Yosemite, *Journey to Ixtlan* was named for one of the books of Carlos Casteneda, which had a dedicated cult following. Many climbers of the 1970s were influenced by these books, evidenced by symptoms such as unusual attentiveness to dust devils and passing ravens, and the adoption of a certain "war-

David Breashears on the second free ascent of the original start to Prayer Book *in 1976, a pitch now known as the* Breashears Finger Crack *(Photo: Dudley Chelton)*

frightening work. The climber would launch into the unknown, edging and smearing on nickel- and dime-size footholds, where a misstep meant a fall of twenty, fifty, sometimes a hundred feet. Protection was from bolts, drilled on lead with hammer and hand drill, a process that could take up to an hour if the stance was poor. Hand drilling on slab climbs was an art in itself, requiring balance and steady nerves. It was not uncommon to fall while drilling. A single pitch—climbable in a few minutes by later parties—might take several days of effort to establish.

One monumental Platte slab route was the work of Colorado Springs climbers Peter Gallagher and Pete Williams. Gallagher was an economics student at Colorado College, bespectacled and high strung. Williams was older and wiser, a recent CC alumnus. The pair did many fine climbs together, and in the spring of 1979 they set out to do their finest.

Fearing route snatchers in the close-knit and contentious Springs climbing community, Gallagher and Williams were tight-lipped about their project. It was known, however, that they were stockpiling sinful numbers of bolts—far more than needed for a good-style ascent on any known dome—and their local reputations suffered. Still, they concealed the reason for so many bolts: they weren't planning an over-protected climb, just a very big one.

Big Rock Candy Mountain is the largest chunk of granite in the South Platte, hidden away in the deep canyons above Cheesman Reservoir. In 1979, few climbers knew of its existence. Earl Wiggins and party had climbed the rock's central weakness in 1975, but the main walls, which looked formidable and blank, had no routes. Williams, however, had inspected the rock from several angles and was convinced that a free-climbing route on the longest, smoothest buttress might be possible.

In April, Williams and Gallagher made their first attempt. Three easy pitches took them up well-featured slabs with protection and belays from nuts. Above, the prow of the main buttress reared to vertical, devoid of features. The flanks were equally steep, but on the right was a long, leaning crack that paralleled the crest of the prow, the only possible access to the upper buttress.

Awkward jamming led to a hanging belay near the end of the crack, where Williams took the lead. Placing a poor nut as high as he could, he stood in slings and began drilling a bolt on the face. The nut ripped and he tumbled backward. Unhurt, he placed a better nut and finished drilling the bolt.

The wall was depressingly blank. Using aid from his first bolt, Williams drilled another and the pair retreated to the ground, disappointed that they had drilled on aid before even reaching the main buttress. Maybe the heck-

Tommy and Mike Caldwell on the final headwall of Cynical Pinnacle in 1999. This difficult pitch was first climbed free by Roger Briggs in winter 1975–76. (Photo: Topher Donahue)

rior" psychology. It might honestly be said that the books' main character, the Yaqui sorcerer Don Juan, helped elevate the free-climbing standards of the 1970s.

Fields of Dreams

The South Platte has the tallest and smoothest granite faces in Colorado. Though not nearly as steep, some far exceed the Diamond in height, with up to 1,000 feet of climbing completely devoid of protection cracks. In the 1970s and 1980s, a handful of climbers established the first exciting routes up these striking slabs.

Leading these climbs for the first time was exacting,

Big Rock Candy Mountain and the South Platte River. The formation, largest in the Platte, was first climbed via the central recess by Don Doucette and Earl Wiggins in 1975. Fields of Dreams takes the long, narrow buttress right of center. (Photo: Ed Webster)

lers at the Cobbler had been right. Were they indeed mad bolters, unworthy of the privilege of great first ascents?

The next weekend they arrived late, with just enough time to climb to their high point and fix a line around the strenuous crack so they would not to have to struggle up it again. The next morning a cold wind awakened them. As they prepared to embark, their sleeping bags blew into the river, and once at their high point they made no progress on the face above.

"It was obvious to me that our failure was due to offending the Rock Gods," Williams later wrote. They resolved to placate the deities and improve their style. They returned in June. Even with good conditions, Williams was still forced to use aid on the two bolts above the crack, but from the highest bolt, he stepped out of his slings and free climbed up onto the prow of the buttress. Several times he stopped to drill from thin, scary stances.

Fifteen feet into the next pitch, with nearly a thousand feet of featureless granite stretching above, Williams was once again standing in slings. After a three-bolt ladder, he reached a point where he believed he could free climb to whatever stance might await. He had broken all but one drill bit. If he were to break that one high above protection on the fierce-looking slab before him, he would

be in deep trouble. Would the Rock Gods favor him? He pondered his bolt ladder and aid slings and called off the attempt.

Three days later Williams and Gallagher were back with enough bits to finish the climb. Above the last bolt ladder, the climbing became progressively easier. The next pitch went all free at 5.9. The slabs above were gentler still, climbable now by pure friction. Four more long pitches remained, just difficult enough to be exhilarating. It was a dreamlike place, with flawless granite falling away on all sides. Late in the afternoon they stood atop their route—*Fields of Dreams Growing Wild*.

A week later they returned to climb the route all free. They left the Springs at 6:00 A.M., and by noon they stood atop *Fields of Dreams* once again, successful. On the free ascent, their bolt ladders had provided just about the right amount of protection for the 5.11 climbing, and the rest of the climb had plenty of long, bold runouts. It was a respectable effort, undertaken with reverence. The Rock Gods smiled.

The Inscrutable Sphinx

As Williams and Gallagher were working on the longest free climb in the Platte, others set their sights on the hardest. Splitting an overhanging block on a granite crag above Pine, the *Sphinx Crack* was, bar none, the wildest looking crack in Colorado. Above a vertical section and a small dihedral, the fissure split a big roof before tracing a razor-cut line up a twenty-degree overhanging wall. At the roof's lip, the crack was thin-finger sized, but quickly widened—enough to ruin the finger jams, but not enough to admit a hand or foot. In short, it was the worst possible size for free climbing. For some, that was its charm.

Although the entire climb was less than a rope length, most climbers who tried the crack used a hanging belay below the roof to avoid rope drag over the sharp edge at the lip. Such precautions were generally unnecessary—few climbers managed even to clear the lip of the roof. Although the roof was as hard as any existing climb in the Platte in 1979, it was merely the approach to the *Sphinx Crack*. On the main headwall, there were almost no footholds, anywhere. Many who tried the route found they could not even let go to move a hand, much less continue without rests for fifty more feet.

Of all the climbers who sampled it, one became obsessed. Steve Hong had grown up in Madison, Wisconsin, and, like Jim Erickson, learned to climb at Devil's Lake. Apparently he got his fill of thin, bouldery climbs there and once in Colorado did his best to avoid them. He

Opposite: *A party on the upper slabs of* Fields of Dreams Growing Wild, Big Rock Candy Mountain *(Photo: Ed Webster)*

Leonard Coyne and Mark Sonnenfeld attempting Sphinx Crack *in 1979* (Photo: Jeff Achey)

considered the Eldorado face routes "trick climbing." Strenuous endurance climbs were Hong's forte, especially cracks. In 1979, he and Ed Webster made the first free ascent of the *Primrose Dihedrals* on Moses, at the time the most difficult crack climb in Utah's Canyonlands. Later, Hong, with his wife Karin Budding, went on to pioneer the first 5.12s and 5.13s on desert sandstone at a time when but a handful of climbers had ever visited the remote valley called Indian Creek.

Small and powerfully built, Hong could hold on forever. He ran, did calisthenics, climbed a rope ladder, and worked out on a special "crack machine." Constructed from two-by-six boards bolted together and separated with spacers to simulate jam cracks, crack machines are relics of the 1970s and early 1980s, when the hardest climbs were cracks. These instruments of torture could be found in places such as the old Camp 4 gym in Yosemite, the attic of the IME mountain shop in North Conway, New Hampshire, and Steve Hong's Colorado Springs garage.

Hong adjusted his crack machine to the off-finger size of *Sphinx Crack* and used every other tactic he could think of to succeed on the climb. He repeatedly top-roped it and preplaced the gear when he began attempting to lead. These were unprecedented tactics in Colorado, and they were working. Hong's attempts gradually improved until he could lead the crack with a few, and then one, rest on the headwall. Finally, after two years of training and attempts, in April 1981 he succeeded. *Sphinx Crack* was solid 5.13—by far, Colorado's hardest free climb. In fact, it shared the honors with Tony Yaniro's 1979 California climb *Grand Illusion* as the hardest pitch of free climbing in the world.

Steve Hong on the headwall of Sphinx Crack (Photo: Ed Webster)

15. A Woman's Place

In the 1970s, paralleling a redefinition of the role of women in society, a number of Colorado women emerged as skilled rock-climbing leaders. Still, in the mid-1970s there were very few women anywhere able to lead 5.10. Among the talented women rock climbers around Boulder in the early 1970s were Molly Higgins, Connie Hilliard, Jean Ruwitch, and Sue Giller. For the few years she graced the crags, one of the most impressive of the Boulder women was Diana Hunter.

Hunter worked hard at climbing. Her style was graceful, and the influence of her training as a ballet dancer was evident. She was barely able to do a single pull-up, yet compensated with articulate footwork.

In 1973, Henry Barber and Hunter teamed up to attempt the second free ascent of *Wide Country,* Duncan Ferguson's testy free climb on the Bastille in Eldorado Canyon. Barber led up to the bolt below the first-pitch crux, then stalled out. After a number of tries, he lowered off from the bolt. By this time a small group of onlookers had gathered. Diana pulled on her climbing shoes, feeling that she might as well at least climb up to the bolt. With a dexterous display of footwork, she led the pitch—the crux of the route. A slightly crestfallen Henry followed Diana up. A few days later, Hunter pulled the same trick again, taking Bob Carmichael up the *Northwest Corner* of the Bastille after Carmichael was unable to lead it. Colorado climbing lost a remarkable spirit when Hunter was killed in Rocky Mountain National Park in the summer of 1975, in an unroped fall on easy ground at the top of the Cathedral Wall.

There were other talents. In Colorado Springs, Karin Budding took part in many high-standard ascents, and soon developed into one of the pioneer Canyonlands crack climbers. One of the very best female rock climbers of the later 1970s was Beth Bennett. She grew up in Wisconsin, and while at Duke University, learned to climb at Stone Mountain, Whitesides, and other North Carolina areas. She moved to Colorado in 1974, climbed in Eldorado, and soon felt what she called "the siren-like lure" of the finger crack of the first pitch on *The Naked Edge,* which had never been free climbed by a woman. Here is her account of her foray in October 1976:

Molly Higgins on the Green Spur, *Eldorado Canyon, 1975*
(Photo: Bob Godfrey)

> *Hanging out on the cement pad by the ramshackle pump house and plotting the day's adventure, I foolishly mentioned my fascination with the finger crack to the older boys. There was some winking and nodding, most of it*

Connie Hilliard on Outer Space *in 1975* (Photo: Dudley Chelton)

sotto voce, but Kevin Donald voiced the prevailing sentiment in a loud aside: "No woman will ever climb The Edge!" Needless to say, this not-so-gentle rebuke spurred my determination.

I'd moved to Colorado shortly after finishing college. Like most girls growing up in the pre-Title IX era of the '60s, I had no upper body strength. Eldorado is the perfect place to develop and utilize good footwork, which I did.

The finger crack may have occupied a prominent

position in my fantasies, but the chimney pitch was the stuff of nightmares to me. Which is why I jumped at the offer Pat Adams made one beautiful fall morning. Pat Adams, Buck Norden, and I were drinking tea on the porch of my house in Eldorado Springs. As we sat in the October sunshine, trying to decide what to do with ourselves (again), Pat grinned in his inimitable fashion, poked Buck and said, "Let's go do The Edge. Buckwheat can lead the fourth pitch," the chimney. Buck, never one to back off from a challenge replied, somewhat defensively, that of course he'd lead the chimney.

We soloed up some easy pitches to the base of the finger crack, which I eagerly volunteered to lead. No one offered any opposition and in fact the boys settled in, obviously expecting a siege. The pitch is broken by a small ledge about halfway up. Reaching that ledge was relatively easy. From there, the crack thins down. If you're tall, it's easy to reach the arête with a left hand and the crack with your right. But, if you're tall, your fingers are probably a little too big to fit comfortably in the crack.

Diana Hunter on the crux of Wide Country, *Eldorado Canyon. She led the second free ascent of this pitch in 1973.* (Photo: Tim Loose)

Beth Bennett on the first pitch of The Naked Edge. *After making the first female ascent, Bennett returned to the climb many times including this one—for the making of a film with Lynn Hill in 1981.* (Photo: Jeff Lowe)

My fingertips fit into those jams pretty well. Which is not to say that the moves weren't strenuous for someone who could crank off a grand total of four pull-ups, but I pulled through. I remember latching onto the good face holds at the end and standing there breathing rather loudly for a few minutes, to raucous cheering from the tag team on the belay ledge.

The next few pitches are now a blur, but the chimney pitch looms large in my memory. Buck made a few moves up it and backed off. Pat led it in typical style, clipping the manky fixed pins and one fixed wire at the base of the chimney and running it out till the belay at the top. I went for it and managed to wedge myself in the chimney. Once in, it was a smooth squeeze to the belay. Down on the ledge, Buck groaned about his back being out, and then followed laboriously, grunting his way into the chimney. The last pitch, an overhanging hand crack, was his lead. He bailed, pulling out his "bad back" excuse. Pat harassed him unmercifully as we traversed off onto the easier upper pitches of T2, around the corner to the west.

I would have liked finishing the climb, but to tell the truth, I really didn't care. My goal had been to lead the first pitch, which I did without falling. I didn't care that I was the first woman to lead the finger crack. It was more important to me that I could decipher the sequence to move up gracefully and cleanly, picking the right nuts off my rack, feeling focused and in control. I'll never forget the euphoria I felt looking down

from the face holds where I could stand just above the crack. The sky was the incredible clear bright blue of fall, the wind was blowing my hair and shirt into the east, and two boys I loved more than anyone else at the moment were cheering for me.

The next summer, Bennett went back to *The Edge* with Michael Hoffman, the German climber who, with Adams, free climbed the *Prayer Book* in the South Platte. This time Bennett also climbed the last pitch for the first free ascent of the complete *Naked Edge* by a woman. Bennett, Jean Ruwitch, and the Australian climber Louise Shepherd made the first all-female ascent of the route in 1978.

Bennett was also pushing her limits on Longs Peak. During the summer of 1976, the year after the first free ascent of the Diamond (see Chapter 16), she teamed up with seventeen-year-old Pat Adams and attempted to link the Diagonal Wall and the Diamond. On one effort a storm hit them high on the *Diagonal* route. Their rain-lashed rappel across to the *Gray Pillar* and finally to Mills Glacier was an experience neither wanted to repeat.

Summer 1977 was more stable. In July, Bennett and Adams set off up the *Yellow Wall*, a bit unclear about the free-climbing variations that had been used previously. Bennett set off on what the guidebook described as the "A4 traverse." This proved to be a ledge—narrow, but easily traversed. It led her to a steep, smooth, left-facing corner with a fingertip-size crack, which also looked free climbable.

The thin crack took nuts, quite small but good, so Bennett pressed on. At first she could edge on tiny footholds. When these holds ran out and the layback proved too strenuous, she tried face climbing around the crack. Her first attempt ended in a plummet of fifteen feet. The next fall was longer still. Darkening skies, thunder, and Adams' heckling brought Bennett back to the belay ledge. Adams took over the lead and powered through the crux. Bennett followed. Two pitches of easier climbing brought the pair to Table Ledge as raindrops started to fall. They had freed Kor's original *Yellow Wall* aid line, and the Diamond got its first free ascent by a woman.

Also in 1977, another phenomenal female climber arrived on the Boulder scene. Most people thought Coral Bowman was Australian, since she arrived in Boulder married to Chris Peisker, the Australian who distributed RP micronuts, and she had picked up the accent after two years Down Under. In a quick flurry in 1977 she made on-sight ascents of impressive free climbs, including *Vertigo* and *C'est la Vie* (both 5.11), and first female ascents of some of the more powerful climbs such as *Kloeberdanz*.

A freak accident on *The Naked Edge* in 1978 nearly cost Bowman her life. She detached from her rappel line and fell free for twenty feet before grabbing a thin haul line and miraculously arresting her fall. Her badly burned hands recovered, but her head for hard leading never returned. She continued to climb, however, and later opened a successful climbing school.

The women of the early 1970s were the first generation to make significant inroads into the chauvinistic, male-dominated world of Colorado rock climbing. The psychological obstacles posed by the opinions and prejudices of the day were as real and as daunting as the rocks themselves. It was unclear that women could develop sufficient physical strength to climb at a high, modern standard, and these early women climbers were true pioneers of the unknown and the untested. From this time forward, female climbers became more and more common—a state of affairs not necessarily evident in our subsequent history. In general, women were less active than men in seeking out first ascents and the top women were climbing just off the elite standard, thus evading the historical record. Nevertheless, from the 1970s on, women climbed side by side with men, in ever-increasing numbers, the best of them at a standard that left most male climbers far behind.

Coral Bowman on Flagstaff Mountain in 1978 (Photo: Steve Levin)

16. Freeing the Walls

The 1981 ascent of *Sphinx Crack* represented a distinct high-water mark in Colorado cragging. *Sphinx* was a short climb, fiercely difficult, but with little danger or commitment. Other landmark Colorado free climbs had completely different characteristics. The story must jump back a few years to pick up a related thread of history—the longer free climbs, which had a psychology of their own.

The free ascent of *The Naked Edge* in Eldorado Canyon in 1971 was extremely influential. No mere "roped boulder problem," *The Edge* threw open the doors of perception. If a nearly relentless five-pitch line composed of thin A4 and radically overhanging cracks could be climbed all free, what else might be possible? The question would soon be explored on the walls of Rocky Mountain National Park and the Black Canyon of the Gunnison.

The Diamond—Free

In the early 1970s the major faces and features of Rocky Mountain National Park were approached anew, with a crags-style emphasis on free, all-nut ascents. The height of these explorations came in the summer of 1974. That year, Roger Briggs and Chris Reveley freed *Directissima* on Longs' Chasm View Wall, and Briggs and Larry Hamilton put up the impressive *White Room* on Notchtop. Dan McClure and Robert Gulley freed *The Barb* on Spearhead, and McClure and Mark Hesse did the *Central Ramp* route on the remote east face of Mount Alice.

Higher and much steeper than any of these walls was the Diamond, the only face in the park that crossed that imaginary line defining a "big wall." The Diamond routes were well-known and well traveled—usually via multiday ascents—and in the early 1970s much talk was devoted to debating the possibilities of free climbing this queen of high-country walls. Consensus was that free climbing the Diamond would be very hard—a double *Naked Edge* at altitude—and require considerable luck with the weather.

In the summer of 1972, Duncan Ferguson and Bill Putnam made an impressive free attempt on *D7*, the easiest and shortest route on the Diamond. They managed to free climb 500 feet of the wall before being turned back by wet cracks on the sixth pitch. A week later, Roger Briggs and Scott Stewart reached a slightly higher point, spent an hour searching unsuccessfully for a dry variation to the left, and also retreated.

The Diamond, showing the 1975 free routes. Goss and Logan began on D7 (left), moved right, then exited at Table Ledge. Dunn and Wood climbed Yellow Wall, *with several variations including an easier exit pitch up the final headwall.* (Photo: Jeff Achey)

The summer of 1973 was so wet that no free attempts were made on the Diamond. In 1974, Briggs and Reveley went up, again without success. Ferguson returned with Kevin Donald and Jim Logan. They too were repulsed by wet cracks.

In the course of these many attempts, the remaining aid on *D7* had been whittled down to about fifty vertical feet. It seemed inevitable that someone would succeed in free climbing the Diamond in 1975, and that all-out attempts would begin when the summer months arrived. The race was on, with different parties quietly preparing and weighing their chances.

Wayne Goss and Jim Logan had not figured in the free-climbing developments of the 1970s. Young climbers vaguely remembered that Goss had done the first winter ascent of the Diamond with Kor, and Logan tended to be remembered as the skinny climber who had chimneyed up behind Chris Fredericks on *Crack of Fear*. Neither climber had done the newer 5.10 and 5.11 routes.

141

Logan had accompanied Ferguson and Donald on their 1974 Diamond attempt more as a tourist than a participant, but the experience whetted his appetite. During the fall and winter, he and Goss considered free climbing the Diamond themselves.

Anyone running a wager would probably have given odds of a hundred to one against Goss and Logan. Nevertheless, they began climbing together regularly in the spring of 1975 and managed a free ascent of *Country Club Crack* in Boulder Canyon. In early July, in Eldorado Canyon, Goss made one of the first no-falls leads of *Guenese*, and after a day of rest the pair did *The Naked Edge*, also in good style. After another rest day they headed up to Longs Peak.

Goss and Logan were both savvy Diamond veterans. Wet rock had stopped many parties, and the pair had some ideas about how they might avoid the same fate. They also knew that speed would be essential. The sun left the wall around noon, making free climbing more difficult, and afternoon thunderstorms were common. They banked all of their hopes on making a fast ascent.

In the best modern style, they left behind pitons, hammers, and jumars, and both planned to climb every pitch.

They hiked up in the afternoon for a lightweight bivouac. At Broadway they encountered their first obstacle: Molly Higgins, Stephanie Atwood, and Laurie Manson already bivouacked, intent on making the first all-female ascent of the Diamond. Both parties hoped to start up *D7* first thing in the morning, and it was obvious that a conflict of interest existed.

The women had arrived first, so the right to be first was theirs. Goss and Logan knew, however, that if they started behind a party of three, their chance of making a light and fast ascent was zero. Goss tactfully inquired if they might be allowed to go first. In the end, diplomacy won the day. Goss and Logan somehow presented themselves in such a good light that the women took pity on them for their meager rations and fed them hamburgers.

The next morning, Goss and Logan were away at first light, swinging leads up the first five pitches. The difficulty increased as they moved up the wall, with 5.10 climbing on pitches four and five. The sixth pitch, which had turned back all previous attempts, was Goss's lead. Again, the pitch was wet.

Previous attempts had gone left, which looked easiest. Goss knew that this route had failed. Instead, he traversed right on a narrow, hidden ledge toward the *Black Dagger* and *Forrest Finish* routes. Reasonable climbing took Goss to a dirt-filled section of crack. The crack looked impossible, but Goss thought that he might be able to climb the wall to the right. His account of this section follows:

Steve Shea free climbing on the Diamond in 1976 (Photo: Michael Kennedy)

"Logan! Watch my ass! I'm right on the limit." The climbing is no worse than before, but I am. Up into a layback. Ever wonder why there's not a book called The Joy of Laybacking? *Water running down the wall makes a wake around a swimming RD. Concentrate, motha. Right toe to nubbin. Peek-a-boo round the corner reveals a misplaced chess problem. Possibilities are chalked . . . three . . . four times, to absorb the water. Left hand turns white on its own. Exit out on little holds. This is where it's at! Eyeballs wide. Two inches away, a tenuous hold . . . still out of reach. Some hero, squinting because it's too wet to wear glasses, reaching across a gulf of fear to deliberately finger an eighth-inch indentation just two fingers wide. Which ones to put there? Decisions, decisions. Left foot lifts off the pucky in the crack, and with pluck defying better judgment, belaying a mind of its own, replaces the right. Right is relegated to a newer, but not better, bump. This is art? Climbing on zits. Switch fingers one at a time. Contrapuntal elegance. Left foot slides—*

up, now or never, and place it under the same side's fingers . . . in slow motion cartwheel upwards thinly . . . a vertical hold slips by . . . "Got it!" Ape-like up on buckets.

Goss belayed and Logan followed, climbing straight up the dirt-filled crack. A nut jammed as he was seconding the pitch, and nearing the end of his reserves, Logan left it hanging from the crack, complete with a carabiner.

Logan led a strenuous 5.10 pitch up the *Forrest Finish* to the Yellow Wall Bivy Ledge. They were now above the fifty feet of aid on *D7*, but well to the right, on uncharted free-climbing terrain.

Clouds moved in and it began to rain, then hail. Both climbers were feeling the effects of the first seven pitches, and the altitude contributed to their fatigue. They sat dismally on the ledge for almost an hour, shivering and trying to rest. Finally, hail or no, they had to move.

Table Ledge was less than a rope length away, and from their belay ledge they had a choice of several cracks. It was Goss's lead, and he first chose an inside corner full of fixed pitons (now the normal route up from the bivy ledge), deciding quickly that he could not climb it free in his tired condition. Eventually he chose a line that took him into the hand and fist crack splitting the wall above the *Black Dagger* chimney. The storm had by now abated, but hail covered many of the holds. Still, the climbing unfolded with surprising ease. One final fifteen-foot pitch led to Table Ledge, from where they could traverse off the face. Exhausted but exuberant, they grinned at each other. The Diamond was free.

Goss commented, "If freed routes had new names, we'd call it the *Komito Freeway*, and if they had dedications, this one would be dedicated to all the young hotshots who made it conceivable for us old farts to come steppin' out of the old rocking chair."

The next day, Higgins, Atwood, and Manson successfully completed *D7*, for the wall's first all-female ascent.

A week later, Jim Dunn and Chris Wood drove to the Longs Peak trailhead from Colorado Springs and hiked in to the Diamond. All summer this pair had been climbing on Pikes Peak, where just a few days earlier they had made the first free ascent of *The Flame,* then the hardest crack climb in the Colorado high country.

They approached the Diamond in more traditional style, with hammer and pitons, jumars, and bivouac gear. Dunn and Wood knew nothing of Goss and Logan's ascent or of the routefinding details worked out by the various Boulder teams. They began free climbing straight up Kor's *Yellow Wall* route. Stalled by snowstorms, they fixed lines on the first few pitches above Broadway, and their climb extended over three stormy days. "I remember brushing five inches of snow off the holds, thinking, 'This is crazy,'" Dunn said.

They persevered, and eventually connected with Goss and Logan's line, near where that pair had traversed right from *D7*. They encountered the nut and carabiner Logan had abandoned. It looked as if someone had been stopped by the dirt-filled section of crack and lowered off. They knew Boulder climbers had been trying to free climb the Diamond and they speculated that this was the high point. Dunn aided up, cleaned the dirt from the crack, rappelled to the ledge, and led the pitch free. They reached Table Ledge, then continued up for two more moderate pitches in the vicinity of Forrest's finish. Soon, the pair stood atop the Diamond, triumphant at the thought of having made the great wall's first free ascent—the second party to feel that way in a week.

The free Diamond was to be Goss and Logan's last great Colorado rock climb, although Logan would go on to a distinguished career as an alpinist. Logan, a complete novice on snow and ice, climbed a few of the standard classics in Chamonix with Bob Culp the next year, and the pair then embarked on a casual sightseeing tour to Grindelwald to see the famed Eiger North Face. As it happened, the face was in great shape, and the weather report was for three days of fine high pressure. The Colorado team had little choice but to attempt the notorious "Nordwand." Logan placed his first ice screw somewhere on the Eiger's Second Ice Field, and a day later they stood atop the North Face.

Logan's best alpine climb came several years later, in the Canadian Rockies, with the first ascent of the range's "last great problem," the coveted Emperor Face of Mount Robson, with Mugs Stump. Logan ended his alpine career there, but as of this writing, at age fifty five, he was still rock climbing—at the 5.12+ level— often accompanied by his son Michael.

North Chasm View Wall—Free

In 1975, in addition to the first free ascent of the Diamond, *Free Blast* and *Astroman* were done in Yosemite Valley. These ascents heralded the start of modern big-wall free climbing. One of the most important early venues for this audacious new genre of climbing was the Black Canyon of the Gunnison. Though much lower in altitude than the Diamond, the walls of the Black Canyon were half again as high. Black Canyon free climbing began very suddenly and dramatically, in 1976.

By the mid-1970s, Kor and Dalke's 1964 South Face route on North Chasm View Wall had been repeated once. The third ascent was conceived in April 1976, after Earl Wiggins' first trip to the Black Canyon. Wiggins, John Sherwood, and John Baird had attempted the Chasm

The southeast face of North Chasm View, showing the line of The Cruise *(Photo: Jeff Achey)*

tion of pegmatite face climbing led to a ledge. Several options were possible above, none of them appealing. To the right, where the rock was less steep, a seam led up through more pegmatite. From Kor's route description it appeared that the aid ascent had gone that way. Wiggins led up the seam, climbing unprotected at first. On the unreliable pegmatite, any positive hold was likely to break away, but Wiggins' Garden of the Gods skills saw him through. Small stoppers provided better protection for the hardest moves. (Wiggins' pitch is seldom repeated. An overhanging corner to the left has much better protection, and the passage of many climbers has removed its original crumbling veneer.)

A few pitches higher they joined the *Goss-Logan* line, finding sustained climbing but nothing harder than 5.9. In early afternoon, they stood on the rim. The ascent had taken only six hours, even slowed by the hauling. There were no fisticuffs. Wiggins called it "the first time Jimmy and I jelled as a team." Dunn was elated. "We cruised it!" he told friends in Colorado Springs. Soon, the free route was being called *The Cruise*.

Earl Wiggins, Black Canyon free-climbing pioneer, shown here on the second ascent of the free variation to the Goss-Logan *route, in 1979* (Photo: Ed Webster)

View Nose. A direct finish to the Nose thwarted them—just as it had Goss and Logan in 1972—and the trio finished up the Goss-Logan line. Wiggins immediately noticed that the long section shared with the Kor-Dalke *South Face* route offered surprisingly reasonable free climbing. By the time he reached the rim, Wiggins envisioned climbing the *South Face* all free.

The logical partner for his scheme was Jim Dunn, who had major Black Canyon ascents under his belt, as well as a free ascent of the Diamond. Wiggins hesitated to ask him, remembering their fights in Canyonlands and Yosemite. What if Dunn punched him out high on the wall and left him hanging from a couple of knifeblades? Wiggins weighed the risks and recruited Dunn.

In May, they left the North Rim with a haul bag containing bivy gear, hammer, pins, bolt kit, and enough food and water for two days. Both climbers knew the descent gully, and as was common until the mid-1980s, they downclimbed the 250-foot fifth-class section that now sports fixed rappels.

Moving fast, the pair easily free climbed the first 400 feet, made quick work of a chimney and off-width pitch, and then encountered the first 5.10 climbing, a steep, thin, stemming corner. Above, a frightening sec-

Jim Dunn on the first free ascent of The Cruise, *1976* (Photo: Earl Wiggins)

New Apprentices

Another historic Black Canyon day transpired before the end of 1976. In October, Dunn and Wiggins were back, hoping to free climb the *Diagonal*, the unrepeated original route on the main face of North Chasm View Wall. They had brought with them two young neophytes from Colorado Springs—Ed Webster and Bryan Becker—and talked them into trying *The Cruise*.

Webster and Becker had met two years earlier in North Cheyenne Canyon when Webster was a freshman at Colorado College. Becker, a senior in high school at the time, was a gymnast, adept at tumbling and on the rings, short and stocky, and an excellent boulderer. Webster was taller and weaker but more experienced, having made hard first ascents in his native New England. They quickly became regular climbing partners.

Becker had been kicked by a rodeo bull just a few days before the Black Canyon trip and was still having dizzy spells. Both climbers got dizzy spells from looking into the canyon. "If this climb doesn't blow you away," Dunn said as they peered over the edge, "nothing will."

There was an unprecedented crowd at the canyon—eight climbers, all from Colorado Springs. At the campground Dan Morrison and Bryan Teale had just crawled out from an attempt on the Chasm View Nose, which had ended when Morrison zippered down forty feet of an aid pitch. Down-canyon, Dean Tschappat and Steve Miller were nearing the top of the notorious *Dragon Route* on the Painted Wall, making the second ascent. At camp, the veterans told horror stories to inspire the novices, who soon settled into their sleeping bags, taking refuge from the chilly October night. Fresh images of the appalling chasm played before their closed eyes, accompanied by the distant roar of the river, far below.

In the morning, Dunn and Wiggins were off early, racing down the Cruise Gully with one rope and a rack of a dozen nuts for their attempt on the *Diagonal*.

Becker and Webster lagged behind, carrying a haul line and a little food, water, and extra clothing. They would need everything they had for their attempt on *The Cruise*. They struggled with the 5.10 pitches; on the pegmatite seam they used a point of aid. They climbed on, but eventually lost the race with darkness and fashioned a cramped bivouac behind a large flake some 400 feet below the rim. Webster later wrote of that night in *Mountain* magazine (July 1977):

> *Storytelling and dreaming, aching and laughing, never sleeping, we sat and watched the roaring blackness, where the raging flow of the Gunnison and the deep black of the canyon became one, a torment to our thoughts. My feelings went out to Earl and Jim. Were they off their climb? Had they been benighted like us? They had no food, no extra clothing, and no water. They had put all their chips on the table, laid their lives on the line, bringing only a single rope and a rack of nuts—for a 2,000-foot wall!*

Dunn and Wiggins were, in fact, safely on the rim, partying with Tschappat and Miller, who had succeeded on the *Dragon*. They had not reached that point easily, however.

The *Diagonal* ramp system had gone quickly for Dunn and Wiggins, as expected, though one pitch was difficult and rotten and required a point of aid. Just 200 feet from the top of the wall, the ramp, and the team's progress, ended abruptly amid large overhangs.

From a hanging belay on questionable wired stoppers, they tried desperately to find protection for the climbing above. Dunn tried to slot a hex in an out-of-reach crack by twirling it on the end of a fifteen-foot sling. No luck. Wiggins took over and made a determined effort to free climb out of their impasse. "When Earl says he's going for it, he pushes right to the limit," said Dunn. "When he said he couldn't do it, it was really kind of scary."

It was getting late. They were tired, thirsty, and nearly out of options. Dunn proposed retreat. Wiggins looked down—at the sheer, unclimbed wall below, and at the diagonal of their ascent route. He glanced at their meager rack and single rope. Retreat was not an option. Grimly, Dunn took the lead.

Dunn tried the rodeo move again, swinging the hex until, miraculously, it stuck. The placement looked horrible, but when he jerked on it he couldn't pull it out. Dunn hesitated. His eyes met Wiggins'. "Get us out of here," Wiggins said. Dunn leaned back on the hex placement and tension traversed out of sight around the corner.

Alone now, Dunn fought sideways, scrabbling across the wall as loose flakes broke free and skittered into space. Twenty feet out, he gained a precarious stance. Suddenly, two of Wiggins' belay nuts ripped. The jerk on the rope yanked Dunn, nearly pulling him from the stance. Dunn screamed at Wiggins. Wiggins heard only the river.

Desperate, Dunn moved even farther right. Pegmatite crumbled away underfoot. He placed a #1 Stopper and kept climbing. On disintegrating rock and facing an unthinkable fall, he finally lunged into a rotten chimney. Miraculously, he found belay anchors. The chimney took them to the top, half an hour before dark.

Eighteen hours later, Becker and Webster stumbled in to join Dunn and Wiggins in the campground. Each climber was thankful to have escaped with his life—and each would soon be planning his return to the Black.

17. Boulder: End of an Era

In the Boulder area, the last half of the 1970s began off-key. Diana Hunter died, and the same year, 1975, word got out that the Conda Mining Company was negotiating a deal to mine Eldorado Canyon for gravel. Climbers envisioned the *Bastille Crack* and *The Naked Edge* drilled full of blast holes, detonated, and carried out of the canyon by dump truck. The canyon was owned by Bill Fowler. Many climbers now had second thoughts about how, "as a matter of principle," they had hidden under seats and in trunks, or hiked around behind the Bastille, to avoid paying the twenty-five cents Fowler used to charge for a day on his land. Fowler had been trying to get the state to buy the land for some time, and in all probability the mining negotiations were a ruse. The scare set the wheels in motion, but the fate of Eldorado remained uncertain until 1978, when Colorado State Parks paid Fowler $436,400 for a 272-acre tract of the inner canyon.

During this same era, climbing made one of its rare appearances in the national headlines—when George Willig climbed New York City's World Trade Center. In 1977, Willig brought the media circus to Boulder for a televised ascent on the Bastille. The same year, Mike Munger and Charlie Fowler devised their own climbing stunt: they anchored 150-foot ropes to the top of the overhanging *Diving Board* wall, tied into the ends, and jumped off.

Ray Jardine's Friends, the first commercial spring-loaded camming devices, hit the market. The back-to-nature aspect of clean climbing was dealt a blow as climbers' racks began to bristle with space-age devices. Controversy raged about how such technology fit in with the higher goals of rock climbing, but in the end, the only lasting objection to cams concerned their price.

Friends, though popularized in Yosemite, were actually a Colorado invention, first refined in the Denver shop of Forrest Mountaineering. Jardine, a Colorado climber, often climbed with Kris Walker and Bill Forrest. The camming action of the Jumar rope clamp had gotten several climber-engineer types thinking. Several crude camming devices had been floating around at the time, including a two-cam unit devised for the parallel cracks of Zion that one of the Lowe brothers brought in to show Forrest. Jardine also saw the unit and asked Forrest and Walker to help refine the concept and develop an "ultimate climbing anchor."

"Ray's motive was not business driven," Walker said. "His absolute passion was to be the first party to climb *The Nose* on El Capitan in less than twenty-four hours. He wanted to have a strong, stable, lightweight anchor device that would immediately fit the confines of the cracks and require only one hand to place or remove in one second or less. He was sure that if we could come up with such a device he would be able to pull off the *Nose-in-a-Day*."

In spring of 1974, Jardine, Walker, and Lou Dawson of Aspen started up the *Nose* with the prototype Friends, the code name used when field-testing the secret devices on the crags of Colorado's Front Range. The team was thwarted by rain high on the wall, enduring a chilling bivouac at Camp IV, but the Friends had proven themselves. They proved themselves further over the next few years as Jardine used them to revolutionize Valley free climbing. In the end, Forrest Mountaineering, committed to a new ice ax, couldn't front the money to tool up and build the inventory for Friends, and Jardine eventually had them produced in England.

A simpler new tool came from Australia, seemingly made for Eldorado climbing: Pauligk Nuts, the first true micronuts, produced by the Australian climber Roman Pauligk and soon to be known as RPs. A couple of bootleg sets of these tiny brass wedges with silver-soldered wires appeared around 1976, and the next year Chris Peisker moved to Boulder from Down Under and began distributing RPs (as well as establishing a string of hard climbs). The smallest RPs would hold only a few hundred pounds, but that was enough to protect a move or two and allow a new crop of climbs to be safely freed.

By this time, the new Boulder free climbs had been widely covered in *Mountain* and *Climbing* magazines. The first edition of this book had come out, and Eldorado Canyon had gained an international reputation that was based on style rather than on sheer numerical difficulty. *The Naked Edge* was the most famous free climb in the world, but outside Colorado, times were changing.

In Eldorado—where freeing old aid routes was the

norm and where there were quite a few old aid bolts to clip—placing bolts or pitons was shunned. In California, land of granite slab climbing and steep cracks, the situation was different. Climbers were pushing onto steeper, unclimbed granite faces, and the laws of gravity were generating a new bolt controversy: must protection bolts be drilled from stances, or could aid be used if the rock was too steep to free both hands?

In Yosemite, where strenuous cracks reigned, Henry Barber, Ron Kauk, John Bachar, and Ray Jardine were ushering in a new grade: 5.12. It had a seductive ring to it, just as 5.11 did to a previous generation. *Hotline* and *Fish Crack* in 1975, *Tales of Power,* the *Rostrum* roof, *Owl Roof,* and *Phoenix* in 1977—these were the new ultimate climbs. Jim Bridwell's a-b-c-d rating subdivisions were instrumental in an increasingly dominant concept—that the difficulty of a climb could be precisely determined, and that this difficulty was purely gymnastic. Previously, 5.10 and 5.11 were treated more as vague psychological realms, and protection factors often figured in. *Jules Verne,* for example, with good protection, would have been considered a 5.10 climb.

A controversial free-climbing tactic appeared in the later 1970s—resting on the rope to work out moves. Though standard practice on hard climbs today, in Eldorado in the 1970s this tactic was strictly taboo. An elaboration may shed some light on the evolving nature of free climbing.

With physical and psychological difficulties very much intertwined in the minds of 1970s Boulder free climbers, repeated roped falling could be accepted only if it could preserve an essential free-climbing tenet—the idea of the rope as a safety net. The rope should not aid the climber, even in problem-solving. Jim Erickson took this concept to its logical limit, and all climbers went to great lengths—not always so logically—to differentiate between knowledge gained by free climbing up and falling off and knowledge gained through intentionally hanging on the rope.

Common practice was thus: if you fell while trying to lead a free climb in the 1970s, you were immediately lowered. Viewing the move that had ejected you was not permitted. If you protested or pulled back up to your high point, you would be guilty of a dire taint, given a name worthy of its lowly nature—*hang-dogging.*

By 1978, a few Californian climbers, notably Tony Yaniro, were hang-dogging with abandon and establishing magnificently hard climbs. Hang-dogging soon went on national tour with Wyoming climber Todd Skinner, who put up extremely difficult routes in areas all over the country, generating considerable ungenerous discussion. The first Eldorado free climb to employ this tactic was *Genesis,* done in 1979 and to be recounted shortly.

Only much later was hang-dogging generally accepted in Colorado, at which point the tactic was given a more positive name—"working" the route.

The Eldorado masters of the early 1970s were drifting toward other pursuits: David Breashears into mountaineering and filmmaking, Duncan Ferguson toward ice and mixed climbing (a wide-open field in which he became a brilliant pioneer). Steve Wunsch would soon be working on Wall Street. Jim Erickson and Art Higbee's ambitions now lay in trying to free climb the Northwest Face of Half Dome in Yosemite, which except for a few heartbreaking feet at the top they succeeded in doing in 1976, making a film of the adventure with Bob Godfrey in the process. Erickson and Higbee later top roped a free variation to the aid section, bolted it, but never returned. After 1975, none of these climbers pushed cragging standards in Boulder. The refined concept of difficulty, and the changing of the guard, would soon bring big changes to Boulder climbing.

Roger Briggs, now in his mid-twenties, remained on the scene, branching out into what might be called "endurance free climbing." In 1975 he linked *Kloeberdanz* to *The Naked Edge* with Rob Candelaria for the state's "first all-free Grade V." (Ample motivation came from the obvious name for the link-up: *The Naked Danz.*) The next year Pat Ament and Bill Briggs had a remarkable endurance day in Boulder Canyon with the "Castle Rock Marathon," a one-day blitz of every 5.10 and 5.11 on the cliff: *Athlete's Feat, Radio Andromeda, Country Club Crack, Tongo, Comeback Crack,* and *Final Exam.*

Among the more serious new Eldorado routes of the late 1970s was *Inner Space* on the Bastille, done in 1977 by Jeff Lowe. Originally from Ogden, Utah, Lowe had learned to climb in the Tetons as a young boy. He was among the earliest pioneers on the great walls of Zion National Park in Utah, and in 1971, shortly after making the first ascent of Zion's famed *Moonlight Buttress,* Lowe moved to Colorado to work for the Outward Bound school. In 1976 he opened the International Alpine School in Eldorado Springs with his brother Mike and with Kevin Donald. Jeff Lowe climbed widely in Colorado—in Telluride, on Lumpy Ridge, on various high-country walls, and in the Black Canyon—but his most outstanding contributions would be in the realm of ice climbing and alpinism, and in the organization of climbing events such as the televised Snowbird sport-climbing competitions of the late 1980s and the Ouray Ice Festivals of the 1990s.

New names began to appear beside the most outrageous Boulder climbs. In 1977, teenager Pat Adams free soloed the *Kloeberdanz* roof, and Ken Duncan of Fort Collins free soloed *C'est la Vie.* Some of Eldorado's last

Greg Lowe in 1976 on his route Clever Lever *(Photo: Pat Ament)*

well-protected aid lines were ticked off. The same year, Jeff Lowe's brother Greg free climbed an old bolt ladder that spanned the huge overhang between *Kloeberdanz* and *T2*. This twenty-foot problem, dubbed *Clever Lever,* was Eldorado's second 5.12. In 1978, John Bragg finally completed the strenuous finger-jamming crux of *Cinch Crack,* a gymnastic twelve-foot roof climb, remarkably similar to, if shorter than, Bragg's famous masterpiece *Kansas City,* the first 5.12 in the Shawangunks. *Cinch Crack* was Eldorado's first 5.12 that did not rely on old aid bolts for protection. One of the best Eldorado free climbs of the late 1970s, however, combined difficulty, heady runouts, and airy exposure.

The Wisdom
A Kor-Ament aid line, done on a snowy day in 1962, *The Wisdom* was perhaps the most spectacular of the Roof Routes. It crossed the lower Redgarden roof where it was widest and highest off the ground, and then continued out more roofs above. A rope dangling from the top would touch the ground twenty-five feet out from the rock.

The first pitch of the route was led free in 1975 by Ed Webster, who had hitchhiked to Eldorado from Colorado Springs on one of his first trips to Eldorado. He lacked a partner, but was gregarious by nature and introduced himself to Jim Erickson and Roger Briggs, who had a rope partway up the pitch and were waiting for Art Higbee. Webster asked if he might have a try, and he finished the pitch. Higbee arrived and the party of four was soon assembled below the huge second-pitch roof, but they made no further progress.

Later in 1975, after a few spectacular falls, Higbee mastered the main roof via a diagonal path of holds that required twenty feet of roof climbing. The next overhang jutted out only about three feet, but it shut him down cold, as it did numerous subsequent attempts.

In a very uncharacteristic move, Jim Erickson aided out the main roof and placed a bolt to establish a hanging belay station halfway through Kor's original aid pitch. Erickson claimed he would only use the belay if he could do so without weighting the anchor—a noble thought that would never be tested. Higbee, David Breashears, and others thought the bolt degraded the climb and berated Erickson, who dropped out of the *Wisdom* effort, realizing that his dire "taint" would prohibit him from harassing his partners about using chalk or taking falls.

Wunsch and Bragg included *The Wisdom* on their regular circuit of projects in 1975. They belayed at Erickson's stance and worked on the second roof, which had a distinct lack of holds and only an upward-driven, broken-eyed fixed pin for protection. They also tried to traverse right from the belay and connect to the aid line higher up, but it was scary, strenuous, dubious terrain and they made little progress.

A year elapsed, and in 1977, the legendary Southern Californian John Bachar came to town. Athletic, blond, suntanned, and aloof, Bachar was among the strongest free climbers in the country, and he acted the part. He loved to make casual ascents of the area testpieces, and in this spirit he approached one of Eldorado's two 5.12s, *Clever Lever*, declared it a boulder problem, and tried to free solo it. He fell from near the lip, crashing to the ground twenty feet below and rolling down a rock slab for forty feet more. His tumble ended near a startled party at the base of *T2,* who assumed he had fallen from high on Redgarden Wall. As the *T2* climbers looked on in amazement, Bachar stumbled away, escaping with just scrapes and bruises.

Bachar made several attempts on *The Wisdom* in October 1977, the last with Jeff Lowe. He planned to skip Erickson's hanging belay and try the rightward-traversing variation first explored by Bragg. Bachar cruised out the big roof, and after a final look at Kor's aid line, underclung right, placed a poor nut, and reached over the bulge.

From strenuous fingertip layback holds, he pulled a stopper off his rack, but it was the wrong size. He tried a second nut, which also didn't fit. Bachar's considerable endurance neared its end. A third nut went halfway in. He grabbed it, clipped in the rope, and fell. The nut twisted, but held. Bachar quickly climbed back to Erickson's bolt.

Matt Samet and Steve Dieckhoff on The Wisdom *in 2000. Dieckhoff is at Jim Erickson's controversial bolted hanging belay, while Samet is on the crux moves.* (Photo: Jeff Achey)

He hung on the bolt long enough to untie, pull his rope through the nut that held his fall, and tie back in. Determined now, he climbed back up, clipped his nut, and kept going. Five feet higher he was on good holds, back on the original Kor line. Steep but easy climbing led to a belay and then the top.

Fine points of style were the subject of endless discussion in the 1970s, and the feats of rival Californians were subject to special scrutiny. Some criticized Bachar for hanging on Erickson's bolt, while others were impressed that he had tried to skip the belay at all. Today, the hanging belay has become standard.

Many big falls have been taken from *The Wisdom*'s

Opposite: *Art Higbee on* The Wisdom. *Higbee made the first free ascent of the main roof in 1975. Kor's original aid line continued straight up over the small roof above Higbee, while John Bachar's 1977 free variation moved out to the right edge of the roof and then up.* (Photo: Bob Godfrey)

crux. The record was set during an attempt at the third free ascent by Rob Candelaria. Candelaria led over the main roof and, to reduce rope drag, skipped all the protection after Erickson's belay. He had climbed past the crux when a foothold broke. Candelaria flew over the roof and beyond—almost seventy feet.

Genesis

From Ament on *Supremacy* to Erickson on *The Naked Edge,* the story of Eldorado free climbing is speckled with obsessions, but no obsession before or since has matched that of Jim Collins. The object of his desire was *Genesis,* a rock climb done on aid by Jack Turner in 1961 and the first route in Colorado to be rated A5. Of all the Eldorado projects that saw so many attempts in the mid-1970s, *Genesis* was perhaps the most compelling, a flawless shield that rose directly above the path of any climber hiking up to Redgarden Wall.

As a freshman in high school, Collins, a Boulder native, wore a silver necklace inscribed *Genesis*. By the time he began college at Stanford, Collins had worked his way through the area's harder climbs. He set out to repeat the *Pyscho* roof, and in 1978, after a protracted effort, he succeeded, using a new set of holds five feet to the right of Steve Wunsch's line.

After *Psycho*, Collins set his sights on free climbing *Genesis* and trained relentlessly toward that single goal. He desperately wanted to succeed before returning to college in the fall of 1978. Summer break neared its end. After nearly a hundred attempts he knew the route cold, and one crisp morning he had it in the bag. He felt powerful and precise as he moved into the crux, and in a smooth flow he linked together the hardest moves. Suddenly, he felt a *ping* in his finger, and a moment later he was dangling from the rope. A tendon injury kept him grounded for more than a week.

Collins forced himself to rest his injured finger until the last possible day. As he began his final attempt, a crucial foothold broke. Devising an alternative sequence consumed the rest of his energy. Break was over. Collins flew back to California. He had accomplished one great deed over his summer break, however. Though not widely known as a free soloist, Collins was quite prolific in unroped climbing. In summer 1978, he made the first unroped ascent of *The Naked Edge*.

Collins' fall program at Stanford was demanding: it consisted entirely of training for *Genesis*. He found a bouldering project on campus so long and grueling that he carried a needle in his pocket, which he would grasp in his teeth to drain blisters on his fingertips so that he could continue without getting off the wall. He called his project *Genocide*.

Mark Sonnenfeld on Genesis *in 1985. He is in the same position as Collins in the photo at right.* (Photo: Jeff Achey)

Collins devised a mental trick to make *Genesis* seem less extreme. In the future, he imagined, *Genesis* would be repeated—often, even by fairly average climbers. Collins bought a date book and scratched out the year, revising it to the 1990s. He used the book as his training log and daily planner, pretending that *Genesis* had already been done, and that the best climbers didn't consider it exceptionally difficult.

It was an interesting tactic, but unsuccessful in reducing his anxiety. At Stanford, Collins dreamed of *Genesis* almost every night. Once he had a nightmare that he climbed past the crux only to find the finishing holds impossibly loose. Layton Kor had saved him by clutching a loose block between his knees so Collins could pull through.

In May 1979, Collins returned to Colorado and went directly to *Genesis* to put his demons to rest. Stemming his feet on tiny smears, he stretched up to a sideways hold, using a grip that today would be called a Gaston, but at the time had no special name. A shuffle of feet and a stab to a fingertip pin scar followed, then several short lunges to slim edges. For a brief minute, Collins was living his dreams, adhering to the smooth, gently overhanging, diamond-shaped slab of the *Genesis* headwall. Then it was over. No Kor, no loose blocks. He was alone at the belay atop the headwall.

Collins' description of *Genesis* in the September 1979 issue of *Climbing* was effusive: "two B1+ cruxes followed by a 5.11 crux with no rests between, and this is after doing two 5.10 and one 5.11– cruxes to get to that point. In short, the pitch is 140 feet of sustained climbing with virtually no rests, two 5.10 cruxes, two 5.11 cruxes, and

Jim Collins beginning the crux moves of Genesis, *Eldorado Canyon's hardest free climb in 1979* (Photo: Bob Barron)

two B1+ (5.12+) cruxes, with a possibility of a 40- to 50-foot fall on the final 5.11 crux. The two most difficult cruxes were so difficult that I knew it was over when it 'eased off' to 5.11."

Understatement this was not. Some climbers smirked. Collins was young and enthusiastic, but his words also indicated the shape of things to come—an increasingly athletic, "sport" approach to rock climbing.

Outside the Arena

Wisdom, Cinch Crack, Psycho, Genesis—these ascents were the front-page stories. In the shadow of the newsmakers were the explorers. Chris Reveley, Dan Hare, Scott Woodruff, Brad Gilbert, and Wendell Nuss were among those who roamed Eldorado's West Ridge and Rincon Wall, the Flatirons, and the obscure crags of Boulder Canyon in the late 1970s. *Xanadu* on the West Ridge, *Center Route* on Rincon, and *Where Eagles Dare* in Boulder Canyon date from these days.

Dan Hare was a particularly enduring explorer. He had learned to climb in the late 1960s in Fort Collins while at Colorado State University. He roomed on the same floor as Mark Hesse, the accomplished Colorado Springs climber, and did much of his early climbing at Lumpy Ridge before moving to Boulder. In the 1970s and '80s Hare worked at the Boulder Mountaineer and become a familiar figure to all Boulder climbers, slow-talking, slow climbing, handlebar mustachioed like an old-West outlaw. When he wasn't in the shop he was out doing new routes. Hare was so famously prolific in Boulder Canyon that certain routes got their names because he *didn't* find them—*The Route That Dan Missed, Hare Loss*, and others.

The Dynamic Duo

Two of Boulder's more colorful characters of the late 1970s spent little time roped climbing. A seemingly inseparable pair, they ruled the boulders of Flagstaff Mountain.

A group of climbers might be standing below a problem on Cloud Shadow Rock, chalk on their fingers, when the two figures appeared. One would be slightly built, freckle-faced, red hair pulled into a ponytail—that would be Jim Michael. The other, Jim Holloway, was lanky and tall—six-foot-four—with long hair flowing from beneath a back-turned white painter's cap. Both would be wearing white painter's pants. Climbing independently (they never spotted), they would silently breeze through a circuit of the rock's hardest problems, adding a few variations the other climbers had never seen or imagined. They were friendly, but spoke little, to each other or to onlookers, who would catch themselves standing and staring instead of climbing.

Jim Holloway at Cloud Shadow Rock, Flagstaff, in 1978 (Photo: Jeff Achey)

Although the difficulty of the routes the pair climbed was impressive, more striking was the smoothness of their movements. Their style was similar, smooth and elastic, tiptoes always finding a precise position on tiny nubbins. There was never a sound, of a foot dragging on rock, or of breathing. In a few minutes they would have finished with the boulder and disappeared, moving on to the next. In a few hours the duo would likely each have climbed nearly every difficult problem on Flagstaff.

Flagstaff Mountain already had a long tradition of outstanding boulderers, from Ray Northcutt and Bob Culp in the 1950s, to Pat Ament, Paul Hagan, Richard Smith, Bob Poling, and Bob Williams in the 1960s. In the 1970s, Holloway in particular brought a new standard of difficulty to the area, and to the boulders of Morrison and of Horsetooth Reservoir.

Holloway never climbed on a rope, but his Flagstaff problems included *Just Right* on Capstan Rock, the *Undercling Traverse* on Cloud Shadow, and a ridiculously hard straight-up problem on the same bulge called *AHR (Another Holloway Route)*. AHR, *Slapshot* in the Flatirons, and *Meathook* at Horsetooth Reservoir are sometimes known as the Big Three, and all were climbed by Holloway in the mid-1970s. Little-appreciated at the time, these short climbs represented some of the hardest sequences of moves ever climbed on rock. By the end of the century, only *Meathook* would be repeated, and this by a significant variation to the sequence used by Holloway.

18. Second Bloom in the Garden

In 1976, a new generation of climbers came of age in Colorado Springs. Colorado College had a bumper crop, including Pete Williams, Karin Budding, Steve Hong, and Ed Webster. From town, there were Bryan Becker, Ken Simms, Mark Rolofson, and Leonard Coyne.

Cheyney, McClure, and crew had turned to the local granite, and the second-class status of the Garden gave the new generation free reign. They took advantage of the plentiful opportunity for new routes, and 1976 saw a revival in Garden climbing.

The movement was led by Earl Wiggins, who simply loved the hazardous work of pioneering difficult new routes on soft sandstone. In 1976, with Jim Souder, Wiggins eliminated the aid on Auld and Ziegler's *Pipe Route*. Appalled by the decrepit hardware that protected the route, he led Steve Hong and Ed Webster up a new line nearby, *Pipe Dreams*. The "bombproof" drilled angles he placed as he climbed inspired some thrilling runouts, and the resulting 5.10+ route is a classic period piece.

On North Gateway Rock, a team effort produced one

Earl Wiggins following Amazing Grace *on a repeat ascent in 1977* (Photo: Ed Webster)

of the best-known Garden climbs of 1976. Above a pothole about ten feet off the ground, a bolt was obviously needed, but the steep wall made it impossible to free both hands to drill. Not to be deterred, Leonard Coyne and Ed Russell climbed together into the pothole, and one held the drill while the other wielded the hammer.

More antics followed. Attempting the lead, Wiggins climbed past the bolt, but the precarious moves above took him into ground-fall range. Wiggins pressed up into a mantel, and Coyne readied himself. Suddenly, a hold broke. Like lightning, Coyne reeled in an armload of slack and leaped backward, arresting Wiggins' face-first plunge about three inches from the ground. An elderly tourist had been standing nearby and witnessed the incident. Her shocked exclamation gave the climb its name—*Amazing Grace*.

Kindergarten Rock, also known as Gray Rock, is composed of an unusual layer of Lyons sandstone, harder but more brittle than the Gateway rocks. Its fluted edges make some very steep climbing possible, and one of the steepest was *Footloose and Fancy Free*, done by Coyne and Webster in 1977. Much effort went into placing the

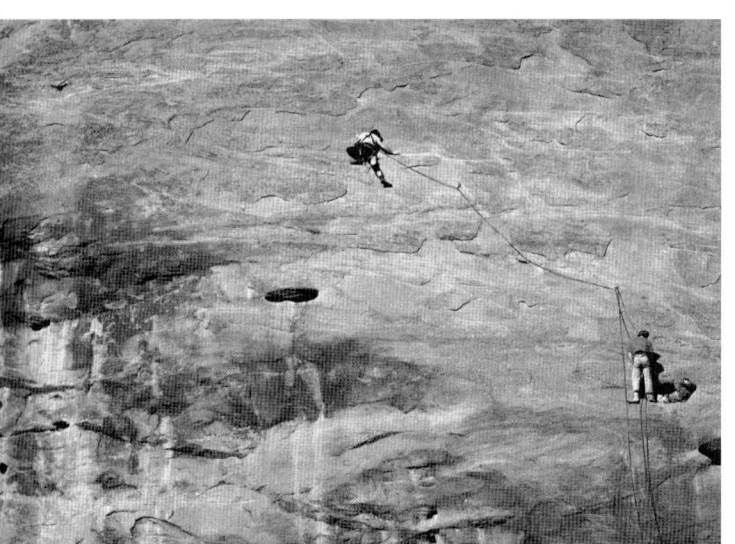

Ed Webster, Bryan Becker, and Leonard Coyne (seated) on the first ascent of Over the Rainbow, *North Gateway Rock, in 1978* (Photo: Ed Webster collection)

climb's fourteen drilled angles and removing the sheets of loose rock that lined an overhanging dihedral. Coyne was fond of flinging rocks and shrieking in mock terror, and he found ample opportunity for both on *Footloose*.

Garden climbing regularly employed tactics that were completely taboo in Boulder: hammering, drilling, and using aid to place protection. "Good style" had a different meaning to Springs climbers, one that reflected the rougher, scrappier requirements of climbing on soft stone. Coyne summarized Springs sentiments succinctly in Glenn Randall's book *Vertigo Games* (W. R. Publishing, Sioux City, IA 1983): "I consider placing bolts while hanging from dubious things behind dubious flakes with a dubious belay to be more truly free climbing than placing cute little nuts in cute little cracks at cute little cosmic crags."

Coyne was one of Colorado's more eccentric climbers. He climbed at the world standard but made his own rules. He collected crystals and fossils, and nameless demons seemed to haunt him. On one day, Coyne might show cool mastery of a difficult jam crack or unprotected face; on the next, he might cringe in terror on the same climb. Coyne moved to Boulder in the early 1980s to study computer science and soon became famous for his Black Canyon climbs, to be recounted later.

One remarkable Garden climb was Coyne and Simms' 1977 circumnavigation of North Gateway. For those who might want to repeat this historic Garden tour, a route description follows: Begin with all of *Anaconda*. Descend from the Tower of Babel and traverse Hollywood Ledge. Work right, with difficulty, across the *Pete and Bob's* section of the west face, then duck into the upper Tourist Gully. Reverse *Psychic Grandma* for three pitches and do the *Tidrick's* finish. Gain the east side of North Gateway and descend the *Boucher-Twombly* chimney to the East Ledges. Traverse to Hidden Valley and finish at the South Ridge of Babel, just around the corner from *Anaconda*.

Coyne and Simms raised a stir the same year with their antics on an obscure old fifty-foot bolt ladder on Keyhole Rock. Using several old bolt holes as handholds, they managed to free climb the route on top rope. The climbing was the hardest in the Garden, and they resolved to create a lead climb by bolting the line on rappel.

The Garden of the Gods—and all of Colorado—had a strict ground-up ethic for establishing new free climbs. The adventure of the first ascent was all-important, and preprotecting routes on rappel obviously eliminated much of the challenge. *The Waterchute Route* was one of the first rappel-bolted climbs in Colorado, and it generated significant controversy.

Almost immediately the bolts on the *Waterchute Route* were chopped, leading to major stylistic discussions among the local climbers. Rappel bolting was rejected—temporarily. The issue came to a head again in 1979, when several free routes, including Mark Rolofson's *Mighty Thor*, were protected by drilling closely spaced bolt ladders on aid. This tactic adhered to tradition but rendered it pointless. Rolofson, in his later guidebook, summarized the aid-ladder debate:

> It was felt that such a style resulted often in an overprotected climb. The alternatives to this style of establishing a vertical to bulging line on soft sandstone without such aids were often not felt possible without taking horrendous risks. Hooks had to be used most carefully if at all, because they could sheer flakes off.

"I consider placing bolts while hanging from dubious things behind dubious flakes with a dubious belay to be more truly free climbing than placing cute little nuts in cute little cracks at cute little cosmic crags." Leonard Coyne free climbing in the Garden of the Gods in mid-1970s (Photo: Ed Webster)

The decision to pre-protect future climbs in the 1980s on rappel after top-rope rehearsal came largely after seeing the results and shortcomings of climbs that were pre-protected with bolt ladders.

In 1979 Coyne established the Garden's first 5.12 climb—the first pitch of *Kor's Corner*—again amid contro-

Steve Hong on an early ascent of Cocaine, *South Gateway Rock, 1977* (Photo: Ed Webster)

versy. In one key section, Coyne found the holds lacking and pounded out a thin pin scar until it was large enough to use as a fingerhold. After a few days work, he free climbed the pitch. Coyne invited several top climbers to repeat the route, without the hole if possible, and when none succeeded, he let the climb stand, as did others.

Late 1970s Garden climbing stood out for the boldness of its protagonists, and their outrageous antics, on and off the rock. For some, transgressions of climbing etiquette were merely forms of entertainment, akin to bull sessions at The Cobbler, margaritas at Henry's Mexican restaurant, or shocking the throngs of summer tourists with some hare-brained stunt. It was the Garden of the Gods, after all, and who really cared about how a bolt was drilled or if someone scratched out a handhold or two in the soft stone, which was always breaking and changing anyway? Yet history was in the making here. The Garden was an important training ground for the climbers who would establish the hardest climbs on some of the West's wildest cliffs—the sandstone of Utah's Canyonlands and the huge walls of the Black Canyon. The Garden of the Gods also became the first Colorado area where routes were routinely bolted on rappel, and the practice would move directly to other areas in the hands of the same climbers.

Leonard Coyne free climbing the first pitch of Kor's Corner *in 1980* (Photo: Jeff Achey)

19. A Gentler, Freer Diamond

The Diamond of Longs Peak repelled repeated attempts at a free ascent until the successful effort of Wayne Goss and Jim Logan in 1975. Modern climbers might wonder why the Diamond held out so long. Hard 5.11 was well established on the low crags in the early 1970s, and several of the Diamond's lines now go with only a spot or two of 5.10.

One reason was the mistaken assumption that *D7*, the Diamond's easiest aid route, would be the line of least resistance for free climbing. In fact, the crux pitch of *D7* would prove to be one of the hardest on the Yellow Wall, and Goss and Logan devised a major traverse to avoid it.

More significantly, the wall itself has changed. Wet rock and vegetated cracks were major stumbling blocks, but beginning with Dunn and Wood's ascent in 1975, free climbers began to "garden" the main cracks. Today the whole Yellow Wall area is cleaner and drier, and modern free climbers often are baffled at why so many early attempts had been turned back by wet climbing.

Chip Salun, a dedicated climber and naturalist, spent several years in the late 1970s studying the Diamond's alpine plants—some quite rare—often camping near the top of the Diamond for a week or more. His plea for low impact in *Climbing* magazine (May–June, 1978) is timeless: "Only an egotistical desire for some relatively obscure first in free climbing could warrant gardening in any remaining cracks." Free climbing left its mark, but beautiful hanging gardens of alpine wildflowers still abound on the Diamond. Having claimed the main crack systems, modern climbers on Longs Peak now take pride in leaving the remaining plants to live in peace, bypassing them with face climbing or choosing other lines.

A final obstacle to free climbing the Diamond was less tangible than routefinding or vegetated cracks. The Diamond was widely considered Colorado's ultimate wall, and a major expedition. Except for a few one-day climbs by the fastest experts, ascents of the Diamond were multiday affairs. Thus, before the free-climbing era, most Diamond climbers endured violent afternoon storms, as well as frigid nights on the wall. The warm sunny mornings were relatively brief windows of comfort in what was otherwise a harsh climbing environment. Under such conditions, lightweight free-climbing tactics seemed dangerously brash.

With rising free-climbing standards came speed. As free or mostly free ascents became the rule, the "window" of warm, sunny mornings often provided sufficient time to complete the entire climb. More and more Diamond climbers eluded the elements, returning home warm and dry. The great wall's fierce reputation began to soften. The early free ascents of the Diamond, however, still struggled under the weight of the wall's early reputation, and the story returns briefly to those times.

The Complete Yellow Wall

By 1976, the Diamond had had three free ascents, Goss and Logan's, Dunn and Wood's, and *Pervertical Sanctuary* near the wall's left edge, climbed by Bruce Adams (Pat Adams' older brother) of Boulder and Tobin Sorenson of California in the summer of 1975. Only Dunn and Wood, however, had climbed beyond Table Ledge, and even they had skirted the main 300-foot headwall that led to the apex of the Diamond. To some Colorado climbers, the wall had yet to see a "complete" free ascent.

One of those climbers was Roger Briggs, who had the disadvantage of knowing the wall's more violent moods. By late July of the 1976 season, Briggs and Rob Candelaria (who Briggs had nicknamed Emilio) had already failed twice on the Diamond, thwarted by storms. Briggs wrote of their successful climb in the September 1976 issue of *Climbing*, including this account of the final push:

Looking up anxiously at the last 400 feet of the Diamond, thirsty, tired, scared of the pitch off Table Ledge, and aware that it's getting much colder with the sun gone, we make our summit bid. It's one pitch to Table Ledge where we could get off, but we know that we won't be satisfied unless we can free the rest of the Yellow Wall.

My hands are numb with the cold as I start up the

Roger Briggs, enduring Diamond free-climbing pioneer, on the second free ascent of D1 *in 1980* (Photo: Jeff Achey)

sixth pitch. Forty feet up, a difficult section takes me by surprise. I almost fall off when my frozen hands refuse to work. Some exotic stems on tiny crystals save me and I enter a grungy chimney. The effort of the difficult section has increased my circulation and my hands start to come back to life. I get out of the chimney, pass another touchy section, then I'm on a nice stance at Table Ledge. As Emilio follows I study the wall above. We're so close . . . an all too familiar feeling.

I begin to get hungry for this climb; I've wanted it for five years. When Emilio arrives I tell him that I'm psyched to lead the next pitch. He agrees to let me lead it, sensing the sudden energy that's come over me. I am aware that he will have to endure the cold while I climb, and now as never before I sense the feeling of teamwork.

A traverse fifteen feet right with 800 feet of space between me and Broadway takes me to a faint crack system. The next 120 feet took us hours to nail on our earlier ascent. I move up with determination, knowing that every foot I gain brings us that much closer to the top. I get good protection but have to use it sparingly to avoid running out of equipment. I make steady progress, past a wet section, past a sickening loose block, then things seem to blank out. I'm only twenty feet away from the summit overhang and we know we can make it from there. I move left into a wet area and get further and further from good protection. Hanging uncomfortably from slippery, sloping holds, I'm unable to piece together the next section. Emilio is uneasy and tells me to get moving because a storm is nearly upon us. I look to the northwest and see a wall of white moving our way. As successively closer mountains disappear I know it will be a matter of minutes before we are swallowed whole.

New life shoots through my body at the thought. Some slippery jams and wet sloping footholds get me to a belay point. Emilio starts up the pitch but his hands are really frozen. I remind him about the storm and somehow he follows the pitch with almost non-functioning hands. As he reaches me a swirling snowstorm engulfs us. Now the only way off is up. Emilio's hands are no warmer, so we decide that it will be quickest for me to lead. I take off with nuts hanging all over me—no time for organization. Emilio keeps coaxing me to keep moving. My focus is on one thing only: going up, as quickly as possible. It's a wet, mossy corner with blocks of ice hanging on it. The snow doesn't bother me—it's too cold to make the rock any wetter. Soon I'm breathing like a distance runner in the 14,000-foot thin air, my hands are going numb, my arms and legs are screaming with fatigue . . . we've got to make it!

The storm rages but I'm almost up. Then I know we've got it so I pause for a moment to relish the absurdity of the whole scene: the two of us dressed like summer tourists and scurrying like ants to escape the wrath of the gods. I laugh to myself because we've squeezed by, our bluff has worked and it no longer matters that it's snowing. As I stretch the rope out 160 feet we're up the Diamond, home free.

D7

In 1977, the Southern California climber John Bachar took a guiding job with the Fantasy Ridge climbing school in Estes Park. Bachar had been part of the first free-ascent team of *Astroman* in Yosemite two years earlier, and was recognized as one of the top free climbers in the world.

Bachar and Richard Harrison, another Californian, enjoyed their first good look at the Diamond as they made the approach hike and set up camp above Chasm Lake.

The pair had only some sketchy information on the routes, but planned to meet their friend John Long, who was making an extended stay in Colorado. Long planned to hike in separately with a woman friend and meet Bachar and Harrison at Mills Glacier. Long claims that he "got off route on the approach"—a dubious story—and for whatever reason, he didn't show. Bachar and Harrison headed up without him.

Unfamiliar with the variety of crack systems on the Yellow Wall, the pair picked one that looked good and started up. Several hours later, they had free climbed *D7*. When first done in 1966, this route's A2 rating ushered in a new era of ease on the Diamond. When freed by Bachar and Harrison at hard 5.11 in 1977, it ushered in a new level of difficulty. The elegant thin-crack crux was one of the hardest pitches of alpine free climbing in the country, and the route as a whole comprised some of the most continuously beautiful climbing on the Diamond.

The Directagonal
Relatively low angle and easily accessible, Ray Northcutt's *Diagonal* on the lower east face of Longs was much attempted during the big free-climbing push of the early 1970s. The lower pitches were often wet, but by 1977 they had gone free with a few spots of hard 5.10 or 5.11. The best free attempts on the *Diagonal* had been thwarted by a smooth section on the long traverse high on the face, the mysterious history of which has been discussed earlier.

In 1977, Roger and Bill Briggs devised a new plan to free the *Diagonal*. They hoped to piece together a rightward-trending line that would hit the summit dihedral system more directly, shortcutting the *Diagonal*'s problematic traverse. After free climbing the lower cracks and surmounting the *Diagonal*'s obvious roof, the brothers struck out right onto unclimbed terrain below the *Diagonal* traverse line.

A spectacular hand traverse and wandering, poorly protected face climbing took the team within a pitch of the junction with the original route. Bill took the lead. Face climbing led to a thin dihedral, which accepted only the smallest wired nuts to protect insecure moves on muddy fingertip jams. The last thin moves led to a rest stance—if one was comfortable resting on soaking wet rock.

An overhanging, hand-size crack loomed above. On dry rock, it would have been a low-end 5.10 free-climbing problem, but the entire face was a sheet of running water. The crack was full of an icy, milk-shake-like mixture of algae and moss. After mastering his disbelief, Bill plunged his hands in and started climbing. He laybacked strenuously, feet smeared high on the slick sheet of wet granite

Jeff Achey on the Directagonal, *1979* (Photo: Chip Chace)

as small wakes formed around the toes of his climbing shoes. Near the end of his strength he shot his left foot out to a hold, stretched, and manteled up onto a belay ledge. The dihedral and cracks above went at easy—and dry—5.10, and the great Diagonal Wall had its first free climb, the *Directagonal*.

The next year, Bill Briggs returned to the wall with John Bragg and free climbed the other prize line on the face, the *Gray Pillar*, a slightly shorter and easier climb that was almost as good.

The Epic Direct

In December 1976, two Fort Collins teenagers set out to attempt the first winter ascent of Longs' *Diagonal Direct*. Shrouded in the aura of Kor and Bossier's epic first ascent, this magnificent route had seen only one repeat. Mark Wilford and Ken Duncan were not well qualified for such an endeavor. Neither had ever done a major aid route, nor any winter climb other than their "practice" ascent, *Hallett Chimney*. As the boys passed through Estes Park on their way to the *Diagonal Direct*, Michael Covington had this piece of encouragement: "Not much chance. Too much ice." Nevertheless, in three days round trip, they pulled it off.

The ascent convinced Wilford that the *Diagonal Direct* would go all free, and when summer arrived he set out with Pat Adams for an attempt. At the level of the *Diagonal* traverse, it was easy to see why Northcutt had left the obvious diagonal crack. The rock suddenly became steeper, glass-slick, and nearly devoid of ledges.

Adams hung in slings on the smooth wall from a nest of wired stoppers. Wilford led through. The climbing became increasingly hard and run-out. Wilford got in one good nut, then, well into the hard climbing, a poor #2 Stopper—one of the smallest nuts then available. He made another move, scratched a fingertip-size divot in the soft dirt that filled the crack, and tried to find better protection, to no avail. Beginning to tire, Wilford sighted an old piton protruding from the crack ten feet above. As he began to move, the dirt fingerhold gave way.

Wilford fell, ripping the tiny Stopper. From below, Adams watched him fly into view. Wilford sailed fifty feet, over Adams' head, then the rope went tight through the only piece of protection on the pitch, yanking Adams into the air and ripping his belay anchors from the wall. Five hundred feet above Mills Glacier, the pair dangled from the single nut that had held Wilford's fall.

The teenagers reestablished the belay and Wilford climbed back up. He replaced the tiny Stopper, climbed quickly to his high point, and worked his fingers into the same now-cleaner holds. He made a long reach for an edge, but halfway through the move he was jerked to a halt by his haul line. Extended between holds with feet smeared tenuously, he screamed for slack. The rope was wedged securely behind an out-of-reach flake, and Adams was powerless to help.

Another fifty-footer seemed inevitable, but Wilford managed to reverse his moves. Gingerly, he hung his weight on the #2 Stopper. This time it held. The boys had had enough and Wilford lowered, cleaning all the pieces back to the belay. With some difficulty, they retreated to Mills Glacier.

D1

In 1978, John Bachar was back in Colorado and climbing stronger than ever. On the crags of Lumpy Ridge, he managed a free ascent of an old aid route on Twin Owls called *West Owl Direct*. The route, a steep dihedral laced with discontinuous flared seams and cracks, had the same sort of gritty granite as Bachar's home area in Southern California, Joshua Tree National Monument.

Climbing with his trademark confidence, Bachar fired up the 160-foot pitch on his first try. The free climbing involved much twisting into wild positions and stemming between flared seams, and he offered the name *Silly Putty*. Bachar rated the pitch 5.11, calling it "more scary than hard." Subsequent ascents—and failures—suggested that it was Lumpy's first 5.12, but indeed, more scary than hard.

Bachar and Billy Westbay approached the Diamond with an objective far more ambitious than anything that had yet been done in the Colorado high country: to free climb the original Diamond line, *D1*. As a beginning climber in the L.A. area, bouldering at Stoney Point, Bachar had met Bob Kamps, who with Dave Rearick had made the original Diamond climb in 1960. Bachar thought that it might be "sort of a family thing" for another Southern Californian to free the climb. His ace in the hole would be Billy Westbay.

The first 300 feet of *D1* are relatively low angle. The payback comes on the upper wall, where the climb overhangs continuously for 600 feet. General consensus was that the odds of free climbing *D1* were zero.

Westbay was feeling ill the morning of the climb, so Bachar led. The character of the upper route quickly became obvious—overhanging, ever-so-slightly rotten, but amazingly free-climbable. The steepest pitches went at about 5.10+. The position was spectacular as the pair reached a small stance at Table Ledge crack, just a pitch from easy climbing. Here, the original line had aided left to a steep knifeblade crack. The obvious free-climbing alternative loomed above—the direct continuation of the main crack system. It was clear why Kamps and Rearick had not gone that way. The overhanging crack, slime-covered and dripping with ice water, varied from four inches to off-width chimney size. Bachar and Westbay had no gear to fit it.

The climbers discussed their options. A deep chill had settled across the wall, and they were already wearing all their clothing. Storm clouds were building fast. Westbay was feeling no better. In fact, he felt too ill to endure a long and storm-lashed rappel. He took the lead, choosing the grim but direct line.

Westbay started up the slippery, unclimbed fissure. At forty feet he reached a crux section where it appeared he would have to move onto the face next to the crack.

With no protection since the belay, the maneuver was unreasonably dangerous. In his trademark style, Westbay remained quietly determined. The first move put him past the point of no return. Another hard face followed. Risking a 100-foot fall, Westbay was finally able to jam an arm, and then a leg, back into the wet crack, and slither upward in relative security. He found protection and ran the rope out to belay among the ice blocks that lay melting in the depths of the exit chimneys. *D1* was free.

On the second free ascent of *D1* in 1980, Roger Briggs free climbed the original aid line, via thin but dry and well-protected 5.11+ climbing. All subsequent parties avoided Westbay's variation. The *Westbay Crack* stands as a lasting testimony to one of Colorado's great climbers, who died in July 2000 of liver cancer at the age of forty-seven. In Westbay's obituary in *Climbing* magazine (December 2000), John Long wrote: "Because Billy always stuck to doing it rather than talking about it, his magic was known mostly to his peers, which makes him perhaps the least-known pioneer of this generation—which suited him just fine."

The Casual Diamond
Before the 1978 season ended, Duncan Ferguson and Chris Reveley climbed an unlikely line that would soon become the Diamond's most climbed route. The idea was to reach a large dihedral system on the *Grand Traverse* by traversing left from the easy start of *D1*.

Ferguson, Michael Covington, and Ken Duncan had all worked on the traverse, becoming the first of many climbers to be lost on it. Ken Duncan finally found the correct line, but a storm chased him off just above it. In the end, the remarkable new route allowed the Diamond to be climbed to Table Ledge with only one pitch harder than 5.8—assuming no routefinding errors were made.

Ferguson called the climb *The Integral,* since it combined several routes, or the *Old Man's Route,* which indulged his fondness for self-deprecation, but it would be known as the *Casual Route*, a name bestowed by Charlie Fowler.

In late summer, Fowler and Dan Stone stopped in at Komito's Boots in Estes Park. They had just made the third ascent of *The Path of Elders* on Chiefshead, a route still cloaked in mystery, so Ferguson and Reveley paused in their work to hear the tale. The cobblers shared a tale of their own, of the easy new Diamond route. "You know," Ferguson commented, "it would be a really secure thing to solo."

In 1978, with the hard-won first free ascent only three summers old, an unroped ascent of the Diamond was an outrageous idea. But Ferguson was speaking to

Climbers on the Casual Route *in the 1990s. They have completed the tricky traverse left from* D1 *and are now in the corners of Bob Boucher and Pat Ament's 1964 route* Grand Traverse. (Photo: Jeff Achey)

Charlie Fowler, who made the first unroped solo of the Diamond, on an early free ascent of D7, *1980* (Photo: Jeff Achey)

two climbers supremely qualified for such a venture: they would make the second and third ascents of Boulder's ultimate mind-control route, *Perilous Journey*. Fowler was particularly accomplished in soloing. The previous year he had shocked the climbing world by soloing the famed *Direct North Buttress* of Middle Cathedral, a 1,600-foot 5.10 climb, the most audacious free solo yet done in Yosemite.

Neither climber said much to Ferguson's remark. The next weekend, Stone had other plans. Late on Friday night, following a climbers' party in Eldorado Springs, Fowler drove to the Longs Peak trailhead. He caught a short nap, packed his climbing shoes, chalk bag, swami belt, camera, cagoule, headlamp, and a handful of nuts and slings for an emergency, and hiked in to the Diamond.

Clouds were already building when he reached Broadway at 6:00 A.M. He started up the Diamond anyway and soon reached the crucial traverse. Remembering Ferguson's advice, he stayed high, testing holds carefully as he went, and reached the *Grand Traverse* dihedral without incident.

From the security of a chimney he surveyed the terrain he had passed. Retreat across the maze-like face looked improbable. Above, the dihedral loomed steeply, but the cracks looked good. They were. Secure hand cracks and good footholds quickly took Fowler to the Yellow Wall Bivy Ledge.

Above lay the pitch Ferguson had called the crux. Fowler had climbed it only two weeks before with Stone, during an ascent of the *Yellow Wall*. He worked up the steep twin cracks to a small overhang with several fixed pins. At the crux moves, he clipped a long sling into one of the pins, moved past, then unclipped and continued easily to Table Ledge. It had been only an hour and a half since he left Broadway.

Fowler scrambled up over the top of the Diamond and back down to Chasm View. He found a sheltered spot where he could see his friends Steve Levin and Chip Chace, now halfway up *Yellow Wall*. He shouted and waved, and they waved back. Then he curled up for a well-earned nap.

When Fowler awoke he could just make out Levin and Chace reaching Table Ledge in the rain. They met up at Chasm View an hour later, and the storm had subsided to a drizzle. The three exchanged greetings and observations, looking out over the sweep of the Diamond.

Levin pointed to the *Grand Traverse* corners and asked if that was Ferguson and Reveley's new route. Fowler nodded. "Are you up here to climb it?" Levin asked. Charlie smiled and replied, "I just did."

20. Rockaneering

Eerie gully descents, belay ledges that fall off, river crossings, poison ivy in the jam cracks—such are the hazards and hardships that face Black Canyon climbers, interspersed with extremely difficult climbing. Leonard Coyne summarized it all well by calling it *rockaneering*.

To go along with this term was a catchy phrase coined by Dunn and Wiggins for the new Black Canyon free-climbing style of the 1970s and 1980s: "a rope, a rack, and the shirt on your back." Ironically, the first time this style was ever tried led to a full-blown epic—Dunn and Wiggins' ascent of the *Diagonal* route on North Chasm View Wall. It is telling of Black Canyon climbers that after this ordeal, the one-rope, no-bivy-gear approach caught on, instead of being discarded as madness.

The Arêtes of the Black Canyon of the Gunnison. The Russian Arête *(Layton Kor, Dick Dorworth, 1962) is the sun-shadow line in the right foreground.* The Hooker *(Michael Covington, Billy Westbay, 1974) is to the left, taking the crack and chimney system on the left edge of the smooth, sunlit slab.* Diagonal Will *(a.k.a.* Swallow Wall, *Kor, Wayne Goss, 1967) takes the obvious right-facing corner system on the large buttress left of* The Hooker. *The left-most formation on the escarpment is the Painted Wall.* (Photo: Jeff Achey)

From 1976—the year of *The Cruise*—through 1979, some of the Black Canyon's best routes were first climbed, or climbed free, including *The Journey Home* and the *Goss-Logan* route on North Chasm View, and *The Flakes* on South Chasm View. In addition, there was considerable rockaneering on the Arêtes downstream from SOB Gully. Most of the routes on these 1,500- to 2,000-foot buttresses had not been repeated since their first ascents. The section of canyon from the Arêtes to the Painted Wall became notorious for its huge pegmatite bands. Climbing across these crumbling pinkish swaths of rock could be horrifying, and they figured in many a gripping tale.

Two side-by-side buttresses—each with one unrepeated multiday route—featured some of the most daunting pegmatite bands in the Arêtes. Ed Webster and Bryan Becker set out to explore both over one remarkable weekend in May 1978.

The Hooker and Diagonal Will
The plan was to meet in the North Rim campground on Friday night, but by late evening Webster hadn't shown—his car had broken down near Blue Mesa Reservoir, an hour away, and he spent the night camped by the side of the road. At first light, Becker set out hitchhiking in search of Webster, who had begun hitchhiking toward Becker and the canyon. Webster flagged down Becker as he passed by in a hay truck. The pair headed back to the canyon together, managing to sweet-talk one driver into taking them all the way out to the North Rim campground, where they arrived at 10:00 A.M.

It was very late to begin a major climbing day, but they threw together their climbing gear and raced down the SOB Gully toward *The Hooker*, a Grade IV climb done by Michael Covington and Billy Westbay four years earlier—touted as "the last major unclimbed wall in the canyon."

The upper buttress looked reasonable. The lower wall sported one very broad pegmatite band that stretched across the steepest part of the wall. Sheer momentum kept Becker and Webster moving down the gully, along the river, up several hundred feet of scrambling, and on up through a 5.7 groove pitch to a small stance where the wall steepened. They roped up, and Webster took the first pitch, quickly finding 5.10 climbing. He turned a small roof and emerged onto the pegmatite band.

They had learned from Westbay that there was some sky-hooking on this pitch, and Webster carried a hook on his rack. He clipped a spinning quarter-inch bolt, climbed a little farther into the pink, flaky rock, and draped his sky hook on a flake. He weighting the hook with some carabiners to help it stay on its perch, and with this protection, scratched out several more hard moves.

Ed Webster on the first free ascent of The Hooker *in 1978* (Photo: Bryan Becker)

Webster's crux lead took them to a stance above the pegmatite band. Becker's pitch crossed a smaller and slightly less frightening band. On easier ground now, they moved left into a large chimney system that shot 600 feet straight to the rim. The chimney allowed much faster climbing, and they made it to the top and back to the campground before dark, elated with their unlikely success.

The next morning at first light, they dropped down the gully, passed beneath the previous day's climb, and scrambled on downstream. Three hundred yards later they stopped in their tracks.

Through poor record keeping and various misprints in climbing magazines, the climb that rose above them had become known as *Diagonal Will*, a catchy name it thus retained. It was quite a piece of stone. The main weakness on the buttress was a long, slightly diagonal corner system that shot up for approximately nine rope lengths, ending in a huge roof that hooked off to the right.

Layton Kor and Larry Dalke had climbed the buttress in 1967 and no one had set foot on it in the eleven years since. The route was long, steep, and extremely intimidating—a much more serious undertaking than *The Hooker*. "When we got to the bottom of *Diagonal Will* we were pretty terrified," Webster said. "It's a *huge* route—over twenty pitches, I think. We were both having serious butterflies."

The initial corners looked reasonable. A small roof two-thirds of the way up looked a little less reasonable, and the roof at the top of the corners looked huge. Above, the cracks seemed to continue a short distance before ending below a massive pegmatite headwall.

Becker and Webster began climbing, soon finding

some of the strangest rock in the canyon—much of it less than confidence inspiring. The seventh pitch was a rotten 5.8 squeeze chimney. It is unsettling to note that when Rob Slater climbed the route in the 1980s, he reported loose and desperate climbing here, but no chimney. The chimney had been formed by one side of a pillar, perhaps 100 feet tall. Apparently sometime in the early 1980s this pillar had simply fallen off.

The lower corners went fairly easily, and the pair gradually gained height on the wall. Webster led around the top roof with surprising ease. Soon they reached a small ledge below the big pegmatite band.

"It was probably about four in the afternoon at that point," Webster recounted in an interview. "You can always gauge how well you're doing in the Black by looking at the other side of the canyon and figuring out how far below the rim you are. I'm sitting on that little ledge—we're now in the shade, it's starting to get late—and looking at the other side of the canyon thinking, 'This is not looking good.'"

In fact, they had more than 700 feet still to go and just over two hours of daylight. When Becker arrived at Webster's belay, the memory of their *Cruise* bivouac two years earlier was already speaking to him. "He was really fired up," Webster said. "He had this incredible adrenaline going—'Hand me the rack. Put me on.'"

The pegmatite band was flaky and steep. Sharp-edged holds couldn't be trusted—they would peel off unexpectedly. Becker called upon his Garden of the Gods experience, smearing on down-sloping edges and spreading his weight out as evenly as possible. After a twenty- or thirty-foot runout, he'd put a sling over a horn or place a poor nut and keep going. It was uncertain where exactly to go. (Kor and Dalke had followed aid seams several hundred feet to the left). As Becker worked through the pegmatite, Webster snapped a picture that later appeared on the cover of *Climbing* magazine.

Finally, Becker reached a belay. "I followed it and I remember thinking it was one of the most outrageous pitches I'd ever done," Webster said. Above the pegmatite band, the climbing got suddenly easier. The next five pitches took just over an hour. They topped out at dusk, their coup accomplished—the second ascents, and first free ascents, of two major Black Canyon routes in a weekend.

Scenic Cruise

One spring evening in 1979, Leonard Coyne, Ken Simms, and Ed Webster lounged around a campfire at the North Rim preparing for a day in the Black Canyon. Coyne and Simms hoped to finish their big project: the first all-free route on the main face of North Chasm View. Webster was hoping to photograph the last few pitches, which included the off-width crack that Jim Dunn had climbed virtually unprotected on the first ascent of *Eighth Voyage of Sinbad*.

Two other climbers approached the fire, Glenn Randall and Joe Kaelin from Boulder. Boulder climbers rarely showed up in the Black in the late 1970s, but Randall, a journalism student at the University of Colorado, was an exception. He and Charlie Fowler made the third free ascent of *The Cruise*, and in a multiday ordeal had repeated Dunn and Wiggins' variation to the *Diagonal*. As talk turned to Webster's plans to photograph Coyne and Simms, Randall stepped forward and said, "Actually, I'd like to photograph them."

Webster hesitated. Coyne said, "Hey, you guys could

Bryan Becker on the crux lead of Diagonal Will *during the first free ascent in 1978* (Photo: Ed Webster)

Joe Kaelin on the first ascent of The Scenic Cruise *in 1979. The route quickly became the most popular in the Black Canyon.* (Photo: Ed Webster)

go try that little crack to the right of *The Cruise.*" Webster remembered seeing the crack from the Cruise Gully, and quickly relinquished his photographic duties. Kaelin, who had never climbed in the canyon, was game.

Kaelin and Webster headed down the gully together the next morning, as did Coyne and Simms. Randall stayed topside, readying his ropes and camera.

From Kaelin and Webster's vantage in the Cruise Gully, the line looked steep and smooth—and ended in the middle of nowhere. By now, Webster knew how Black Canyon climbs often managed to work themselves out, and they started up. They swapped leads up the first section of *The Cruise,* then branched right into the new crack. The climbing was excellent—never too hard, never too easy. A thin section would lead to perfect jams, or a face hold would appear just where needed. Webster called it "the most well-designed climbing you could dream up." After a few pitches, however, they needed to find a way back left onto *The Cruise.*

They paused about thirty feet below a small triangular roof, above which the crack thinned and died. Showing better intuition than many later parties, Webster scanned the wall to the left. There were seams and grooves that looked like they might offer passage—if he could reach them. Patting around with his hand, he found a small crack on the left wall, blindly placed a nut, then swung out onto the face. Protection was sparse, but Webster persevered and soon turned a corner and reached a ledge on the familiar ground of *The Cruise.*

Naming climbs was almost as important to Ed Webster as climbing them, and he was already scheming. "I felt kind of pressured," he said. "Like, man, we've got to think of a good name for this climb!" Superb rock and picturesque passages, close to its mother climb *The Cruise:* before Kaelin and Webster even reached the rim they had the name—*The Scenic Cruise.* And what of the partnership that began so promisingly on what would become the Black Canyon's most famous climb? "I have never, ever seen Joe Kaelin again," Webster said.

Air Voyage

Of the many superb Black Canyon free climbs that were done in the 1970s, one stands head and shoulders above all others in difficulty. Since the mid-1960s, Yosemite had set the standard for long, hard free climbs—the North Buttress of Middle Cathedral, the *Rostrum, Astroman*—and none of the Diamond or Black Canyon routes were quite as demanding. This would change in 1979, with the first all-free route on the main face of North Chasm View, the brainchild of Leonard Coyne.

As Webster and Kaelin pondered what to name their variation to *The Cruise,* Coyne and Simms were around the corner, working up the wide cracks of a climb called *Air City* on the main face of Chasm View. Near the top of the long corner system, Coyne laybacked up an overhanging six-inch crack to a ledge that would take him left toward *Eighth Voyage.*

This fantastically exposed pitch of free climbing was familiar ground for Coyne. The previous year, with Ed

Russell, he had been in the same place, finding the way barred by a huge, sickeningly loose flake. Coyne could neither avoid nor climb the precarious feature, and the ensuing 1,000-foot retreat consumed half their rack. They crawled out of the canyon in the dark, and Russell vowed never to return.

A few weeks after this retreat, Coyne took the shortest and most logical approach to the impasse: he shouldered a rope, strolled 100 yards from the North Rim campground to the rim, and rappelled down until he was level with the flake. Dangling in space, he threw his hammer behind the flake and reeled himself in. With a gentle tug, the massive rock broke loose. Coyne swung out as the rock catapulted from its perch. He watched it fall, eerily silent, and waited in anticipation. After a free fall of 1,000 feet, the flake smashed into the lower slabs with a silent puff of smoke. A second later came the sound, an explosion that echoed down past the Painted Wall.

The next morning, Coyne and Bryan Becker scrambled through the rock fragments to the base of the climb, spent most of the day climbing through the blistering heat, past the trundled flake, and collapsed in exhaustion on the ledge below the *Eighth Voyage* off-width. They had no energy to continue the free attempt. One long retreat had been enough for Coyne, however, and he had planned ahead. Ken Simms, waiting in support on the rim, tossed the team a rope, which they climbed on a pair of wooden ascending devices Coyne had whittled.

Coyne returned with Simms a week later. They rappelled to the ledge below the off-width and free climbed it, a serious wrestling match that even fresh off the rappel required all of Coyne's considerable strength and wide-crack skill. Number 4 Friends, the largest camming units made at the time, were too small; Coyne protected the pitch with tube chocks. Above the crux section of the crack the pair headed left, onto the face. Placing several bolts, they set up a belay and worked out a 5.11 traverse line that linked into easier exit cracks and the rim. The pitches were now all in place, and only a continuous ascent remained.

Coyne and Simms took a day off, hung out by the campfire with Webster, Kaelin, and Randall, and then while Webster and Kaelin were on the *Scenic Cruise*, linked together the hardest long free climb yet done in the country—the *Air Voyage*. The crux off-width, positioned atop more than 1,000 feet of steep and strenuous climbing, remains one of the most testing free pitches in Colorado, still rarely climbed without resort to direct aid.

The Nose of Chasm View
Despite the focus on free climbing, aid climbing had not gone completely out of fashion in the late 1970s. In fact, some of the country's most famous big-wall routes date from this time. In American wall climbing, all cliffs pale in comparison to the great south face of El Capitan in Yosemite, but Colorado has its own scaled-down version, the Black Canyon's North Chasm View Wall. By the mid-1970s, the face had some fairly demanding aid lines, and in 1977 it finally saw a direct ascent of its most-attempted feature, the Nose.

The Nose had been tried perhaps a dozen times since the late 1960s. The daunting atmosphere and logistics of

Leonard Coyne on the crux off-width crack of Air Voyage *during the first complete free ascent in 1979* (Photo: Glenn Randall)

North Chasm View Wall, showing the lines of Air Voyage *(left), and* The Nose *(Photo: Jeff Achey)*

Black Canyon climbing had stopped many early attempts, while the unexpected difficulty of the climbing had turned back the stronger parties.

In April 1976, Earl Wiggins, John Sherwood, and Jim Baird, on their first visit to the canyon, tried to improve upon the line pioneered by Goss and Logan in 1972, but failed. Early on, Baird was hit in the head by a small rock, and after every pitch he would appear at the belay bleeding alarmingly. The team pushed on, but after exploring the same dead-end that had stopped Goss and Logan, they too escaped right and finished on the Kor-Dalke *South Face*.

By spring 1977 Wiggins had more first-hand knowledge of the Nose line than any climber, and he was obsessed with it. The previous fall he had done the nearest flanking routes on the southwest face, the *Diagonal* and his own route *High and Dry*. He had made two abortive attempts to solo the Nose, and in April 1977, as he prepared for another solo effort, Bryan Becker offered to go along. Becker had spent the past summer in the Alps and the winter ice climbing back East. He was strong and fit, and Wiggins welcomed him on board.

It was to be a happy, if lopsided, team effort. A short way up the wall, Becker offered to let Wiggins lead, and he would belay and jumar in support.

Wiggins knew that the large *Goss-Logan* dihedral was a trap, but out left, near the prow of the Nose, were thinner features that appeared to lead higher on the face. There were blank spots, however, the first of which lay directly above their first bivouac terrace.

Wiggins led off left onto a smooth slab, immediately encountering A4 climbing. At one point he called for the drill, which was deeply buried in the haul bag. By the time Becker dug it out, Wiggins had made a tension traverse from a RURP and reached another crack. A bit of free climbing, a bolt, and another tension traverse led to a belay.

Above, the new line unfolded, thin but promising. They were now a few hundred feet left of the *Goss-Logan* dihedral, following discontinuous cracks and hanging corners. The eighth and ninth pitches were A4, with hooking, copperheading, and some dangerously detached flakes. The eleventh pitch went through a decomposed band. Sustained hooking on poor rock led to a tension traverse, then more A4. Becker took in the grand scene, dozing occasionally, as Wiggins worked slowly upward. "I remember a golden eagle flying by, coming really close to me and looking me over," Becker said. "I was wondering, 'God, do I look like a meal to him or something?'"

The weather was perfect. In the evenings they feasted on freeze-dried shrimp cocktail. On one hooking pitch, Wiggins took a short fall, awakening Becker. On the first night, Wiggins had unfurled a cushy, three-inch-thick foam pad, fully six feet long, "to pad the haul bag," he claimed. At night, of course, it padded his hammock.

High on the wall there was one frightening pitch through large, hanging blades of rock wedged together in an overhang. Breathing gently, Wiggins passed through by nutting on large hexes. Five days after leaving the ground they reached the top of the buttress a few feet from The Nose guardrail. *The Nose* was finally climbed—the most difficult and spectacular wall climb in Colorado.

Becker and the Dragon
Unlike North Chasm View, the Painted Wall did not sprout many new routes in the 1970s. In 1977, John Pearson, Jim Newberry, Tom Pulaski, and John Rosholt brought the total to three, adding *Journey Through Mirkwood*. This crew, based out of the Gunnison region to the south of the canyon, was involved in many Black

Canyon adventures in the late 1970s that became campfire legends. Pulaski and Pearson made the second ascent of Forrest and Walker's Painted Wall route, Pearson and Newberry established the beautiful *Goldberg Special* on South Chasm View, and Rosholt, a professional gambler, did a new Chasm View route appropriately called *The Plunge*, on which he took an eighty-foot fall that cut halfway through his rope.

After belaying Wiggins on *The Nose,* Becker wanted to strike out on his own. In October 1978, after a Black Canyon climb with Brian Teale, Becker hoisted a packed haul bag and said goodbye to his partner. Teale headed back to Colorado Springs. Becker headed down SOB Gully toward the Painted Wall. His plan was to make the Black Canyon's first major solo ascent, via the *Dragon Route,* one of the most feared climbs in the canyon.

Becker owed his enchantment with the *Dragon* to Dean Tschappat, who had finished the route's second ascent the same evening Becker and Webster had bivouacked on *The Cruise.* At camp, and later in Colorado Springs, Tschappat had beguiled Becker with tales of the *Dragon.* That winter, Becker had a girlfriend in Tucson. While visiting her in Arizona he met Scott Baxter, a member of the original *Dragon* ascent party, who further kindled his imagination.

Becker spent the chilly autumn night alone at the bottom of the canyon, and moved his gear up to the upper terrace the next day. With no distracting talk from a partner, Becker's senses were sharpened. The walls seemed to sparkle, the spray from the rapids stood out in relief. The poison ivy was vivid yellow.

On the terrace, Becker searched in vain for signs of the route. There were no visible cracks, either to start in or to head for. Finally he picked a lower-angled place and began free climbing. After a pitch of uncertain wandering he arrived at belay bolts, much relieved. He climbed another pitch, fixed the two ropes he carried, and spent the night on the terrace.

The next day's climbing was much steeper. Overhanging cracks and dihedrals that had been invisible from below formed the next half-dozen pitches, climbed mixed free and aid, with sections of loose blocks that had to be passed by careful stemming. Late in the afternoon Becker reached the big roof of Kor's Cave and bivouacked.

The next day, in the vague area that had turned back Kor, Becker lost the route. Poor cracks led everywhere and nowhere among streaks of pegmatite and sharp-edged blocks. Halfway through the lead, Becker found a tiny ledge and sat down. Since leaving the rim he had been pushing hard, always moving. He sat and watched the river for almost an hour. When he resumed climbing, the correct route fell into place. He spent a quiet night in his hammock.

A bit higher he began the Stygian Traverse he had heard about. Traverse pitches are particularly complicated for a solo climber, especially to follow and haul, and at one point Becker's haul bag swung roughly across the lead line. While following the pitch, Becker noticed a big white puff in the middle of his rope—a cut, of uncertain severity. He quickly clipped into a piton and unweighted the rope. A moment's thought made it clear that his options were limited.

Becker tested the damaged rope with a couple of stout jerks, then continued, moving quickly and smoothly until he could slide his jumar past the nasty cut. Becker had no spare rope. He tied off the cut and continued the climb.

Becker spent four nights on the wall. He got lost one last time near the Summit Crack, but only briefly. By then he felt completely in tune with the wall and the canyon. On top, he was quietly elated and at the same time sad that the great adventure was over. Late in the day, he hiked his load back to the campground. Jimmy Newberry and Jenny Goldberg were there to meet him with cold beer. As Becker raised a third toast, a bird landed on his shoulder.

Part Four

THE EIGHTIES: GYMNASTICS IN THE SKY

The early 1980s was a pivotal period in Colorado climbing. We would say now that an era was coming to an end, but this wasn't evident at the time. As always, there were controversies and wild new climbs, and all of these and none of these seemed significant.

Eras are the product of retrospect, invented by singling out certain events and ignoring others. Occasionally, however, something will define an era with particular clarity. For many climbers, one such "something" was the first edition of this book, which painted a vivid picture of 1970s Colorado climbing. How to describe it? Perhaps as a crystallized moment—a cool spring day in Eldorado Canyon in 1975, with two climbers dressed in painter's pants and rugby shirts with a rack of stoppers and hexes hiking up toward *The Naked Edge*.

Some version of that image was imprinted upon the collective consciousness of an entire generation, and it defined Colorado rock climbing. Its power drew young climbers to Colorado from all over the world, and the story of how that image passed into history begins here.

Opposite: *A new concept took hold in American rock climbing in the 1980s—the bolt-protected arête, symbol of the "line of strength." Christian Griffith on his 1987 route* Lakmé *in Eldorado Canyon.* (Photo: Charlie Fowler)

21. Winds of Change

The traditions of the 1970s were held so fiercely in Boulder that the catalyst for change had to come from outside. The key outsider was Alec Sharp, a British climber who moved to Boulder in 1977. Sharp came from Wales, where he had many first ascents to his credit. He had authored guidebooks to the famed Welsh crags of Gogarth and Clogwyn d'ur Arddu. Sharp's eye was tuned to British crags, dense with routes and variations. He saw unclimbed lines everywhere, and he was shocked at how little new-route activity was going on in the Boulder area.

There were several reasons for this lull. Since the late 1960s, Boulder free climbing had revolved around freeing old aid routes. On these well-traveled climbs, vegetation and loose rock had been removed, and fixed protection was likely in the blank sections. By 1979, however, most of the good aid lines had been free climbed and the remaining ones were very difficult or dangerous. The surge of new climbs of the early 1970s was slowing down.

Sharp, however, was used to dealing with lichen-covered rock and uncertain protection. In Britain, where the rock was sometimes completely overgrown, climbers routinely roped down new routes to clean cracks, brush lichen, and inspect holds or nut placements. These tactics were alien to Boulder climbers, but Sharp used them extensively.

Sharp set off on a new-route spree, beginning on the most densely climbed crag in Boulder Canyon, Castle Rock. Rappel inspection revealed thin protection cracks in a dihedral system that joined *Country Club Crack* near its final roof, and *Englishman's Home* was quickly dispatched. Barely twenty paces away, *Never a Dull Moment* was another route that Boulder climbers had ignored—in part because its main crack was choked with bushes. Sharp dropped a rope down, removed the bushes, and placed several bolts to protect a short approach pitch below the crack and another blank face on the third pitch. A few days of effort produced another fine new climb.

In Eldorado Canyon, rappel bolting would not have been tolerated, but then and now, Boulder Canyon climbing has operated at a much more lenient stylistic standard. In 1982, Sharp summarized his views in a news report for *Mountain* magazine: "New philosophies developed concerning how the routes could be legitimately protected, and in the absence of a general consensus, individuals carried a lot of responsibility in their decisions." In fact, Sharp stood alone in his willingness to take this responsibility—at first.

Sharp loved the smooth Boulder Canyon granite, so unlike the rock of Wales, and while the critics grumbled,

Alec Sharp on the first ascent of his Castle Rock route, Never a Dull Moment *in 1979* (Photo: Dan Hare)

he went climbing, putting up dozens of short routes. Sharp was skilled and bold, and his routes began to earn grudging respect. Among his climbs are Boulder Canyon classics, including *Grand Inquisitor* on Bell Buttress and *Divine Wind* on Blob Rock.

After getting a ground-floor job in a Boulder computer company, Sharp began compiling a computer list of the new climbs, and he occasionally printed out a small staple-bound "guidebook" from his database. This guide, which could always be found behind the counter at the Boulder Mountaineer, was anathema to many climbers to a degree that is hard to fathom today. Computers still seemed futuristic even in popular culture in 1979, and among most climbers they symbolized everything climbing was not. Nevertheless, "The List" had power. New-route fever broke out. Boulder Canyon saw a landslide of routes. They were mediocre, but significant: many were done by fairly average climbers, eroding the unspoken 1970s rule that unclimbed ground was reserved for the elite.

The New Eldorado
Eldorado was not immune to the changes taking place in Boulder Canyon. Numerous high-standard routes were done in early 1970s style—free ascents of *Night, Revelation, and Practice Climb #101*. Other routes tested the rules, including one on the Rincon Wall, climbed in 1979 by Ed Webster and Leonard Coyne, both Colorado Springs climbers, and Bill Feiges of Boulder.

Webster led, starting up a striking arête and arranging a few of the new Australian Pauligk nuts to protect the first hard moves. Balanced at a stance about twenty-five feet off the ground, he called for the drill. With some difficulty, he placed a bolt, then attached a sling, stood in it, and drilled another bolt. After a third bolt, he returned to his stance and free climbed on up the arête. Coyne and Feiges followed.

Aerospace was an exciting face climb, with challenging moves and dramatic position up the most compelling unclimbed feature on Rincon. Yet the style of the first ascent was considered deeply flawed. After Ferguson and Erickson's example on *Jules Verne*, Eldorado climbers had been strictly committed to a pure "clean climbing" ethic. Some writers would call it a style based on boldness, but to many climbers it was a style based on conforming to nature. Safe climbs were welcomed, but where cracks were absent, the challenge was to make do. Forcing the issue with hammers or drills not only sidestepped the challenge, but was considered disrespectful and destructive to the natural beauty of the rock.

Aesthetic concerns aside, there was the matter of how this practice might affect advancing standards. The moves on *Aerospace* were difficult, but not *that* difficult,

Derek Hersey on Night, *in Eldorado Canyon in 1989. Freed in 1980,* Night *was one of the last of the Eldorado aid routes to be free climbed in traditional 1970s style before the approach fell out of fashion. A devoted traditionalist, Hersey made the second through sixth free ascents.* (Photo: Steve Dieckhoff)

and the climb thus posed a fundamental question. Should such lines be left unbolted, to become the *Perilous Journeys* of the future, or was it better to bolt these into fun climbs that many could enjoy? Was climbing pure recreation, or a more serious quest? Could the two philosophies coexist?

Another issue that helped chip away at the hammerless ethic was the need to upgrade 1960s hardware, which was never designed to hold falls and was now becoming dangerously old. On *Genesis*, Jim Collins had replaced an old bolt with a stronger new one, and the same was done a few years later for the free ascents of the early Eldorado 5.12s such as *Apple Strudel* and *Salvation*. An extension of such "maintenance" was the addition of a bolt where none was originally used. "Retro-bolting" had tamed the aid climbing on some of the testpieces in the 1960s, including Turner's landmark A5, *Genesis*. The first aid climb bolted to protect a free ascent was *Fire and Ice,* in 1981.

Roger Briggs on his route Scary Canary *in 1980. This route, one of the most demanding in Eldorado at the time, was established on aid then quickly freed—early evidence of changing tactics in the canyon. (Photo: Glenn Randall)*

In 1980, Jim Erickson published a new Boulder guidebook, *Rocky Heights*, which had several interesting features. First, it omitted any route that used direct aid, rendering the book useless for the Jim Ericksons of the future looking for old aid climbs to free. More important, *Rocky Heights* introduced new symbols to identify poorly protected climbs—the now widespread R and X system, which Erickson lightheartedly borrowed from the motion-picture industry.

As early as the 1950s, Harvey T. Carter had objected to the Decimal System grades and their potential effect on American climbing. In the late 1970s there had been much discussion about introducing a rating system that would give proper standing to climbs such as *Jules Verne* and *Perilous Journey*, whose decimal grades were modest, but whose psychological challenge represented state-of-the-art climbing. There was some regional rivalry involved. As the Yosemite 5.12s multiplied, Boulder climbing needed something to show that it was indeed keeping pace. The R and X system, however, wasn't it. Catchy as it was, Erickson's system did not legitimize "mind control" routes. To some people, it merely labeled them as obscene.

Alec Sharp also left his mark in Eldorado Canyon, where he held to a different style than he used in Boulder Canyon. He placed no bolts, and his routes such as *The Human Factor* and *Ministry of Fear* rivaled the most serious climbs of Duncan Ferguson and David Breashears. Sharp did inspect most of his harder routes on rappel, but he might have been better off without this tactic. He would often spend a sleepless night obsessed with climbing his new line but trembling at the difficulties and lack of protection he had discovered.

On the Veil, high above Eldorado Canyon, Sharp established two of the most beautiful and heady face climbs in the Boulder area. The 5.10 route in the center of the slab, *Forever*, was led without pre-inspection, with only one piece of protection. To its left is perhaps Sharp's most daunting route in Boulder, *Way Honed and Gnarly* (5.11+). He inspected this sixty-foot line on rappel, and then led it with the protection of two sky hooks placed on small edges and duct-taped to the wall.

Climbing Like Mad

Other new climbers arrived in Boulder, among them Skip Guerin, from New Jersey, and Bob Horan, a young climber from Devil's Lake, Wisconsin. In 1981 this pair was sharing a four-room house on Ninth Street with a revolving list of other climbers and climbing like mad. The pair's earliest new routes were the short, steep, very difficult cracks that still remained in Eldorado—line such as *Blues Power, Crazy Fingers,* and *Silver Raven*.

Like most of the climbers who helped advance Boulder free-climbing standards in the 1980s, both Horan and Guerin were dedicated boulderers. Horan would prove to be a tireless explorer of the Front Range's boulders, authoring several bouldering guidebooks and hundreds of demanding problems. He also took up "bouldering out" some of Eldorado Canyon's shorter lead climbs, and was probably the first climber in Boulder to solo 5.12, with *Horangutan* on the Whale's Tail above the Eldorado pump house.

Guerin could be aloof and competitive, and he had a cutting sense of humor. One of his masterpieces was a grueling traverse of the Pebble Wall boulder on Flagstaff Mountain, which he named *Over Yourself*. He enjoyed asking his friends and rivals, "Did you get *Over Yourself* yet?" They hadn't. Another Guerin creation, unrecognized at the time, was a short Eldorado route called *Superfly*, probably the canyon's hardest pitch when he did it in 1983, still unrepeated in 2001, and possibly Boulder's first 5.13.

Guerin, Horan, and the Fort Collins climber Mark

describe its history than anyone in the country. His Colorado boulder problems are legion, but the best are perhaps *Germ Free Adolescence* in Eldorado Canyon and *The Ineditable* on Independence Pass near Aspen—the latter on the home turf of his editors at *Climbing* magazine, who loved to rewrite his prose but could not touch this problem.

Another remarkable Californian living in Boulder in the early 1980s was twenty-year-old Randy Leavitt, who had several unique skills. In California, on the concrete ceiling of an underground garage, he and Tony Yaniro had perfected a method for climbing overhanging wide cracks—called Leavittation—which took the discipline of off-width jamming to new levels of difficulty. Leavitt also had an uncanny willingness to take huge falls, calmly and in control, and he would later make BASE jumps of El Capitan and the Black Canyon's Painted Wall.

Leavitt's most distinctive Boulder route was *Limits of Power* on Blob Rock in Boulder Canyon. Climbed without bolts, this 5.12 route was protected by a complicated

Bob Horan unroped on his Whale's Tail climb Horangutan, *probably the first 5.12 in Colorado to be free soloed, in 1985. He is wearing an early pair of Spanish-made Fires, the first "sticky rubber" climbing shoes, which replaced EBs as the rock shoe of choice in about 1984. (Photo: Charlie Fowler)*

Skip Guerin, sans shoes, and Bob Horan on the thin 5.12 dihedral of Wendego *in 1984. This energetic pair nearly doubled the number of top-standard routes and boulder problems in the Boulder area in the mid-1980s. (Photo: Glenn Randall)*

Wilford were among the core residents of the Ninth Street house. Eventually, fearing for his health, Wilford moved back to Fort Collins, but not before the house gained a wild reputation and provided lodging to visitors such as Jerry Moffatt and Chris Gore, about whom more will be said shortly.

Some strong new climbers came from California, among them John Sherman and Harrison Decker, roommates at the University of Colorado. Over the next two decades, John "The Vermin" Sherman would write profusely for the climbing magazines, in a colorful, ribald style that earned him loyal fans, passionate critics, and nothing in between. Sherman was a pioneering boulderer at Hueco Tanks, Texas, and in his guidebook to the area he introduced the now-international V-scale for bouldering difficulty—a rating system he later disowned.

Sherman would do more to promote bouldering and

Randy Leavitt on his Boulder Canyon route Limits of Power *in 1983. Despite the complicated system of four ropes, Leavitt still took several thirty-foot falls while attempting the first ascent in 1981.* (Photo: Glenn Randall)

system of four ropes but still required Leavitt to take several thirty-foot falls off the crux to succeed. This was a new genre of challenge, requiring skill both on the rock and in the air. It might have caught on, had Leavitt stayed in Boulder, or had someone else shown an equal love of flying, but as it turned out, the route was one of a kind.

If *Limits of Power* epitomized Leavitt's aerial skills, *Animal Magnetism* proved his mastery of off-width cracks. At the now-closed Split Rocks area, between Boulder and Estes Park, Leavitt climbed what is probably the hardest off-width crack in the state, an appalling eighteen-foot roof problem. Sadly, this climb is now off limits, on strictly patrolled private property.

Leavitt would eventually return to California, where he went on to great deeds on El Capitan and at Joshua Tree and at Arizona's Virgin River Gorge, but he wasn't yet done in Colorado. More will be said of him later when the story turns to the new climbs afoot in the Black Canyon of the Gunnison.

The Natives

A new batch of climbers from the local high schools appeared on the Boulder scene in the early 1980s. At Boulder High, the ringleader was Eric Doub. Two years behind Doub was Christian Griffith, who followed Doub up *The Naked Edge* at age thirteen, as well as Dale Goddard. At Fairview High was another group of young climbers, foremost among them Eric Goukas.

Doub and Griffith put their names on the line in 1981, with a rappel-protected climb in Eldorado Canyon on the arête between *Vertigo* and *Super Slab*. The boys' style of ascent flew in the face of the old ethics, and their name for the route, the *Doub-Griffith,* was equal parts youthful brashness and sarcasm about the ethical debates of the day. The name was derived from the famously runout *Bachar-Yerian* in Tuolumne Meadows, California, a climb then recently completed by John Bachar and Dave Yerian. Though this route set a new standard for boldness, Bachar was getting some heat for bolting his route from hooks instead of free stances as was the traditional California style. Bachar defended his approach by appealing to mountaineering principles, and thus named the *Bachar-Yerian* in the eponymous style of the great alpine routes. Griffith, who had recently climbed with Bachar in Tuolumne, suggested that he and Doub name their defiant new Boulder route in the same style.

One of the important gathering spots for Boulder climbers in the early 1980s was the University of Colorado field house, where climbers often trained in the days before commercial and home climbing gyms. On a typical snowy winter evening, one group of climbers would be engrossed in a pull-up marathon, while others hung by fingertips from the metal beams. Others would traverse the brick stairwells, while others still would watch college women on the indoor track.

Invasion from Across the Atlantic

One October day in 1982, Christian Griffith ran into a scruffy-looking character in stained long johns bouldering on Flagstaff. The visitor looked like a good climber and Griffith, always outgoing, asked him what he had climbed. "I did *Psycho*," he replied in a thick British accent. "Oh, you tried *Psycho*?" replied Griffith, emphasizing the "tried." The route had gone unrepeated

Opposite: *Todd Skinner at the "pause" between cruxes on* Rainbow Wall. *Skinner was one of many wandering climbers lured to Eldorado by the new bolted routes of the late 1980s.* (Photo: Charlie Fowler)

since 1979, not for lack of attempts by the best climbers in Boulder. "No, I *did* it," replied the Brit matter-of-factly. The young climber's name was Jerry Moffatt, and a few days later he made a quick second ascent of *Genesis,* Boulder's hardest climb.

The reputation of *Genesis* had grown to massive proportions, and local climbers had been completely daunted by the route's aura of difficulty. Moffatt repeated *Psycho* and *Genesis* so easily that the psychological barrier was shattered. Skip Guerin quickly repeated *Genesis,* as did Moffatt's British partner Chris Gore. In a final *coup de grace,* Moffatt top-roped the climb in his running shoes.

The Brits' visit made it clear to local climbers that Boulder had fallen off the world pace, diluting its energy with stylistic squabbling. What was needed was less guilt and clinging to tradition, and more pure effort on the rock. This was obviously what was going on in Britain.

The goings-on across the Atlantic increasingly influenced ambitious Colorado climbers. In France, starting at the end of the 1970s, the traditional, alpine-based speed emphasis in rock climbing had given way to a new breed of rock gymnastics—steep, limestone face climbs, protected by bolts placed on rappel. Free-climbing standards were rising fast, and French names such as Tribout, Edlinger, and Le Menestrel would soon be known in faraway Colorado. In 1980 the 7c+ grade was opened in France—the equivalent of American 5.13a—and by 1982 Tony Yaniro's *Grand Illusion* and Steve Hong's *Sphinx Crack* were eclipsed by more difficult European climbs.

Rappel-bolted face climbing made its first big splash on the American scene in 1983 and 1984, when Alan Watts catapulted the backwater area of Smith Rock in central Oregon into an internationally known rock-climbing destination. By 1985, Smith Rock would be home to the climbs of the hour, blank faces and steep arêtes with names like *Last Waltz, Chain Reaction,* and *Latest Rage.*

These were the world climbing currents, and they would soon take over in Colorado. For now, they simply made climbers restless and hungry for gymnastic difficulty. Shameless hang-dogging and overt competition accompanied the next Boulder testpiece, a short aid climb called the *Rainbow Wall.*

Griffith first tried to free this short wall on Eldorado's Wind Tower in spring of 1984. After several days of effort he had managed to climb the two hardest sections but had not yet linked them. Griffith returned one day with Bob Horan, who soon began working on the route himself, over Griffith's protests. Griffith left for Yosemite, and Horan continued the effort, as did others.

Horan eventually linked the two crux sequences and latched a layback flake at the end of the main difficulties. Suddenly, both Horan and the flake flew off the wall. With the flake gone, the climb became significantly harder. More attempts ensued, with Horan and Harrison Decker now vying for the ascent. Horan finally prevailed. With a twenty-five-foot section of unrelenting, bouldering-style moves, *Rainbow Wall* was Boulder's first official 5.13.

Despite the popularity of Smith Rock and the trendy European limestone, Boulder held out against rappel bolting—but only with some ambiguity. *Psycho, Clever Lever, Genesis, Rainbow Wall*—each new "hardest" Eldorado free climb had been bolt protected. In a sense, Boulder was pretending: many climbers wanted to break from tradition and try harder, safer climbs, but no one wanted to take the rap for putting in the bolts. Whereas Boulder was at the international cutting edge in the mid-1970s, its technical standard was now embarrassingly low. In 1985, the visiting Frenchman Patrick Edlinger drove this point home when he climbed *Genesis* on-sight.

The New Wave

Dale Goddard was a Boulder native, but he began climbing at a high standard only after starting college in Colorado Springs and doing an exchange program in France in 1984. Goddard was scientific in his training and diet, and his build earned him nicknames such as Skeletor and the Stick Insect. Goddard's climbing philosophy was Darwinist. In an interview in *Climbing* magazine, December 1987, he said: "Any given set of ethics will prevail in a particular area as long as the sport can continue to develop. But when the ethic becomes an impediment to evolution, it will be dropped in favor of one that will allow growth."

Goddard would be best known for his climbing in areas outside Colorado, but he helped push Boulder standards with two important climbs in 1985—*The Evictor* on the face left of *Center Route* on the Rincon Wall, and *Space/Time Inversion,* on a Flatirons crag called the Backporch. Though extensively rehearsed and preprotected, both climbs were done without resorting to rappel-placed bolts.

Space/Time Inversion, an old Roger Briggs aid route, was one of the most impressive natural lines in Boulder, a razor-cut fist-to-finger crack through a huge overhang. After many tries, Goddard managed to free climb the route at mid 5.13. A patient, diligent, project free climber, Goddard poked fun at the time he put into the route by renaming it *The Five Year Plan.*

Goddard's climbs were mostly on out-of-the-way crags, but the climber who really yanked Boulder climbing into a new era preferred his climbs to be center stage. Christian Griffith was as passionate and flamboyant as Goddard was practical and analytic. He had grown up at the base of Flagstaff Mountain, and sustained his first bouldering injury at the age of four.

Dale Goddard on Space/Time Inversion *around the time of his free ascent in 1985. After a protracted effort, Goddard suceeded, renaming the route* The Five Year Plan. *It was the hardest free climb in Boulder at the time, and remains one of the state's hardest nonbolted routes.* (Photo: Dan Hare)

Griffith had his eyes opened when, on Jerry Moffatt's invitation, he made an extended trip to the U.K. in the fall of 1984. For several months he lived and trained with some of Britain's top climbers, and visited the Frankenjura in Germany with Ben Moon. There he met the German climber Wolfgang Güllich, who had just opened the 8b (5.13d) grade in Europe.

Güllich was a pioneer in training methods, and he showed Griffith a special apparatus he had assembled at a health club called Campus on the outskirts of Erlangen. It was a hanging wooden board with fingertip-width edges screwed on, ladder-like, and numbered both vertically and horizontally. While hanging by fingertips from the board, a climber could lunge from rung to rung, either straight up or diagonally. Güllich was fantastically strong on the board, sometimes moving from rung to rung with only two fingers. He had measured the vertical and horizontal distance between holds on his project climbs in the Frankenjura and could simulate the moves on his "Campus board." Griffith returned from Europe that winter a changed climber.

On a February day in 1985, Griffith returned to his old nemesis, *Rainbow Wall*. It felt so easy that he started

Eric Winkleman attempting Red Dihdedral *in 1984* (Photo: Jeff Achey)

laughing midway through and almost fell off. A short time later he repeated the climb, then rounded out his climbing day with ascents of *Genesis* and the *Psycho* roof.

Griffith had continued climbing with Eric Doub, whose aid-climbing skills would come in handy on their next project, the towering *Red Dihedral* on Mickey Mouse Wall. Two approach pitches led to the base of the main feature, a 100-foot double-overhanging dihedral with an A4 seam in the back.

On aid, Doub arranged protection from poor pins and thin wired nuts. Over the next few hours the pair convinced themselves that the protection would hold short falls, and eventually, with lots of nervous hanging on gear, they worked out a series of hard stemming sequences up the dihedral. They rappelled off for the day, and on the way down they passed very near *Perilous Journey,* David Breashears' famous unprotected face climb.

Griffith had attempted *Perilous Journey* before. While rappelling off *Red Dihedral,* he sighted the tiny ledge between the difficult lower wall and the final crux move on the slab. The discovery inspired him. Griffith figured that if he climbed to that point and chickened out, he could stand on the ledge for as long as it took for Doub to solo around and throw him a rope. A few minutes later Griffith made *Perilous Journey*'s fourth ascent.

Griffith and Doub soon returned to Mickey Mouse and managed to free climb the first pitch of *Red Dihedral* at 5.12+. An intimidating roof pitch remained, but Griffith had been assured that the pitch was easy 5.11. Unfortunately, the climber who volunteered this information had assessed the difficulty from the comfort of aid slings. It was now late afternoon. At the hanging belay, Griffith shouldered the tangled rack, not bothering to sort it, and headed out underneath the huge roof, hoping to quickly finish the climb before dusk.

With overhanging rock dropping away underfoot, Griffith realized quickly that his friend's assessment had been flawed. He clipped a fixed RURP, a pin, then an ancient bolt, and made increasingly strenuous moves out across the overhanging wall. Near the end of the roof, Griffith reached back to clip into an old bashie, but when he tried to clip in the rope, he discovered that he had accidentally clipped in a Friend instead of a quickdraw. Flaming out fast, he clipped the cam back on his rack, reached for a quickdraw, clipped, reached for the rope, and fell.

Twenty feet down he felt a light jerk. Twenty-five feet farther he bounced to a halt, dangling in space well below Doub. On the rope at his waist hung the old bolt, which had ripped out in the fall.

Griffith grabbed the lines hanging down from Doub and hand-over-handed to the belay. The first pitch had been desperate, and Griffith did not want to have to do

Chistian Griffith on his route Paris Girl *in June 1985. Perhaps no climb in Colorado has been the center of so much rhetoric and controversy. Ironically, of all the bolted Eldorado climbs of the contentious 1980s,* Paris Girl *is one of the most tactful.* (Photo: Charlie Fowler)

it again on another day. Gauging the amount of daylight remaining, he rested as long as he dared. Then, stripping down the rack to the bare essentials, he launched out on the traverse, gunned past the now-empty bolt hole, clipped the bashie on his way by, and turned the lip to easy ground. *Red Dihedral* was free.

Boulder's last great problems were falling fast to Griffith's technical prowess and European-trained fingers, but one free-climbing project repeatedly frustrated him—*Tourist Extravagance* on Castle Rock. The ordeal would make it clear to Griffith where the old ethic had taken climbers of the mid-1980s.

The sole obstacle of the climb was contained in the first fifteen feet—a glassy, water-polished, near-vertical slab originally passed with a few aid bolts. Almost every serious free climber in Boulder had tried the impossibly thin edging moves. Griffith joined their ranks, bloodying his fingers by popping off a few dozen times. He resorted to trick footwear. He found a pair of old super-stiff green Chouinard shoes at a garage sale and filed down one of them until it had a hard, precision edge that would perch on dime-thin holds. He used this shoe for the thin right-foot edges and a sticky-rubber Fire for smearing on the other foot. Still, Griffith popped off the moves.

Finally, after many attempts spread out over months, Griffith's foot stayed on its hold. He reached his victory stance, twenty feet off the ground. The crack above was much more fun, but it had already been climbed free years ago at 5.11+.

Griffith felt relieved—and foolish. So much time and work to follow the careless aid bolts of climbers past, just to reach a position where a picnicking tourist kid might pelt him with stones. "It was a horrible route," Griffith claimed. "Excruciatingly thin, painful moves protected by a bolt at your waist—it was kind of like the scraps that were left to us."

Griffith's early accomplishments were all but forgotten in the wake of his next Eldorado route, a one-pitch face climb on the west face of Redgarden Wall. Griffith rehearsed the line on top rope, bolted it on rappel, and then made the difficult and quite serious lead. These tactics were not unprecedented in Eldorado, but this was the first time they had been used to protect the entire length of a climb.

It was a route carefully conceived to be an overall test of rock mastery. The unprotected start gave a stiff opening challenging in the style of *Jules Verne* and was enough to turn back many. "For me that automatically made it OK," Griffith said. "If you got there you proved you were a good enough climber to have evolved to the next level." The "next level" meant using rappel-placed bolts. Four of these protected 5.12+ climbing; then easier rock and a ground-fall runout led to three more bolts through another 5.12 section. The finish involved a thrilling 5.10+ runout to the top.

Griffith named the climb after an image he had seen in a slide show given by Charlie Fowler, featuring a visit to Chamonix and subsequent tour of Paris. One slide that captured Griffith's imagination was of a striking thirteen-year-old girl sitting cross-legged, in roller skates, in front of the Eiffel Tower. The pout on her face was of a variety known only in France. Smitten, Griffith named his climb for her—*Paris Girl*.

The ascent of *Paris Girl* did not add bolts to an existing aid line, as other free climbs had. The route was very bold, and on rock that no one else had dreamed of climbing. Ironically, the route became a symbol of the new trend that was threatening the more traditional style. Soon, it would become a war zone.

22. Mountain Madness

The summer of 1980 was a fine season in the mountains. The weather was unusually stable, leaving the walls warm and dry. The Diamond was as impressive as ever, but it had lost its big-wall aura. One-day ascents were now the norm, and humping huge loads to Broadway and heavy hauling were things of the past.

The year saw the first all-free, one-day link-ups of

Climber in the Black Dagger *chimney on the Diamond. The* Black Dagger *was one of the many Yellow Wall climbs to be done free in the early 1980s.* (Photo: Jeff Achey)

the Diagonal Wall and the Diamond. From a camp at Mills Glacier, Leonard Coyne and Jeff Achey linked the *Gray Pillar* to the *Casual Route*, finishing at Table Ledge. Within a week, the ascent was eclipsed by Roger Briggs and Kim Carrigan, the latter a supremely talented and fit Australian who was making an extended visit in Boulder.

In a grueling day, round trip from Boulder, Briggs and Carrigan linked the *Directagonal* to the complete *Yellow Wall*. Briggs commented: "In the '60s, during the big-wall era, we thought of this as the first Grade VI in Colorado. I made various unsuccessful attempts in big-wall style, but the one-day free push made much more sense. The actual climb went pretty smoothly—of course, Kim was one of the best climbers in the world at the time. I remember we were on the climb from 6:00 A.M. to 6:00 P.M."

Another notable ascent on Longs Peak involved Carrigan's Australian traveling companion, Louise Shepherd, who teamed up with Jean Ruwitch of Boulder for the Diamond's first all-female free ascent, via the *Casual Route*. This was the same pair who, two years earlier with Beth Bennett, had made the first all-female ascent of *The Naked Edge*.

The *Diagonal Direct* was finally done all free in 1980, and the ascent party discovered that Mark Wilford and Pat Adams' impressive 1977 effort had come within ten feet of completing the crux climbing. On the hardest pitch, Charlie Fowler climbed up toward the old stopper from which Wilford had lowered. A fixed piece in this strenuous section was much welcomed, but when Fowler reached the nut he found it barely worth clipping. Fowler kept his cool, and a few more feet of slippery moves led to a stance above the hard climbing.

There had long been some confusion about the exact line taken by Layton Kor and Tex Bossier. The *Diagonal* cracks continue, faintly, all the way to Broadway, but this was not the original *Diagonal Direct* line. In the vicinity of the crux free climbing, Kor had followed an arch out right, reaching a dihedral that took a shorter course straight up to Broadway. The first free ascent party traversed the

Opposite: *Roger and Bill Briggs on the second free ascent of* Diagonal Direct, *in 1981* (Photo: Glenn Randall)

The east face of Longs Peak, showing the 1980 one-day link-ups (Photo: Bob Godfrey)

face above the arch and found the final pitch up the dihedral still full of old pitons—relics from Kor and Bossier's stormy epic in 1963.

Late in the season, *D1* got its second free ascent, this time finishing up the original thin crack that avoided the Westbay Crack. As Roger Briggs and Jeff Achey started up the approach pitches, they noted with some concern a huge icicle hanging from the exit chimneys. They would be safe once they reached the overhanging wall, but would first have to negotiate several pitches exposed to a potentially massive ice fall.

The ice remained in place as Briggs started up the crucial section. Preparing for a sprint, he swung out around the roof and onto the final slab, now directly in the line of fire. As if on cue, the icicle cut loose from the chimneys 600 feet above. Both climbers watched in horror as huge blades of ice windmilled through the air. They smashed into the slab fifty feet above Briggs, and a thousand pounds of ice splintered into fragments and cascaded down the wall. Miraculously, Briggs was unhurt. On the ledge below, Achey's chalk bag was filled with crushed ice. The rest of the ascent passed without incident.

Seven Arrows

It was an active season on Longs, but one of the best Rocky Mountain National Park climbs of 1980 took place in Glacier Gorge. Charlie Fowler worked for Fantasy Ridge that summer, as did John Harlin III, son of one of the most famous American alpinists of the 1960s, killed while climbing with Kor on the Eiger Direct in 1966, when John III was just a boy. The young Harlin now lived in Estes Park. A talented all-around climber, he guided, climbed, and made several notable extreme ski

Seven Arrows, the second route to be completed on the northwest face of Chiefshead and one of the finest in Rocky Mountain National Park (Photo: Steve Bartlett)

descents, but he is probably best known for his ambitious three-volume series *The Climber's Guide to North America* (Chockstone Press, Denver), a first of its kind, which came out in the late 1980s.

The northwest face of Chiefshead had been climbed only a handful of times by 1980, and only by its original route. The wall retained an intimidating aura. Harlin and Fowler had ample opportunity to study the face during their guiding outings, and on a cold day in June, they made their first attempt on a new line to the left of the *Path of Elders*, Kor and Culp's original line up the center of the northwest face.

Path of Elders had taken the only obvious weakness through the steep lower section of the face, a two-pitch dihedral. Harlin and Fowler began atop the highest alternative feature they could find, a flake that cleared the snowfield by only about twenty-five feet, leaving the steepest part of the wall to be climbed with few helpful features. Steep and devious climbing quickly ensued. The rock was ice cold, and the protection poor. Half a pitch up, when Harlin finally reached a place where he could place a solid piton, he lowered off and they quit the effort.

They returned on a much warmer July day and Harlin dispatched his pitch much more easily. Above lay a short corner, then a worrisome blank section, then another corner. By the end of the pitch the pattern would be set—follow a short dihedral, be grateful for any gear placement found there, then strike out across blank granite toward the next feature. When you get there, fully committed, you may or may not find more protection. Repeat until you reach anchors good enough for a belay—or until you run out of rope.

At about the halfway point, below a particularly long blank section, Harlin and Fowler discussed route options. Fowler thought the smooth slab directly above looked good. Harlin argued for moving to the left end of their ledge and taking a slightly less direct line. It was Harlin's lead and he took the left-hand choice. He was far out from protection when he ran out of rope. Fowler had to climb up thirty feet before Harlin found a belay stance, but they had made the right decision. The direct line would have required 100 feet of unprotected simul-climbing.

Ten hours after setting out they reached the slabs and boulder fields on top of the face. They had found 5.10 climbing on three of their pitches, nothing either of them considered extreme, but the journey into the unknown had been thrilling. At no point had success been assured, and one of the hardest leads was the last. After the third pitch, the thought of rappelling from their various equalized belay anchors was disconcerting. The simul-climbing pitch put an end to any thought of retreat. Their line was elegant and direct, and they had placed no bolts. In keeping with the Native American theme of the Glacier Gorge peaks, they named their route after the book *Seven Arrows*, by Hyemeyohsts Storm.

Risky Business
A few years later, Chiefshead would see another notable climb. In 1984, the summer after doing a solo winter link-up of the Diagonal and Diamond faces of Longs, Mark Wilford hiked in to Glacier Gorge to meet Jeff Lowe, who was then his boss at Lowe's Latok company in Lyons. Lowe arrived separately; he had dropped down over the ridge from Longs after climbing the Diamond with Duncan Ferguson earlier that day.

The northern aspect of Chiefshead forms a huge cirque, divided in the middle by the jutting spur of Spearhead. Chiefshead's so-called northwest face is on the west—the climber's right—while on the east sits the so-called northeast face. In fact, all three walls have approximately the same aspect, similar to that of the Diamond—north/northeast.

Chiefshead as viewed from Longs Peak, showing the northeast face. Risky Business *follows a line up to and through the right end of the prominent horizontal break.* (Photo: Jeff Achey)

For whatever reason, climbers had overlooked the northeast face. A short detour from the usual Spearhead approach provides an excellent vantage, and the tall, right-hand portion of the face reveals itself to be steeper and just as smooth as the more famous northwest face. When Wilford and Lowe started up in 1984, no new routes had been completed on the northeast face in the twenty-one years since Kor and Bob Bradley first climbed it.

The first three pitches went quickly and easily with a bit of 5.10. Lowe then worked up a long, tricky, and strenuous corner, with 5.11 climbing near the top. He tied off a knifeblade piton, and then continued thirty feet, passing several difficult moves. Lowe's progress slowed, and after over an hour he finally declined to push it further. He painstakingly down-climbed to his tied-off piton, lowered, and turned the lead over to Wilford. When he arrived at Lowe's high point, however, Wilford continued easily to the belay. Lowe had already climbed the worst section—both up and down.

The next pitch looked like an impasse: the dihedral they had aimed for was running with water. Wilford took the lead again, stepped neatly out onto the arête of the dihedral, and face climbed it at 5.10+.

A large horizontal break that marked the upper face proved to be a sloping ramp, with no easy exit to the top. The next pitch was the technical crux, strenuous but well protected. One more lead took them to the top.

At nine pitches and 5.11+, Lowe and Wilford's *Risky Business* was the most challenging climb in Rocky Mountain National Park outside the Longs Peak cirque. The route remained something of a mystery into the 1990s and would later be crossed by several new routes and variations, all employing considerably more fixed protection. The original line has been all but lost. A few years later, Chiefshead's northwest face, too, would be tamed, sprouting a bolt-protected climb, *Birds of Fire,* whose most significant effect was to install a quick rappel route down the length of the face, attainable from most of the northwest face routes. Times change, and the new routes are excellent, but the adventure and commitment of the early ascents of the Chiefshead routes *Path of Elders, Seven Arrows,* and *Risky Business,* can now be found only in imagination and history.

Road Warrior
Some of Colorado's 14,000-foot peaks are fairly remote and inaccessible. Mount Evans, the "fourteener" closest to Denver, is not one of them. It is a gentle peak with a paved auto road to its summit, visited by thousands of tourists on a typical summer weekend. Hidden along the summit road, however, is a deep cirque with a sheer face known as the Black Wall, home to a unique high-country climb.

Ken Trout was the first serious rock climber to examine the face, in the late 1970s, and he enlisted Mason Frichette for an attempt on the wall's most striking line. Frichette was an accomplished off-width climber, and Trout picked him with good reason.

The pair motored up the Mount Evans road, parked, and hiked down into a cirque below the 500-foot wall. Running nearly from top to bottom, eclipsing all other features on the face, was a single, wide crack. Their attempt ended forty feet up, when Frichette thought bet-

The Black Wall on Mount Evans. Road Warrior *follows the very obvious wide crack.* (Photo: Jeff Achey)

Jeff Lowe following the crux pitch of Road Warrior *during the first ascent in 1984* (Photo: Dan Hare)

ter of continuing unprotected with no break in sight for another 200 feet. The line would sit idle for years.

In 1984, Frichette was working for Lowe Alpine Systems and mentioned the Mount Evans line to Jeff Lowe. A few years earlier, LAS had started producing their line of Tri-Cams, the largest of which could provide excellent protection on seven-inch cracks such as the one on Evans. Lowe approached the wall with Dan Hare, but they had packed only one of the big Tri-Cams. It proved to be the only piece that fit the crack.

Hare took the lead, sliding along the Tri-Cam as he climbed. He was in constant fear of nudging the gangly nut out of the crack or fumbling it while moving it along. He imagined it rattling down the rope, leaving him stranded in the off-width. At the 150-foot mark, Hare found a few sketchy wired nut placements to back up the tipped-out Tri-Cam, convinced himself that he had an adequate belay, and brought Lowe up. Above, the crack continued even more fiercely, bulging past vertical, still seven to ten inches wide. They called off the attempt.

Trout soon got wind of Lowe and Hare's attempt. After years of disinterest, he immediately enlisted Bill Dob-

bins to try the crack. This pair drilled a bolt anchor at Hare and Lowe's high point, climbed another thirty feet to the base of an overhanging section of crack, and retreated.

Lowe and Hare returned with more off-width gear. They climbed back up and happily noted Trout's bolted belay anchor and his retreat gear in the crack above. Hare set off up the second pitch and was soon facing the bulging section. The next twenty feet were daunting, but features and face holds appeared inside the crack to ease the struggle. Above, the crack narrowed and entered a series of corners, and more conventional 5.10 climbing landed the pair on rolling tundra. They strolled back to their car, a mere fifteen minutes away, naming their unusual route *Road Warrior*.

That same summer, Trout claimed his consolation prize when he and Eric Winkleman climbed the thinner cracks to the left of the *Road Warrior* off-width—the popular *Good Evans*.

The King

For seven years after its free ascent, *D1* remained in a league of its own, steeper, more intimidating, and more committing than any other Diamond free route. By the mid-1980s the Yellow Wall shield—which was merely vertical—was laced with free routes, but the overhanging Right Side was like a different wall, off limits to free climbers. Here, Roger Briggs recounts the story of the Diamond's first free route to the right of *D1*, the *King of Swords*.

> *In the summer of '85 I was making a comeback into climbing after finally "retiring" from coaching. It was the very beginning of the sport-climbing boom and everyone was going for the big numbers. As always, that kind of climbing is not my cup of tea (because I'm no good at it, of course) but I still wanted to push some kind of standards.*

The Diamond, showing Eroica *(left) and* King of Swords (Photo: Jeff Achey)

Steve Levin on the crux pitch of King of Swords in 1993 (Photo: Kennan Harvey)

    After D1 was free climbed, it seemed like everything on the Diamond had been done and no one had any interest in climbing up there. But I had this hope of finding the "last great climb." Billy Westbay gave me a tip about Its Welx *that Hesse and McClure had passed along to him—that a lot of it would go free. So I grabbed Jim Logan, who was totally coming off the couch, and we went up to look at it.*

    We found a two-pitch alternative start to avoid a 200-foot overhanging A4 section, which put us at the base of what I came to call the Torture Chamber—an incredibly rotten, twenty-foot overhanging crack. I struggled up this, pulling out at least 100 pounds of crumbly, decomposed rock, until I could finally traverse left to avoid an overhanging off-width section that was just as rotten. I remember looking up and thinking, "That's about the most horrible looking nightmare I can imagine and no one would ever be able to climb it."

    Jim led the next pitch with a little aid through some wide cracks, then I tried the crux pitch. Instead of going straight up the smooth corner, I moved left to a parallel crack. I was out of gas and couldn't do one five-foot section, so we bailed—a major adventure in itself.

    Jim and I had made a very respectable on-sight attempt. I came back with Dan Stone later that summer and finished it. I can't remember who did the second ascent a couple years later . . . but Michael Gilbert did an early ascent with Alan Bradley. When he [Gilbert] got to the Torture Chamber he went straight up the off-width section. It really blew my mind when he told me that—he thought that's where the route was supposed to go. When he got to the crux pitch he looked straight up and thought, "That's totally a Roger stemming pitch," and climbed directly up the beautiful corner, thinking that was how I did it. That's how everyone does it now. The left-hand variation is still super good, but the Gilbert direct is brilliant.

Briggs' account highlights a few memorable passages without quite capturing the unrelenting nature of *King of Swords*. After five and a half pitches, most of them overhanging and 5.11, you reach Table Ledge—a horizontal crack not even warranting a belay station. On the Yellow Wall to the left, other parties can be seen easily traversing off at this level, but on the *King*, there is no escape. More 5.11 climbing lies above, and by this time the wall has long been in the shade and it is usually storming.

Eroica

Briggs spent the summer of 1986 exploring the Diamond for more free climbs, trying the *Enos Mills Wall, Dunn-Westbay,* and *Jack of Diamonds,* all to no avail. Near the end of the summer, with his brother Bill, he pushed a line partway up the smooth face between *The Casual Route* and *D1.*

Late in the day, after several unlikely 5.11 pitches, Roger placed a bolt at his high point, envisioning a runout up the blank face above. The brothers rapped off, and the next week the first snowstorms of autumn ended the 1986 Diamond season.

That winter, Briggs coauthored an article on Longs Peak free climbs for *Rock & Ice,* the new climbing magazine that had started up in Boulder in spring of 1984. His partner on this project was Eric Goukas, who had been a student of Briggs at Fairview High School. The pair planned to try Briggs' new line as soon as the Diamond came into season.

Goukas never made the attempt. In the late spring of 1987, he was killed in a fall in Yosemite Valley. Eric was a popular young figure in Boulder and his death was a blow to local climbers. In summer 1987, Briggs and Eric Doub—also a friend of Goukas—went up to finish the tribute climb.

Briggs succeeded in leading the runout (a later climber took a forty-foot fall here). Doub mastered a short 5.11 section, but cut the pitch short and belayed from an alcove. Above the cramped, semihanging belay, Briggs led the next section—the technical crux—falling on the hardest moves but continuing up the pitch. Two spectacular 5.11 pitches up the upper Diamond headwall right of *Yellow Wall* finished off the climb. With the questionable belay stance and Briggs' fall at the crux, the pair did not claim a free ascent. They did, however, declare the route a free climb, and they called it *Eroica*, their tribute to Eric Goukas.

Subsequent ascents continued to thwart an "official" first free ascent. Attempts to lead the crux in one long pitch in 1988 and 1989 both resulted in falls at the last move. On the Diamond, with its short windows of warmth and its exposure to storms, repeat attempts are rare. Most hard pitches are freed first try of the day, or not at all.

On the fourth ascent in the mid-1990s, Alan Lester made a no-falls lead of the route, belaying at the alcove as advised by his partner—Eric Doub. "I'm sure someone must have done it the right way by now," says Briggs.

The Super Direct

Though he had spent decades climbing all over the east face of Longs Peak, Roger Briggs had never climbed the *Diagonal Direct*. After the route's first free ascent in 1980, he held the opinion that the free climb had traversed off Kor's original line, which he believed continued up the faint diagonal cracks. He had not seen the telltale pitons in the final dihedral that testified to Kor and Bossier's epic. What he did see was the thin extension of the *Diagonal* crack running all the way to Broadway.

In July 1987, Briggs and Chip Chace began at the base of the *Diagonal* and in five hours free climbed the entire crack system bottom to top, including the upper section, which was previously unclimbed. This ascent added the final touch to the many free variations on the *Diagonal* line, and was done in peerless, almost effortless style.

The lower east face saw another notable ascent in 1987—*Question Mark Wall,* on the smooth face to the left of the *Diagonal*. This mixed free and aid climb was done without any attempt to push free-climbing standards and might seem like a throwback to old times. Indeed it was. The ascent party was Dan McGee and Layton Kor.

23. Back in the Black

In Yosemite, the 1970s was the era of the great "blank" El Capitan routes—*Zodiac, The Shield, Mescalito,* the *Pacific Ocean Wall*. A few Colorado climbers had sampled these climbs, and the experience was addictive. The only comparable piece of Colorado rock—steep and unbroken from base to summit, composed of features discernable only through spotting scopes—was in the Black Canyon of the Gunnison, the smooth expanse of the North Chasm View Wall to the left of *The Nose*. Several climbers had looked over this wall—Wiggins, Trout, others. In 1980 it would finally be climbed, amid a local media extravaganza.

In the same year, the Painted Wall pioneer Bill Forrest, with Bill March, completed a longstanding project climb at the east end of the Narrows, *Wild Bill's Wall,* which he called his hardest wall route ever. In 2001, it remains unrepeated. In general, however, the Black Canyon had become a hotbed of high-adventure free climbing, and the early 1980s saw the first free ascents of high-standard climbs both popular and horrific.

Canyon Climbers Conquer Perilous Route

In 1979, in Yosemite, Bryan Becker climbed *Mescalito* and Ed Webster did the *Pacific Ocean Wall*. In the fall of that year they set out to find a local version of these climbs on North Chasm View. Their first attempt was just before Thanksgiving, late for a Black Canyon climb, and the cold drove them off the wall at the beginning of the hard climbing, five pitches up the wall. They rappelled, leaving a large cache of gear at their high point, had a Thanksgiving feast with their friend Jim Newberry in Cimarron, and left the project until spring.

In April of 1980 Becker and Webster returned. They descended the Cruise Gully, turned the corner of the wall, and peered up toward their highpoint. At their cache, they saw an unfamiliar speck of color. "Did we leave anything orange?" Becker asked Webster. They hadn't. Two climbers were on the ledge with their cache.

Becker and Webster ascended rapidly toward the cache. When they arrived they found Ken Trout and Bruce Lella, two climbers they had never seen before. It was an awkward meeting. "We'd already split up your gear," offered Lella as an icebreaker. Soon, in an admirable display of diplomacy, the foursome joined forces.

The large features of the lower wall ended abruptly and the next pitch gave the team their first taste of Black Canyon hooking. Flakes were plentiful, but dangerously fragile. Becker finished the pitch with a long pendulum left to a remarkable ledge they would come to call Fantasy Island, the last ledge they would see for quite some time. They increased the living space considerably by erecting Becker's two-man Gramicci Cliff Dwelling, the first time a portaledge had been used on a Colorado wall. Above, the climbing became progressively thinner. Snow and rain continued intermittently for several days, slowing their progress. Fantasy Island became home.

The route began to show its true character: long blank sections crossed mostly by hooking, with the occasional copperhead and free-climbing move. Becker took the first A5 lead. He was short, about five-foot-seven, and in order to reach between rivets on El Cap he had become expert at stepping high in his aiders, a technique he used even on sketchy hooks. At 130 pounds, Becker could move over the most fragile flakes. Sometimes he would equalize several hooks before trusting his weight to them. As he progressed, the potential fall pushed into the hundred-foot realm. Occasionally a free move was required to span a gap between hooks, a free-and-aid combination Becker called "fraid climbing." The lead took him sixteen hours, spread over two days.

The team worked from fixed lines strung down to Fantasy Island. Progress was very slow, and a party atmosphere reigned at the ledge. Trout realized that they would not reach the top before a mandatory college exam he had coming up in Durango, and he decided to descend. As Trout began the rappels, Webster (playing off Chris Bonington's famous book *I Chose to Climb*) said, "When we write it up we'll tell people you chose to graduate."

Progress continued to be slow. Becker had already dropped out of college, but Webster also had school commitments. Not long after Trout left, the whole team bailed. On the drive out, they stopped at Newberry's Store in Cimarron, where they discovered that the local newspaper had been asking about the climb, which kindled some extra enthusiasm.

have been a great night for a party, but Webster and Lella had descended the fixed lines to retrieve gear at Fantasy Island, and a two-day storm pinned them there. During the storm, Becker led off on the wildest pitch yet, traversing underneath a large roof and turning the lip onto a steep headwall leading toward the Beak, a large landmark roof.

The Beak pitch was much steeper than those below; even staying low in his aiders, Becker found he could not help pulling out on the hooks, which were often placed on flat and slippery edges. After much fretting Becker finished the Beak lead, and the rest of the team reassembled on Happy Trails. As had become their habit, they tuned their transistor radio to the local station to hear a report on their progress. "The climbers are now approximately 300 feet from the top."

Becker had been averaging eight hours or more on his pitches. Now, eight days into the attempt, they were virtually out of food. The top was within reach and summit fever took hold. Webster took the next lead. He found better cracks, and promptly drilled a bolt ladder when these blanked out. Newberry led off on another steep aid pitch, and was soon out of earshot.

Newberry's progress became so slow that Lella started releading the pitch. It was getting late. Finally, a somewhat frazzled Newberry rappelled into sight, calling down that there was a rotten chimney above and that they wouldn't make the summit by dark. As he was delivering this disheartening news, the jumar he was using to back up his rappel jammed out of reach. At the end of his patience, Newberry thrashed in vain to free himself, then drew a knife to cut the sling. The others saw the blade, the tensioned rope, and the frenzied Newberry, and screamed at him until he put away the knife. Newberry finally managed to free himself and finish his descent.

Lella and Webster pushed for the top. Lella struggled up the rotten chimney, pummeling Webster with flakes and small rocks and running out of rope on a ledge just thirty feet from the top. Webster headed up.

When Webster reached the rim, he heard a strange roar. Across the canyon on the South Rim, a crowd was cheering. As he stood up, he was greeted by a Denver TV news crew. The other climbers arrived, one by one. Champagne was served, and interviews conducted. The next day, in huge type they had not used since World War II was declared, the *Montrose Daily News* ran the front-page headline: "Canyon Climbers Conquer Perilous Route."

The team called their route the *Hallucination Wall*, after the elusive nature of the features, but common usage soon changed the name to the equally appropriate *Hallucinogen Wall*. The route was given the impressive rating of VI, 5.11, A5. The 5.11, Becker confides, was a

Bryan Becker on the pendulum to Fantasy Island during the first ascent of the Hallucinogen Wall *in 1980* (Photo: Ed Webster)

After a day of rest the team returned, this time inviting Jim Newberry, who stocked them with supplies from his store.

The second A5 pitch had a short section of copperheading about twenty feet off the belay. Above that, Becker placed a bolt, and another one thirty feet higher. Otherwise, every other placement on the pitch was a hook.

An easier pitch took them through a hanging cactus garden to a small ledge they called Happy Trails. It would

Jim Newberry, Bruce Lella, and Bryan Becker after the Hallucinogen Wall *(Photo: Ed Webster)*

short section on pitch eight above their Fantasy Island camp that Ed Webster re-led on fixed copperhead protection, for the specific purpose of boosting the rating. All subsequent parties have aided this section. By the end of the century the route would gain a few bolts, settle down to a more modest modern rating of 5.10, A3+, and become the most popular multiday climb in the canyon, receiving a small handful of ascents in a typical year.

The Stratosfear

By 1980 only one major Black Canyon wall remained to be free climbed. It was a conspicuous exception, the same huge, shattered, pegmatite-streaked precipice that had resisted Layton Kor and others all through the 1960s: the Painted Wall. Bill Forrest and Kris Walker's original route had been repeated only twice. The most recent of these had been a fast ascent in June 1980 by Stan Mish and Dan Langmade, a motorcycle-riding pair also known as the Banditos, noted for wild ascents of remote desert spires and for the pin-ups from biker magazines they often left inside empty whiskey bottles on top. Mish and Langmade started up the Forrest-Walker with little more than a free-climbing rack, three quarts of water, and a few raw potatoes, and barely lived to tell the tale.

In the spring of 1981, Leonard Coyne made his first attempt on the same route. Coyne was never a recre-

Opposite: *An abandoned Fantasy Island camp at one-third height on North Chasm View, during a reprieve in the effort. This 1980 climb was the first use of portaledges in Colorado. Previous wall climbers used either hammocks or natural ledges for their bivouacs, greatly limiting the amount of time most were willing to spend on a wall.* (Photo: Ed Webster)

ational climber. He often claimed to hate rock climbing, but it provided an outlet for his lunatic energies. At the end of 1980 he was on a roll, with recent ascents of the first 5.12 in the Garden of the Gods, *Air Voyage* on North Chasm View, and the first Diagonal Wall/Diamond linkup on Longs Peak. He would soon focus the full force of his fanaticism on the Painted Wall.

Coyne recruited Randy Leavitt for the effort, and the pair brought to bear a combined wealth of Colorado and Yosemite climbing experience—as well as a taste for the outrageous. Kristian Woyna, with one arm in a cast, signed on to jumar behind Coyne and Leavitt and carry a small pack of supplies. The trio arrived at the rim at midnight and started down the gully at 2:00 A.M. On the climb, the three-man system proved too slow and cumbersome. A few pitches up, Woyna rappelled, taking most of the bivy gear.

Coyne and Leavitt were high on the wall by late afternoon. Twenty pitches up, Coyne scraped through a desperate and unprotected pegmatite pitch. At 6:00 P.M. it started to rain. As they hunkered down for a long and miserable night, they discovered that Leavitt's cagoule leaked and cowered together beneath Coyne's. "I was so screwed up I was convinced that if we rappelled down 150 feet, a cat in this 1950 swooped-back car would drive us along this little road right to the rim," Coyne said in Glenn Randall's book *Vertigo Games*. In the morning, they made a harrowing 2,000-foot rappel to the ground, but had the presence of mind to fix a twenty-foot length of knotted sling to protect the pegmatite death pitch. They hiked out of the canyon in their climbing shoes.

Their epic reconnaissance had convinced them that free climbing through the *Forrest-Walker* overhangs was not feasible, and on their next trip they hiked to the top of the Painted Wall and made a rappel inspection of their options. They discovered a continuous line of lower-angle rock, sandwiched between layers of massive overhangs, leading from below the overhangs on the *Forrest-Walker* route to the 5.10 exit cracks of the *Dragon Route*. They smashed a few copperheads into seams to help with the task of prying off dangerous loose blocks, and left the heads as landmarks. At one likely belay point, they drilled a quarter-inch bolt. The traverse was about as exposed as Colorado rock climbing could get, but it looked like reasonable climbing.

Coyne and Leavitt planned their attempt for the cooler days of fall and asked a couple of friends to hike out to the rim and act as support team. The pegmatite pitch, with its twenty-foot new sling, was Coyne's lead. When he arrived at the pegmatite, he found his sling blown by the wind and snagged on a rock spike, completely out of reach. He had to relead the pitch unprotected.

Once again, bad weather caught Coyne and Leavitt

Rob Slater on the second ascent of Stratosfear *in 1983. Slater, a go-for-broke Boulder climber, was probably best known for his Yosemite wall route* Wyoming Sheep Ranch. *(Photo: Randy Leavitt)*

near the beginning of the traverse, 250 feet below the top. Blowing rain made conditions too cold and wet to continue. After much yelling, they managed to communicate with their friends, who tied together two ropes and eventually succeeded in lowering one end to the climbers.

The line stretched as Leavitt lowered out. He bounced and spun in space, 2,000 feet above the river. The rescuers had been careful to protect the rope from the razor-sharp rock at cliff's edge, but just below the rim, the line ran over an edge that was invisible from above. As Leavitt jumared higher, he could see a fray in the line. "The rope's cutting!" he shouted. When he finally slid his jumar past the fray, he slumped into his harness, almost sick. The edge had lacerated the rope's sheath and cut several core strands. The rim team rearranged the rope and lowered a doubled length over the sharp section. They slid the jumars back down to Coyne, but they hung up partway down. Two hours later, Coyne slid his makeshift prusik slings over the rim.

The battered team made no further attempts that year, but in May of 1982 they were back. The lower climbing was familiar and they avoided countless small routefinding errors. On their previous attempt, they had pinned the sling in place at the pegmatite pitch, which they now passed in comfort. The traverse started well, and they felt a surge of confidence that the worst was behind them.

Soon the climbing became steeper. On rappel, among so many overhangs, they had misjudged the traverse as a ramp. Now the reality was apparent: the 200 feet of rock separating them from the *Dragon* chimneys was vertical, more difficult than anything below, and perhaps not even possible.

The twenty-fifth through twenty-seventh pitches were complex and scary. The first 5.11 section was protected by a copperhead, and a downward traverse led to unprotected 5.10 up a sharp arête. From their belay bolt, another section of 5.10 down climbing led to a 5.11 traverse. Finally they gained the exit cracks.

Several hundred feet of easier climbing followed, with a few overhanging fist cracks thrown in for good measure. Eighteen hours after starting up the wall, Coyne and Leavitt reached the rim. Leavitt proposed the name *Stratosfear,* for the exposure and the frightening climbing, and they called it a Grade VI. It would be Coyne's parting gesture in the state's climbing history, and it soon grew into the most feared free climb the state had ever seen. Leavitt would repeat the climb the next year with the adventurous Rob Slater, who was killed in a storm high on K2 in 1995. Shortly after their *Stratosfear* ascent, the pair also BASE jumped the Painted Wall.

By the early 1980s the main formations in the Black Canyon had been free climbed. As in the high country of Rocky Mountain National Park it was a time for filling in the blanks and climbing some of the neglected walls. In 1981 Jim Dunn and Leonard Coyne free climbed the original line of *Eighth Voyage of Sinbad,* climbing directly up to the grueling crux off-width of *Air Voyage.* Later, Dunn would make several free-climbing forays onto his other mid-1970s North Chasm View route, *Stoned Oven*, eventually whittling down the aid to just a few points. The all-free ascent, however, went to the Boulder climbers Mark Sonnenfeld and Eric Winkleman, in May 1985.

Ed Webster was a particularly active explorer, seeking out shorter or more moderate formations that had been neglected during the big-wall quests. One visit in October 1982 showed his typical level of enthusiasm. On three consecutive days, Webster and Chester Dreiman climbed three new routes—*Escape Artist, Checkerboard Wall*, and *Leisure Climb*.

Other Black Canyon adventures of the early 1980s were masterminded by Earl Wiggins. His exploits went

After a hiatus of twenty years, Layton Kor makes another Black Canyon first ascent, the Gothic Pillar, 1987 (Photo: Ed Webster)

largely unknown, but among the few, his legend grew. One particularly notable Wiggins tale dates from 1979. Webster had been delighted to tell his mentor Wiggins of his new route *The Scenic Cruise*. Good hand cracks avoided the off-width and thin stemming sections on *The Cruise,* Webster said. Wiggins' imagination had already been churning, and the slight advantages tipped the mental scales. In the fall of 1979 Wiggins descended the Cruise Gully wearing a pair of old Kronhoffer boots, carrying no rope, climbing equipment, or chalk bag. An hour and a half later he was back on the rim—by way of the *Scenic Cruise*. This ascent was the longest, hardest, and boldest free solo then done anywhere in the world.

In 1983, Wiggins teamed with Michael O'Donnell for another Black Canyon first—the ascents of two 1,600-foot Grade Vs, *The Cruise* and *Goss-Logan,* in a day. The next year he and Katy Cassidy added a new free climb called *Cheap Shot* on the *Hooker* buttress that, though little known, rivaled *Stratosfear* in seriousness. Soon af-

South Chasm View Wall as seen from the bottom of the Black Canyon. The Flakes *and* Astrodog *routes begin in the long, jagged flake system in the center of the photo.* (Photo: Jeff Achey)

Climbers on Comic Relief, *one of the popular shorter routes first done in the early 1980s* (Photo: Ed Webster)

who did it. In fall of 1987, a canyon pioneer made the first ascent of a striking buttress near *The Hooker* that he had long admired during the 1960s. After a hiatus of nearly twenty years, Layton Kor, now fifty, returned to the Black Canyon, and with Ed Webster climbed the *Gothic Pillar,* a fine mixed free and aid route done over two days. That summer, Kor had also done a major new route on Longs Peak, *Question Mark Wall,* up the slabs left of the *Diagonal.* After these impressive first ascents, Kor once again vanished from the Colorado climbing scene.

South Chasm View

The South Chasm View Wall is a shadowy cliff located directly across the Narrows from the North Rim campground. This huge face drops directly into the river, and steep slabs bar easy approach from the nearby gullies, necessitating frightening traverses above the river, which crashes down among house-size boulders.

A few early climbs had been done in the vicinity, including Kor and Bob LaGrange's first Black Canyon climb, in 1960, on a more easily accessible sector just downstream from the sheerest part of the cliff. The main face had been first climbed via a line known as the *Flakes* route. This compelling line, marked by a series of massive flakes, was done almost simultaneously by two parties, first as a multiday wall-style ascent by Ken Trout and Bob Sloezen in spring of 1977, and then again as a light-and-fast free

ter, Wiggins put his wall-climbing skills to work in Hollywood. He worked on numerous commercials and films, including Sylvester Stalone's *Cliffhanger,* and in 2001 was still running a thriving aerial rigging company.

One Black Canyon ascent of the mid-1980s stood out not so much for the difficulty of the climb, but for the party

Robert Warren and Peter Gallagher at the North Rim campground in 1983 (Photo: Earl Wiggins)

climb by Ed Webster and Steve Hong. The wall's most popular route, however, was not climbed until 1986. The line was the brainchild of Robert Warren, another alumni of Colorado College. Warren would rack up numerous high-standard first ascents in the Black Canyon, and the first was a line to the right of *The Flakes* on South Chasm View. His initial two attempts—with Mark Hesse and Chuck Grossman—were foiled by rain, and the high point was about 500 feet up the wall. For his third attempt, Warren recruited Peter Gallagher, then fresh from a month on the Ruth Glacier in Alaska.

On the day of the climb they met at the bottom of the canyon—on opposite sides of the river. Warren approached on the south side, while Gallagher descended the Cruise Gully. With a short rope toss they established a Tyrolean traverse line across the Gunnison River, ensuring a relatively safe and expedient escape back to North Chasm View camp should they need it.

The pair scrambled upward and as they neared the base of the climb they came upon the empty form of a dog. The top of his head and back were intact, while the lower body was missing. The poor beast had obviously made a miscalculation at the South Chasm View overlook 1,800 feet above, perhaps while chasing a chipmunk.

That evening found Warren, Gallagher, and two large rocks sharing a spacious ledge half-height on the wall—a perch the climbers named the Two-Boulder Bivy. The route above was clear: above camp lay a beautiful hand crack in a dihedral. The next day began with two superb 5.10 crack pitches, and their hopes for an all-free route soared. Partway through the next lead, Warren encountered leaning dihedral—a pitch that Ken Trout had nailed, at A4, on the first ascent of his version of the nearby *Flakes* route. "My heart sank," recounted Warren. "I called down to Peter that we had come to the end of the line and that he should send up the hammer and few pins we had."

Warren attempted to place one of their pitons but was unsuccessful. As a last ditch effort, he hung the heavy rack at his feet and moved up into the dihedral with just a few small nuts on his harness, hoping to free climb up to a nut placement he could use for aid. The climbing began to unfold in a series of stemming and chimney moves. There were almost no holds but every few feet he was able to place a small nut that inspired the next move. After twenty feet he was still free climbing, but his rack was now far out of reach. Another steep crack, nearly unprotected with his skeleton gear selection, led to a shal-

Tracy Martin and Jonathan Thesenga face the leaning dihedral on Astrodog (Photo: Jeff Achey)

low cave, where he wedged himself and belayed Gallagher. The rock above proved gently angled, and about 500 feet of easy climbing led to the top. In tribute to the hapless canine they had found near their rope-up point, Warren and Gallagher named their route *Astrodog*.

24. Trashy Little French Crags

In the mid-1980s, Boulder climbers were warring over the use of bolts to protect new free climbs. Colorado Springs experienced a completely different history. It was easy to bend early 1970s clean-climbing ethics in the Garden of the Gods—the area had no clean climbs. Bolting on first ascents was standard, and though a rappel-bolting controversy flared up in 1979, it was quickly resolved.

In 1981, an Eastern climber named Bob D'Antonio moved to Colorado Springs. High-strung and always keen for first ascents, he quickly became a well-known figure on the Colorado climbing scene. Over the next fifteen years D'Antonio would put up hundreds of new climbs, from the Garden of the Gods, to Aspen, to new crags yet unexplored. D'Antonio hailed originally from blue-collar Philadelphia, a child of the streets. He was hot-tempered, and on more than one occasion an argument over some climbing issue led to fisticuffs. On the other hand, D'Antonio was highly gregarious, befriending visiting climbers, local ranchers, and land managers alike. This quality would prove significant in early dealings with the Bureau of Land Management that determined the fate of what are now some of Colorado's most popular climbing areas.

D'Antonio and Mark Rolofson became the most active Garden climbers of the early 1980s. In 1983 alone they did dozens of new climbs. These included *Horribly Heinous*, the Garden's third 5.12; *Rocket Fuel* on the Drug Wall, an extreme 5.11 smearing problem that heralded a new arrival on the climbing scene—the original "sticky rubber" rock boots, Fires; and *Men at Work*, up the steep potholes near *Pete and Bob's,* a popular 5.11 that helped win acceptance for rappel-placed bolts.

Even with rappel bolting, Garden of the Gods climbing soon reached a plateau. The sandstone was simply too soft to allow more difficult routes. By 1984, D'Antonio and crew had begun to look elsewhere.

New local areas saw a surge of exploration, including Eleven-Mile Canyon, along the South Platte River just off Route 24 west of Woodland Park. The canyon had seen climbing since the 1950s, and there were many easy routes on its granite domes, as well as good camping and fishing. In 1979, Brian Teale had done a striking two-pitch dihedral that was Eleven-Mile's first 5.11. In 1982, Chris Peisker, the Australian who distributed RPs out of his home in Boulder, did an overhanging finger crack that was one of the harder climbs in the state at the time. In keeping with the backwoods nature of Eleven-Mile, these routes were known as the *Teale Route* and the *Peisker Crack,* respectively. Though not much to look at, the Eleven-Mile routes soon included some of the hardest in the Springs area.

Colorado Limestone

It was a spring morning like many others in the mid-1980s. Harvey T. Carter had left Aspen and was back in Colorado Springs, living beneath Pikes Peak, and he had convinced a dubious group of local climbers to accompany him on an outing to another one of his "new crags." Having been through this routine before, the enlisted climbers resigned themselves to a day of assaulting an obscure cliff that had been long ignored for good reason.

Their expectations did not rise as they entered Cañon City, a town distinguished by its looming state prison. Right-angle turns through rural neighborhoods followed. They left the town limits and drove ten miles out a winding dirt road before a collection of scruffy limestone

Shelf Road crags (Photo: Michael Kennedy)

outcrops finally came into view. They parked the car along Fremont County 9, also known as Shelf Road.

Carter, Tom Eisenman, Tom Austin, and Art Wiggins did a few mixed free and aid climbs that day. It was a pretty place, quiet and isolated, with red-tailed hawks soaring on thermals and a dry landscape of cactus and shrub stretching north toward the old mining town of Cripple Creek. There was limited enthusiasm for a return trip, but the group passed on word and other Springs climbers visited. Steve Cheyney brought various partners out to climb the crack lines at what came to be called Cactus Cliff. Peter Gallagher and Harvey Miller brought Maureen Gallagher (no relation to Peter) and Boulder climber Charlie Fowler to Cactus Cliff in 1985. Climbing from the ground up and drilling from hooks, this crew did Shelf Road's first bolted route, *Limestone Cowboy*.

Mike Johnson, a young climber who had visited Shelf Road with Cheyney, was the first to see the crags with a more modern eye. Limestone, after all, was the medium of all the hot new European climbs. Johnson enlisted Dale Goddard to help bolt a climb he had top-roped with Cheyney.

Goddard, in school at Colorado College, was only mildly impressed with Johnson's climb. He had recently returned from an exchange program in France, where he had seen really good limestone. At the time, he was spending most of his climbing time in Eleven-Mile Canyon with D'Antonio. After one of the trips to Eleven-Mile, however, Goddard took D'Antonio and Gene Smith on a detour to Shelf Road.

At the time, there were no significant limestone climbing areas in the United States. The rock at Shelf Road seemed marginal at best, but Goddard had noticed a section of gray limestone that reminded him of the rock he had seen in France. Goddard led the team up two routes on this section, *Line of Strength* and *Mannequin*, on a cliff that would soon be known as the Dark Side. The routes proved superb, better and longer than the Eleven-Mile fare, and the climbers planned to return.

By the fall of 1986, D'Antonio, Darryl Roth, Richard Aschert, and Dave Dangle were making regular trips to Shelf Road. Through the fall and winter they put up numerous rappel-bolted face routes on Cactus Cliff, with names to match their philosophy—*The New Ethics, The French Are Here*. One day they met a local rancher, George Robertson, a friendly, longtime resident. Roberton asked the climbers to stay off Cactus Cliff, which was on his land, but steered them toward the crags now known as the Bank, Sand Gulch, and the Gallery. More of today's classic climbs appeared—*Unusual Weather, Back to the Future, Taping Tendons*.

Word spread and the new-style climbing at Shelf

Chris Beh on Thunder Tactics *in 1987* (Photo: Michael Kennedy)

Road—safe, convenient, and difficult—gained a following. On weekends a dozen climbers might be found at the campsite above the Bank. One chilly morning, a large group including Colin Lantz and a few other Boulder climbers, D'Antonio and friends, and the *Climbing* magazine crew of Michael Kennedy, Mike Benge, and John Steiger were standing around a campfire. All were clad in the climbing attire of the day. At the crest of the hill appeared a rider, Robertson, clad in Carhartts, hat pulled low, herding cattle through the juniper and sage. He looked up and beheld the gaggle of a dozen climbers, their skinny legs psychedelic in a dozen neon hues of skin-tight Lycra. Robertson's expression told all.

In April 1987, Richard Aschert became the first Colorado climber to purchase a battery-powered hammer drill—a Bosch Bulldog. A bolt hole that had taken half an hour to drill by hand could now be bored in seconds. Aschert strung his rappel rope, armed the Bosch, and in a matter of minutes installed the first power-drilled climb in Colorado, *Welcome to the Machine,* a five-bolt 5.11 on the shady side of the Bank. D'Antonio immediately ordered his own Bulldog.

Until that point, drilling had been a lot of work, so bolts were placed sparingly and many of the original Shelf Road routes had thought-provoking runouts. Once power drilling arrived, bolts could be quickly installed en masse, leading to a new quandary—the cost of hardware. As the number of bolts swelled to hundreds, cheesy homemade hangers graced many early climbs.

By that fall, some of Shelf Road's most popular climbs had gone up: *Surreal Estate* and *Sparkle in the Rain,* by Roth, D'Antonio, and Bob Murray; *Heavy Weather* and *Thunder Tactics,* by D'Antonio and Roth. The University Wall—on private land and now closed—was a favorite, with routes such as the early classic *Le Pumping Bull,* and Roth's *Critical Mass,* one of the area's first claimed 5.13s, done in August 1987.

Regular news dispatches went out, and in December 1987, *Climbing* magazine ran a flashy article titled "Surreal Estate," by Roth, whose story began:

> *The grinding whir of the drill spun to silence. In seconds the last bolt was tapped in. After lowering to trade the Bosch for the sharp end and tighter lacing, the slightly built climber danced up to the third bolt, struggling to failure just above, and sagging onto the rope. "Merde," he uttered in a thick American accent. Frustrated, he hung, mentally rehearsing the sequence—stuff two fingers in the pocket high left, clip right, crank like a mutant ape to the sleazy layback, step high into the finger pocket, set, dyno for . . . But his image blurred. "How would Le Menestrel do it?"*

The answer, of course, was the French way, with a minimum of sweat and fuss, with elegance and an eye to convenient, civilized climbing. Shelf Road was the first sport-bolted limestone area in the country, and there was no end to the comparisons with France, whose limestone routes were the talk of the climbing world. Roth continued:

> *In a tempest of energy that began in late 1986, a small, obsessed core of Colorado Springs locals are creating a tidal wave of very difficult routes and transforming the area into Colorado's Euroclone. . . . Eurotactics are applied exclusively at Shelf Road; cleaning on rappel, bolting with Bosch power drills, marking key holds with chalk, smoothing down razor-sharp edges, and hang-dogging are all considered appropriate.*

The Francophilia was a bit much for many Colorado climbers, and the whole enterprise seemed a bit immoral. Some referred to Shelf Road and other early bolted cliffs as "trashy little French crags."

Los Hermanos de la Penitente

Extending for more than 120 miles from southern Colorado across the New Mexican border to the hills above Taos, the San Luis Valley is one of the largest high-mountain valleys in the world. On the east lie the Sangre de Cristos, a long knife edge of high peaks including nine over 14,000 feet, some of which, such as Crestone Needle, have attracted rock climbers since Albert Ellingwood's day. On the west, the La Garita foothills rise more serenely, gradually gaining height and also reaching 14,000 feet as the San Juan Mountains. The huge aquifer beneath the valley floor feeds the headwaters of the Rio Grande.

Footage for the old TV show *The Big Valley* was shot here, and the show *Bonanza* took its name from the old mining town at the valley's north end. The valley also contains the oldest European settlement in Colorado, the eighteenth-century Spanish mission site of San Luis, and the region has an unmistakable New Mexican feel. With its artesian springs and flocks of exotic migrating waterbirds, the massive Great Sand Dunes, and sparse, strongly Hispanic population, it is an enchanted landscape.

There are a few conspicuous volcanic fins and plugs in the valley itself, but nothing to tempt the climber. Hidden in the hills, however, are deposits of a welded volcanic ash called Fish Canyon Tuff, similar to that of the famous Smith Rock climbing area in Oregon. Some of the tuff canyons were visited by members of a Catholic sect called the Penitentes, whose painful rituals including cross dragging and self-flagellation. Odd relics of their activities remain, most conspicuously a painting of the Virgin on a rock wall in what has become known as Penitente Canyon.

In the 1970s, a happy-go-lucky group of climbers including Peter Karasz resided in the San Luis Valley, based out of the Balloon Ranch near the tiny town of La Garita. "Their efforts," wrote Lew Hoffman in *Climbing* magazine in February 1985, "if not always consistent and sustained, were most often colorful, replete with tales of disintegrating belay ledges and top-rope rescues."

The early 1980s climbing scene in San Luis was equally relaxed. Hoffman was a dedicated boulderer, and also did many short, roped climbs with friends including Jim Dinapoli, a doctor in the nearby town of South Fork. Their climbs were scattered—some in today's popular San Luis canyons, others on obscure rocks such as Collier Crag west of South Fork.

In late spring of 1984, on a bouldering visit to the Garden of the Gods, Hoffman met the ever-gregarious Bob D'Antonio, whom he invited to sample the unknown climbing of San Luis Valley. A few days later, D'Antonio showed up at the Balloon Ranch.

Unlike Penitente Canyon, many of San Luis's cliffs had quite a few crack lines. Strange coincidence led to one of Hoffman and D'Antonio's first climbs. They were discussing Hoffman's meager collection of gear. Hoffman owned only one camming device, he said, which he had found on a roadside climb in the Needles of South Dakota. D'Antonio recalled that he had left a Friend—*that* Friend—on that very climb. Hoffman related that the cam now hung at the high point of one of his crack projects on the La Garita Creek Wall. Later that day, D'Antonio made the first ascent of the crack, recovering his long-lost Friend.

D'Antonio spent most of June in San Luis, with Bob Murray and visiting Australian Kevin Lindorff as well as the small local crew. San Luis climbing entered modern times. *Feet Don't Fail Me Now* in the canyon called the Rock Garden was San Luis's first 5.11, and *SST,* an elegant thin crack not far from the lost Friend on the La Garita Creek Wall, became the area's first 5.12. All of these were crack climbs. The changes in climbing style that were soon to come in San Luis would doom these fine lines to obscurity.

With the intensity of sleepy San Luis climbing now bumped up to an unprecedented level, the local climber Jim Dinapoli jumped in and added many hard cracks of his own, including *Who Dunnit Crack* in the Rock Garden, and *True Penitence,* one of the first lines in Penitente Canyon proper. (Modern climbers will recognize this as the crack next to *Jabba the Hut.*) Another classic from the summer of 1984 was Lindorff's *California Crack* in the Rock Garden, one of the last of the obvious unclimbed jam cracks. Thinner seams were soon climbed, such as *When the Whip Comes Down,* an RP-protected 5.11+ in Penitente, done by D'Antonio in September of 1984.

With the Colorado Springs crew's climbing in the nearby Shelf Road region now entering the picture, bolted climbing made its way to San Luis. One of the first routes to break away from the cracks was D'Antonio and Richard Aschert's *Come a Time,* a 5.12 arête in the Rock Garden, done in October 1985. By now, D'Antonio, Aschert, and other Colorado Springs activists were splitting their time between San Luis, Eleven-Mile Canyon, and Shelf Road.

Top Shelf

Standards rose quickly at Shelf Road. One of the climbers responsible was Colin Lantz. Originally from the Philadelphia suburbs and later to be owner and manager of the climbing shoe company Sportiva USA, in 1987 Lantz was living without heat or running water in a converted chicken coop outside of Eldorado Springs. While his wife Cathy worked through grad school in physical chemistry, Lantz picked up carpentry work and climbed.

The Gym, near Cactus Cliff, had about ten existing lines when Lantz began work on one of Shelf Road's best climbs. Appalled by the homemade angle-iron hangers on the neighboring routes, Lantz equipped his line with fashionable new Metolius stainless-steel bolts. Hoping that others would follow suit and use better-quality hardware, Lantz named his route long before he was able to climb it—*The Example*.

After ten trips, Lantz still could not link the moves. Like many of the top Boulder climbers, Lantz was active in the budding competition-climbing circuit and had been invited to a competition in Snowbird, Utah, in June. This was a big event that was drawing the top European climbers, and in May, Lantz got wind that the French team had arrived in Colorado for a bit of climbing before the competition. In fact, the next weekend they were planning a visit to Shelf Road.

Lantz panicked. Among the French entourage was J. B. Tribout, one of the best climbers in the world, who was famous for snagging the pet projects of weak Americans. By now Lantz was on day thirteen of his project at the Gym and the route was thrashing him. A friend chided, "Jibé is coming and he's gonna flash your route, dude!"

With the French arrival imminent, Lantz enlisted Chip Ruckgaber, cut a day at his construction job, and headed for Shelf Road for one last try. In an inspired, all-out effort, Lantz linked his moves on the tiny edges and one-finger pockets, and succeeded on his route.

The Example was Shelf's hardest route. Later ascents would find a variation that drifted a bit right at the crux, shaving off a letter grade from its original 5.13b/c, but the route remains among the area's most prestigious. Tribout did eventually climb the route, though not in 1988. On another visit in 1995, the Frenchman walked up to the

Gym, tied in at the base of *The Example*, and flashed it.

By the end of 1988, most of the Shelf Road rock had been explored and climbed. In 1990, Mark Van Horn published a guidebook. The hardcore elite drifted on, but others arrived to take their place. Shelf Road soon became one of Colorado's most popular rock climbing areas, the first truly European-style limestone crag in the country. Climbers befriended the local Bureau of Land Management officials, and the area soon had trails and campgrounds designed specifically for climbers—another first in the state.

Penitente Comes of Age

By 1987 the crack lines of San Luis had all been climbed—most of them never to be climbed again. In May of 1987, with bolting already in full swing, D'Antonio and Aschert climbed a feature they had admired ever since they first walked into Penitente Canyon. Though at mid-5.12 it did not set a new standard of difficulty, this stunning arête has been called the most beautiful sport pitch in Colorado.

The story of the climb began the previous February, with an alarm call from Lew Hoffman. "Hey, man, you gotta get down here and do that route. Somebody put a bolt in it!" This was troubling news. D'Antonio and friends considered Penitente Canyon their private climbing area. Boulder climbers had already taken over Shelf Road, and D'Antonio was worried that they would start showing up in Penitente.

Wasting no time, D'Antonio enlisted Dave Dangle. They drove from Colorado Springs to the canyon, mired their car in the mud on the final dirt road, hiked through the snow, and reached the base of the arête. It was untouched. At a certain time of day, sunlight hits a small mineral deposit on the wall, making a reflection—the "bolt."

Greatly relieved, the pair managed a climb or two in the Rock Garden, where conditions were less wintry. On the drive home, in a snowstorm, they went into a spin and flew off the road. They escaped unharmed, but D'Antonio likes to claim that he almost died for his route.

In May, when the weather improved, D'Antonio and Aschert returned for the arête. They followed a now-familiar procedure: they hiked to the top, put in anchors, strung a rope, tried the moves on top rope, and dotted the route with chalk smudges to mark the bolt placements. Then they put in the bolts and began trying to lead the pitch. The next day, climbing yo-yo style, they succeeded, naming the route after a song off their favor-

Opposite: *Wolfgang Schweiger on Colin Lantz's 1992 route* The Example, *still one of Shelf Road's best and hardest. Note the exemplary bolts.* (Photo: Beth Wald)

Bob D'Antonio on the first ascent of Bullet the Blue Sky *in Penitente Canyon, 1987* (Photo: D'Antonio collection)

ite U2 album, *Bullet the Blue Sky*.

Penitente Canyon saw some early tentative experiments in hold manufacturing, a tactic that had made a clandestine appearance with the advent of rappel bolt-

Sue Wint on Los Hermanos de la Weenie Way, *one of the excellent, popular climbs established by Kevin McLaughlin and Glen Schuler in the late 1980s* (Photo: Charlie Fowler)

ing and power drills. In 1987, D'Antonio claimed the San Luis Valley's first 5.13, *Virgin No More,* on the steep face next to the Virgin painting. Shortly after this ascent, some of the holds on the upper crux were "improved" by another climber, reducing the difficulty. *Cassandra,* another early Penitente 5.13, had been doctored by a visiting climber before its first ascent by Christian Griffith in 1988. Dan Michael of Boulder—little brother of the legendary boulderer Jim Michael—drilled finger pockets for his 1989 Rock Garden climb *Just Do It.* Hold chipping was generally shunned, but it had become widespread in France, where many up-and-coming American climbers took their inspiration.

Michael was also responsible for two of Penitente's hardest and most beautiful lines, *Color of Emotion,* a vertical face sparsely dotted with pockets, done in 1988, and *Sitting in Limbo,* a striking vertical seam that, at 5.13b, remains the area's hardest route.

In the mid-1980s, Penitente Canyon was considered a hotbed of high-standard climbing. Along with Shelf Road, the area introduced a new all-bolt-protected way to climb rock. So different was the experience that it earned a new name: "sport climbing"—a European term coined to differentiate the safe and sane activity from more serious and risky alpine climbing. Today, Penitente is one of the state's most historic and user-friendly "sport crags," known more for its enjoyable routes than its desperate ones. Many of the popular moderate climbs were first done by D'Antonio and crew, and for climbs such as *Brown Sugar, Forbidden Fruits, Love Snake,* and *Rocket Man,* climbers can thank another prolific pair, Kevin McLaughlin from Alamosa and Glenn Schuler from Colorado Springs.

25. Bolt-er, Colorado

Shelf Road and Penitente became extremely popular climbing areas, and won acceptance for sport climbing in Colorado. The atmosphere at the crags was one of positive energy and fun. In Boulder, at the same time, a truly vicious bolt war was heating up.

The years 1986 and 1987 saw the first ascents of some of Boulder's best extreme free climbs, but it was a time tainted with hard feelings. The Boulder climbing scene was so big that it had long ago split into subgroups. Few friendships were at stake to help with the diplomacy.

Christian Griffith was the leading advocate of the new style. Though Griffith's climbs, for the most part, were very tactful examples of rappel bolting, his personality and presentation were inflammatory. In the spring of 1986, someone crowbarred out the bolts on *Paris Girl*. Griffith was climbing at Smith Rock at the time and replaced the bolts as soon as he returned. During the ride home, he had scribbled a draft of an article titled "Manifesto," which appeared in *Climbing* magazine in October 1986.

In the form of a parable, Griffith presented his basic convictions—and a call to arms. The narrative device was a gnarled old man handing his manifesto to a dubious young climber, who reads the old man's words:

> *Like a bull crashing from the hands of its tormentors through the walls of the arena, a new generation shakes its horns and parts the crowd. They are free. They are the new power that will decide what direction climbing should go. . . . This revolution is spurred by a rebirth of responsibility. Its ideas are not new, but reflect those primary to every stage in climbing's development. What is possible? What can be braved? How can new heights be reached and old barriers dissolved?*

The manifesto continues:

> *What petty waste of time the old pursuit of "What's hardest?" and the begged questions of "Who's best?" These are crippling, insignificant questions! . . . Respect for the past should be measured by respect for the future. Where there is none, neither should respect or mercy be! To hold proud the heritage which gives*

Christian Griffith on his 1987 route Lakmé, *originally thought to be Eldorado's first 5.14* (Photo: Dan Hare)

footing is important, but where the intent is to trip, vengeance must be felt! . . . Climbing needs no shaggy watchdogs, whose low growl disguises their worn teeth, teeth worn through snapping in their own selfish interests. Let the tyrants burn, the climbing dynamic must live!

The furor that arose over rappel bolting—in Colorado and elsewhere—would be hard to overstate. Talk among climbers was divisive as never before. Fistfights broke out in Yosemite. Across the country, climbing communities were in civil war. Words and threats flew, but bolted climbs kept going up, at an accelerating pace. In 1986 alone, more bolts were drilled in Eldorado Canyon than in its entire previous history.

Controversy aside, many of the new climbs were remarkable, produced by a small group of talented climbers including Mark Sonnenfeld and Dan Michael. Unlike modern sport climbs, many were positioned high above the ground—a second pitch to *Genesis,* a variation to the fourth pitch of *The Naked Edge.* Griffith produced a steady stream of climbs, the most famous of which was center stage in Eldorado Canyon, spanning the overhanging wall of the *C'est la Vie* dihedral.

Griffith bolted his new line in 1986, first on lead from hooks, then finishing on rappel. The subsequent effort to free climb the route was impressive but personal: uninteresting to describe, composed of many visits, flashes of explosive movement, minor experiments and discoveries, construction of muscle memory, and subtle shifts of mind leading from hope to determination and eventually to success. The climbing was like bouldering at its best, with iron-cross moves, heel-hooking, and wild dynamics. When complete, *Desdichado* proved to be exactly what Griffith had sought. At 5.13c, or French 8a+, it was Boulder's hardest free climb. Better yet, it was the antithesis of *Tourist Extravagance*—not the stale leftovers of a past ethic, but something altogether new, fantastic and powerful, in a commanding position in Eldorado Canyon.

The name derives from Sir Walter Scott's nineteenth-century novel *Ivanhoe,* which Griffith thought reflected his role in Boulder climbing. In Scott's novel, the son of a Saxon nobleman is renounced by his family as he rides off to fight for Richard the Lionhearted. The son later returns incognito, dressed as a black knight, and finds that the Normans have subjugated his people. A jousting match is in progress. The mysterious black knight makes a late, surprise entry, defeats the arrogant Normans, and then rides away. His shield bears an emblem of an uprooted oak, and below, the Spanish word *desdichado,* "the disinherited."

The Wild Brit

At this time there were few signs that old-school Eldorado climbing was progressing. Mark Wilford established several fierce climbs, including the 5.12+ "X" route *Spinal Tap,* but these were on more obscure Front Range crags, and easily overlooked. One outstanding exception in Eldorado was the 1987 route *To RP or Not to Be,* a wildly unprotected journey up the wall to the right of *Vertigo* that remains mysterious and feared, more a myth than a

Christian Griffith on Desdichado, Eldorado Canyon's hardest free climb in 1986 (Photo: Charlie Fowler)

Mark Wilford on an early attempt on his route Spinal Tap *in Big Thompson Canyon, one of the fiercest of the non-bolted Front Range climbs of the late 1980s. Note the protection from anchor-shaped Crack 'N' Ups, period-piece devices designed to fit cracks too thin and intermittent for the smallest wired nuts.* (Photo: Steve Mammen/Mark Wilford collection)

milestone. It was the work of a British climber named Derek Hersey.

If few new climbs of the late 1980s upheld the time-honored Eldorado tradition of calm and control in the face of great danger, this one climber did. Hersey arrived in Boulder in 1983 from England, and almost immediately began climbing the classic hard routes of the 1970s—unroped. He did a scattered collection of new free climbs, but he was known less for these than for his constant, outrageous free soloing. Fun-loving, outgoing, and a friend to expert and beginner climbers alike, Hersey made an impression on everyone he met. He had countless friends, including Annie Whitehouse, who wrote the following brief profile for this book.

Derek was different. The lively, proud expatriate from Manchester was ragged and disheveled, full of jocular banter. He started climbing in the Peak District of northern England, where many gutsy gritstone climbers are born. After years of climbing and living on the dole, he moved to Boulder and his notoriety grew considerably.

According to Chris Archer, a gregarious local climber, when Hersey arrived in Boulder in 1983, he was "a wild, unkempt Brit, who looked like D'Artagnan after a particularly hard sword fight with the Queen's men. Shirt ripped, pants torn, but with a quick smile and incredible good nature." Archer recalls Derek falling repeatedly on a 5.10 crack on Practice Rock in Boulder Canyon, and then shortly thereafter on-sight free soloing two much harder routes: the Northwest Corner of the Bastille *and the* Diving Board *on Redgarden Wall.*

Derek continued to up the ante in his free soloing. In July 1989 he started up the Yellow Wall *on the Diamond of Longs Peak. Finding the fourth pitch running with water, he moved over to the* Forrest Finish, *which he had never climbed, and followed that to*

Derek Hersey, the wild Brit (Photo: Pat Ament)

Table Ledge. Then he down-climbed the Casual Route. He completed his "Triple Crown" with an on-sight ascent of Pervertical Sanctuary. Hersey recalled the day as "really on high gear . . . a meeting of mind and body. Very satisfying, high adrenaline, very simple." He was fueled by three Fig Newtons and a Snowball.

Soon after, Hersey free soloed The Scenic Cruise, Journey Home, and Leisure Climb in the Black Canyon—4,000 feet of climbing and three long gully descents in three and a half hours. The day's efforts, said Hersey, left him "buzzed and in need of plenty of beer."

Just as impressive was Derek's daily fare at "The Office," a.k.a Eldorado Canyon. Notations in Derek's guidebook reveal his voracious appetite for soloing: Jules Verne—solo; Naked Edge—solo; Le Toit—solo; Northcutt Variation to the first pitch of the Bastille—solo; Sidewall—solo; Boomerang—solo.

Steve "Crusher" Bartlett, Derek's roommate at the infamous "British Embassy" on Spruce Street in Boulder, says Derek "was a walking, and definitely talking, encyclopedia of Eldorado Canyon. He had incredible drive and an uncanny memory for climbs." Derek once told Crusher, offhandedly, that he'd soloed Outer Space probably one hundred times.

Derek had strong opinions about training, diet, and climbing style. "Training?" he'd say, "I stay away from that. . . . We lift pints at Old Chicago." He'd insist "vegetables make you soft in the head." He disdainfully called vitamin supplements "horse pills."

Hersey continued his soliloquy: "The '90s word is 'working.' Work the route, work the moves.' Naaa, I think to enjoy climbing is to be nearly at your limit, but not over it. That's why I don't hangdog and stuff. Because for me it's over the limit, out-of-context. . . . And also, I'm kind of lazy. Mention work, and I run away."

Few climbers anywhere have ever soloed as close to their leading level as Derek did. Hersey stated, "Ya, I'm soloing 5.11c and me leading limit is like 12a/b on-sight. Ya, I'm very comfortable in me mind, I guess. Very comfortable and I know when to back off. I can down-climb most 5.11s."

When pressed about his motivation, Derek was forthright:

"Soloing is a very selfish way of climbing, but I enjoy it meself. One of the reasons I want to solo is because I want to do it by meself. Not to be antisocial, but I just love climbing by meself. I know me talents and me skills, and all the experience to boot. I never take it for granted. That would be dangerous for a soloist. I got a very good temperament and you have to have a little bit of ego to go with it, for sure. You have to have that drive. Soloing's definitely kind of an ego thing. But you're the one at the steering wheel who races around the track."

Derek was full of contradictions. He had amazing tenacity and strength despite binge drinking and a woeful diet. Although social and gregarious, he thrived on climbing alone. He loved to travel, but never learned to drive a car. He often talked about his mum and dad in Manchester, but only went back to visit once in ten years.

Hersey's diary affords a glimpse into one of his days:

"Had a great night and a bad morning. What shall I do today? The art of great thinking is not dead, yet. I know . . . I'll go to the office, a.k.a. Eldorado Canyon. No punters to go with, all at work, or saving

Derek Hersey unroped on the fifth pitch of The Naked Edge *(Photo: Derek Hersey collection)*

Hersey on one of his many hair-raising adventures, the first free solo ascent of Prayer Book *in the South Platte* (Photo: Steve Dieckhoff)

themselves for the (rock) gym. Might as well go with myself and Bag of Courage (chalkbag). Off I toddle down the road to hitchhike and look who's picked me up. Dale Goddard and Chris Hill. Must stop at the store for a cup of tea and a hot dog. Are you O.K., Dale, you look white! Dale and Chris went to Massiff Wall (The Web). So I thought, I'll free solo Le Toit. Seems like a good sketch. Kind of pokey 5.11a moves. This took me up to the start of The Naked Edge. Well, I am here. I'll do this 5.11, 5.10, 5.8, 5.11, 5.11 and come down via Blackwalk to my two Twinkies left at my sack. The Edge was only twenty-five minutes. I thought I was doing well. Had my Twinkies and proceeded up to Rincon. Free soloed Climb of the Century and Center Route. Then, it was back to Boulder for a chicken curry and Toothsheaf Stout."

Some of Derek's other frightening free solos were the Crack of Fear *on* Lumpy Ridge, Prayer Book *in the South Platte, and* Quarter of a Man *in Indian Creek, Utah, all on-sight. After falling numerous times from the famous* Butterballs *in Yosemite, Derek free soloed it a few days later.*

On May 28, 1993, in Yosemite Valley, odd mists began to swirl, followed by roiling gusts and sprinkles of rain. The next day, when Derek had not returned from his attempt to free solo the Steck-Salathé *on Sentinel Rock, friends found his body below the face. No one will ever know exactly what happened. Derek died a soloist's death.*

Derek Hersey beginning his "Triple Crown" Diamond solo in 1990. (Photo: Steve Bartlett)

There are other things that we will never know about Derek. What drove him to free solo thousands of rock climbs so very near his limit? How did he compute the risk/reward ratio for soloing? And from where did he summon the courage?

Hundreds attended Derek's memorial service in Eldorado Canyon. Testimonials poured from damp-eyed mountain men and women. For days after news of Derek's death reached Boulder, Liquor Mart (which Derek had dubbed "The Shrine") was sold out of Derek's beloved Toothsheaf Stout.

The Great Debate
In December 1986, the American Alpine Club held its annual meeting in Denver. Traditionally, the New York-based AAC had been of little interest to rock climbers, and vice versa. In the 1950s, the club completely ignored the "non-summit" routes that were going up in Yosemite and the Tetons, and on into the 1980s, archaic bylaws still barred admission even to many accomplished experts. The organization was perceived as more of an aristocratic old-boys club than a vehicle for active rock climbers.

In the mid-1980s, the club decided to do something to change its suffering image—and boost its membership. Jim McCarthy was elected president. McCarthy had rock-climbing roots. He was a pioneering Gunks climber of the early 1960s, author of classic new routes on the north and west faces of Devil's Tower, and compatriot of Layton Kor on the first ascent of North Chasm View in the Black Canyon. Under McCarthy's leadership, the club reached out to rock climbers, and one of its early moves was an attempt to provide some badly needed arbitration in the "bolt wars" that were ripping apart the country's climbing community. The main event of the American Alpine Club's 1986 annual meeting was the so-called "Great Debate," to argue the pros and cons of rappel-bolted climbing.

The country's top rock climbers were invited for a panel discussion. It was an all-star cast—Randy Vogel, Ron Kauk, Lynn Hill, and John Bachar from California; the vagabonds Henry Barber and Todd Skinner; Rob Robinson from the Southeast; Christian Griffith from Colorado; and Alan Watts from Oregon. The meeting's guest of honor was Layton Kor, and John Gill gave the keynote address. It was a spectacular event.

The "debate," held in front of an audience of several

Panelists for the American Alpine Club's Great Debate in Denver, 1986. From left to right: Henry Barber, Rob Robinson, Randy Vogel, Ron Kauk, Lynn Hill, John Bachar, Todd Skinner, Christian Griffith, Alan Watts. (Photo: Michael Kennedy)

hundred well-dressed club members and guests, was more of a polite presentation of opposing views. The dignified setting of the meeting resulted in an admirable level of decorum from even the most hotheaded panel members. Griffith, at the last minute, even slipped a pair of pants over the Lycra tights he had planned to wear on the panel. (He did wear them for his slide presentation.) Nothing, of course, was actually resolved.

The rappel-bolting issue was debated ad nauseum in dozens of climbing communities, at parties, in mountain shops, at the crags themselves. Boulder held its own meeting in March 1987, convened at the auditorium of Fairview High School, where Roger Briggs was a teacher. This was well attended, but almost completely without result.

American crag climbing was headed in a new direction. Earth-tone cotton had given way to neon Lycra tights as the uniform of the new elite. European terms appeared: *monodoight, a vue,* sport climbing, and redpoint. Climbs of 5.13 became commonplace. American rock would no longer be epitomized by the delicate runouts of Eldorado and clean cracks of Yosemite, but by new venues—the vertical faces and arêtes of Smith Rock, and swathes of overhanging limestone. By the 1990s, few road-tripping visitors would even visit Boulder, bound instead for Colorado areas yet untouched and unknown.

26. The Busy Years

So many new rock climbs were done in the late 1980s that a detailed history becomes impossible. The attempt would be doomed to failure, and success would be doomed to tedium. Dozens of skilled climbers will be necessarily slighted in the remaining sections of this book. In a way, this is fitting. In the 1970s, doing hard new routes automatically gave a climber considerable status. By the 1980s, this was a thing of the past. There were hundreds of climbers across the state doing the same thing.

The character of Colorado rock climbing was shifting. The sense of endless possibility of the 1970s was gone, and a rat-race ethic was creeping in. Whenever a new area was found, there was a scramble for first ascents. Standards were very high. Many skilled climbers had swept through the various areas, and the unclimbed lines were either extremely difficult "last great problems," or located on obscure and overlooked crags.

The South Platte
One relatively untapped area of the early 1980s was the South Platte. While elsewhere the pace was slowing, in the Platte it was picking up. In 1985, the area was threatened by a vast dam proposal called Two Forks that would have flooded the valleys below Cynical Pinnacle and dozens of other rocks, but the dam was narrowly defeated, largely through the efforts of flyfishing lobby groups. The Platte was then appreciated even more.

In June 1981, Mark Rolofson brought the British climber John Allen to Turkey Rock, resulting in that area's hardest crack climbs. Near *Journey to Ixtlan* was a project known as *Goomba Turkey,* a fingertip crack splitting a roof and continuing up an overhanging dihedral. After considerable effort, the lithe Brit succeeded, at 5.12c, calling the route *Beauty and the Beast.* Allen and Rolofson also climbed the biggest roof crack in the area, on the backside of Turkey Rock proper—*Sheer Shark Attack,* an easier 5.12.

Perhaps the nicest Platte crack climb of 1981 split the steep wall a few feet right of Ellingwood's 1920s route on the Bishop—Chip Chace and Charlie Fowler's *Craftwork*. On the flipside of this rock was an even more impressive thin crack, tried several times in the early 1980s, most notably in 1984 by Mark Wilford. Photos of this attempt had appeared in the climbing magazines, spreading interest in the amazing crack and giving it an aura of great difficulty, since it was known that Wilford had not succeeded.

The circumstances of Wilford's "failure" were unusual. Jeff Lowe, Wilford's boss, had needed an advertisement photo for his new Tri-Cams. Lowe enlisted Wilford and Steve Mammen to climb the most photogenic crack he knew of.

Lowe set up for photographs and sent the pair up the crack with a rack of tiny Tri-Cams. The nuts were tricky to place, and a bunch of wired stoppers and Friends would have been pretty handy. Wilford made an impressive effort, jamming up the strenuous crack and wiggling in Tri-Cams while hanging from finger locks. Eventually

Mark Wilford and Steve Mammen attempting the Bishop Crack, *1984. Note the rack of Tri-Cams.* (Photo: Jeff Lowe)

Ken Trout, South Platte climbing pioneer, in Yosemite in 1977 (Photo: Ken Trout collection)

the crack thinned and the difficulties kicked in for real. Wilford was exhausted, Lowe had his photos, and the team pulled their ropes and left.

In 1985, Christian Griffith and Henry Lester approached the crack. Griffith went up with a skeleton rack, not expecting to get far. Much to his surprise, he climbed well into the upper difficulties, quickly running out of gear. Inspired, Griffith lowered off, assembled an adequate rack, and fired through the thin finger jamming on his next try. The *Bishop Crack* (5.12b) was not the hardest pitch in the Platte, but it was one of the most beautiful. To make a first free ascent of that prominence and quality in 1985 was nothing less than a gift from the rock gods.

The South Platte domes are a wonderland for slab climbing, and most of their classic routes date from the 1980s. The best-known route of the area was *Topographical Oceans*, which branched off from Duncan Ferguson and Jim Walsh's *Bishop Jaggers* to climb the smooth upper slabs to the right. This 1982 ascent was the best-known of the routes done by Peter Hubbel, who would go on to author several guidebooks to the Platte, the 1988 edition of which lists over two hundred of his first ascents. The hardest early 1980s slab pitch followed the direct line of final bolt ladder on the *Prayer Book,* free climbed in 1983 by Rolf Grange at solid 5.12.

In 1984, the face climb of the year was *Childhood's End,* the second route on the long main buttress of Big Rock Candy Mountain. As with Williams and Gallagher's *Fields of Dreams,* climbed five years earlier, this was a mammoth project, spread out over weeks. Ken Trout spearheaded the ascent, with much help from Brian Hansen, Eric Winkleman, Robby Baker, and Kirk Miller. Winkleman, a talented and unsung climber from Boulder, served as elite rope gun. When climbing *Childhood's End* it is easy to tell when he was in the lead. The span between bolts is noticeably longer, despite Trout's shouted admonishments to drill during the first ascent.

Trout and friends did numerous other superb slab climbs. One typical classic was *El Supremo,* a four-pitch climb on Wigwam Dome done in 1985. Twice during the first ascent, sudden thunderstorms turned the route's landmark water groove into a raging "class 7 rapid," forcing retreat.

These clean granite slab climbs were hand-drilled on the lead, mostly with larger, stronger bolts than the traditional quarter-inch fare of the 1970s. It would often take several days to establish a single pitch. Three or more climbers were assembled for each effort, if possible, and the whole enterprise was carried out in an atmosphere of lighthearted fun, with much partying and harassing of the gripped leader.

Telluride

Modern times came slowly and gently to the West Slope. Royal Robbins' Rockcraft climbing school in Telluride had failed, the Californians had left, and new route activity returned to a more dignified pace. Various aid routes went up on the Ophir Wall between 1980 and 1982. *Magic Mirror, Queezy Street,* and *Neanderthal Wall* weren't terribly hard, or long, but they allowed good hang time on wild sections of the face without requiring too much sweat. Dave Bell and Allan Pattie were the main protagonists. Pattie quotes Bell in his 1988 guidebook to the Ophir Wall: "The truth is, I climbed Mirror Wall because I was bored . . . there was nothing better to do and I had to get away."

MountainFilm brought visitors from all over the world to Telluride, and many stayed—or returned—to climb. This led to the remarkably far-flung roster of people with routes on the Ophir Wall, famous and not so famous, including Rick Sylvester, Mugs Stump, Pete Livesey, Geoff Birtles, Michael Kennedy, Bill Meyers, Charlie Fowler, and Jeff Lowe.

In the early 1980s, exploration of the smoother faces began in earnest, resulting in some classic Ophir wall routes. Bill Kees and Barry Rugo divined their way up *Emotional Rescue* in 1982, and the next year Antoine Savelli, Teri Kane, and Ace Kvale did one of the best and

Opposite: *Ian Spencer-Green on the clean granite of Helen's Dome, South Platte* (Photo: Stewart M. Green)

Mark Sonnenfeld on the second free ascent of Morning Glory, *Ophir Wall, 1988* (Photo: Ace Kvale)

area, and produced some of the hardest and most aesthetic West Slope climbs of the mid-1980s. The best of these are probably the 1986 routes *Morning Glory* and the three-pitch 5.13 *Dingo Maniaque,* and the 1987 route *Weaving Through Golden Waves,* a 5.13 with twenty-five bolts on the crux pitch.

Editors on a Rope

Times were changing in Aspen, too. In 1986, Michael Kennedy hired a second editor, John Steiger from Tucson, to help get a handle on the changing climbing scene. Soon after, the editorial staff swelled to three with the addition of Mike Benge, a Kansas City native and Summit County ski bum of the late 1970s, who introduced the much loved and derided news section of *Climbing* magazine, "Hot Flashes." In 1988 the magazine hired Alison Osius, a trained journalist from New England, and one of the first women of the 1970s to climb 5.11. Much later, in 1997, she would become the first female president of the American Alpine Club.

Once again, Grotto Wall climbs dominated in Aspen history. In May 1987, Steiger and Benge tried a new line next to John Long and Lynn Hill's *Pea Brain*. Benge went

Kurt Smith in 1987 on a project near his Grotto Wall route The Knucklehead, *Aspen's first 5.13. The route shown went unclimbed until 2000.* (Photo: Michael Kennedy)

most popular climbs in Ophir, *Powder in the Sky,* on the Mirror Wall sector.

Savelli, an energetic and ambitious climber and guide, would equal the earlier California invasion in his effect of the Telluride scene. He had a forceful personality, and strong ideas about bringing Telluride climbing up to date. Beginning in 1986, he brought a European touch to the flanks of Ophir, tripled the bolt count of the up first, hooked a flake about ten feet up, and drilled the first protection bolt. He top-stepped the bolt, placed a tiny RP, and stepped up again. As he prepared to drill, the RP ripped. Benge toppled headfirst, narrowly missing the ground. A short powwow ensued. The team put away the hooks and RPs, skipped around to the top, and an hour later, Independence Pass had its first rap-bolted route, which each led shortly thereafter. Awash in mock guilt, they called it *Scene of the Crime*.

Another influential climber made his Colorado debut that year on Independence Pass. In 1987, Kurt Smith was a California teenager already known for hard and scary first ascents in Tuolumne Meadows. He was spending the summer in Breckenridge, and in June the *Climbing* magazine crew gave him the tour of Independence Pass.

Smith was much more experienced than Benge at bolting on the lead, and with a cool head and a good set of hooks he quickly protected a forty-foot line right of *Scene of the Crime*. With the bolts in, he began working on his new free climb, logging some impressive whippers before quitting for the day. Charlie Fowler of Boulder was also present, and while Smith was hooking, Fowler scrambled around to a ramp atop the right edge of the same wall and bolted his own line on rappel. Both climbers swore by the high-tech new hardware they were installing—quarter-inch wedge bolts—but few others had any confidence in the spindly studs. The next weekend, Smith succeeded on his route, *The Knucklehead*, Aspen's first 5.13. Fowler also did his, *Space Sluts in the Slammer*.

Times were changing. Shelf Road and Penitente Canyon were the new hot spots, and Kennedy, Benge, and Steiger had been there. Bolted climbing was in. In 1988, Kennedy and Benge bought their own power drill. The first modest test drives produced the *Fossil Finish* to *Trilobite* on Pass Wall and *A Walk in Central Park* on the Outrageous Overhangs. Power drilling had come to the little high-country crags of Aspen. Indeed, it had come to many areas, and it was changing the face of climbing.

The Changing Faces of the Flatirons

By 1987, new lines in Eldorado Canyon were running out, but acres of sandstone lay untouched and waiting in the hills. The Flatirons had long been a sanctuary where climbers could explore and struggle, far from judging eyes. For all Boulder residents, the labyrinthine canyons and trails were a place to get away from it all, a miniwilderness minutes from downtown.

Throughout the 1970s and early 1980s, classic hard crack lines had gone up—*Ruby Slipper, Superpower, Warlocks, Transgression, Five-Year Plan*. Now, the crackless faces promised even more and harder new climbs. Beginning with Dale Goddard's *Cornucopia* in 1986, the

Dale Godard in December 1986 on his route Cornucopia, *the earliest rappel-bolted climb in the Boulder Flatirons* (Photo: Dan Hare)

Flatirons saw an intense wave of new bolted face routes.

Dan Michael was one of the most active of the early Flatiron sport climbers. He was a thoroughly new-wave climber with a good eye for a line and little inhibition about bolting or even a touch of hold sculpting. In 1987 Michael established two of the hardest and most distinctive Flatirons climbs, *Slave to the Rhythm,* up a pebbly, overhanging wall on the Ironing Board behind the Third Flatiron, and *The Fiend,* a forty-foot overhanging dihedral on Dinosaur Mountain.

Some of the easier early sport climbs were beautiful creations, for example *The Big Picture* on the massive vertical west face of Overhang Rock, by Dan Michael and Paul Piana, and *Farniente* near *Slave to the Rhythm,* done by Bobbi Bensman, recently moved from her native Tuc-

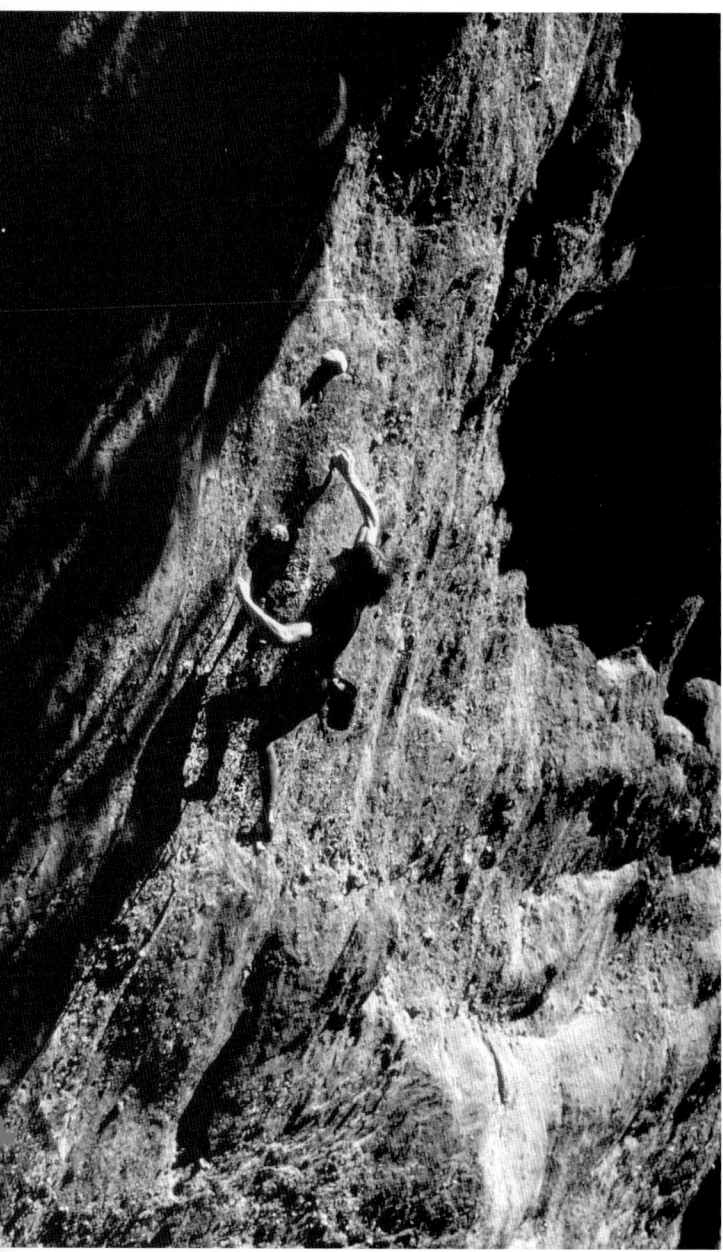

Dan Michael in 1987 on his route Slave to the Rhythm, *one of the best and hardest of the early Flatiron sport climbs* (Photo: Beth Wald)

climbing guidebook. Rossiter explored and climbed extensively all over Boulder, and was married to a professional ballerina, Joyce, who was one of the better face climbers in Colorado. Among Joyce's first ascents were *Radlands of Infinity* in Boulder Canyon and *The Black Face* on Cadillac Crag above Eldorado, both involving 5.12+ micro-edge climbing. "Joyce and I were a good first-ascent team," Rossiter said. "I placed the bolts and she redpointed most of the harder routes."

Routes such as *Radlands* notwithstanding, the Rossiters' climbs showed a subtle shift in psychology that was taking place. The adventure, or lack thereof, derived from the style of the first ascent was becoming less important than creating an enjoyable, safe, high-quality "finished product." This was a revolutionary idea. In an earlier era, as Roger Briggs pointed out, "There was no concept of public service. If anything, you wanted to put your fellow man through hell." A new route was an expression of one's level of personal mastery,

Joyce Rossiter in 1988 on her Boulder Canyon route Radlands of Infinity *(5.12+), at that time the most difficult route established by a woman in Colorado* (Photo: Richard Rossiter)

son to Boulder and soon to become one of the state's strongest climbers.

Sheer difficulty was beginning to play a smaller role in the terrain chosen for bolted climbing. One leader in this movement was Richard Rossiter, author of the 1981 book *Boulder Topographics: A Pictorial Guide to Boulder Climbs*, an artistic vision of Boulder rock as well as a

Colin Lantz, one of Colorado's most prolific sport climbers of the late 1980s, on his 1988 route Your Mother. *This was the first climb in Eldorado Canyon to be equipped using a power drill.* (Photo: Colin Lantz collection)

often composed of a crumbly, unreliable stone. Lantz was a pioneer of the various dubious practices modern Colorado climbers have used to deal with the problem of poor rock, and for the sake of the historical record, he consented to relate his rather unflattering tales.

On one Flatirons route, Lantz reinforced a section of crumbling rock using an epoxy resin intended for repairing fiberglass boat hulls. The results were horrifying. In the right light, the unnatural glaze could be seen from half a mile away. Even this measure, however, proved insufficient to render the wall climbable. Finally, Lantz decided to bolt a climbing-wall hold to the rock. During this process, while fishing for the right grip, Lantz upended the bag of holds he was carrying, and a falling hold landed amid another party of climbers at the base of a nearby route. Already disconcerted by Lantz's antics, and now pummeled by plastic holds, the outraged climbers stormed up the hill. They were outnumbered by Lantz's entourage, however, who faced them down and warned them back.

In the end, Lantz was so disgusted with himself that he removed the bolt-on hold and thoroughly sanded down

Symbol of the bolt wars? The climber is the Frenchman J.B. Tribout, Eldorado Canyon, 1988. (Photo: Jeff Achey)

and perhaps a gauntlet thrown down. A trend in the late 1980s, however, was to produce moderate new bolted routes specifically designed to be enjoyed.

The quest for difficulty was still alive and well, however, Colin Lantz was an extremely active Flatirons climber in the late 1980s, and he sought out the hardest possible climbs. This preference drew him to the larger overhangs of the Flatirons, which unfortunately were the rock surface to return it to near its original appearance. He eventually did climb his creation, at hard 5.13, calling it *Rock Atrocity*.

Another route Lantz equipped during this time—this one with a little more discretion, was *Honemaster Lambada* on the steep wall next to Dan Michael's *Slave to the Rhythm*. This line would resist Lantz's efforts until 1991, when it would become the hardest pitch in the Boulder area.

In 1989, with virgin rock running out, the latest "secret" area for Flatirons new-routers was Fern Canyon. By now, there were probably more than a thousand climbers in Boulder. Of the dozens actively involved in new routes, many did not even know each other. On a fine weekend, there might be several different parties in the pristine confines of Fern Canyon, drilling away. In 1989 alone, over thirty-five new bolted routes were done in the tiny enclave.

The most prolific group was Lantz, Paul Pomeroy, and Greg Robinson, and among their routes were *Chains of Love, Cream Puff,* and Lantz's *Violator,* one of the hardest sport routes in the Flatirons. Their most significant route, however, was called *Superfresh*.

Most of the Flatirons sport routes climbed the flanks of hidden crags, but *Superfresh* took a line up a giant boulder that overhung the Fern Canyon trail. One day at the height of Fern Canyon's development, with power drills whirring in the background, a baffled hiker passed through the canyon. He heard the drills, saw the chalk and the bolts on *Superfresh*, put two and two together, and complained to the Boulder Mountain Parks rangers.

There had been previous uneasy rumblings about the goings-on with climbers in the Flatirons, and after the *Superfresh* incident things happened fast. Within months, bolting in the Flatirons was outlawed. Within the year, Eldorado Canyon was also under a bolting ban. It was the end of an era. Issues of style and freedom to climb were no longer mere matters of opinion among climbers. They had encountered the law.

THE NINETIES AND BEYOND: THE MADDING CROWD

Part Five

If the 1970s were about clean climbing and the 1980s about rock gymnastics, the 1990s were about climbing going mainstream. Convenience became paramount. Even topping out on a crag began to seem like a hassle, and lowering off anchors became the norm rather than the exception. For the first time in the history of Colorado rock, climbers rejoined the masses, spending much of their climbing day standing on the ground.

Climbers and climbing magazines now talked of "developing" a crag, a phrase as disturbing as fingernails on a blackboard to the ears of a 1970s climber. More than just the phrase smacked of urbanization. Developing a crag typically meant cutting a trail to the base and going to work with power tools.

In the 1990s, climbers would find themselves the subject of real environmental concern. The bolting bans had made clear that modern-style "route development" was considered inappropriate in the open space that urban Boulder had set aside for primitive recreation. Rock climbing, once an escape from modern culture, was being assimilated, and becoming that culture in microcosm.

Or was it? All outdoor "risk" sports had become trendy in the 1990s, and despite the drawbacks, and the nostalgia of the old-timers, this reflected a positive shift in the general public's view of these activities. To the participants, rock climbing was still adventurous, rewarding, and close to nature. Yet a certain maverick quality had disappeared.

One of the most important things to happen to rock climbing in the 1990s was artificial climbing walls. "Climbing gyms," long popular in Britain, appeared all over the country, and some of the earliest—including CityRock in the California Bay Area and Paradise Rock Gym near Denver—were designed by Colorado's Christian Griffith. Climbers with full-time jobs and family obligations now had a very efficient way to stay in shape, and a number of old-time Boulder climbers such as Jim Logan would soon be climbing 5.13 as a direct result of gym training.

As for those just learning to climb, Pat Ament once said: "A climber inherits the ability to do 5.10 or 5.11." This was nowhere more true than in the rock gyms. A young teenager might visit the Boulder Rock Club and be immediately surrounded by people casually climbing 5.12 while conversing about aromatherapy or bio-engineeering with their belayers. Imitation hot-wired the learning curve, and it was not uncommon in the 1990s for someone to climb 5.12 after only a month on the rock.

On the other hand, gyms altered the nature-based essence of climbing. Up until the 1990s, entry into rock climbing was through outdoor channels—rock scrambling as a kid, friends who climbed, a rock-climbing course at summer camp or in a national park. In the 1990s, however, one could discover climbing after joining a health club and watching people on the climbing wall across the gym.

Accomplished gym climbers often found themselves frighteningly out of their element on old-style climbs as easy as the *Bastille Crack* or *Ruper*, and an entire population of climbers grew up never learning how to protect a climb using gear and natural features. For these climbers, if there were no bolts, there was no climb.

Along with indoor climbing came formal competitions. In the mid-1980s, when the first European sport climbing competitions appeared in places like Arco, Italy, many American climbers complained that competition would ruin the sport. Overt competition clashed with the general antiestablishment ethos of the 1960s and '70s, but human nature had been wreaking havoc with this official philosophy for years. In the 1960s, when climbing was more free-form, one could "compete" by forging new lines, free climbing a friend's aid route, or simply pulling some outrageous stunt. By the 1980s there was head-to-head competition for first free ascents. The arrival of formal competition added little more than a stroke of honesty.

Opposite: *Tim Fairfield, Pete Zoller, and friend in Rifle Mountain Park. Fairfield is attempting* Lungfish, *a much-tried route that later became the first consensus 5.14 in Colorado.* (Photo: Chris Goplerud)

27. Industrial Rock

In 1990, Colorado sport climbing was in a bit of a funk. Around the world, standards were soaring. J. B. Tribout had climbed America's first 5.14 in 1986 at Smith Rock in Oregon, and with Ben Moon's ascent of *Hubble* at Ravenstor in Britain in 1990, European standards stood at 5.14c. Lynn Hill had abandoned her homeland, moved to France, and in 1990 became the first woman to climb 5.14. Colorado, however, was still looking for its first climb of that grade.

Significant areas were now under a bolting ban, and routes such as *Rock Atrocity* were proving that Boulder rock was somewhat unsuited to standard-setting sport climbs. Not even the limestone of Shelf Road had the unrelentingly overhanging climbing needed for the highest levels of difficulty.

One area that experienced a flare of activity was Clear Creek Canyon, along the busy highway leading into the mountains from Golden and Denver. Here, where teenagers in pickups used to shoot rappel slings off the crags, a new breed of sport climbers went to work. Climbers including Alan Nelson, Kurt Smith, Pete Zoller, Mike Pont, and Scott Frye bolted numerous climbs on crags such as Anarchy Wall, quickly establishing many 5.13s. On one crag, the Nomad Cave, the climbing was almost completely on chiseled and drilled holds. With such tactics, as well as constant traffic noise, Clear Creek's ambience matched the favored music among the climbers—industrial rock. Clear Creek suited a few, but to most it was a desperate, stopgap measure. The modern elite needed someplace better. They would find it in the spring of 1991, in the hills north of a West Slope cowboy and oil town called Rifle.

"Friends Don't Let Friends Climb Slabs"

Box Canyon, as it was known to locals, was a quiet little gorge carved by East Rifle Creek as it dropped from the high country of the Flat Tops Wilderness toward the Colorado River. The canyon, a park for the town of Rifle, had been visited by ice climbers since the 1970s, but none were tempted by the rock. Layton Kor, who had lived for a while in nearby Glenwood Springs, had done a multi-pitch climb near the entrance to Rifle Mountain Park that explored a cave high on the east wall, but that was the extent of the canyon's rock climbing. Until 1991, Box Canyon was the exclusive haunt of local fishermen and picnickers. No one would have believed that within a few years it would become the hottest rock-climbing destination in the country.

Mark Tarrant, a Boulder resident who grew up in Rifle, and Richard Wright, of Denver, were the first "modern" climbers to seriously consider climbing the canyon walls. In the spring of 1991, they found a clean stretch of stone and established the canyon's first sport route, a long 5.11 line that went nearly to the rim. They also drilled a similar-looking line of more than twenty

Will Gadd in Clear Creek Canyon, a climbing area re-explored and reinvented after the 1989 bolting bans near Boulder
(Photo: Bill Hatcher)

bolts that proved much harder—too hard, in fact. The first climb was called *Rumor Has It,* and remains one of the canyon's best easier routes. The latter became the first of many projects on the Project Wall, a 130-foot route, later slightly rerouted and climbed by Phillip Benningfield at 5.13 and called *The Eighth Day.*

After *Rumor Has It,* rumor spread, and the next spring Front Range climbers Pete Zoller and Phillip Benningfield drove to Rifle. Others soon followed—Mike Pont, Kurt Smith, Matt Samet, Colin Lantz, Jim Hall, Brett Ruckman. "We screamed at the top of our lungs and would have thrown a few back flips if we'd known how to," Smith wrote in a *Climbing* magazine article.

European-style bolt protection had drastically changed climbers' vision. So had American Fork Canyon, an area south of Salt Lake City. In American Fork, many of the routes ascended overhanging cliffs that were originally too unstable to climb. Salt Lake climbers had pried off vast amounts of loose rock and secured key holds with industrial adhesives. The resulting routes—heavily hyped in the magazines—were radically overhanging and very difficult, and they revolutionized American sport climbing. American Fork tactics would figure large in Rifle climbing.

For climbers with the right bag of tricks, the potential of Rifle Mountain Park was staggering. The rock formed natural amphitheaters, which climbers called "caves," and the routes often projected outward as much as they ascended. An attentive belayer would quickly develop a crick in the neck, thus giving rise to the classic "Rifle belay," where the belayer would stare at the ground, seemingly oblivious to the leader's gymnastics on the overhangs above. The normal "sport loop" of slack hanging from the belay device—necessary to keep the climber from swinging violently during a fall on overhanging rock—contributed to the careless appearance. Sometimes the sport loop sagged to the ground, perhaps draped across one of the ubiquitous dogs lounging in the dirt. No matter, the long falls were generally safer.

Severely overhanging climbing on relatively large holds became almost a cult, and bumper stickers appeared saying "Friends don't let friends climb slabs." In Rifle jargon, a "slab" was any rock face less than fifteen degrees overhanging—for example any climb at Shelf Road or Smith Rock.

Equipping the Rifle walls for sport climbing was hard and often dangerous work. The climbs ended well below the rim of the canyon and the rock was so overhanging that rappel bolting was sometimes impossible. The standard tactic was to choose a promising wall and establish the first route ground-up, aiding up via a combination of natural features and bolts. Nearby climbs were then equipped by traversing right or left from the first climb's anchors and aiding down.

Rifle's first "steep" routes were done by Benningfield, Zoller, and Pont. Unlike the walls soon to be developed—the Arsenal, the Ruckman Cave, and others—these routes required no American Fork tactics, but spanned a clean, European-looking twenty-degree overhanging alcove of blue and tan limestone. Benningfield writes of his first visits to Rifle:

> A couple of routes already existed in the canyon, but we didn't know that. We spent our first hours standing below the overhangs of the untouched Arsenal in complete awe. Then we moved farther into the canyon and

Rob Floyd on Never Believe, *Rifle Mountain Park's first "steep" route, established by Phillip Benningfield and Pete Zoller in 1991* (Photo: Jeff Achey)

came to the pristine expanse of the soon-to-be-named Wasteland. *In my distorted mind, it seemed clear that T. S. Eliot's poem rang a metaphorical note to what we were about to do.*

We unloaded the necessary arsenal of equipment, stomped out onto the untrammeled ground, and started playing The Ministry to psyche us up for the chore ahead. Pete and I worked the Bosch's magic. It was my first bolted route, there was no way to begin except from the ground up, and I feared every move I made. I placed bolts from precarious nuts wedged in seemingly fragile grooves, and my amazement at the resilient rock spurred me on. After the route was finally loaded with bolts, we began the days of figuring out the difficult moves. Our second weekend out we both sent the line, one right after the other, named it Never Believe, *and proceeded to bolt* The Beast.

A half mile up, on the opposite side of the canyon, Pete and I found our next raison d'être. One line straight up the middle of a tall, smooth, yellow and blue wall was one of the best looking in the canyon. Industrial music helped muster up our energy—in absolute conflict with the pristine surroundings—and we started bolting, again from the ground up. Less than an hour into the project an aid bolt sheered, and I, loaded with hammer, bolts, and power drill, came crashing down. Once on the ground, I found my wrist no longer linear, and I spent the next several weeks jonesing to be back on the rock, while Pete finished the route and aptly christened both it and the wall—the Anti-Phil.

The steepest caves required aggressive work with crowbars, chisels, and glue. With these tools came ample opportunity to create holds. Only later, however, did wholesale hold manufacturing come into practice. As Matt Samet put it, "While many of the chipped routes have put Rifle on the sport-climbing map because of their 5.14 difficulty, they are generally a lot less fun to climb on than their easier, more natural counterparts—the glue routes!" One showpiece crag of original Rifle "glue routes" is the Arsenal.

Colin Lantz and Jim Hall, among the earliest Rifle climbers, had both come to Colorado from the Shawangunks in New York, famous for its roof climbing. On their first trip to the canyon in the spring of 1992 they stopped below a vast, unclimbed swath of roofy terrain—soon to be named the Arsenal. Lantz says it reminded them of the Gunks.

This pair—mostly Lantz—would do over a dozen Arsenal routes. Lantz's first project was a line that he would climb only after much effort—*Colinator,* still the

Shelly Presson, one of the top female competition climbers to frequent Rifle, on Vitamin H *in the Arsenal* (Photo: Bill Hatcher)

Arsenal's longest and hardest route. Hall's first contribution became the wall's most popular route, Vitamin H, named after the power drink he employed for the first ascent—a good German hefeweisen. This route lost some popularity in the late 1990s when an entire three-bolt section collapsed to the ground.

The ultimate Arsenal "glue route" was *Spray-A-Thon*, now probably the canyon's most popular 5.13c. The upper section cleaned up nicely after a few hundred pounds of blocks were pried off, but the lower section was hollow and rotten. Lantz, however, was expert in such matters. Following his misadventures on *Rock Atrocity* in the Boulder Flatirons, he had devised much better resin and glue technology with the help of his roommate, Chas Fisher, who manufactured plastic climbing-wall holds. Lantz brought home rock samples from Rifle and Fisher produced a sand/resin mix that matched the rock color. Using a squirt bottle and rubber gloves, Lantz worked the resin into the hollow, scaly section of rock on *Spray-A-Thon*, reinforcing large sections of the climb that otherwise would have broken away under a climber's weight.

Ghetto Life

Rifle was more than hard climbs. It became a way of life, a postmodern version of Yosemite's Camp 4. The climbers were urban refugees from the Front Range, but they were not only escaping from mainstream society, as were Yosemite climbers of the 1960s. They were escaping from mainstream climbing—the affluent gym and sport climbers who were now crowding places like Shelf Road.

Rifle climbers were the punk elite, as harsh as their music. Matt Samet was there and describes the scene:

In the early days, if you weren't out there putting up routes you were a "bottom feeder." This term was coined by Alan Lester, a self-professed bottom feeder who, like many Front Range climbers, came out to Rifle to repeat routes rather than sink any time into the momentous task of unearthing new ones from beneath Rifle's shell of blocky choss. In fact, most of the early climbers in Rifle were bottom feeders. This only drew us new-routers closer together and we soon became the snottiest clan of locals at any American sport-climbing venue, putting even the hecklers at Smith Rock to shame with our attitude and vitriol.

Our favorite camping spot was the Ghetto Meadow, a large, sunny pullout just upriver from the climbs. Camping was free and unregulated, so we would pile as many cars as we could into the meadow. On weekends there would be twenty or more vehicles.

If we didn't like someone who pulled in, we'd sit in our cars and say horrible things about them, laughing as hard as we could with the windows rolled up, sometimes pointing. Eventually they'd go away.

There were hardly any women around. If a girl flying solo were to show up she was hounded, feted, and pursued. If she showed up with her boyfriend she was pursued anyway. Those of us who didn't have girlfriends at home (e.g. myself) suffered an overabundance of testosterone, which made us want to climb harder, spray louder, and drill more bolts. We were a desperate, dirty, vice-ridden crew but we managed to put up some of American's finest and hardest sport climbs despite ourselves.

We knew we were lucky—how could we not? We had stumbled onto a canyon of virgin limestone, climbable along its entire two-mile length, littered with blue- and black-streaked walls and outrageous caves that rivaled the finest stone in Europe. Even the ugliest walls—such as the Arsenal and Bauhaus—yielded bullet routes, mega-classic twenty- to thirty-meter pitches up to 14b.

Every one of us wanted to bag the canyon's first 5.14. When the dust cleared after the 1992–1993 season, many of us had come close. Colin Lantz had polished off Colinator *in the Arsenal. Kurt Smith had done* Slice of Life *in the Wicked Cave. Scott Frye put the hurt on his extensively "cleaned" Project Wall masterpiece* Living in Fear. *Mike Pont sent* Der Stihl, *the first route out the main Bauhaus Wall. Jimmy Surette had done the wildly steep* Cracked Open Sky, *first route to actually exit the main Skull Cave. I contributed the diminutive and bouldery* Dumpster Barbecue.

Slice was the only route to emerge at 14a—a grade it held for over a year until Chris Knuth found seven knee bars along the way, including a hands-off rest and a kneecap-grinding method of avoiding the crux dyno that had been bouting everyone. In doing so Knuth started the "Knee-bar Revolution." The blocky, convoluted nature of Rifle rock made it possible to scum one's knees up under lips and against rails, resulting in both a new style of climbing and blanket downgrading of most of the existing hard routes.

Since there were so few of us, we tended to respect each other's projects. One route consistently beckoned, however: Eric Fedor's project out the central cave on the Project Wall, one of Rifle's sweetest sweeps of stone. After watching Eric work the first ten moves for three years, Phillip Benningfield became so upset that Eric still hadn't bolted the top section that he rapped down and drilled it for him. Still we stayed off the route—but we were not above talking a visitor,

Scott Frye on his 1993 route Living in Fear, *one of Rifle's early 5.13+ climbs* (Photo: Chris Goplerud)

Scott Franklin, into grabbing the first redpoint of Simply Read.

A couple of articles ran in the mags and visiting climbers began to show up. Most of us, being from Boulder, were sure we were the coolest, if not the strongest, climbers in the country. We would spend entire rest days parked below the Arsenal, poking fun at people dogging up routes we had ruthlessly wired. In the name of mean-spirited fun, we would send visitors' redpoint projects in our tennis shoes, including all of the routes we called "warm-ups" (anything less than 5.12d), and even some harder routes like Vision Thing. *We figured if we burned off enough people and acted like big enough assholes, eventually people would stop coming to our area. The first guidebook to Rifle, by Hassan Saab, featured the most offensive preface in climbing literature, beginning, "Rifle is truly a pile," and degenerating from there.*

In fact, Rifle was a pile, and we knew it. Many of our routes took days to clean. We would hang in our harnesses for hours, prying off blocks and watching with perverse joy as they crashed through the canopy of trees. One of my finest memories is of the hours I spent on the lip of the Skull Cave, pulling off a VW-size shield of rock that I had bolted my way up.

If we hadn't sunk all this work in, there wouldn't be anything in the canyon to climb. There would be no Rifle. *And without Rifle there would be no good sport climbing in the state of Colorado.*

There was a general taboo on bolting sub-5.12 climbs, for fear that the "riffraff" would invade Rifle. The "Girlfriend Rebellion" prompted some of the first easier bolted climbs. Annie Smith was one of several women responsible for sounding the battle cry. Annie commuted from Denver to Rifle almost every weekend with Kurt Smith, then her husband. Since she couldn't climb 5.12+, belaying was soon her main activity. Finally she gave Kurt the ultimatum, and in response he bolted a short, slick, and scary 5.9 in the Ice Caves—arguably the worst route in Rifle. *Bumble Bee* was named in reference to the "bumblers" Kurt feared would soon to be buzzing into the canyon.

Alan Nelson and Richard Wright, acting outside the testosterone cult, added other, better easy climbs, such as *Merry Maids*. Soon, as predicted, Rifle's popularity soared. Certain advantages accrued. Visits from talented Europeans secured local contacts for trips to Buoux and Ceuse. Road-tripping Americans stopped in, and more invitations were exchanged—Vegas, Salt Lake, Bend. A significant percentage of the "riffraff" turned out to be female. The bad boys chilled out. On weekends the campground would brim with cars and climbers of all nationalities. Crowds were a problem only on the "warm-ups," so the inner circle warmed up on 5.12+ and learned to love the audience. Standards slowly climbed until Rifle had a greater concentration of hard routes than any place in the country.

By the mid-1990s, Rifle was showing signs of abuse. The local residents, who used to love Box Canyon, had almost abandoned it, and at one point it looked like the city might close the canyon to climbing.

Phillip Benningfield recalls the controversy:

As more and more climbers congregated to do such classic routes as Pump-O-Rama, *the* Anti-Phil, Beer Run, Der Stihl, *and* Dumpster Barbecue, *the fragile riparian ecosystem was trampled. No longer did waist-high stinging nettles and native grasses brush up against the limestone. Trails became a mass of tangled trees and blocks that had been torn from the cliffs. Rifle locals began to detest the skinny, self-serving climbers who showed no respect. Something had to be done.*

A few wise souls helped calm the storm—Kurt Smith and Colin Lantz in particular, who formed the Rifle Climbers' Coalition and tried to tone down the noise, over-bolting, parking, and general chaos. Boombox blare died a quick death, but the banging and cussing still echoed up and down the canyon and people continued to park in bad spots and stand in the road while belaying. Only with time, posted signs ("No Climbing Here"), and entrance fees did the situation seem to come to a reasonable balance.

Realizing that the town of Rifle needed an olive branch from the nefarious climbers, we started the Rifle Mountain Park Clean-up. Since then, climbers from around the world have taken part in rebuilding trails and picking up trash. These efforts have led to relative peace in the canyon, and preserved climbers' freedom to express themselves on Rifle's hard limestone.

A bolting moratorium instituted in 1994 proved very beneficial to climbing standards at Rifle. With new bolts outlawed, pressure mounted on the route developers to either complete their lines or give up and let the bottom feeders try. Some climbers auctioned off their projects for beers or cash. Climbers did less hanging, bolting, and dreaming—and more climbing.

One open project was a short but viciously hard line spanning the so-called Nappy Dugout. It was the scene of much high-pitched yelling and many near ground-falls as Timmy Fairfield of New Mexico repeatedly came close,

Mike Pont, accomplished competition climber and early Rifle pioneer, on his Der Stihl, *the first route on the main Bauhaus Wall* (Photo: Chris Goplerud)

certainly not failing for lack of intensity. In the end, Jeff Webb of Salt Lake City redpointed *Lungfish,* the canyon's—and Colorado's—first consensus 5.14.

By 1995, the canyon had become *the* sport-climbing destination in America. If you were a Coloradan traveling in Europe, the local climbers would say, in German-, French-, or Spanish-accented English, "Ah, so you know Rifle!" Professional European competition climbers such as François Legrand would stop at Rifle to on-sight as many hard climbs as possible—often several 5.13 routes per day. One highlight was the Italian Christian Brenna's ascent of *Spray-A-Thon,* at 8a+ or 5.13c, one of the hardest on-sight ascents yet in Colorado.

The Rifle scene, though still intense, was fun even for "sub-5.13 riffraff," and some of the classic "easy" climbs deserve mention: Lori Mason and Eric Johnson's *Eighty Feet of Meat;* Kadie Johnston's *Defenseless Betty;* Rob Floyd's *James Brown's Wild Ride;* and Rob Candelaria's *Feline* and *Ricochet.*

The summer of 1996 was pivotal, as Rifle was assaulted on all fronts by visitors from afar. First to make a stir was the Frenchman J. B. Tribout, who was working on a short but explosively difficult climb in the Winchester Cave. A few days into the effort, rumor spread that success was near. On the evening he hoped to make the final ascent, Tribout was a bit dismayed when a large crowd, some packing cameras and video equipment, followed him out to the climb. In true French style, he rose to the occasion and redpointed the route, calling it, appropriately, *The Seven P.M. Show.*

The climb was originally rated 8c, or 5.14b, which would have made it the hardest in Colorado. It was so short, tricky, and technical, however, that later consensus held that it could be "learned down" to 5.14a, and it soon became the most repeated 5.14 in Rifle.

The next disturbance was caused by a relatively unknown fifteen-year-old Californian, whose visit announced the arrival of a new breed of American rock climber. Chris Sharma climbed all of the canyon's hard routes in about a week, and then redpointed an open project called *Zulu,* a consensus 8c, Colorado's first.

It became obvious that a new generation had arrived when another up-and-coming youngster showed up: Tommy Caldwell, from Estes Park. Caldwell also repeated Rifle's hardest routes, and unlike Sharma, he didn't go away. His continuing exploits will be covered in a later chapter.

Many Boulder climbers commuted to Rifle every weekend of the summer to work their way through the grades, and the social scene was a circus all its own. The climbing jargon of the 1990s colored every conversation. To "send" a route was to redpoint it; "beta" was the tricks

J. B. Tribout on the first ascent of The Seven P.M. Show (Photo: Jim Surette)

ing hard at Rifle. Many of the female climbers on the competition circuit frequented the canyon, carving out their own list of achievements that eclipsed all but the hardest male ascents. A few standout climbs by Colorado women were Shelley Presson's ascent of *Apocalypse,* Hillary Harris's of *Cryptic Egyptian,* and Mia Axon's of *Living in Fear.*

Antics abounded at Rifle, especially at the Arsenal, center stage above the dirt road. Herman Gollner of Aspen, at age sixty-something, popularized time trials and "sport jumping." For the latter, a climber would head up the popular Arsenal 5.13 *Pump-O-Rama*, skip two or more bolts on the upper headwall, and then jump off from the anchors—preferably with enough slack to allow a fall of fifty feet or more. Also at the Arsenal, following a late-night challenge fueled by too many beers, Charlie Bentley, one of the top Rifle climbers, stripped down naked, dangled a watermelon from his harness, and climbed the 5.12+ route *Vitamin H.*

Bobbi Bensman on Fluff Boy (5.13c). *Bensman, one of country's most dedicated professional rock climbers of the mid-1990s, moved to the town of Rifle in the mid-1990s and became the area's most accomplished female climber.* (Photo: Bill Hatcher)

and techniques for sending; "spraying" was to talk too much about your beta or your send.

When trying to "tick" the next grade, part of the art was to find a route that was "soft" for its grade, but not too soft. This struggle led to comical confrontations and tragic down-ratings. The most conspicuous example was the original Rifle 5.14, *Slice of Life*. As Smith climbed it, *Slice* was an honest 5.14, Colorado's first, but the climb was repeated that way only once. Then came knee bars and the grade dropped. In fall 1996, Bobbi Bensman climbed *Slice of Life*—at 5.13d, a landmark for women in Colorado sport climbing. A few days later, Don Welsh discovered a variation at the crux that dropped the grade to 5.13c and fueled an absurd and heated debate: if you sent *Slice of Life* before the variation, could you still claim a 5.13d redpoint, or had you merely made a routefinding error? Conversely, could you claim an ascent of *Slice* if you used the new variation? In an emotional moment, Bensman threatened to chip the holds off Welsh's variation. A resolution came when the new sequence was given its own name: done the "easy" way, *Slice of Life* became *Piece of Cake.*

Bensman was by no means the only woman climb-

Opposite: Kurt Smith on Vision Thing, *Rifle's hardest route after his first ascent in 1991* (Photo: Chris Goplerud)

28. Big Walls in the Nineties

Despite the new trends that had changed the public face of rock climbing, the old ways hadn't died. Climbers still loved the old haunts of Eldorado Canyon, the Garden of the Gods, the South Platte, and Lumpy Ridge, and traditional big-wall climbing was alive and well. Internationally, the wall-climbing news was of Yosemite tactics taken to the huge cliffs of the Arctic and the Karakoram, and El Cap routes being free climbed at 5.13. Nevertheless, throughout the 1980s and 1990s, first ascents of big, super-thin aid climbs accounted for many great adventures in Colorado, in venues such as the Right Side of the Diamond and the North Chasm View Wall.

The Face

On North Chasm View in the Black Canyon, one very conspicuous thin-aid challenge remained unclimbed in the late 1980s—a direct start to the *Hallucinogen Wall*. The original route had followed obvious free-climbing corners for five pitches before swinging left to Fantasy Island ledge, where the "real" climbing began. The new line—or lack of line—would make a direct approach up the blank face below Fantasy Island. Linked to the *Hallucinogen*, it would create a continuously invisible line for the entire height of the North Chasm View Wall. It had been eyed by several parties.

Steve Quinlan of Durango was probably the most intent of the aspirants. Though adept at avoiding the limelight, Quinlan was one of Colorado's most accomplished wall climbers. His ascents included a dozen trips up El Cap; a new Grade VI route, done solo, on the north face of Mount Hooker in the Wind Rivers; and first ascents in Alaska, such as the south face of Broken Tooth in the Ruth Gorge with Mugs Stump.

Quinlan hoped to cap the lower *Hallucinogen* variation with an independent finish to the rim. In the fall of 1989, Quinlan and Les Hutchinson made an abortive attempt, climbing one hard aid pitch into the lower face before retreating. Their false start would cost them the first ascent. On the very day of Quinlan and Hutchinson's retreat, Bryan Becker and Brad Schilling scrambled down the Cruise Gully to try the same line, a bizarre occurrence indeed in the obscure realm of Black Canyon wall climbing.

Becker had spent little time in the canyon since the first ascent of the *Hallucinogen* nine years earlier. For the last several years he had been involved in exploring the renowned Lechuiguilla and Carlsbad cave systems with the Colorado Springs climbers Don Doucette and Art Wiggins. This pair had brought in Becker as the minimum-impact aid-climbing specialist, and he put his skills to work on delicate subterranean headwalls, creating state-of-the-art technical spelunking passages such as the *Aragonitemare,* a 100-foot A4 pitch up feathery aragonite formations deep underground.

The direct start to the *Hallucinogen* proved to be very similar to the climbing Becker had led on the original route—mostly hooking and copperheads, with a bit of Becker's beloved "fraid climbing." After six pitches they reached Fantasy Island and continued up the original route. Becker had spent so much time in Lechuiguilla that he led many of the hard hooking pitches on the *Hallucinogen* at night, by headlamp, apparently preferring the familiar womblike darkness to the dizzy exposure of day. On the pitch off Happy Trails, one of the hardest on the original *Hallucinogen,* Becker found rivets that he had not placed on the first ascent—a common occurrence on aid routes. Clipping one for protection, he hooked past the offending additions, only to pull off a flake near the end of the hooking and take a spectacular fall. As of 2000, the severely bent rivet that caught his fall remains, striking fear in the hearts of repeat climbers, who must use it.

Becker and Schilling had packed for two weeks on the wall, but needed only four days to reach the top. They called their variation *Le Visage*—"The Face."

In June 1993, Quinlan returned to North Chasm View with Ken Sauls. The pair repeated *Le Visage* to Fantasy Island, branched left from the *Hallucinogen* on the next pitch, and continued for nine new pitches to the rim. The complete route, *Paint It Black,* is generally considered the hardest wall route in the state.

A macabre incident occurred during a winter attempt on another Quinlan/Sauls route on North Chasm View between the Nose and the *Hallucinogen*. In stormy weather, Quinlan, Sauls, and Lyle Dean fixed several ropes on the wall, and then hiked out of the canyon to resupply before the next push. Along the snowy road a few miles in from the roadhead they came upon the body of a local girl, a suicide. Shortly thereafter the climbers abandoned their attempt. Quinlan and Sauls returned in June 1997 to finish the route, *Mark of Cain,* another of the Black's most difficult wall climbs.

Parties of One
The other contenders for hardest wall route in Colorado belong to one of the state's most enigmatic climbers. Jim Beyer began his career as a big-wall soloist in 1973, at age seventeen, with a first ascent on the Diamond. Four years later, in Yosemite, he made the first solo ascent of *The Shield* on El Capitan. In the 1980s and 1990s Beyer drifted into competitive kayaking, radical environmentalism, and solo ascents of some of the hardest and most dangerous aid lines ever done in Utah's Canyonlands, including notorious climbs such as *Deadman's Party* and *Intifada* on the mud walls of the Fisher Towers.

Beyer climbed all over the West, seeking out the most impressive walls. In Rocky Mountain National Park alone, he established solo aid routes on the east face of Mount Alice (1978), the lower east face of Longs Peak (*Anti-Nuclear Tide,* an A4+ route, 1987), and the Diamond (*Smash the State,* the wall's only claimed A5, 1989).

In 1989, in preparation for a trip to Pakistan, Beyer set out to do a low-key practice climb on the right side of the Painted Wall in the Black Canyon, up an obvious diagonal crack system that joined the *Northern Arête.* He brought no bolts and a fairly scanty aid rack, but the lower climbing proved to be anything but low-key. *Climb Bold or Fly* involved A4+ through huge pegmatite bands on the lower wall. Progress was unexpectedly slow, and Beyer quickly found himself desperately low on food and water. Once he reached the easier ground of the main crack system, he tied off his ropes and gear and sprinted free-solo to the rim. In 1990, Beyer did another Black Canyon route called *Black Planet* (A4+) on North Chasm View between *Air City* and *High and Dry,* again solo and without bolts. In summer of 1999, he soloed a new variation to the *Hallucinogen* that began on the original route, and then went straight up to Happy Trails ledge instead of making the pendulum to Fantasy Island.

Beyer played his own game and made his own rules. His reports to the *American Alpine Journal* (never to the popular magazines) were cryptic and without fanfare, and Beyer's solo mode involved no partners who could help demystify his climbs. He had his own version of the aid rating system, subdividing the A4 and A5 grades with a, b, c, and d, each of which had a specific definition. He also designated the A6 grade to indicate a situation where even the belay would be stripped from the wall in the event of a fall. Beyer did more than hypothesize the A6 grade. He climbed it.

From 1989 through 1991, Beyer made three trips to Pakistan, resulting in solos of two Grade VII routes on 19,000-foot granite spires—and a permanent expulsion from the country after a violent showdown with a liaison officer. Beyer, who lives in Durango, is among the most respected big-wall soloists in the world, and his routes continue to proliferate to this day.

One other notable Black Canyon solo ascent occurred in June 1997. Amanda Tarr, a twenty-two-year-old video game programmer living in Boulder, visited the canyon, which she knew from girlhood, having grown up in the nearby town of Gunnison. Her objective was a solo ascent of the *Hallucinogen Wall.*

The hauling on the initial low-angle pitches of the climb was a heartbreaking task that had stopped teams cold. It was a particularly exacting test of will for a slightly built climber working solo. After descending to free the bags for the fifth time, Tarr figured she had jumared 800 feet on the first pitch alone. Daytime temperatures reached into the nineties.

At night, with the physical struggles over, fear worked its magic. Tarr wondered what would happen if she got hurt. "Maybe I'm still scared of the dark," she wrote in her diary. "All I know is that as soon as I settled into my ledge, a deep, chilling fear took over all my thoughts." Even with the sound of her Walkman playing full volume, the roar of the river filled her ears.

A few days into the effort, Tarr blew a hook placement and fell—fortunately not far. There were many places above where a blown hook would be unthinkable. She assessed her mistakes. Moving too quickly. Improper testing. One of the crux hooking pitches was next. She wrote in her diary: "Slowly and carefully, I balanced my way up the pitch, exfoliating flakes crunching under my toes. There were many times that I wasn't sure which way to go, and had to just follow my nose and hope I'd find the way. Maybe I was lucky, for every time I thought I'd hooked myself out into a dead end, I'd get into my top steps and find another placement to send me on my way." Three pitches later, after five days on the route, Tarr reached the rim and became the first woman to solo a Black Canyon wall route.

Winter
Winter rock climbing is close enough to alpine climbing that its history has been largely ignored here. Winter ascents of big rock climbs such as those on the north face of Capitol Peak near Aspen and the big faces of the San

The Black Canyon in winter (Photo: Jeff Achey)

Juan range must wait for a different book, but a few notable big-wall ascents can be mentioned.

Winter climbing in the Black Canyon involves difficult conditions both on the wall and on the rim. A long ski approach is often required to reach the descent gullies, isolating the expedition considerably. Winter conditions on the wall can range from pleasant to bitter cold, with the chance of ice and snow storms. The first winter ascent of the main face of North Chasm View, via the *Hallucinogen Wall,* was accomplished in 1992 by the renowned expedition wall climbers Mugs Stump and John Middendorf. The first winter ascent of the Painted Wall was made via the *Dragon Route* in early March of 1996 by Mark Synnott and Jeff Achey.

On Longs Peak, the Diamond was first climbed in winter in 1967, by Layton Kor and Wayne Goss as previously recorded. The first winter solo was by the Czech climber Thomas Gross over thirteen days in 1977. The remnants of Gross's homemade plywood bivy platform graced the *D1* route for several years, Colorado's own modest version of the Maestri compressor on Cerro Torre. A few of Mark Wilford's various winter excursions on Longs have already been noted, including his solo link-up of the lower east face and the Diamond in 1984. Two winter ascents of the 1990s deserve mention. In January 1997, Topher Donahue and Craig Luebben climbed *D7* round-trip from the Longs Peak parking lot in just under twenty-one hours for the first one-day winter ascent of the Diamond. In early March of that year, while training for the televised Survival of the Fittest contest (in which he placed second), Kennan Harvey repeated this feat solo, in seventeen hours.

Footloose

By the 1990s, free climbing had evolved into subdisciplines, each with its devotees. Bouldering gained unprecedented popularity, partly due to the advent of "crash pads," which greatly increased the comfort and safety of falling. At the other end of the spectrum, long free climbing—the subject of the rest of this chapter—had its own currents and trends. Standard-setting new routes were climbed, and massive endurance days took link-ups to exhausting new lengths.

The decade began with a bang in 1990 when Mike

Pennings and Topher Donahue made an enchainment that would comprise an ambitious week for most climbers visiting Rocky Mountain National Park. The pair climbed five of the park's major faces—the Diamond, Spearhead, Petit Grepon, Hallett Peak, and Notchtop—in just under twenty-three hours. Technical climbing comprised only a portion of this effort. Connecting the peaks required covering over twenty miles of extremely rough terrain. The highlight of the pair's outing came when they inadvertently found themselves the first party to climb what remained of the *Northcutt-Carter* route on Hallett after a multipitch section was obliterated by rockfall.

One hypothetical Longs Peak link-up stood out as the ultimate "line," easily discerned from any vantage with a view of the east face. *D1,* the original Diamond route, shoots arrow-straight and dead-center up the wall. Below and to the left lies the equally eye-catching *Diagonal Super Direct,* an unbroken line running the full height of the Diagonal Wall. Each 1,000-foot route is a taxing day in itself, with sustained climbing and multiple pitches of 5.11, all above 12,000 feet.

The link of these two routes had been much discussed, and tried several times. In 1994 it still had not been done. Finally, in one very long and tiring day that summer, with much simul-climbing and a single point of aid each, Chip Chace and Roger Briggs pulled off the link-up.

A few weeks later, Alan Lester and Steve Levin did an equally demanding combination, linking the *Super Direct*

Chip Chace caught in the act on the last pitch of the Diagonal Super Direct-D1 *link-up* (Photo: Topher Donahue)

to *King of Swords*. If slightly inferior in line, this link was probably harder, and Lester, who had not previously climbed either route, managed the day 100 percent free.

The Joker

Many good pitches and variations were free climbed, but there was only one big project done on the Diamond in the 1990s. Not surprisingly, the driving force behind it was Roger Briggs. In 1986, Briggs' plans to do a new Diamond free climb with Eric Goukas had ended tragically when Goukas was killed in Yosemite. Briggs went on without Goukas, establishing *Eroica*. Briggs' next Diamond project would prove an eerie déjà vu.

Over the fall and winter of 1992 in Boulder, Briggs climbed frequently with Derek Hersey and they planned to climb a new Diamond route together the next season. They never made the attempt. Hersey was killed in Yosemite in the spring. Briggs would go on to complete the new Diamond climb and dedicate it to Derek, one of whose nicknames was The Joker.

The east face of Longs Peak, showing the Diagonal Super Direct-D1 *link-up,* The Joker *(far right), and* The Honeymoon is Over *(lefthand Diamond line)* (Photo: Bob Godfrey)

Briggs' proposed free line started on Kris Walker's route *Christopher Robin* on the right side of the Diamond. His first attempt was in the summer of 1993 with Chip Chace. The pair went up and, according to Briggs, "got utterly slammed on the second pitch—11+ right off, with A3 pro on sketchy rock . . . no way."

Briggs returned and rope soloed the pitch, placing two bolts and fixing numerous wired nuts. On the next attempt, Briggs and Chace climbed thirty feet into the next pitch before retreating in the face of more loose and overhanging climbing.

Undeterred, Briggs made another rope-solo trip, adding a bolt and a few fixed wires to the third pitch and pulling off about a hundred pounds of loose flakes. By now Chace had lost all interest in the climb. Briggs recruited Steve Levin, who supplied this account of their 1993 climb of *The Joker*:

Roger Briggs on pitch three of The Joker *in 1993* (Photo: Steve Levin)

Roger swims up North Chimney *in twelve minutes wearing his sneakers. I follow, gasping for breath. On Broadway we head right. Above rises an overhanging granite tombstone that spits ice water in intermittent dribbles.*

Roger grabs the rack and is off, gliding up a wet 5.10 pitch. Seconding in one exhalation, I reach the belay hypoxic and try to down a bar, but can't chew. Pitch two is mine, hard moves on rotten flakes right off, then harder moves above, the rock getting worse. A bunch of fixed wires stick out—courtesy of Roger's last foray up here. Without them I doubt I could protect this. I fight, trying not to pull off holds while pulling as hard as I can. As I near the belay, the moves get even harder. I throw for a bucket just below the anchors, miss, and sail into space. I lower to a hand jam and pretend to recover. Take two, same result. When I finally clip the anchors the forearm lactic acid meter is off the scale.

Roger follows, then scratches up the next pitch, horrendous overhanging stemming protected by two fixed pins and a bolt. Seconding takes all I have. Just when I've climbed myself into a pretzel I grab the bucket above the crux—and almost pull it off. Will this climb even exist after a few ascents?

My lead again and, amazingly, twenty feet of climbing that is only 5.10+. Then a puzzling traverse left, out of the crack and across a blank wall. If only there were holds! Twenty feet higher there are holds—tight finger locks between good rock and a plug of something else, a decomposing imitation rock. I place a #0 TCU and reach the belay, feeling bouted and spent.

Above is an overhanging corner that meets Table Ledge at a four-foot roof. Roger is stemming it at full extension with his left foot at ear level. He looks completely in his element—at almost 14,000 feet and a thousand feet off the deck, dinking in an RP in a stem that would make a circus performer proud. On the follow I almost dislocate my groin, but manage to keep it together as the climbing eases to 5.11.

Tucked in a semi-hanging belay, I can see in his eyes that some kind of victory awaits us. Looking up, however, I'm filled with doubts. It looks impossible—soaking wet moss covers the rock. I start up and start digging. Twenty feet higher I'm covered with mud and my shoes are soaked in slime. This isn't even rock climbing anymore, so I justify pulling on a piece. I've gotten what I came for and I'm ready to be out of here. I look down and Roger is laughing, one last laugh before his turn at the mudslinging. Diamond climbing doesn't get any better—or worse.

Briggs and Levin had completed the line, but not all free. Subsequent ascents of *The Joker* also defied a definitive "first free ascent"—which in Colorado generally means an ascent where every pitch of the climb is led free by some member of the party during a continuous push from the bottom to the top of the route. Perhaps Briggs and Pat Adams' ascent in 1994 will be judged sufficient, where all the pitches were led free except the second, on which Briggs used a point of aid, but Adams followed free.

Minute stylistic analysis seems necessary to designate "firsts" in a climbing history, but it also obscures the reality of such remarkable free-climbing days, so different in character from sunny afternoons in Eldorado Canyon, or the controlled environment of a one-pitch sport climb. On these Diamond ascents, one climber hangs shivering at a sling belay above 13,000 feet while the other struggles overhead with continuous 5.11 and 5.12 climbing, often on wet or crumbling rock. Climbing the pitch on-sight is almost mandatory—there is little time for working a pitch. Half an hour later the belayer shakes some warmth into his hands, does his best to follow the pitch, and then starts up the next lead as a storm sweeps in over the summit of Longs.

Although *The Joker* was the hardest big free climb done in Rocky Mountain National Park in the 1990s, the poor rock will likely prevent it from ever becoming the classic testpiece of the wall. In the future, that distinction probably will go to a new route just right of *Eroica*, established over many days with much aid and fixed protection by Eric Doub. This route, called *The Honeymoon is Over,* spent most of the 1990s as a project and was climbed with aid several times—enough to discern that a free ascent would be much harder than anything yet done on the face.

Black Canyon Free Routes

By the 1990s, the Black Canyon had become Colorado's most important refuge for "trad" (traditional) or "adventure" climbing, strange new terms in climbers' vocabularies that spoke volumes about the influence of sport climbing.

Most of the canyon's new routes were approached from the North Rim campground, Colorado adventure climbers' equivalent of the Ghetto Meadow in Rifle. Some were on new walls in the less visited gullies while others were free versions of old classics.

In the latter category, Cary Gunter and Ed Pearsalls of Colorado Springs made a near free ascent in 1992 of the historic *Diagonal,* the original line on the main face of North Chasm View. This route had been the scene of the canyon's second big free-climbing venture, the near-disastrous attempt in 1976 by Jim Dunn and Earl Wiggins. Exotic routefinding and placement of a half dozen bolts led Gunter and Pearsalls to an unplanned bivouac and consumed enough energy to defeat the free-climbing effort at the route's crux—one of the final aid sections of the *Hallucinogen Wall*. This attempt paved the way for the all-free ascent in 1994, accomplished by Dunn, once again in top shape to revisit the site of his epic eighteen years earlier, partnered by Eric Decaria.

Over two days in 1993 Kent Wheeler and Greg Lomme climbed *Lost Cities* on an untouched wall upstream from North Chasm View. This was a particularly sustained free route, as well as a testament to how much excellent unclimbed rock remained in the canyon—for those with the correct temperament.

The next year, on his third attempt, Robert Warren finished *Trilogy,* probably the most demanding of the early 1990s new routes, taking a spectacular arête rising above the Cruise Gully. Though short (800 feet), *Trilogy* was fierce, with forty-foot falls possible on 5.10+, and 5.11+ arête climbing protected by RURPs, bashies, and widely spaced quarter-inch bolts.

Harder still, and also "spicy," was a nearby line picked out by Wheeler up the smooth buttress right of *Ament's Chimney.* Finished by Wheeler and Scott Lazar in 1996 after several attempts (and several long falls), *Apparition* had one of the single most difficult free-climbing pitches in the Black Canyon. "Scott deserves all of the credit for the two crux pitches," Wheeler said. "Mind-boggling watching him thirty feet out on 5.12 placing hooks to drill from." The route epitomized the high level of adventure maintained on first ascents in the canyon.

The most publicized Black Canyon climb of the 1990s

Australian climber Steve Monks on Trilogy, *Robert Warren's daunting 1994 route on North Chasm View Wall* (Photo: Topher Donahue)

Scott Lazar on The Apparition (Photo: Topher Donahue)

was the *Free Nose* of North Chasm View, accounts of which appeared both in *Climbing* magazine and the 1997 *American Alpine Journal*. This remains the most sustained free climb in the canyon, and it involved a massive siege. Jeff Achey gives a firsthand confession:

I was one of a long line of Black Canyon climbers enamored with the Nose of Chasm View, and my first attempt to free climb it was in 1983. I'd never attempted a multiday climb before, and this effort was a joke, ending in exhaustion on the easy terraces near the bottom of the wall.

In 1995, now considerably more experienced, I drove out to the North Rim to photograph some friends on High and Dry. *They weren't on the route. That day, with a lot of rope and time on my hands, I made my first rappel down what would become the* Free Nose.

It was not unusual to scope the upper sections of hard Black Canyon projects on rappel, but the Free Nose *involved a quantum leap in rappel recon. The rappels were so steep that we had to place all kinds of sketchy intermediate gear, and the ropes constantly dislodged loose flakes, suffering numerous nicks and cuts. Once, wearing a massive pack, I sat back into an overhanging rappel, heard a click, and found myself teetering in balance, holding the rope in my hands, completely unclipped.*

Chip Chace was my main partner for these escapades, and he mastered the crux rope maneuver, a diagonal tension traverse about 800 feet below the rim that involved hook moves and A4 pins to cross a face covered with loose, bladelike flakes. Chip fixed a rope across this traverse, and not long after that he dropped out of the project, fed up with my overriding obsession with the climb. Chip never got any credit, but these epic rappels were the hardest and most dangerous part of the Free Nose *ascent.*

Over three days in October 1995, Steve Levin and I made the first ascent of the general line which began on the Goss-Logan and connected with the Wiggins-Becker. We used a fair amount of aid and jumared Chip's fixed rope, which crossed the same crackless expanse that had stopped Goss and Logan and the other aid-climbing parties in the early 1970s. Just before the snows closed the canyon for the winter I returned with Baptiste Briand, a French sport climber who had no idea what he was getting into, and made the rappels one last time. We spent the day hook-bolting the long blank section, which went free at 5.11. Rappel bolting was and still is shunned by Black Canyon climbers, and I tried to make up for the epic siege by doing all the bolt placements on lead.

In early May 1996, Steve and I returned. By this time we had managed to add a documentary film to the already overblown project. Brian Morrato and Jim

Opposite: *Steve Levin on the crux pitch of the* Free Nose, *North Chasm View Wall, in 1996* (Photo: Jim Surette)

Jeff Achey on the first ascent of The Serpent, *the second free route on the main face of the Painted Wall* (Photo: Kennan Harvey)

Surette shot footage while Steve and I climbed various pitches of the route. This was critical rehearsal time for us, as the route was proving all too near our limit. We finished the filming, pulled all our ropes, and then free climbed the route in a two-day push, bivouacking halfway up with supplies we had stashed. Finally, the route was free—and so were we.

In March 1996, just before the completion of the *Free Nose*, Achey climbed the *Dragon Route,* which was still the only line on the overhanging central section of the Painted Wall. This ascent convinced him that much of the *Dragon* would go free. Years passed and no one tried it. In October 1999, Achey enlisted Kennan Harvey for an attempt.

Harvey, recently moved to Colorado from Salt Lake City, was one of the state's best all-around climbers. He could do the scary Eldorado climbs, flash 5.12 cracks in Canyonlands, and had put up huge free routes in the Bugaboos of Canada and on Shipton Spire in Pakistan.

Harvey could spare only four days for the climb, so the pair chose the fastest style possible. Though the leader would free climb, the second would follow in standard big-wall style, on jumars. They packed a portaledge, the usual wall gear, and a free-climbing rack, supplemented with pitons and about twenty bolts.

The crux crack climbing came about six pitches up, where Harvey deviated from the regular *Dragon* line and led a jagged crack that ran beneath the massive Kor's Cave roof. The next five pitches involved poorly-protected Eldorado-style open face climbing and some unusual belays, including one solely from slings draped over a huge spike. No bolts were placed. The free variation joined the *Dragon Route* midway through the Stygian Traverse, struck out left onto new ground again, then rejoined the original line just below the Exit Cracks. The pair spent a second night on the wall just below the final chimneys and topped out the next day, completing the route in four days round-trip from the campground.

The pair dubbed their climb *The Serpent,* and it was repeated just a week later by Topher Donahue and Jeff Ofsanko, in similar big-wall style. As of 2001, a one-day free ascent of this route remained one of the canyon's outstanding challenges.

Black Canyon Link-ups

Some of the most impressive climbs in the Black Canyon in the 1990s were not new routes. Instead, classic hard routes were repeated—several in a day. Earl Wiggins and Mike O'Donnell had done the first big two-route day in 1983, climbing *Scenic Cruise* and the *Goss-Logan*. In 1991, Derek Hersey did a triple combination—*Scenic Cruise, Journey Home,* and *Leisure Climb*—climbing solo and unroped.

The team of Jeff Hollenbaugh and Mike Pennings took the enchainment game to its highest level yet. Hollenbaugh began climbing as a student at Glenwood Springs High School on Colorado's West Slope, while Pennings was originally from California. Both were superb all-around climbers and together they made a powerful team.

In June 1993 they were the first to do a classic link-up—*The Cruise* and *Astrodog*—in an adventurous day that took them up both the North and South Chasm View Walls. This "rim to rim to rim" idea was Derek Hersey's, who had died in Yosemite just the month before. The mad Englishman was a hero to the pair, and it became Hollenbaugh and Pennings' habit to celebrate their Black Canyon climbs with Hersey's favorite brew, Toothsheaf Stout.

In 1997 they linked *Stoned Oven* and *Air Voyage*. These climbs were no longer than earlier enchained routes, but they were much more difficult, with extremely physical climbing. Featuring long sections of hard off-width climbing, each was considered a brutal day in itself for even the best climbers. *Stoned Voyage* is a link-up destined to be repeated by few.

On this and other speed ascents, Pennings and Hollenbaugh free climbed almost everything, but would aid the odd move. This was typical of speed climbers, and to call it "poor style" is to misunderstand the new passion for freedom of movement and the shift in goals. In the 1980s, free climbing had become such a dogma that a single move of aid could generate a sense of failure on a 2,000-foot climb. By the 1990s, high-end free-climbing sieges often involved more aid-climbing and rope-hanging time than conventional big-wall ascents. Hollenbaugh and Pennings didn't take the hackneyed old game so seriously. They wanted to cover ground. They climbed the wall, as fast and free as expedient, then headed down the gully to climb another—and perhaps a third.

Hollenbaugh and Pennings got faster: fast enough to aspire to what they called the Trifecta, a one-day link-up of the Black Canyon's three largest and most difficult formations—the Painted Wall, and South and North Chasm View. The feat would require 5,600 feet of high-standard rock climbing, plus thousands of feet of gully descents and rappelling, two river crossings, and substantial night climbing. The *Southern Arête* route on the Painted Wall alone was notorious for taking parties longer than the available daylight hours. The other routes would be *Astrodog* on South Chasm View and *The Cruise* on North Chasm View.

By 1999, a young climber named Cameron Tague had joined the fray. Living in Boulder, Tague was giving the local adventure climbing a shot in the arm, with exploits in Eldorado such as the first ground-up lead of Dale Goddard's 1986 route *Evictor* and the first ascent of the extremely serious *Weeping Willow* near *Jules Verne*. Tragically, in 2000 Tague would be killed in a fall from Broadway on Longs Peak during a routine approach to the Diamond.

Tague loved the Black Canyon and added several high-standard new routes. With Hollenbaugh, and then with Pennings, he too tried the Trifecta. These efforts were thwarted by fatigue or flood conditions on the river, but they solved some fine points of logistics. The climbers had now logged very fast times on each of the three routes. In the summer of 2000, Hollenbaugh was preparing to move to Montana, and Pennings to California. Hollenbaugh was out of rock-climbing shape, but the pair realized it was now or never for the Trifecta. Hollenbaugh gives this account of their day:

Derek Hersey soloing Scenic Cruise, first climbed unroped by Earl Wiggins in 1979 (Photo: Dan Hare)

Sitting on a glacier in Alaska wasn't exactly Trifecta training. I would have to rely on enthusiasm. Mike, on the other hand, was in top shape and the only person in the world that I could possibly team up with to pull this off.

Four A.M. and we were on autopilot and down the gully. The sun let us know it was game for another day as we tied in at the base of the Painted Wall. Climbing as fast as possible, I still took time to enjoy the pitches and gaze out at my awesome surroundings. The climb disappeared below us and we changed into our walking shoes for the four-mile jaunt back to camp.

Astrodog was soaking up the heat, and we relaxed and rehydrated at the campground, waiting for the sun to head west. We could not complain. The weather was perfect, on the cool side for mid-June. We talked about the heat of the Stoned Voyage as we made our way down the Cruise Gully to the river.

Huge stoneflies guarded the boulders on the approach to the Tyrolean. The mist from the river cooled our bodies on the outside and the final gulps from the river quenched the inside as we changed back into climbing shoes and made our way upward. The Dog was as good as ever—one of best free climbs in the Black. I knew the day was taking a toll when we reached the crux pitch. I wish it were for the sake of speed that I pulled on the gear as I seconded the pitch, and perhaps it was, for if I had not I would have been hanging on the cord.

We topped out on the South Rim as its shadow topped out on the North Rim; it was time to return to the river. Rappelling down the Dog was the least enjoyable portion of the day. Several times the rope threatened to get stuck, several times I was tentative about the anchors, several times I thought that this was the stunt that could compromise the vision. The relief I felt back on the banks of the river was odd. Here I was in the throat of the beast and utterly relaxed and at home. The chill of the river spray pulled me from my stupor as I pulled across the Tyrolean. All we had to do now was claw our way up The Cruise.

I assumed the tiredness I felt at the base would disappear as soon as we started climbing. I was mis-

Mike Pennings and Jeff Hollenbaugh enjoying the Black Canyon in the 1990s. Pennings is shown settling in for a forced bivouac near the top of the Painted Wall, off-route on Stratosfear, *1993; Hollenbaugh inspects* The Nose *(Photos: Jim Surette, Jeff Achey)*

The Trifecta: The Painted Wall, and South and North Chasm View, climbed by Pennings and Hollenbaugh in just over twenty-four hours in summer 2000 (Photos: Jeff Achey)

taken. The wide cracks of The Cruise *offered comfort, a womb, a warm place to curl up and sleep as the solar radiation soaked up by day radiated back out at night. The comfortable ledges I would normally welcome became cursed; as Mike would lead out on the sharp end I would readily fall asleep. I was wasted. The Alaska training program was no better than I could have expected. Following and yarding on gear, I arrived at belays in amazement. "How in the hell did you climb that?!" Four pitches from the top, Mike could sense what was going through my head. "Do you want me to take this lead?" On belay and sweet dreams . . .*

We topped out seven minutes in excess of a twenty-four-hour day. Back at camp we passed out before we could even get a Sheaf cracked. Driving away from the Black the following day was an emotional experience. For the first time I was leaving completely content, like there was no way I could have done more. In the past I could never put my finger on the discontent I felt upon departure. Now I knew. Thanks Derek. Thanks Mike. Thank you Black Canyon of the Gunnison.

29. Into the Future

Following a decade characterized by stylistic conflict, the late 1990s were a time of acceptance and synthesis. Indoor competition climbing continued on its halting course, falling short of the Olympic expectations that accompanied its early days in the late 1980s. At the end of the millennium it made another national TV appearance as one of the sexy new "extreme sports" in the ESPN X Games. Even with the lofty, gymnastic bouldering format used in these games, climbing was pretty drab as an extreme spectator sport. Still, the summer 1999 event in San Francisco netted Chris Sharma more than ten thousand dollars in prize money and matching sponsorship bonuses. By now, many of the best rock climbers in Colorado and elsewhere were professionals, and making a fair living.

The on-sight climbing prowess that had come with high-level competition produced results that spilled over beyond the discipline of sport climbing. In Colorado, perhaps the best example was the Japanese climber Yuji Hirayama's ascent of the famed *Sphinx Crack*. In 1995, he walked to the base, loaded his harness with a well chosen selection of nuts and cams, and led the climb bottom to top, first try, no falls, placing protection as he went.

Sport climbing became increasingly popular. Grand Junction, Durango, Redstone, Glenwood Springs, Crested Butte, Vail, Steamboat Springs, Golden—all these towns and others had their own new sport-climbing areas.

Fun, convenience, and craftsmanship were priorities, and a few climbers took these values to the extreme. Beginning in around 1998, parts of Boulder Canyon were "developed" in the fullest sense of the word. At the so-called Sport Park, holds were drilled and sculpted to maximize route density, eliminate hard cruxes, and provide "user-friendly" training. The grounds were extensively landscaped to provide a comfortable staging area. By 2000, Sport Park was one of the most popular climbing areas in Boulder.

Other Boulder Canyon crags were "grid bolted," offering novel route possibilities, as evidenced by the guidebook description of the climb *Walking on a Burning Hillside* on the Solar Dome: "Climb *Walking on the Sun* to 3rd bolt and traverse left past 3rd bolt on *The Homesteader* to 2nd bolt on *Sundance*. At 3rd bolt of *Sundance* go left to 3rd bolt of *Burning up the Hillside* and up this climb's crux and finish to its anchors."

Not surprisingly, Boulder Canyon had its share of controversies. In the late 1990s, the canyon made local headlines when one ice climber assaulted another with an ice ax. In 2000, the Sport Park phenomenon kicked off a major bolt war, resulting in more feature stories in the local newspapers and more strange publicity for the sport of climbing. Another more parochial controversy surrounded Boulder Canyon's most outrageous free climb of the 1990s, on Castle Rock.

The protagonists in this drama were Rob Candelaria and Jerry Moffatt, both well-known characters on the Boulder scene. Moffatt had made regular visits to Boulder since the 1982 visit when he repeated *Genesis*, and he was now a fully sponsored professional climber and globetrotting superstar. Candelaria had been party to many grand free-climbing efforts since the 1970s. A professional athletic coach (he was personal trainer to champion climber Robyn Erbesfield), he gave Boulder its first indoor climbing gym, C.A.T.S., which was *the* place to train at the end of the 1980s.

Candelaria had done countless new routes in the Boulder area since the late 1970s, including a number of alleged free ascents that had been doubted by other climbers. The reported ascents were of world-class severity, often horrendously unprotected, and often done roped-solo. Hard evidence was lacking and gossip played as large a role as fact, but by the mid-1990s, Candelaria's credibility was widely questioned—an unfortunate state of affairs for a talented climber who had done much for Boulder rock climbing.

In 1996, Candelaria was working on Castle Rock's "last great problem," a free ascent of the *Practice Aid Roof* pioneered by Dale Johnson and party in 1950. Moffatt, too, had tried the problem. Ever since the 1970s, free climbers had looked up at this twenty-foot finger-size roof crack and wondered. Now, it appeared, the *Practice Roof* was going to go. Both Candelaria and Moffatt claimed to be close to success.

One can imagine a satisfying scenario that would have gone far in clearing Candelaria's reputation. Candel-

Jerry Moffatt on Life's Too Short, *a.k.a.* Deadline, *a.k.a. the* Practice Aid Roof, *Castle Rock, in 1997* (Photo: Beth Wald)

aria might have claimed the first free ascent. Moffatt, predictably, would doubt his word. If proof was then produced—say, video footage of the ascent—then all of Candelaria's previous feats would be viewed in a more credible light. Unfortunately, this scenario never took place. Candelaria claimed the free ascent. Moffatt also freed the roof, with photographers present, and claimed Candelaria never did it. There was no video. Candelaria's belayer was his girlfriend. Climbing historians remain in a quandary, but one thing was indisputable: Boulder Canyon had its most outrageous free climb yet.

The talent pool of Colorado climbers was deep as never before, and it became increasingly difficult for an individual climber to stand out. By the late 1990s, dozens of climbers could regularly do hard 5.13. Countless climbs were added by both young climbers and veterans.

One interesting Boulder climber of the 1990s was Alan Lester, who had been an early contemporary of Alan Watts just before Smith Rock's sport-climbing spree of the mid-1980s. Lester had remarkable all-around talent, traveled and climbed widely, and by the early 1990s, living in Boulder, he began to tick off an eclectic series of semitraditional "last great problems" in Colorado that stood out even in the elite Boulder scene. These included the hardest climbs in several areas, such as the big roof and headwall of *Exotic Headache* on the Grotto Wall in Aspen in 1993 and Layton Kor's old aid route *Anaconda* on Lumpy Ridge in 1994.

In Boulder Canyon in 1993, Lester climbed the longstanding *Throne Crack* on Blob Rock, another solid 5.13 seam and crack climb. In 1994, with Pete Takeda, he made the first free ascent of what is probably Colorado National Monument's finest line, *Medicine Man* on Sentinel Spire, a four-pitch 5.12 Canyonlands-style tower route. Unlike most climbers making hard 5.13 ascents, Lester excelled in a variety of disciplines, including long link-ups in Rocky Mountain National Park and the Black Canyon.

Also worth noting was the continuing presence of Steve Hong, who had established Colorado's hardest free climb, *Sphinx Crack,* in 1981. In the mid- and late 1990s, Hong was living in Boulder, competing and winning against climbers half his age in the indoor competitions, and establishing a steady string of new climbs at Rifle, some as hard as 5.14.

In Colorado Springs, the scene was considerably more relaxed. In the early to mid-1990s, Dan Durland brought a new standard of difficulty to the region with first ascents including *Damage* (5.13c/d, Shelf Road) and *The Dark Art* (5.13c/d, Eleven-Mile Canyon).

Ian Spencer-Green was another exceptional young Springs climber. Son of the 1970s climber and photographer Stewart Green, Ian began bouldering at age three, led his first 5.10 at age ten, and in 1993 became the youngest American to climb 5.13, redpointing *The Example* at Shelf Road two days before his fourteenth birthday. After working his way through the harder climbs at Shelf Road, Rifle, and elsewhere, he established his own hard routes on the crags around Pikes Peak, including gear-protected 5.13 cracks. His hardest route was *Tallboy*, an overhanging granite face in Engleman Canyon above Manitou Springs, the Springs area's first 5.14, done in November 1999.

With its low-key reporting and seemingly endless supply of new climbing areas, the Springs scene is in many ways unchanged since the 1970s. "Nowadays," said Spencer-Green in a recent correspondence, "the Pikes Peak region is more or less the same as it has always been—a handful of hardcore locals battling away on stellar first ascents on dreamlike stone in secret, hard-to-locate areas of pristine nature. Although from an outside perspective Colorado Springs may seem quiet and inactive, in fact, there is always constant first-ascent activity taking place that goes unreported to all except a few select locals. This is how it will always remain in Colorado Springs."

The Rarefied Realms

In sport climbing, the upper grades filled out considerably in the late 1990s. Many 5.13+ and 5.14- routes went up near the Front Range towns, where huge numbers of climbers lived, and in and around Rifle. In 1996, however, top-end difficulty in Colorado reached a stubborn plateau at 8c (5.14b).

One definitive characteristic of extreme sport climbing in the early and mid-1990s was hold chipping. The practice had made limited appearances in the Garden of the Gods in the late 1970s and in the Boulder Flatirons, Penitente Canyon, and Shelf Road in the late 1980s, and then had exploded in Clear Creek in the early 1990s. It filtered with a bit more subtlety into Rifle, where it mixed inextricably with the cleaning that was necessary to climb the blocky limestone.

In Rifle, as at Shelf Road and Penitente, some top climbers strictly avoided intentional hold manufacturing. Others indulged. One conspicuous example of indulgence was *The Crew,* a sweeping line out the Wicked Cave near *Slice of Life,* which, when done by Chris Knuth of Boulder in 1996, quickly gained acceptance as Rifle's hardest route. Artificial finger pockets dotted the smooth lower section of the wall. Up higher, where natural features were too abundant, the line was "deconstructed" to eliminate good holds and knee bars.

In 1989, *Climbing* magazine editor Michael Kennedy had written, "*Climbing* will no longer give any credence to chipped routes, other than to subject them to the scorn they deserve. Simply put, if people wish to construct training apparatus with chisel and glue, they should do it on artificial walls. No debate, and no exceptions." The vast majority of Colorado climbers agreed.

But what did they know? How could the masses grasp what it was like to climb at the cutting edge of the possible, where artificial holds were the only way to link the barely climbable features that comprised a potential route? Elite climbers, as always, set the rules and the standards. In the 1980s, the majority of climbers were against bolted climbs, and now they couldn't get enough of them. Chipping, too, would probably soon be accepted. The Europeans had already led the way—at crags such as Buoux, in France, some of the most famous climbs were artificial. For example, the original "Rose" move,

Ian Spencer-Green on his route Tallboy, *the Colorado Springs area's first 5.14* (Photo: Stewart M. Green)

on *La Rose et le Vampir*, was manufactured by Antoine Le Menestrel.

Yet chipping struck at the core concept of free climbing: meeting an impossible-looking natural challenge. If the challenge was constructed, something fundamental was destroyed—the sense of wonder at discovering an esoteric natural choreography in the rock. The uncertainty of success was also squelched. On a chipped route, the precise overall difficulty could be predetermined. It could be made just hard enough for the creator to succeed, and tailored to match his strengths and avoid his weaknesses.

For a while, a concerted effort was made to omit manufactured routes from magazine news reports. This proved impossible. There were ambiguous shades of gray—if you crowbarred off a loose rock but glued some of it in place, was that an artificial hold? There was also the problem of detection. Most top climbers were either loath to admit to chipping, or hesitant to point the finger at friends. The reporting policy soon waned.

Beginning in the mid-1990s, a new generation of climbers appeared to whom chipping was not just a philosophical issue, but a tangible threat. Chipping was not opening up new possibilities. Rather, for Chris Sharma of California, David Graham of New England, and Tommy Caldwell of Colorado, chipping had trivialized some prime 5.14+ climbs.

In Colorado, Caldwell was living proof of the hypothetical "climber of the future" who would do what the elite climbers before him had deemed impossible. Caldwell summarized his approach thus: "I've bolted a few routes that I don't know will ever go, but I've also bolted a bunch of routes that I thought would never go—that I've done."

The success of this remarkable Colorado climber deserves elaboration here.

Mountain Boy

Not long after he learned to walk, Tommy Caldwell learned to climb. Outdoor living ran in the family. Born in 1978, Tommy was the son of Mike and Terry Caldwell, of Estes Park. Mike was a climbing instructor and guide, as well as an active Lumpy Ridge climber, and his young son loved family outings in the mountains, which became progressively more adventurous. One memorable summer day in Rocky Mountain National Park, Mike and Tommy climbed the *Northcutt-Carter* route on Hallett Peak, and then hiked into the next valley and did the Petit Grepon the same day. Tommy was twelve years old.

That same summer, Tommy made his first trip up the Diamond. He also began sport climbing, and in 1994 he entered a few Front Range competitions. Until then, climbing was a "family fun" thing. After his success in the com-

Father and son on Renaissance Wall. Though overshadowed by the fame of his son Tommy, Mike Caldwell (belaying) was a prolific new-route climber himself and established this Lumpy Ridge climb with Randy Farris in 1992. (Photo: Craig Luebben)

petitions, Tommy started to take climbing more seriously.

At one of the contests he met another young star, Chris Sharma, and with the help of some folks who were old enough to drive, the pair went road-tripping. They swapped falls and redpoints at Logan Canyon, Wild Iris, Rifle. By 1996, Caldwell had climbed his first 5.14s.

He quickly repeated some of Colorado's hardest routes, including *Honemaster Lambada* in the Boulder Flatirons and *The Crew* at Rifle. He began ticking off any open project he could find on Colorado's Front Range. These, in no particular order, include *Interstellar*, one of the hardest routes at Clear Creek, which he did at age seventeen; *Stiletto*, a stunning 5.14 arête in North St. Vrain Canyon; *Mr. Stiffie*, one of the harder routes in Boulder Canyon; *Gomorrah* on the Bauhaus Wall in Rifle; and *Third Millennium* (5.13d) and *Grand Old Opry* (5.14b), projects of his own at an area called the Monastery. Caldwell's 5.14 routes ranged from severely overhanging limestone lines to super-technical vertical faces.

Mostly he climbed with his dad, and father and son alike loved to bolt and climb new projects. Bad weather seldom stopped them. One chilly winter they repeatedly made the hike up to try a climb on the Industrial Wall on Mickey Mouse Wall south of Boulder. The final day, near Christmas 1998, was bitter cold and overcast, but Terry had hiked up, too, through shin-deep snow, and Tommy didn't want to let his mom down. After warming up by a fire, he succeeded on *Vogue*, at 5.14b the Boulder area's hardest route.

A few months earlier, Caldwell had found a project at Rifle, next to *Gomorrah*. To call this an open project would be misleading. The line had looked so unpromising to the person who equipped it that it had been used only as an access route to bolt other climbs. Nevertheless, Caldwell tried it. "I remember it being different than anything I'd ever been on," he said, "because it doesn't really have holds." Knee pinches and other exotic tricks were required, and the only rest on the pitch required turning around to face the river. In November 1998, Caldwell redpointed *Tomfoolery*, perhaps Rifle's hardest route.

The next summer, Caldwell did an even more unusual climb. In the early 1960s, when climbers were allowed to stay at the shelter cabin below Longs Peak, many short climbs went up on the Ship's Prow, a small formation on the shore of Chasm Lake. In 1998, Pat Adams and Jim Redo established a two-pitch, 5.12 sport climb, *Baloney Pony*, up a spectacular arête near the formation's right side. They made a bet about the very unlikely direct start they had left unclimbed—a fifty-foot glass-smooth section of arête. After studying it from a rappel rope, Adams, a seasoned 5.13+ climber, declared the arête impossible. Redo disagreed, and they bet a dinner at the posh Flagstaff House in Boulder.

Visions of fine wine and filet mignon prompted Redo to call Tommy Caldwell, and in summer 1999 Tommy and his dad went up to have a look. A rope inspection convinced Tommy he could do it, and he proceeded with the hard labor of hand-bolting the pitch. Climbing 5.12 at an elevation of nearly 13,000 feet is quite an experience, but climbing two number grades harder proved a physiological odyssey. The explosive, relentless climbing left Caldwell hypoxic and dizzy. Still, he loved the project—the long hike in, the unlikely moves of the climb, the stark alpine setting. Finally, Caldwell climbed the pitch—*Sarchasm*, the country's highest 5.14.

The Rifle bolting ban had sent climbers exploring the nearby canyons, and Caldwell and Nick Sagar discovered an impressive-looking new crag in nearby Elk Creek. It had been spotted before, but few Rifle climbers were willing to make the hour-long hike to reach it. When Caldwell and Sagar reached the base, they found a 200-foot-high amphitheater of smooth, overhanging limestone, monumental and remote. They called the crag the Fortress of Solitude.

Tommy spent eight hours bolting the crag's first line, aiding from the ground up with hooks and Tri-Cams. He was looking for something of middle difficulty, but by the time he drilled his anchors he realized he had stumbled onto something else entirely. When lowered down, landing fifty feet out from the base, he said, "Wow, that looks pretty hard."

That September he started working on the climb, first with Sagar, then with his dad. It took six days before Caldwell could do the individual moves. It would take twenty days, spread out over two months, to link them. Often Mike and Tommy would come up the night before and camp at the base of the crag. "I had to get into a routine where my whole life centered around trying to do that thing," Tommy said.

Tommy linked progressively longer sections of the route. By mid-October 1999 he had tried the route sixty times. His dad had named the route *Kryptonite*.

One Saturday, on his last try of the day, Tommy came close to the redpoint. His dad told him that they needed to be headed back to Estes Park by four the next afternoon. Crisp conditions were essential, and the climb didn't go into the shade until three.

"I got up and got on it at like eight in the morning and it felt horrendous," Tommy said. "I couldn't do anything. So I was like, well, try it again . . . and I think sometimes that mindset is really good. You don't get nervous." Next try, he succeeded.

Having climbed several 8c+ routes in other areas, Caldwell felt *Kryptonite* was harder. He rated it 9a, 5.14d, which would make it the hardest pitch of rock climbing in the country, and among the hardest in the world.

Tommy Caldwell on his route Gomorrah *in Rifle, a few days before the first ascent* (Photo: Jeff Achey)

Equally remarkable, it was one of the few 5.14s that was completely free of chipping or gluing.

Sadly, this status would soon change. In 2001 a pair of the world's best professional climbers—Yuji Hirayama of Japan, François Legrand of France, plus their assorted photographers and companions—came to attempt *Kryptonite* on a bid to climb "all of America's hardest routes." Legrand failed, but after a six-day effort, Hirayama succeeded, suggesting a grade of 8c+, a notch below Caldwell's claim. During the *Kryptonite* attempt, however, the sharp natural holds were enlarged and "comfortized," and at least one new pocket was drilled outright. Apparently, this was the work of Legrand, renowned mostly for his artificial-wall climbing. Incredibly, the masterful *Kryptonite,* in all its uncomfortable, natural brilliance, was no more.

The Route Ahead

With the first ascent of 100-foot *Kryptonite (may it rest in peace),* and huge multi-formation link-ups in Rocky Mountain National Park and the Black Canyon, Colorado rock climbing entered the new millennium with vigor. In addition to high-end sport routes and high-speed linkage, there are several other interesting new trends.

On the smaller crags, there is new interest in "mind control" climbing. The poorly protected routes that put Eldorado Canyon on the free-climbing map in the 1970s were still widely respected throughout the 1990s, but the art had advanced little since the early 1980s. For a while, bolt protection provided new route possibilities, but that era ended with the 1989 fixed-hardware regulations. Climbing a new bolted route in Eldorado in the late 1990s required a lengthy application process, and few new climbs were approved.

There was no prohibition against new climbs using nonhammered gear, but the remaining possibilities seemed to lie in a realm that even the most talented and dedicated were unwilling to enter. On British gritstone, international ground-zero for "necky" routes, climbers had reached a similar impasse at about the same level as the 1980s Eldorado plateau. Using the decimal rating system, this level is a vague realm—"unprotected 5.11," "poorly protected 5.12," or just plain "desperate." It is less vague to the British, who represent it by the grade E5. On gritstone, few E6 climbs were led without rehearsal on top rope. In Boulder, only *Perilous Journey* and a few of Alec Sharp's preinspected routes pushed the E5 standard.

On the riskiest gritstone routes, British climbers first safely master the climb on top rope and build up the confidence—or the illusion—that they can pull off a go-for-broke lead. Someone proposed the perfect name for this scary kind of redpoint: a headpoint. Headpointing was popularized in this country by a dramatic British climb-

Topher Donahue on Locks of Rages, *a 1999 "headpoint" route on Rock of Ages in Rocky Mountain National Park* (Photo: Craig Luebben)

ing video called *Hard Grit,* and at the end of the 1990s the practice came to Eldorado Canyon.

As of this writing, the hardest Eldorado headpoint climb is probably Andy Donson's *The Lion,* on the blunt arête next to *Rainbow Wall* on Wind Tower. At mid 5.12, with a nasty thirty-foot fall possible on the precarious crux, this route is, by Donson's estimate, low-end E7. The potential for harder Eldorado climbs of this style is nearly unlimited. Near Estes Park, Topher Donahue has pushed some hard headpointing routes that feature thin and tricky-to-place protection, with long falls possible, but less risk of serious injury. The new game seems to promise many variations.

There has also been a huge surge in the popularity of bouldering, the history and culture of which could fill a book all its own. With the advent of crash pads and advanced spotting skills, falls of twenty feet or more are being taken safely and routinely, resulting in some very high, very difficult, very exciting unroped climbs. Closer to the ground, new Front Range boulder problems such as Tommy Caldwell's *Turn that Frown Upside Down* at Gross Reservoir and David Graham's *Nothing but Sunshine* and *Centaur* in Chaos Canyon in Rocky Mountain National Park are of world-class difficulty. New crags are increasingly hard to find in Colorado, but there seems to be no end to new boulders.

At the other extreme, the Diamond may still offer groundbreaking firsts for those who can couple old-style mountain savvy with modern world-class free-climbing ability. One such ascent proves the point. In August 2001, Tommy Caldwell pulled off the first free ascent of Eric Doub's project of the 1990s. The Diamond got its first 5.13, *The Honeymoon is Over*.

A Final Word

In the future, in all genres, new challenges will be taken on and mastered—that, as always, is climbing. The new millennium's most important rock-climbing challenges, however, will not lie in establishing 5.15 or longer and faster link-ups. They will involve mastering the sport's growing pains. Rock climbing is no longer esoteric, wide open, and new. Despite its maverick roots, it has become an extremely popular, almost mainstream, outdoor activity. It figures in modern ad campaigns selling everything from pharmaceuticals to SUVs. It has been integrated into the culture and has drawn enough enthusiasts to have a serious environmental impact.

There are danger signs. We are trashier than ever—even the bivy sites of the Black Canyon show signs of carelessness and abuse. Our fondness for bolts has taken us out of the company of hikers, anglers, and bird-watchers and put us in a class by ourselves. We have developed "sport parks" without the permission or knowledge of the citizens with whom we share stewardship of our wild public lands. In 1989, Boulder climbers were blindsided by a sweeping bolting ban in the Flatirons and Eldorado Canyon. Rules that prohibit climbing altogether could hit just as suddenly.

Our infighting has taken an ominous turn. In 2001, *Paris Girl* in Eldorado was once again the whipping boy for bolting ideology. This time the bolts weren't chopped. They were slyly sabotaged so as to set an anonymous death trap for any climber who fell while attempting the route. Fortunately the damage was discovered before anyone got hurt. State police were called in to investigate.

There are also signs of hope. Climbers have created organizations that can both educate the bureaucrats who would control us, and help us control ourselves. We have begun to stop chiseling away the challenges of the future, as the leading sport climbers elect to discover, rather than construct, the hardest climbs. We do chalk-washings and crag clean-ups. We have rappelled off climbs on Longs Peak mere meters from the top because there was no way to continue without harming a garden of alpine wildflowers. Even with wildly disparate views and practices, and participants numbering in the hundreds of thousands nationally, we climbers still speak of ourselves as a community, sometimes even as a tribe.

This book speaks of daring and exploring, of overcoming odds and blazing a new trail—across the rock and through the mind. Now more than ever, that trail must become a middle path, blending the passion for challenge with an equally present reverence for the rock and the hills that make climbing more than just a sport. To meet the new challenge, we will distinguish between the safety that pays respect to life and the safety that drains away life's vigor. We will appreciate the convenience of modern rock climbing without letting it destroy our taste for that ultimate inconvenience called adventure. The stories in these pages can help. It is our hope that they not only record the remarkable path that has brought us this far, but also help us find a worthy path into the future.

Tommy Caldwell during a photo session on The Honeymoon is Over *shortly after the first free ascent in August 2001 (it was nearly dark by the time Caldwell reached this point on the actual free ascent). The route, envisioned and equipped by Eric Doub in the early 1990s, follows* D1 *and* Eroica *for its first half, then takes the imposing headwall left of* D1 *for five very sustained pitches—5.13a, 5.13c, 5.12d, 5.12d, and 5.12b, according to Caldwell. If these grades hold (and even if they slip a bit), this is the most difficult long free route in Colorado—so far!* (Photo: Topher Donahue)

Colorado Rock-Climbing Ascents and Events

1820: Pikes Peak climbed by Major Stephen Long and party. Declared "inaccessible" by Zebulon Pike, this was the first major Rocky Mountain summit to be reached by white men.

1865: *First ascent of the Matterhorn, Switzerland/Italy*

1868: First ascent of Longs Peak, by Major John Wesley Powell and William Byers, the year before Powell's famed Colorado River explorations.

1871: Longs Peak's east face first broached, in descent, by Reverend Elkanah Lamb.

1906: First ascent of the Third Flatiron, Floyd and Earl Millard. Aerialist Ivy Baldwin makes his first walk of the high wire at the posh Eldorado Springs resort.

1911: John Otto ascends Independence Monument.

1915: Rocky Mountain National Park established.
Albert Ellingwood leads the first technical rock climbs in the Garden of the Gods.

1920: Lizard Head first climbed, by Albert Ellingwood and Barton Hoag. This remains Colorado's most difficult "high peak."

1922: Longs Peak's east face first ascended, solo, by Princeton University professor J. W. Alexander.

1927: Joe and Paul Stettner, climb *Stettners Ledges* on the lower east face of Longs Peak, the hardest alpine rock climb in the country at the time.

1931: First ascent of the north face of Mount Sneffels, centerpiece of the activities of Dwight Lavender and the San Juan Mountaineers.

1944: First ascent of the Maiden spire in the Boulder Flatirons, by Roy Peak and Mark Taggart. This rock was a focal point of Boulder climbing through the 1950s.

1947: Joe Stettner—with Jack Fralick and John Speck—once again establishes the hardest alpine rock climb in Colorado, and the first to involve a bivouac, with an ascent of the east face of Monitor Peak in the San Juan Mountains.

1949: First ascent of the *Northwest Passage* route on the Third Flatiron, Boulder's first major artificial climb, by Tom Hornbein, Bob Riley, and Dick Sherman. This ascent also marks the first (and unsuccessful) attempt to use expansion bolts on Colorado rock.

1950: First ascent of *The Window* on the east face of Longs Peak, by Bill Eubanks, Brad Van Diver, first Longs Peak route done by Colorado-trained climbers to match the standard of the 1927 Stettners route.

1952: *Decimal System introduced at Tahquitz, California.*

1954–5: U.S. Army climbers make the first ascent of *Bastille Crack* in Eldorado Canyon and on Montezuma's Tower in the Garden of the Gods.

1956: Two major psychological breakthroughs for Colorado climbers: the first ascent of Boulder's most imposing cliff, the Redgarden Wall, by Chuck Murley, Dick Bird, and Dale Johnson; and a direct route on the intimidating "nordwand" of Hallett Peak in Rocky Mountain National Park, by Ray Northcutt and Harvey T. Carter.

1958: *First ascent of The Nose of El Capitan.*

1959: First ascent of the *Diagonal* on the east face of Longs Peak, Colorado's first Grade V, by Ray Northcutt and Layton Kor.
First wave of major Eldorado Canyon ascents—*T2, West Buttress, Northwest Corner*—by Layton Kor and partners. Also in Eldorado, Ray Northcutt free climbs a variation to the *Bastille Crack*, producing one of the first 5.10s in the country.

1960: The National Park Service opens the Diamond of Longs Peak to climbing, and the face is quickly climbed by Californians Dave Rearick and Bob Kamps via *D1*.

1961: First ascent of the northwest face of Chiefshead by Layton Kor and Bob Culp, a sheer, committing face climb done in remarkable light-and-fast style.
First ascent of Salathé Wall, Yosemite.

1962: A big year in Eldorado Canyon, with first ascents including *Dessert, C'est la Vie, Guenese, Psycho, Wisdom, Le Toit, Rosy Crucifixion, Rover, The Serpent, Italian Arête, Diving Board, Rincon, Tagger, Scotch 'n' Soda,* and *X-M. Genesis* becomes the first Colorado aid route to be given the A5 rating. *T2* is free climbed by Dave Rearick and Bob Culp, the first of Eldorado's major routes to be targeted for an all-free ascent.
Layton Kor and Charlie Roskosz make the second ascent of the Diamond, via the *Yellow Wall*.

1963: Hoping to establish the state's first Grade VI, Layton Kor, Tex Bossier, and Jim McCarthy make the first ascent of the North Chasm View Wall in Colorado's promising new big-wall climbing area, Black Canyon of the Gunnison.
Layton Kor and Royal Robbins make the first one-day ascents of the Diamond, with the second ascent of *D1* and the first ascent of *Jack of Diamonds*.
First ascent of *Crack of Fear* on Twin Owls by Layton Kor and Paul Mayrose. Even with its few points of aid, the route is one of the fiercest crack climbs in the country.

1964: First complete ascent of *The Naked Edge* in Eldorado Canyon, by Layton Kor and Rick Horn. Kor and Bob Culp had climbed all but the last pitch two years earlier.
Tom Fender and Bill Roos make the first ascent of the *Prayer Book* on Cynical Pinnacle, one of the earliest major climbs in the vast South Platte region.
Royal Robbins free climbs an old Stan Shepard aid route on Castle Rock near Boulder. Renamed *Athlete's Feat*, this is perhaps the most sustained free climb in the world at the time, with four consecutive pitches of 5.10.
First ascent of North American Wall, El Capitan.

1966: First free ascents of *Vertigo* and *Supremacy Crack* (top rope), by Pat Ament, among the first 5.11 climbs in the country.

1967: First winter ascent of the Diamond, by Layton Kor and Wayne Goss.
First serious attempts on the Painted Wall, Black Canyon. New Colorado transplant John Gill makes the first

ascents of *Pinch Overhang, Left Eliminator,* and other famous, difficult boulder problems at Horsetooth Reservoir near Fort Collins.

1969: New Boulder resident Jim Erickson makes the first free ascent of *Blackwalk,* the first Eldorado Canyon A4 to be done free.

1970: First solo ascent of the Diamond, by Bill Forrest.

1971: First free ascent of *The Naked Edge* in Eldorado Canyon by Jim Erickson and Duncan Ferguson. With a spectacular line and sustained, varied 5.10+ and 5.11 climbing, this route sets a new world standard in long, hard free climbing.

1972: First ascent of the Painted Wall, by Bill Forrest and Kris Walker. This was Colorado's first Grade VI route, established nearly boltless, an unprecedented achievement in big-wall climbing.

1974: Colorado ice climbing comes of age: Bob Culp makes the first ascent of Vail's *Rigid Designator,* and Jeff Lowe and Mike Weiss climb Bridalveil Falls near Telluride.

The first "Friends" prototypes are tested on Colorado Front Range crags by Ray Jardine, Kris Walker, and Bill Forrest.

First ascent of Supercrack *in the Shawangunks of New York by Colorado climber Steve Wunsch. At 5.12c, this is the world's hardest free pitch at the time.*

1975: First all-free ascent of the Diamond, by Wayne Goss and Jim Logan.

First free ascents of the standard-setting Boulder routes of the mid-1970s: *Jules Verne, Psycho,* and *Perilous Journey.* Also, Roger Briggs and Rob Candelaria climb the *Naked Danz* free link-up, touted as Colorado's first all-free Grade V.

First ascent of Fish Crack, *the first 5.12 in Yosemite, Henry Barber, and first one-day ascent of* The Nose *of El Capitan.*

1976: Earl Wiggins and Jim Dunn make the first free ascent of *The Cruise.* This 1,600-foot 5.10+ route was the first major free climb in the Black Canyon.

First complete free ascent of the *Prayer Book* in the South Platte, by Pat Adams and Michael Hoffman.

After several seasons of attempts, Colorado climbers Jim Erickson and Art Higbee free all but fifty feet of the Grade VI Northwest Face of Half Dome.

1977: First ascent of the Nose of Chasm View in the Black Canyon, by Earl Wiggins and Bryan Becker.

First ascent of The Phoenix, *the first 5.13 in Yosemite, by Colorado climber Ray Jardine.*

1978: First solo ascent of a Colorado Grade VI, the *Dragon Route* on the Painted Wall, by Brian Becker.

Eldorado State Park established.

First free solo ascents of *The Naked Edge,* by Jim Collins, and the Diamond, by Charlie Fowler.

The Diamond's *D1* route free climbed by John Bachar and Billy Westbay.

Wild Country Friends hit the market, sold out of the back of Ray Jardine's van in Yosemite.

1979: Leonard Coyne and Ken Simms climb *Air Voyage* in the Black Canyon, the country's hardest long free climb.

First MountainFilm festival, Telluride.

Earl Wiggins solos the Black Canyon's *Scenic Cruise.*

1980: First major one-day free-climbing link-ups on the east face of Longs Peak: *Gray Pillar/Casual Route* and *Directagonal/Yellow Wall.*

First free ascent of *Ophir Broke* (5.12c) on Telluride's Ophir Wall. This becomes Colorado's hardest crack pitch, led by a young Lynn Hill.

Jim Erickson introduces R and X ratings in his guidebook *Rocky Heights.*

1981: First free ascent of *Sphinx Crack* by Steve Hong. This overhanging crack shares honors with Tony Yaniro's *Grand Illusion* at Sugarloaf, California, done in 1979, as the hardest pitch of free climbing in the world.

1982: Leonard Coyne and Randy Leavitt make the first free ascent of the Painted Wall via *Stratosfear,* Colorado's first free Grade VI.

1984: First free ascent of *Rainbow Wall,* Boulder's first 5.13, by Bob Horan.

1985: European influence on the rise: Patrick Edlinger on-sights *Cinch Crack* and *Genesis,* and repeats *Sphinx Crack* in three hours. Christian Griffith makes the first ascent of the controversial route *Paris Girl* in Eldorado.

Roger Briggs raises Diamond free-climbing standards with *King of Swords* (5.11), and *Ariana* (the wall's first 5.12).

Wolfgang Güllich establishes the 5.14 grade, with Punks in the Gym, *Mount Arapiles, Australia.*

1986: Shelf Road established as Colorado's first sport crag.

The Great Debate is held at the American Alpine Club Annual Meeting in Denver, to discuss the crisis in American free climbing surrounding a new trend, bolted "sport climbing."

1987: Peter Croft free solos The Rostrum *and* Astroman *in Yosemite.*

1988: First free ascent of the Salathé Wall, *Yosemite, by Todd Skinner and Paul Piana.*

1989: Derek Hersey solos three Diamond routes in a day.

Boulder Mountain Parks and Eldorado State Park ban bolting.

1990: Mike Pennings and Topher Donahue climb the Diamond, Spearhead, Petit Grepon, Hallett Peak, and Notchtop in one long day.

1991: First sport routes established at Rifle: *Rumor Has It, Never Believe, Anti-Phil.*

Colin Lantz finally completes *Honemaster Lambada* in the Boulder Flatirons. At 5.13d, this is the state's hardest pitch.

Wolfgang Güllich establishes the world's first 9a (5.14d), Action Direct *in the Frankenjura of Germany.*

1992: First major winter ascent in the Black Canyon: *Hallucinogen Wall,* by Mugs Stump and John Middendorf.

Kurt Smith's *Slice of Life* at Rifle, as originally climbed, becomes Colorado's first 5.14, soon to be downgraded with the advent of the knee-bar technique.

1993: *Lynn Hill free climbs* The Nose *of El Capitan at 5.13+.*

1994: Chip Chace and Roger Briggs link the east face of Longs Peak's ultimate "line," the *Diagonal Super Direct* to *D1.*

1995: Yuji Hirayama on-sights *Sphinx Crack.*

1996: The 5.14b grade opened in Colorado with ascents of *The Seven P.M. Show, Zulu,* and *The Crew* at Rifle, and *Vogue* on the Industrial Wall near Boulder.

First free ascent of the Nose of Chasm View, Black Canyon, by Jeff Achey and Steve Levin.

1999: First ascent of *Kryptonite* (5.14c), Fortress of Solitude, by Tommy Caldwell, currently Colorado's hardest pitch.

2000: Mike Pennings and Jeff Hollenbaugh climb the Black Canyon Trifecta—the Painted Wall, North Chasm View, and South Chasm View—in 24 hours, 7 minutes.

2001: Tommy Caldwell free climbs *The Honeymoon is Over,* the Diamond's first 5.13.

A Note About Sources

Much of the history presented here was gathered directly from personal interviews, those done by Bob Godfrey and Dudley Chelton from 1972 to 1976 and by Jeff Achey between 1994 and 2001. The many instances in *Climb!* of "so-and-so said," though not specifically cited in the text, generally refer to these interviews or to other informal conversations with the authors from the early 1970s to the present.

The other main sources for the history come from the written record: the few books that touch on Colorado rock climbing, climbing guidebooks, and the journals and magazines that have covered climbing more regularly since the 1950s. Where it seemed appropriate or helpful, specific references have been cited in the text, but rock climbing has always been an activity that is informally, inconsistently, and often carelessly recorded. Climbers' memories vary, change with time, and often differ from written records, which themselves contain many verified errors. The only way to gain any verity is through sheer volume of inquiry, to question the elders and activists, and to seek out the existing written sources. The following selected readings are presented in an attempt to assist the interested reader in the latter quest.

One excellent source is the original *Climb!*, published in 1977, which contains many interesting passages, especially on the early history, that were edited out to produce the current volume. Copies of the first edition can occasionally be obtained from booksellers specializing in mountaineering titles. Another out-of-print book, also hard to find, is Glenn Randall's *Vertigo Games* (W. R. Publications, Sioux City, IA, 1983), an excellent treatment of select Colorado rock and ice climbs of the 1970s and early 1980s, rich in classic period photography. Randall's *Longs Peak Tales* (Stonehenge Books, 1981) has some great stories as well. Another superb, out-of-print source is *Beyond the Vertical* (Alpine House, Boulder, 1983), the autobiography of Layton Kor, written in collaboration with Bob Godfrey, with dozens of contributed essays from noted climbers. The photographs alone make *Beyond the Vertical* one of the most valuable books on American rock climbing.

Other books of special historical interest include *Master of Rock* (Stackpole Books, Mechanicsburg, PA, 1998, revised edition) and *Spirit of the Age* (Stackpole Books, Mechanicsburg, PA, 1998, revised edition), Pat Ament's biographies of John Gill and Royal Robbins, respectively. Many other of Ament's writings also offer unique glimpses into the past, including his early *Swaramandal* (Vitaar, Boulder, 1973), the various incarnations of his and Cleve McCarty's Boulder guidebook *High Over Boulder* (Two Lights, Boulder, 1995, fifth edition) and his autobiographical *Stories of a Young Climber* (Two Lights, Boulder, 1996).

Various more general books contain interesting passages on Colorado rock, including *Climbing in North America*, by Chris Jones, recently back in print (The Mountaineers Books, Seattle, 1997); *Stone Crusade*, John Sherman's historical bouldering guide to the U.S. (American Alpine Club Press, 1999 reprint); and *American Rock*, a recent John McPhee-esque treatment by Don Mellor (The Countryman Press, Woodstock, VT, 2001). Steve Roper's *Camp 4* (The Mountaineers Books, Seattle, 1994) is a superb source that focuses on the Golden Age of Yosemite. It contains interesting stories about visiting Coloradoans such as Harvey T. Carter, Mike Borghoff, and Layton Kor, and frequent visitors to Colorado, especially Royal Robbins, as well as chronicles a comparison of Colorado and California during a very creative and fascinating time period. A helpful East Coast climbing history is Laura and Guy Waterman's *Yankee Rock and Ice* (Stackpole Books, Mechanicsburg, PA, 1993), which details the climbs of Jim McCarthy, Henry Barber, Steve Wunsch, Ed Webster, and other activists in *Climb!* Eric Bjørnstad's history-rich guidebook *Desert Rock*, either the original volume (Falcon, Helena, MT, 1988) or the new series (Falcon and Globe Pequot, Guilford, CT, 1997–2001), covers Colorado National Monument as well as the exploits of the many Colorado climbers who made the Canyonlands of Utah a second home.

Finally, there are the periodicals. The *American Alpine Journal (AAJ)* is a consistent source of dates and route information, with short write-ups and the rare feature pertaining to Colorado rock climbing. *Trail and Timberline*, the journal of the Colorado Mountain Club, covered Colorado rock climbing during a time when no other journals did. It is a particularly helpful source for pre-1970s history. Complete collections of both the *AAJ* and *Trail and Timberline* can be perused at the American Alpine Club (AAC) library in Golden, Colorado—a place well worth a visit. *Climbing* magazine has thoroughly covered Colorado rock since 1970, as has *Rock & Ice* magazine, since 1984. Older back issues of these magazines can seldom be obtained through the magazine offices; booksellers or internet searching is a better bet, and the AAC library also collects them.

Index

Pages in bold indicate photographs; "c" followed by a page number indicates a color photo

10th Mountain Division, 19, 112-3
Achey, Jeff, **98**, **159**, 182, 184, 232, 236, **238**
Adams, Pat, 32, 138-9, 148, 160, 182, 234, 246
Aerospace, 173
aid climbing (see also big-wall climbing): early technique, 18, 20-2, 25; classic-era ascents, 29, 34, 36-7, **37**, 41
Air Voyage, 166-7, **167**, **168**, 193, 194, 239
Alexander, J. W., 15
Alexander's Chimney, 15, **17**
Alps, The, 13, 16, 17, 21, 53, 112-4, 143, 168, 181
Amazing Grace, 154, **154**
Ament, Pat, 35-6, **35**, 39, 51-2, **52**, 58-9, 62-6, **63**, **66**, 75-8, 82-6, 96, 129-30, 148, 151, 153, 219, 235
American Alpine Club, 210, 214
American Alpine Journal, The, 19, 27, 45, 103-4, 231
American Fork Canyon, Utah, 223
Anaconda, Garden of the Gods, 74, **74**, 102, **102**, 155
Apparition, 235, **236**
Arching Jam Crack, 97, **97**
Arêtes, Black Canyon, 50-3, **54**, 163-5, **163**, 239
Armstrong, Baker, 13
Aschert, Richard, 199-203
Ashcrofters camp, 113, 116, 119
Aspen, 75, 78, 112-9, **114-7**, 121-2, 147, 175, 198, 214-5, **214**, 231, 243, **c6**
Astrodog, 2, **195**, **197**, 197, 239-40
Athlete's Feat, 36, 58, **58**, 59, 86, 148
Auld, John, 74, **74**, 123, 124-5, 154

Bachar, John, 148-51, 158-9, 160, 176, **210**
Baillie, Rusty, 55, 103, 105, 107-9
Baldwin, Ivy, 25, **25**
Banditos, The, 193
Barber, Henry, 78, 85, **90**, 93, 113, 116-8, 119-21, **120**, 137, 148, 210, **210**
BASE jumping, 175, 194
Bastille Crack, 32, **32-3**, 71, 80, 93, 220
Baxter, Scott, 107-9, 169
Becker, Bryan, 100, 145-6, 154, **154**, 164-9, **165**, 190-1, **191**, **193**, 230, **c7**, **c15**
Benge, Mike, 200, 214-5
Bennett, Beth, 137-9, **139**, 182
Benningfield, Phillip, 223-7
Bensman, Bobbi, 215, 229, **229**, **c13**
Beyer, Jim, 105, 231
Bicentennial and *Bicentennial Roof*, **116**, 117, **117**, 122

Big Rock Candy Mountain, 133-4, **134-5**, 212
Bigger Bagger, 76, **76**
big-wall climbing, 27, 44, 49-55, **50**, 77, 89, 97, 100-1, 103, **104**, 106-11, **106-8**, 167-9, 182, 230-2, 238
Bird, Dick, 25-6, 30, 113
Bishop, 129, **129**, 211-2, **211**
Bishops Jaggers, 130, **130**, 212
Black Canyon of the Gunnison: general, 49-51, **49**, **c10**; early climbs, 17, 49-51, **54**; 1970s free climbs, **144-5**, 163-8, **239**; 1970s big walls, **106-9**, 163, 168; 1980s free climbs, **194-7**; 1980s big walls, 191-3, **195**, 230-1, **c7**; 1990s free climbs, **235-8**
Black Dagger, 142, 143, **182**
Black Wall, 146-7, **146**, **147**
Blackwalk, 34, 81, **81**, 209
bolts and bolting: early use, 19-23, 25; opinions on, 25, 37, 45-6, 59, 106-7, 110, 130, 148, 155-6, 198, 248; bans, 218, 219, 227; chopping, 45-6, 59, 155, 205, 242; ladders, 22, 72, **72**, 74, 114, 129, 132, 134, 149, 155-6, 191; placed on rappel, 30-1, 148, 155-6, 172, 178, 181, 198-206, 210, 215; "retro," 59, 149, 173, 193; "grid," 242; drilled angles, 20, 72-4, **72**; drilling tales, 72-4, 76, 109, 133-4, 154, **155**, 203, 212, 223-6
Bossier, Tex, 45-6, **50**, 50-1, 62
Boulder Mountaineer, 41, 153,
Boulder, Colorado (see also specific climbs), 6, 10, **12**, 20, 71, 147-8, 172, 205
bouldering, 20, 26, 32, 51, 56, **66**, 66, 69-70, **70**, 114, 118-9, **118**, 151, 153, **153**, 174-5, 201, 232, 247
Bowman, Coral, 139-40, **140**
Bragg, John, **88**, 91, 95, 149, 159
Breashears, David, **66**, 84, 93-5, **94-5**, 122, 132, **132**, 148, 149, 174
Bridwell, Jim, 100-1, 127, 148
Briggs, Bill, 148, 159, **183**, 188
Briggs, Roger, 51-2, **52**, 60, **64-5**, 66, 79, 86-9, **86-8**, 91, 93, 132, 141, 148-9, 157-161, **158**, **174**, 182-4, **183**, 187-9, 210, 216, 233-4, **234**, **c6**
Bruce, Larry, 114, 116
Budding, Karin, 166-7, 154
Bulge, 30-1, **30**, 86
Bullet the Blue Sky, 203, **203**

C.A.T.S. climbing gym, 242
Cactus Cliff, 199
Caldwell, Tommy, 227, 245-8, **245-6**, **248**
Campus boards 179
Candelaria, Rob, 148, 151, 157-8, 227, 242-3
Canyonlands, Utah, 45, 71, 102-3, 111, 123-5, 128, 130, 136-7, 156, 193, 231

Carter, Harvey T., 20, 26-7, 71, 74-6, 96, 103, **112**, 113-6, 124-5, 174, 198-9
"Castle Rock Marathon," 148
Casual Route, 161-2, **161**, 182, 208
Chace, Chip, 162, 189, 211, 233-4, **233**, 236
chalk, 69, 78, 85, 142, 200, 218, 248
Chelton, Dudley, **58**, 80, 93, **127**
Cheyney, Steve, 71-6, **96**, 96-7, 100-1, 154, 199
Chiefshead, 41-3, **43**, 56, 77, 161, 184-6, **184**, **185**
Childhood's End, 212
chipping (see hold manufacturing)
chocks (see nuts)
Chockstone Chimney, 26, **26**
Chouinard, Yvon, 27, 35, 39, 113, 117, 121
Cinch Crack, 95, 149, 153
cleaning (see also hold manufacturing), 101, 128, 143, 157, 172, 200, 223-6, 244-5
Clear Creek Canyon, 222, **222**, 244-5
Climbing magazine, 78, 113, 118, 147, 175, 199-200, 214-5, 244, 252
climbing shoes: early, 12, 16, **19**; Kronhoffer, 76, 78, **124**, 195; EBs, **68**, 78, **114**; sticky rubber, **175**, 181
Cobbler, The, 96, **96**, 134, 156
Collins, Jim, 151-3, **152**, 173,
Colorado College, 13, 19-20, 71, 97, 133, 145, 154, 197, 199
Colorado Mountain Club, 13, 129, 251
Colorado National Monument, 74, 123-5, **123-5**, **c8**
Colorado Nut Company, 130
Colorado Springs, 10, 13-4, 20, 71-6, 96-102, 127, 129, 154-6, 198, 244
competition and competitions, 20, 45, 56, 70, 78, 114, 148, 178, 201, 220, 224, 227, 229, 232, 242-3, 245
Cornucopia, 215, **215**
Cosmos, 100-1
Country Club Crack, 58-9, **59-60**, 65, 82, 83, 142, 148
Covington, Michael, 47, 52-3, 109, 126-8, **127**, 160-1, 164
Coyne, Leonard, **98**, 100, 132, **136**, 154-6, **155-6**, 163-7, **167**, 173, 182, **182**, 193-4
crack machines, 136
Crack of Fear, 61-2, **62**, 126, 209
Cracked Canyon, 120-1
crash pads, 232, 247
Crew, Rifle, 244, 245
Croff, Pete, 71-6, **74**
Cruise (and *South Face* route—see also *Scenic Cruise*), 51, 144-6, **144**, **145**, 165-6, **166**, 169, 195, **239**, 239-41
Cryogenic, 115-6, **115**
Culp, Bob, **31**, 34, 36-7, 41-3, **41**, 45, 47, 54-8, 62, 143, 153
Cynical Pinnacle, 129-32, **129-33**, 209, **209**, 211-2

252

Index

D1, 39-41, **40-1**, 44-5, **158**, 160-1, 184, 187, 232-3, **233**
D7, 89, 141-3, 157, 158-9, **162**, 232
Dalke, Larry, 34-5, **35**, 39, **50**, 51-5, 65-9, **67**, 75, 86, 90, 129, 164
D'Antonio, Bob, 198-204, **204**, **c2**
Dawson, Lou, 113-6, **114**, 147,
Dean's Day Off, 117-8, **117**, 122
Death and Transfiguration, 86-9, **88**, 127
Desdichado, 206, **206**
Diagonal, Longs Peak, 36, 38-9, **38**, **40**, 43, 45, 62, 139, 159-60
Diagonal Direct, 45-7, 160, 182, **183**, 189, 233, **233**
Diagonal, Black Canyon, **49**, **50**, 50-1, 110, 145-6, 163, 165, 168, 235
Diagonal Will, **163**, 164-5, **165**
Diamond, Longs Peak (see also specific routes): general, 15, **16**, 46, 157, **c4**, ban, 38; early forays, 24-5, **24**; vs Black Canyon 50; first ascent, 39-41, **40**, **41**, 56; first free ascents, 141-3, **141**, 157-8; first one-day ascents, 43-5, 182, 232; first female ascents, 139, 142, 143, 182; solo ascents, 103-5, **104**, **105**, 231, 232; winter ascents, 47-8, **47**, **48**, 185, 232; Right Side, 104-5, 187-8, **188**, 230-1, 233-5, **234**; unroped ascents, 162, 207, **209**
Directagonal, 159, **159**
Diving Board, 34, 66, **83**, 86-8, **87**, **88**, 207, **c6**
Donahue, Topher, 232-3, 238, 247, **247**
Doub, Eric, 176, 180, 189, 235, 248
Doucette, Don, 76, 97-9, 100, 134, 230
Dragon Route, 107-9, **108**, 145, 168-9, 193, 194, 232, 238
Drumstick Direct, 100, **100**
Dudley, Michael, 97-100, 125
Duncan, Ken, 148, 160, 161
Dunn, Jim, 37, **97**, 97, 100-2, **101**, **102**, 103, 105, 109, 110-11, 128, 143-6, **145**, 157, 163, 194-5, 235
Dylan, Bob, **52**
dynamic belay, 19

Edlinger, Patrick, 178
Eighth Voyage of Sinbad, 110-11, 165, 166-7, **167**, 194
El Capitan, 28, 50, 97, 100-3, 110, 122, 147, 190, 230-1
Eldorado Canyon: general, 24-5, **25**, **26**, **c9**; comments on the climbing, 96, 136, 147-8, 210; early climbs, 25-6, **26**, 30-7, **30-7**, 56-8, **56**, **57**, 62-9, **63-9**, 71, 72; 1970s climbing, 80-96, **137-9**, **149-52**, **c1**, **c5**, **c6**; state park, 147; 1980s climbing, **173-7**, **180**, **205**, **206**, **217**, **c3**, **c15**; 1990s climbing, 239, 247-8
Eldorado Springs, Colorado, 25
Eleven-Mile Canyon, 198-9, 201, 244
Eliminator Boulder, 69, **70**, 119
Ellingwood Arête, 14, **15**, 25, 129
Ellingwood, Albert, 13-4, 19-20, 129, 200
enchainments, 24, 148, 182, **184**, 185, 232-3, **233**, 238-41, **241**
Enos Mills Wall, 47-8, **48**, 188

Erickson, Jim, **62**, 69, 80-95, **81**, 116, 148-9, 173-4
Eroica, **187**, 188-9, 233, 248
Estes Park, Colorado (see also Lumpy Ridge), 126-8
Evans, Mount, 146-7, **146**, **147**
Example, 201-3, **202**, 244

Fantasy Ridge, 105, 126, 158, 184
Fast Draw, 124-5, **125**
Ferguson, Duncan, 69, 80-4, **82**, 88, 91, 93, 127, 130, **130**, 137, 141-2, 148, 161-2, 173, 185
field house, University of Colorado, 42, 176
Fields of Dreams Growing Wild, 133-4, **134-5**, 212
Fiend, 215, **c14**
films and filming, 93, 96, 113, 121, 122, 129, 139, 148, 196, 212, 236, 238
Finger Face, 72, **73**
Fisher Towers, Utah, 103, 105, 114, 125, 130, 231
Five Year Plan, 178, **179**, 215
Flagstaff Mountain, **12**, 26, 56, 66, **66**, 82, 90, 153, **153**, 174, 176, 178
Flakes, Black Canyon, **195**, 196-7
Flame, 97, **98**, 143
Flatirons (see also specific climbs), **11-13**, 20-3, **21-3**, 215-8
For Turkeys Only, 100, **101**
Forrest, Bill, 103-7, **104**, 115, 126, 147, 190
Forrest Mountaineering, 103, 147
Forrest-Walker, Painted Wall, 105-9, **106-8**, 169, 193
Fowler, Bill, 147
Fowler, Charlie, 161-2, **162**, 165, 181-5, 199, 211, 215
free climbing: in the early days, **38**; in the 1960s, **35**, **67**; crack climbing, **85-8**, **97-100**, **102**, **115**, **122**, **125-32**, **136**, **167**, **172**, **179**, **187**, **196**, **209**, **211**, **243**, **c1**, **c6**, **c15**; slab climbing, 11, **59**, **73**, **130**, **133**, **135**, **154**, **156**, **175**, **213**, **216**, **c11**; spicy routes, **81**, **91-4**, **151**, **173**, **176**, **207**, **247**, **c5**; in the high-mountains, **17**, **18**, **27**, **38**, **43**, **76**, **142**, **159**, **161**, **162**, **182-4**, **209**, **233**, **234**, **248**, **c9**; in the Black Canyon, **144**, **145**, **164-7**, **194-7**, **235-9**; early 510 climbs, 33; early 5.11 climbs, 59-66, **63**, **64**, 81, 89, 102, 116, 117, 120, 128; early 5.12 climbs, 91, 94-5, **95**, 101, 116-7, **117**, 119, 122, 126, 132, 148, 149, 160; early 5.13 climbs, 136, **136**, 174, **177**, 178, 200, 201, 204; early 5.14 climbs, 205, **221**, 222, 225, 227, 229, 244-5, **244**
Free Nose, 236-8, **237**
free soloing, 13, 15, 30, 53, 69, 72, 82, 99, 114, 132, 148, 151, 162, 174, 195, 206-10, **208-9**, **238-9**
Friday's Folly, 21, **22**, 25
Friends, 126, 147, 167, 201, 211

Gallagher, Peter, 133-4, **196**, 197, 199
Garden of the Gods, 10, 12, 13-14, **14**, 16, **18**, 19-20, 71-5, **72-4**, 96, 101-2, **102**,

154-6, **154-6**, 198, 244
gardening (see cleaning)
Genesis, 95, 148, 151-3, **152**, 173, 178, 180, 206
Gill, John, 33, 66, 69-70, **69**, **70**, 78, 96, 118-9, 210
glue and gluing, 217-8, 224-5, 244-5
Goddard, Dale, 176, 178, **179**, 199, 209, 215, **215**
Golden Book of Bullshit, 96-7
Goss, Wayne, 47-8, **48**, 52-5, 105, 109-10, 127, 141-3
Goss-Logan, Black Canyon, 109-10, **109**, 144, **144**, 164, 168, 195, 236
Goukas, Eric, 176, 189, 233
Grand Giraffe, **31**, 33-4, 41, 56, 130, **c1**
Grandmother's Challenge, 80-1, **81**
Gray Pillar, 45, 159, 182, **184**
Great Debate, The, 210, **210**
Greenman, Ernest and "Ma", 13
Griffith, Christian, 66, **171**, 176-81, **180**, 204, 205-6, **205-6**, 210, **210**, 212, 219, **c12**
Grotto Wall (see Aspen)
Guenese, 34, **83**, **88-9**, 89-90, 94, 142
Guerin, Skip, **128**, 174, **175**, 178
guidebooks, 13, 19, 66, 77, 80, 81, 97, 100, 114, 155-6, 172-5, 185, 203, 212, 216, 226
gyms (climbing), 136, 176, 209, 219-20, 242

Hallett Peak, 26-7, **27**, 160, 233, 245
Hallucinogen Wall, 190-3, **191-2**, 230-5, **c7**
"hang-dogging," 148, 178, 200, 208, 226
Hare, Dan, 153, 187
Harlin, John, 47, 55, 184
Harlin, John III, 184-5
Harvey, Kennan, 232, 238
"headpointing," 247, **247**
Hersey, Derek, **173**, 207-10, **207-9**, 233, 238-41, **239**
Hesse, Mark, 97, 100, 105, 127, 141, 153, 188, 197
Higbee, Art, 94, 95, 148, 149, **150**
Higgins, Molly, 97, 114, 137, **137**, 142, 143
High Over Boulder guidebook, 77
high wire, Eldorado Canyon, 25, **25**
Hill, Lynn, 121-2, **121**, 139, **210**, 222
Hirayama, Yuji, 242, 247
hold manufacturing, 156, 203-4, 215, 217, 222-5, 242, 244-5, 247
Hollenbaugh, Jeff, 238-41, **240**
Holloway, Jim, 153, **153**
Honemaster Lambada, 218, 245
Honeymoon is Over, **233**, 235, 248, **248**, **c9**
Hong, Steve, 154, **156**, 178, 197, 243-4
Hooker, Black Canyon, 134-6, **136**
hooking: for aid, 37, 55, 88, 97, 100-1, 107-8, 168, 190-1, 230-1, **c7**; for free climbing, 155, 164, 174, 176, 199, 206, 215, 235-6, 246
Horan, Bob, 174, **175**, 178
Horn, Rick, 34, 37
Hornbein Crack, 24
Hornbein, Tom, 20-5, **21**
Horsetooth Reservoir, 69-70, **70**, 118-9, **118**, 153-4

Howells, Art, 71, 97-9, 100, 125
Hunter, Diana, 130, 137, **138**, 147
Hurley, George, 33-4, **34**, 93, 103, 128
Huston, Cary, **17**, 22, 25-6, 30

ice climbing, 82, 103, 113-4, 143, 148, 198, 222, 242, 250
Independence Monument, **123**, 124-5, **125**, **c8**
Independence Pass (see Aspen)

Jack of Diamonds, 44-5, 188
Jackson, Dallas, 25-26, 30
Jardine, Ray, 104, 126, 147-8, **c1**
J-Crack, 126, 128
Johnson, Dale, 21-6, **23**, 30, 38-9
Joker, 233-5, **233-4**
Journey to Ixtlan, 132
Jules Verne, 62, **83**, 90-4, **91-2**, 148, 173-4, 208, **c5**
Jumars, 67, 103, 147

Kamps, Bob, 39-41, **41**, 45, 160
Karlstrom, Karl, 105, 107-9
Kees, Bill, 120-1, **120**, 212
Kennedy, Michael, 113, 115-6, **115**, 118, 200, 214, 215, 244
Kieners route, 14, 17, 24, 45
King of Swords, 187-8, **187-8**, 233
Kissing Camels, 16, **18**, 71, 72
Kloeberdanz, 34, 66, **83**, 90, **90**, 93, 94, 132, 139, 148
knee bars, 225, 229
Knucklehead, 215
Knuth, Chris, 225, 244
Komito, Steve, 37, 50, 126-7, **126**, 143, 161
Kor, Layton; as a novice, 30; general descriptions, 34, 44-5, 55; Eldorado climbs, 30-37, **35**, **37**, 72, 149; Garden of the Gods climbs, 74, **74**; Black Canyon climbs, 49-55, **50**, 105-7, 164, **195**, 196; Rocky Mountain National Park climbs, 31, 38-48, **43**, **44**, 61, 126, 186, 189; Colorado National Monument climbs, 124-5, **124**; quitting and returning to climbing, 55, 189, **195**, 196
Kor's Corner, 74, 156, **156**
Kryptonite, 246-7

Langmade, Dan, 121, 193
Lantz, Colin, 199, 201, 217-8, **217**, 223-6, **c13**
Lavender, Dwight, 17
Le Visage, 230
Leavitt, Randy, 175-6, **176**, 193-4
Leavittation, 175
Lester, Alan, 189, 225, 233, 243
Levin, Steve, 162, **188**, 233-4, 236-8, **237**
Limestone Cowboy, 199
Limits of Power, 175-6, **176**
link-ups (see enchainments)
Lion, 247
Living in Fear, 225, **226**, 229
Lizard Head, 14, **15**, 17, 25
Logan, Jim, 61-2, 109-10, 130, 141-3, 157, 168, 188, 219

Long, John, 118-9, **118**, 121-2, 127, 159, 161
Longs Peak, 10, **13**, 14-7, **16**, 24, 47, **47**, 69, **185**, 246
Lowe, Greg, **149**, 149
Lowe, Jeff, 103, 106, 148, 149, 185-7, **187**, 211-2
Lumpy Ridge (see also specific climbs), 61, 126-9, **126**, 160, 245
Lungfish, **221**, 227

Maiden, Flatirons, 20, 22-3, **23**, 26, 69, 72, 74, 89
Mammen, Steve, **85**, 132, **211**
Martyr, 75-6
Mayrose, Paul, 34, 61, 126
McCarthy, Jim, 33, 43, 50-1, **50**, 210
McCarty, Cleve, 59, 77
McClure, Dan, 43, 97, 100, 105, 127-8, 141, 154, 188
media coverage of climbing, 34, 40, 43, 147, 190-1, 242
Michael, Dan, 204, 206, 215-6, **216**, **c14**
Michael, Jim, **95**, 153, 204
Mickey Mouse Wall, 37, 93-4, **93-4**, **179**, 180, 245, **c13**
Mirror Wall, Black Canyon, **49**, 51-2
Moffatt, Jerry, 175, 178, 179, 242-3, **243**
Monitor Peak, 17-8, **18**, 25
Montezuma's Tower, **14**, 20, 71, **154**
Morning Glory, 120, **214**, 214
Mountain magazine, 75, 77-8, 145, 147, 172
MountainFilm festival, 120, 121, 212

Naked Danz, 148, 250
Naked Edge, **28**, 31, **36**, **37**, **66**, 66, 84-6, 89, **139**, 141-2, 147, 176, 206, 255, **c1**; first ascent, 36-7; first free ascent, 82-6; first female ascents, 137-40; unroped ascents, 151, 208-9, **208**
New England climbs and climbers, **90**, 100, 101, 111, 120, 145, 214, 245
Newberry, Jim, 168-9, 190-3, **193**
North Chasm View Wall (see also Black Canyon and specific climbs), **49**, 51, **109**, **144**, **168**, **c10**
North Cheyenne Canyon, 100, 101, 145
Northcutt Variation, 32-3, **33**, 58, 82, 208
Northcutt, Ray, 26-7, **27**, 32-3, 36-9, **38**, 45, 56, 153
Northcutt-Carter, Hallett Peak, 26-7, **27**, 233, 245
Northwest Corner, Bastille, 33, **33**, 65, 75, 88, 137, 207
Northwest Passage, 20-1, **21**
Nose of Chasm View, 109-10, **109**, 144, 167-8, **168**, 236-8
nuts and nut stories, **58**, 63, **68**, 78, 91, 101, 104, **110**, 111, 114, 130, 133, 141-6, 155, 159-60, 167-8, 187, 197, 211, 242, 246

Olevsky, Ron, 105, 125
Ophir Broke, 122, **122**
Ophir Wall (see also Telluride), 119
Ormes, Robert, **15**, **19**, 19-20
Osius, Alison, 214, **c2**
Otto, John, 123-4

Outer Space, **33**, 34, 35, 36, 66, **138**, 200
Outward Bound School, 55, 105, 115, 148, 255

Paint it Black, 230
Painted Wall (see also Black Canyon and specific climbs), **54**
Paris Girl, **180**, 181, 205, 248
Path of Elders, 41-3, **43**, 56, 77, 161, 185, 186
Peaches and Cream, 128, **128**
Peisker, Chris, 139, 147, 198
Penitente Canyon, 200-4, **203-4**, 215, 244, **c2**
Pennings, Mike, 233, 238-41, **240**
Perilous Journey, 93-4, **93**, 132, 162, 173-4, 180, 247
Pervertical Sanctuary, 105, 125, 157, 208
Pete and Bob's, 72-4, **72-4**, 101, 155
Pikes Peak, 10, 14, 20, 71-6, 97-8, 143, 244
Pinch Overhang, **118**, 119
pitons: soft iron, 14, 20, 35, 39, 45, 72, 96, 119; European, 15; chrome-moly, 35, 39; Colorado-made, 17, 72; pitons vs clean climbing, 77-8, 85, 89, 91, 93, 142
Pont, Mike, 222-3, 225, **227**
portaledges, 190, **193**, 238, **c7**
Post Office Crack, 119
power drilling, 200, 204, 215, **217**, 218, 224
Practice Aid Roof, 21, 242-3, **243**
Pratt, Chuck, 33, 58, 61, 62
Prayer Book, 129-32, **131**, 139, 209, **209**, 212
Psychic Grandma, 72, 155
Psycho, 34, 56, 67, **83**, 94-5, **95**, 101, 151, 153, 176, 178, 180
Putnam, Bill, 90-1, **91**, 141

Quinlan, Steve, 230-1
Quivering Quill, **99**, 100

Rainbow Wall, **177**, 178-9, **c3**
Randall, Glenn, 155, 165-7, 193, 251
rating systems, 71, 114, 148, 174-5, 231, 247
Rearick, Dave, 28, 34, 39-41, **40**, **41**, 56-62
Red Dihedral, 37, **93**, **179**, 180
Redgarden Wall (see also Eldorado Canyon and specific climbs), **26**, 31, **83**, **c9**
Redguard, 26, **26**, 30, 31, 80, 113
Redstone, Colorado, 242, **c2**
Renaissance Wall, **245**
Reppy, John, 115-6
Reveley, Chris, 95, 127, 130, 141, 153, 161
Rifle Mountain Park, **221-9**, 246, **c3**, **c12**
Ripper Traverse, **70**, 119
Risky Business, **185**, 185-6
Road Warrior, 186-7, **186-7**
Robbins, Royal, 39, 44, 48, 58-66, **58**, 78, 81, 86, 100, 103, 108, 121, 212
Rock & Ice magazine 188-9
Rock Atrocity, 218, 222, 225
"rockaneering," 163-9
Rockcraft climbing school, 121, 212
Rocky Heights guidebook, 174
Rocky Mountain Climbers Club, 10, 12-3

Rocky Mountain National Park (see specific climbs and formations)
Rolofson, Mark, 100, 154, 155, 198, 211
Roos, Bill, 129-30
roped soloing, 66-7, 100-1, 103-5, **105**, 125, 169, 185, 230-4, 242
ropes: early fibers, 14, 16, 19; rope stories, 12-13, 18, 39, 42-3, 46, 111, 115-6, 145-6, 147, 169, 176, 194
Roskosz, Charlie, 32, 43, **44**
Rossiter, Joyce, 216, **216**
Rossiter, Richard, 216
Roth, Darryl, 199, 200
RPs, 139, 147, 173, 198, 201, 215
Rumor Has It, 223, **c3**
Ruper, **35**, 41, 62-3, 220
RURPs, 35-6, 69, 111, 235
Ruwitch, Jean, 137, 139, 182

Samet, Matt, **151**, 223-5
San Juan Mountaineers, 17, 119
San Juan Mountains, 10, 14, **15**, 17, 18, **18**, 25, 119, 121, 200, 231
Sarchasm, 246
Savelli, Antoine, 212, 214
Scary Canary, **174**
Scene of the Crime, 215
Scenic Cruise, 165-6, **166**, 195, 208, 238, **239**
Serpent, Black Canyon, 238, **238**
Seven Arrows, 184-6, **184**
Seven P.M. Show, 227, **229**
Sharma, Chris, 227, 242, 245
Sharp, Alec, 172-4, **172**, 247
Shawangunks climbs and climbers, 20, 33, 43, 69, 80, 82, 90, 91, 117, 149, 224
Shea, Steve, 113-4, 116-7, **117**, **142**
Shelf Road, 198-203, **198**, **199**, **201**, 215, 222-5, 244, **c16**
Shepard, Stanley, 30, 32, 36
Shepherd, Louise, 139, 182
Sherman, Dick, 20-1, **21**
Sherman, John, 175
Sherwood, John, **72**, 76, 97, 101, 102, 143, 168
Shiprock, New Mexico, 19, 103, 123, 124
Sibley, Paul, 129-30
Silly Putty, 160
Sink, The, 30
skiing, 112-4, 119, 184
Skinner, Todd,148, **176**, **210**, 210
Skyline Ranch, 119-21
Slater, Rob, 165, **194**, 194
Slice of Life, 225, 229, 244, **c12**
Smith Rock, Oregon, 178, 200, 205, 210, 222-5, 243
Smith, Kurt, **214**, 215, 222-6, 229, **228**, **c12**
Snively, Doug, 97, 100, 105, 127, **128**
soloing (see free soloing and roped soloing)
Sonnenfeld, Mark, **136**, **152**, 195, 206, **214**
South Chasm View Wall (see also Black Canyon and specific climbs), **195**
South Platte, 97-101, **99-100**, 126, 129-36, **129-36**, 209-12, **209**, **211**, **213**, **c11**
Southern Arête, Painted Wall, 52-3, 239, **241**

Spencer-Green, Ian, **212**, **244**, 244, **plate 16**
Sphinx Crack, 129, 134-6, **136**, 141, 178, 242-3
Spinal Tap, 206, **207**
sport climbing, early,156, 178, 198-206, **199-206**, 214-8, **215-7 c2, c12-14**
Sport Park, Boulder Canyon, 242, 248
Spray-A-Thon, 225, 227
Stannard, John, 90, 93
Stauch, Bob, 71, 72, 75, 76
Steiger, John, 200, 214, 215
Stettner, Joe and Paul, 15-8, **17**, **18**
Stettner's Ledges, 16-8, **18**, 24, 25, 38
Stone, Dan, **70**, **93**, **116**, 161, 188
Stoned Oven, 195, 239
Stratosfear, 193-6, **194**
Stump, Mugs, 143, 212, 230, 232
style and ethics, 8-250
Sundance Buttress, 31, 61, **61**, **126**
Super Slab, 34, 66, 82, 89, 176
Supercrack, Shawangunks, 91
Superfly, 174
Superfresh, 218
Supremacy Crack, 62-5, **63**, 151

T2, 31-2, **31**, **56**, **57**, 58, 75, 81, 90
Tagger, 80, **80**
Tague, Cameron, 239
"tainting," 86, 90, 148, 149
Tarr, Amanda, 231
Telluride, Colorado, 14, 112, 116, 119-22, 148, 212-4
The Climbers Club (aka TCC), 71, 75
Third Flatiron, 8, **11-3**, 12-4, 20-2, **22**, 25
Tidrick's, 72, **73**, 155
Tidrick, Rick, 72
Tomfoolery, 246
Tourist Extravagance, 181, 206
Trail and Timberline magazine, 12, 13, 18, 41, 47, 77
training, 19, 26, 69, 82, 97, 129, 136-7, 151-2, 176-9, 208, 219, 240-2, 244
Tribout, J. B., 178, 201, **217**, 222, 227, **229**
Trifecta, Black Canyon, 239-41, **241**
Trilogy, Black Canyon, 235, **235**
Trout, Ken, 186-7, 190, 196-7, 212, **212**
Tschappat, Dean, **110**, 111, 145, 169
Turkey Rock, 96-101, **99**, **100**, 129, 132, 211
Turner, Jack, 34, 36, 61, 151, 173
Turnkorner, 61, **61**, 126
Twin Owls, Lumpy Ridge, 61-2, **62**, 128, **128**, 160
Two Forks Dam proposal, 211

Van Diver, Brad, 22, 24
Vertigo, 58, 65, **65**, 75, **78**, 86, 127, 139
Verve, **c12**
Virgin No More, 204, **c2**
Vision Thing, 226, **229**
Vitamin H, **224**, 225, 229
Vogue, 245

Walker, Kris, 103-7, **106-7**, 147, 193, 234
Warren, Robert, **196**, 197, 235

Waterchute Route, 155
Way Honed and Gnarly, 174
Webb, Jeff, 227
Webster, Ed, **76**, 97, 100, **125**, 136, 145-6, 149, 154, **154**, 164-9, **164**, 173, 190-7
Westbay, Billy, 42, 47, 97, 100, **101**, 105, 127-8, **128**, 160-4, 184, 188
Whillans, Don, 63-5
Whimsical Dreams, 101
Whitehouse, Annie, 207
Wide Country, 80, 88, 137, **138**
Wiggins, Art, 199, 230
Wiggins, Earl, 97, **99**, 101-3, **102**, 109, 133-4, 143-6, 154, **154**, 163, 165, 168-9, 190, 195-6, 235, 238-9
Wilford, Mark, 160, 175, 182, 185-6, 206, **207**, 211-2, **211**, 232
Williams, Pete, 133-4, 154, 212
Window Route, 24-5
Winkleman, Eric, **179**, 187, 195, 212
winter ascents, 47-8, 160, 231-2
Wisdom, 34, 95, 149-51, **150-1**, 153
Wright, Richard, 222, 226
Wunsch, Steve, 81-4, **82**, **88-9**, 89-95, **93**, 130-2, 148, 149, **c5**
Wunsch's Dihedral (see *Prayer Book*)

X-M, 34-6, **67-8**, 69, 75

Yaniro, Tony, 136, 148, 175, 178
Yellow Spur, **31**, 33, 34, 62, 66, **67**, 80
Yellow Wall, **40**, 43-4, **44**, 75, 89, 139, **141**, 143, 157-8, 207
Your Mother, **217**

Ziegler, Gary, 74, 123, 125, 129, 154
Zion National Park, Utah, 103, 106, 111, 125, 147, 148
Zoller, Pete, **220**, 222-3

About the Authors

Bob Godfrey, a longtime Boulder resident, was a British native and an accomplished climber, kayaker, pianist, writer, publisher, and filmmaker. He was coauthor of the first edition of *Climb!*, and the motivating force behind *Beyond the Vertical,* the autobiography of Layton Kor. His films include *The Left Wall,* documenting a climb in North Wales; *Outward Bound: Schools of the Possible,* about the Outward Bound schools; *Sherpa,* a study of changing culture in Nepal; and *Free Climb,* which chronicled Jim Erickson and Art Higbee's attempt to free climb the Northwest Face of Half Dome in 1976. In 1987, Bob was diagnosed with Parkinson's disease. Despondent over his gradual loss of muscle control and other events, Bob took his life in June 1988, but not before accomplishing two of his lifelong ambitions: free climbing *The Naked Edge* and kayaking the Grand Canyon. Tragically, Bob's photographic collection was lost during his estate settlement. His photos printed herein were reproduced from the halftone negatives of the original edition of *Climb!*

While coauthoring the first edition of *Climb!* with Bob Godfrey, **Dudley Chelton** obtained an undergraduate degree in physics from the University of Colorado and enrolled at the Scripps Institution of Oceanography in San Diego, where he obtained a Ph.D. in physical oceanography in 1980. He worked at the Jet Propulsion Laboratory in Pasadena until 1983, specializing in satellite remote sensing of the ocean. While in California he climbed extensively throughout Southern California and northern Baja and discovered the spiritual benefits of dawn-patrol surfing sessions before work. Since 1983 Dudley has been a professor of oceanography at Oregon State University in Corvallis. Sailboarding in the Columbia River Gorge has partially filled the void left by a fifteen-year hiatus from climbing.

Jeff Achey moved from Princeton, New Jersey, to Boulder in 1976. He studied intermittently at the University of Colorado for twelve years and also began a ten-summer stint with Outward Bound. He had a hand in a few classic free ascents in Eldorado before earning a master's degree in experiential education and moving to the West Slope to teach at the alternative Colorado Rocky Mountain School, located in Carbondale. After four years teaching he spent eight years as photo editor and contributing writer for *Climbing* magazine. He has remained an active climber and is currently a writer, photographer, freelance editor, and sometime painter and blacksmith, living in Glenwood Springs, Colorado.

Jeff Achey

Dudley Chelton